The African Diaspora

The African Diaspora

Slavery, Modernity, and Globalization

TOYIN FALOLA

UNIVERSITY OF ROCHESTER PRESS

First published 2013
Reprinted in paperback and transferred to digital printing 2014

University of Rochester Press
668 Mt. Hope Avenue, Rochester, NY 14620, USA
www.urpress.com
and Boydell & Brewer Limited
PO Box 9, Woodbridge, Suffolk IP12 3DF, UK
www.boydellandbrewer.com

hardcover ISBN-13: 978-1-58046-452-9
paperback ISBN-13: 978-1-58046-453-6

Library of Congress Cataloging-in-Publication Data
Falola, Toyin.
   The African diaspora : slavery, modernity, and globalization / Toyin Falola.
      p. cm.
   Includes bibliographical references and index.
   ISBN 978-1-58046-452-9 (hardcover : alk. paper) 1. African diaspora.
2. Globalization—Africa. 3. Africans—United States. 4. Yoruba (African
people)—United States. 5. Transnationalism. 6. Slave trade—Africa. I. Title.
   DT16.5.F35 2013
   909.0496—dc23

2013011247

A catalogue record for this title is available from the British Library.

Cover image: Detail from *Birdcall 1* by Victor Ekpuk.

This publication is printed on acid-free paper.
Printed in the United States of America

For Professor Tunde Babawale, for his excellent
leadership in transforming the Center for
Black Arts and African Civilization (CBAAAC) in Nigeria

Contents

Plates follow page 312.

Preface and Acknowledgments

This book connects the history of slavery, the transatlantic slave trade, contemporary migrations, and their legacies, and speaks to the broader issues of the African diaspora in relation to previous and ongoing struggles of black people for rebirth, progress, justice, and racial uplift. It focuses on the African diaspora in the Americas, notably the United States. While some of the concepts and frameworks are surely applicable to other contexts, the book does not make the claim of constructing a blanket history for all diasporic experiences.

The book has four components: First, the power and identity structures created by the Atlantic slave trade; second, the diaspora as a function of this slave trade; third, the diaspora created by a large number of contemporary voluntary migrants; and fourth, the identities that members of the African diaspora have created for themselves from these modern day migrations. In the following thirteen chapters, the historical themes of racism, slavery, domination, resistance, and resilience are framed as the context for understanding diaspora history, linking the past with the present in ways that contribute to discussion of contemporary issues such as the eradication of poverty and the preservation of traditional practices and values.

This work represents a contribution to constructing a longer causal history of the diaspora and its impact on the modern world. It connects black history with black identity and politics. In this long-term history, the book shows the new and old African diasporas and the resulting ideological and cultural differences between the two. In this way, it establishes political and existential histories for members of the slave diaspora, first- and second-generation migrants, migrants from different African nations, exiles, and transnationalists. Finally, the work contextualizes the African history of the diaspora in global networks to correct gaps in African nationalized pedagogies.

For thirty years, I have privileged the writing of history from below. While not ignoring the state and major political actors, I have always been interested in the experiences and responses of people themselves: how policies affect ordinary men and women, how every-day people seek dignity and fight back against power, and how weaker nations respond to stronger ones. In this book, my interest in agency continues: the agency of Africa as a continent within a powerful wider world; the agency of the displaced, enslaved, and free; and the agency of the poor. Power, resistance, and nationalism are the three organizing principles that arrange the data and present the analyses. The conversational tone has been retained for effect, as in chapter 5 where it is crucial to underscore the assumed linkage in identity between the speaker and his audience, and where an academic sub-ject connects to ongoing politics and cultural nationalism.

Various public lectures gave birth to this book, and I am indebted to a rather long list of committed scholars, engaged students, vibrant intellectual settings, and genuine academic spaces where there was a lot of interest in remaking Africa and the world. In 2008 the rise of Barack Obama, the first candidate in the long battle for an African American to win the nomination of the Democratic Party, energized academic discussions of the African diaspora and provided several points of interest to anchor some of the key issues in this book. I must also give credit to Ben Weiss, my undergraduate student at the University of Texas at Austin, who proofread the first draft and checked the endnotes, and who pointed out some aspects of the work that students and the general readers may find difficult. Dr. Shennettte Garrett-Scott, a historian, graciously read the entire draft and made editorial suggestions.

The list of institutions and individuals worldwide that assisted me in various ways is indeed long. Let me begin with the students and faculty of the University of Texas at Austin, where there has been ample intellectual space for a focus on the diaspora that blends per-fectly well with my three decades of interest in African studies. The constant references to diaspora issues pushed me not only to com-plete this book but also to add my voice to a theme that has com-manded attention as a subfield in the last quarter century. My wish to provide a strong interdisciplinary foundation for undergraduate students led to the creation of a popular course, "The United States and Africa," that sparks intellectual curiosity among my students and keeps my focus intact and my passion for diaspora issues strong. My intellectual journey has been enriched by faculty who focus on dias-pora issues, creative scholars who are generous with their wise coun-sel. I am deeply grateful for their collegiality.

I also thank a long list of friends and associates who offered strong words of encouragement. Dr. Vik Bahl is always there for me, in spite of his commitment to his young family. Vik and his wife, Seema, are first-generation migrants from India. Living in the diversified cities of Seattle and Phoenix, they are now witnessing the growth of a third generation who aspire to maintain a connection to Indian culture and values. Their son Ayodele's life illustrates in many ways the contents of this book. By birth an American citizen, and a second generation Indian parent, Ayo is being inserted into multiple worlds. Vik and Seema, in spite of their insertions into American society, are embedded in Indian communities. The celebration of their marriage and the child-naming ceremony for Ayodele were non-Western. I am the chronicler of an interesting experience. Ayodele is a Yoruba name, one that I bestowed on him with a formal ceremony presided over by Professor Simon Ottenberg, who was a professor of African studies for many years at the University of Washington, Seattle. Ayodele as a name, even aside from the naming ceremony, is a reflection of the complex nature of interactions in an age of globalization.

Professor emeritus A. B. Assensoh of the University of Indiana, Bloomington, always has encouraging words of wisdom and engaging stories. He represents the best in collegiality. Fondly known as "Brother A. B.," Professor Assensoh is steeped in that dying Renaissance tradition of encyclopedic knowledge combined with generosity and sharing. Dr. Moses Ochonu of Vanderbilt University posed tough questions that led to new thinking and fresh interpretations. In the same vein, Dr. Bessie House-Soremekun, Public Scholar in African American Studies, Civic Engagement, and Entrepreneurship, and professor of political science at Indiana University–Purdue University in Indianapolis, is a gentle critic who routinely checked on the progress of my work and health. Her remarkable friendship is a gift that I value immeasurably for always demanding acknowledgment of the the practical values of knowledge, demonstrating her unique ability to turn historical narratives into more accessible scholarship.

I have benefited from the support and comments of various professors from different corners of the world. I am especially grateful for the comments, friendship, and encouragement of colleagues in Nigeria, notably Professors Okpeh O. Okpeh of Benue State University, Aderonke Adesanya and Ademola Dasylva of the University of Ibadan, and Professor Ayo Olukoju, formerly of the University of Lagos but now the president of Caleb University, Nigeria. These scholars are all advocates of my work and committed supporters of my "nationalist" and "Pan-Africanist" approaches. As the book took shape, I received critical insights from great minds such as Reverend Attah Agbali as well as Professors Akin Ogundiran, Niyi Afolabi Wilson Ogbomo, and Augustine Agwuele.

The collegiality of the campuses where I presented many of the ideas in this book is impressive, and I can hardly repay the debt of affection and hospitality I owe to hundreds of people, many of whom I met for the first time. In Brazil, where I spent the summer of 2006 lecturing, I am most grateful for the invitation and red-carpet treatment offered by Professor Maria Antoneta Antonacci of the History Department at the Catholic University of São Paulo. Maria showed an unstinting support and kindness, so rare to find anywhere. Maria and her two students, Silvia Lorenso and Nirlene Neponuceno, formed a trio that took care of me daily and sustained an unusual interest in all the lectures. Also in Brazil, the guru at the Federal University in Bahia, João Reis, organized a major university lecture for me with an overflowing crowd beyond the hall. In Bahia, the faculty and students of the Steve Biko Institute were wonderful, and they shared their big hearts and brilliant minds with me. I have been back into Brazil on other occasions, at the invitation of UNESCO and the Center for Black Arts and African Civilization, under the dynamic leadership of Professor Tunde Babawale.

In Africa, I enjoyed the hospitality of colleagues in Accra, Cape Town, Cape Coast, Cairo, Makurdi, Kaduna, Ile-Ife, Ede, Calabar, Gombe, Abuja, Nsukka, Ondo, Ile-Ife, Akungba, Lagos, and Ibadan. At the University of Ibadan, where I gave a keynote address in June 2008, the English Department treated me lavishly, including an elaborate drama performance. In 2007 Dr. Akin Alao devoted an entire week to transport me to five universities to present lectures to large crowds. He and his wife Ireti demonstrated the richness of Nigerian hospitality in all its details and indescribable lavishness. At Adeniran Ogunsanya College of Education, Ijanikin, Mrs. Nike Ajayi handled a university lecture with competence and affection. Professor Okpeh O. Okpeh and Dr. Ademola Babalola, both based in Nigeria, have had to log hundreds of miles in moving me from one location to another. These are two great friends of outstanding human qualities. In May 2012 I returned to Ibadan to give two lectures. I gave the J. F. Odunjo Memorial Lecture at the University of Ibadan, where Professor Philip Ogundeji and his team were very hospitable. At Lead City University,

Professors Jide Owoeye and Ayo Olukotun prepared a hero's welcome and an auditorium-size audience. The Nigerian connection was further cemented by the most generous funding provided by Professor Tunde Babawale of the Center for Black and African Art and Civilization, who hosted an elaborate UNESCO conference on slavery in Calabar in March 2012, as well as the Toyin Falola Annual Conference in July of the same year. Both provided great opportunities to discuss various aspects of this book. Professor Ayandiji Daniel Aina, the vice chancellor of the new Adeleke University, Ede, invited me to give the 2012 Distinguished University Lecture, which generated discussions on migrant networks in globalized spaces.

In the United States, I cannot thank enough the various universities that generously invited me to give public lectures. The list is rather long, but the memory of some are forever implanted in my mind: the University of Illinois, the University of Maryland at Eastern Shore, the State University of New York at Stony Brook, Florida International University, Kennesaw State University, Cornell University, the University of Georgia at Athens, Indiana University, Temple University, the Pennsylvania State University, Delaware State University, Norfolk State University, James Madison University, the University of North Carolina at Charlotte, Rice University, Texas State University, Johns Hopkins, Tennessee State University, the University of Vanderbilt, the University of Indiana at Indianapolis, Xavier University of Louisiana, Central Connecticut State University, Bowling Green State University, Colgate University, Langston University, Kentucky State University, and Marquette University in Milwaukee.

A number of academic associations were gracious in their invitations to me to deliver keynote addresses, notably the Canadian African Studies Association, which held its annual conference in Queens in 2009, where Professor Marc Epprecht served as the excellent host. I must also thank Dr. Jamiane Abidogun, who invited me in 2008 to deliver the keynote address at a conference in St. Louis, Missouri. Dr. Abidogun is a scholar who has turned Africa not only into her home but also into a commendable passion, both in the generosity of her spirit and the grandness of her affection.

In Europe, my gratitude goes to the African Studies Program at Hannover; the German Anthropological Association, which invited me to Halle; the Casa Africa in Gran Canaria, Spain; the Wilberforce Institute at Hull and the Department of History, Warwick University, the United Kingdom; and a host of other organizations in Germany and Spain. In France, I cannot thank enough the generous hospitality of Dr. Jean-Luc Martineau and the late Dr. Brigitte Kowalski. Dr. Marisa Pineau of the Department of History, Universidad de Buenoes Aires, facilitated an enjoyable trip to Argentina. Professor Paul Lovejoy is always gracious in hosting me in Toronto once a year. His library, one of the best in the world, supplies me with an endless stream of ideas.

I am happy to acknowledge this large intellectual and social debt to the aforementioned institutions and scholars, the majority of whom I met only once in my life. Indeed, I cannot write a book of reflections such as this one without incurring innumerable debts. I have had to draw from the scholarship of various generations of scholars since the nineteenth century, many of whom will go uncited but remain as part of this blanket acknowledgment. My apologies to anyone that I have failed to recognize.

The University of Rochester Press believed in my projects. Suzanne Guiod, their former editorial director, was meticulously committed to every manuscript from the proposal stage to the book in print. I am very gratified by my association with the press, and I thank everyone for their constant encouragement and support.

I wish to thank the Office of the Vice President for Research and the Office of the President of the University of Texas who provided a generous grant to support the publication of the book.

Finally, I am grateful to my family for their support and love. Bisi, my wife, has been a major source of support for three decades. My three children, Dolapo, Bisola, and Toyin, add to the joy of living.

Toyin Falola
University of Texas at Austin
Summer 2012

Introduction

The Old and New African Diaspora

This book pulls together three dominant themes in the history of Africa and the African diaspora since the fifteenth century—slavery, migrations, and contact with the West—to reflect on their cumulative impact over the years. The consequences of the interactions of Africa and the West transcend the boundaries of Africa itself and extend to locations where black people have been scattered over time and are now labeled as the "African diaspora." Some other labels have emerged, such as the "black Atlantic" and the "Atlantic World," incorporating the four continents of Europe, the Americas, and Africa: all localities united by contacts, interactions, migrations of peoples, and exchanges of commodities, and all made possible by the use of the Atlantic Ocean to move goods, peoples, and ideas. The diaspora addressed in this book is in the Americas, and most examples are drawn from the interactions between Africa and the United States. The chapters focus on the relationships between and among people; the postscript points to the relations between states, which shape the future of migrations and transnationalist projects.

To be sure, the African diaspora extends far beyond the United States; there are also communities of African origin in the Caribbean, the continental South and North America, Asia, the Middle East, and Europe. While there are commonalities in the experiences of these various diasporic communities, there are also important differences set in the context of regional histories, economics, and politics. In a recent essay, the historian Paul Tiyambe Zeleza has warned against the danger of imposing our knowledge of the African American representatives of this diaspora onto our understanding of other diasporic communities in such places as Iraq and India.[1] Before him, the historian Pier M. Larson noted how the Atlantic scholarship dominates our understanding of the African diaspora in spite of the evidence that millions were also forced to migrate to the Mediterranean and the Indian Ocean.[2] The caution by Zeleza is borne in mind, although my work extends the point made by Larson about the centrality of the Atlantic. In both past and present histories, the focus and examples are drawn mainly from West Africa and the United States without losing sight of other relevant cases.[3]

The three issues of slavery, migrations, and contacts are united in terms of how they were all instigated by the expanding and extensive power of Europe (and also the Americas) in creating dynamic global forces of interactions, and of how Africans have had to respond to many circumstances, some of which they were able to control, some beyond their control. In these interactions, Africans have served as subjects (when they were dominated), as agents (when they shaped the events), as victims (in the case of forced migrations), and as the instigators of their own miseries that have given rise to the wave of contemporary immigrations.

The generations of African migrants in the years of the transatlantic slave trade are different from contemporary migrants. Although now homogenized as "black" people, the history of the individuals of the successive waves of migration is not the same. Thus, this book focuses on the diaspora created by the Atlantic slave trade (now called the "Old Diaspora," which led to such identities as Afro-Brazilians, African Americans, Afro-Cubans, and the like) and of the diaspora of individuals of the contemporary period, known by various names as the "transnationalists," "recent migrants," and the like, of the "New Diaspora."

With respect to the Old Diaspora, this book deals with a history of misery and reflects on the burdens of slavery, racism, and domination, but also resistance and the collective genius of survival. The dispersal of Africans to other parts of the world created a black diaspora, studied as part of the "Atlantic World," "world history," the "black Atlantic," and a host of other labels that link space, time, and people together to explore the history and forms of interactions in different continents. Slavery, in whatever form, involves the punishment of a powerless victim captured by acts of violence and kept in bondage. Racism was about persecution, using the "color line" to separate human beings, and to enable those of "superior" color to abuse and degrade those of "inferior" color. This book is also about the lingering impact of displacement brought about by the slave trade, which relocated Africans against their will to the Americas, Europe, and Asia. Part 1 examines the formation of identity and identity politics in the context of the transatlantic slave trade and the plantation complex.

The colonial conquest and the insertion of Africa into the consciousness of the Western world after 1885 and the Berlin West Africa Conference added significantly to displacement; millions of Africans left as voluntary migrants. A "new diaspora" had been created, which forms part 2. The number of voluntary migrants has increased since the 1980s and is currently estimated at over ten million Africans scattered in different parts of the world. A larger percentage of these migrants maintains connections with Africa,[4] thus strenghtening the forces of globalization. A new set of knowledge is being generated to understand this "new diaspora," including established and new literary works on the tropes of alienation, abandonment, suffering, and new opportunities.[5]

All diasporas have to be managed once they have been constructed by the migrants, slave traders, owners, and host societies. To be managed they have to be imagined, which involves complex networks and relations between Africa and the various places that have a black presence. The loss of actual location becomes the profit of reflection, the ruptures of dislocation are turned into the value of network formation. The consequences of the diaspora are enormous and long-lasting. Distance and space are overcome in such a way that the past (history) informs the present (politics). If the West traumatized Africans in slavery and conquest, the African diaspora keeps the memory of slavery alive in the politics and practices of black solidarity. Therefore, part 3 is the formation of identities in response to displacement.

The generation of knowledge about Africa and the African diaspora has equally been influenced by issues of slavery, race, exploitation, and domination. There is an intellectual coherence to the study of Africa and blackness as units of identity, space, and boundaries. Knowledge has made it possible to point to areas of domination and exploitation in different historical eras and places. An opportunity has been provided to generate nationalism, thus making Africa and the African diaspora both a category of analysis (academic knowledge) and of practice (politics, actions, and nationalism). This book reflects the unity made possible by the historical circumstances that connect Africa with the places where the Africans have migrated.

In analyzing the representation of Africa, a myriad of issues and social processes are crucial. Whether related to slavery, colonialism, or race relations, scholarly thinking and social actions tend to be combined. The "modernity" constructed by Wilmot Blyden, one of the most prominent African scholars of the nineteenth century,[6] cannot be understood without also regarding his theories as political. Kwame Nkrumah, the first president of independent Ghana, was not just operating as a theoretician of Pan-Africanism, but also as a political activist.[7] K. O. Dike, a historian of the post–World War II era, was not just writing academic history, but was also advancing the agenda of nationalism and nation building.[8] Knowledge about Africa, as this book makes clear, is not disconnected from the real world of politics.

Knowledge about the diaspora is connected with African history. Ideas spread in a transatlantic and transnational manner. An intellectual connectedness has delivered ideas on race and slavery from Bahia in Brazil to Accra in Ghana, and ideas of cultural nationalism (e.g., Négritude) from Harlem in New York to Lagos in Nigeria. The concept of blackness, the phenomenon of race, and the "invention" of Africa are part of a package of ideas that have been circulating for over one hundred years. This package is analyzed in some of the following chapters as a history that enables us to connect the past with the present, and also develop it as a political idea that allows us to understand how society is constructed through the prism of identity and the consequences of the intervention of the West in Africa.

Some of the diverse topics in this book include slavery, the impact of Africans on American cultures, the linkages between the diaspora and Africa, and the emerging ideas on the new generation of African immigrants that I call the "transnationalist diaspora." The themes are organized around an older history and an emerging one. I will make brief comments on the old and new diaspora, using knowledge that is familiar to many readers to frame the overarching context.

The Old Diaspora: The Atlantic Slave Trade and Identity Issues

Slavery and the slave trade connected Africa to the world economy and to global history. The grand narratives of world history cannot be accurately written without including the slave trade, and an understanding of the global economy and politics since the fifteenth century cannot omit the role played by Africans. Africa was an integral part of the Atlantic World and played a crucial role in the history of early modernity, the industrialization of Europe, and the plantation economies in the Americas.[9] If the beginning of the new field of Atlantic history is dated to the fifteenth century, then it means precisely the beginning of the connections between Europe and West Africa and the subsequent extension to the Americas following the "discovery" voyages of Columbus in 1492. If the end of Atlantic history is dated by some scholars to the abolition of the slave trade during the nineteenth century, a very contested position since connections to the slave trade continued into the twentieth century, Africa was still integral in terms of the stoppage of the slave traffic. Thus, for four hundred years Africa was connected with a larger world, being shaped by and also shaping that world.

The areas along the sea were profoundly affected, and the impact reached far into the interior where economies and politics were restructured to meet the demands and pressures of the Atlantic World. Africans were linked to the Atlantic World in their greater role as slaves, cheap labor that was used in various aspects of the ecomomy and society. Those who left Africa could not have imagined the long distances they were to travel to their new destinations. They took with them ideas and cultures. Those left behind received imported items, new food crops, and new cultures. Diseases were also exchanged. Africans in the interior used the new products of the Atlantic World even though most were unlikely to have any idea where the products came from, giving them generic names that associated the makers with a race different from their own.

The improved capacity to navigate the world drew Africa into a huge Atlantic economy from the fifteenth century onward. In 1444 the Portuguese pioneered the slave trade, forcefully capturing some Africans at the mouth of the Senegal River. Not only were Europeans now able to travel south of Cape Bojador, which had been the limit of navigation for years, but Africa was also to be connected to the large development of the plantation systems in the Americas. The ability to navigate the sea was linked to the European desire and search for commodities, and the extensive production of sugar and the labor to produce it. Europeans competed with one another in a so-called spirit of mercantilism that sought resources from other lands using means that were both ethical and unethical. Members of the political class sought wealth and control, while merchants and entrepreneurs did the same. Piracy was considered legitimate for some time, as was as ruthless ambition to take profitable land away from others.[10] The access to a limitless pool of land after the "discovery" of the Americas and the availability of African labor established the foundation of an Atlantic system that lasted for centuries.[11] Slavery had been an old institution in different parts of the world. For instance, slaves were used for large-scale farming and domestic work in various parts of Europe and the Mediterranean. In African societies with complex agriculture, the use of an unfree labor force, akin to the institution of slavery, was also practiced, as in the example of pawnship and clientship.

However, the Atlantic slave trade and slave system redefined the practices of slavery and enlarged its scale of operations. In a chattel form of slavery, the slaves in the American plantations were property, lacking in rights and privileges except as defined by their masters. The production of sugar in Brazil and the Caribbean consumed the majority of African slave labor; about another 5 percent worked in the Old South of the United States on cotton, rice, and tobacco plantations. As various studies of the slave trade have revealed, virtually all aspects of it were brutal and dehumanizing. Captured by acts of violence, human beings were turned into commodities by slave dealers. The trauma and horrors in the Middle Passage, the journeys from Africa to the Americas, were no less than genocide and brutal war.[12]

The Atlantic slave trade created the "diaspora of slavery," producing the established histories of the black presence in the Americas, Asia, and Europe. Africa is the source from which they originated, a continent originally organized into hundreds of nations. Africa is implicated in the memory and consciousness of many migrants, and is expressed in their notions of historical origin, land of ancestors, and place of dispersal.

Our conceptions of racism, underdevelopment, wars, and other issues have been shaped by African encounters with the West in particular and modernity in general. A number of black identities outside of Africa began their history with the trauma of the slave trade—they did not begin with the Stone Age and the natural cycle of human evolution that we associate with African history. The post-fifteenth-century encounter of Africa with the West has equally distorted its long history, so much so that scholars of the nineteenth and twentieth centuries spent considerable time and space providing evidence of a much longer history—the emergence of agriculture and settlements, the place of Egypt in global civilization, and the formation

Figure I.1. The passage slaves would exit through before crossing the Atlantic at the Portuguese and later Dutch Elmina fortress, Ghana. Photograph courtesy of Ben Weiss.

Figure I.2. A holding cell in the Elmina fortress, where rebellious slaves and foreign pirates would be detained. Photograph courtesy of Ben Weiss.

Figure I.3. Elmina fortress moat. Photograph courtesy of Ben Weiss.

Figure I.4. Elmina fortress from afar. Photograph courtesy of Ben Weiss.

Figure I.5. The British Cape Coast slave fortress, Ghana. Photograph courtesy of Ben Weiss.

Figure I.6. Graves of former fortress administrators, Ghana. Most died from malaria. Photograph courtesy of Ben Weiss.

of a number of great kingdoms—to prove the point that Africans were not stupid and docile, and that they had established institutions and states that ran well before contact with the West. The necessary response to racialist thoughts and derivative writing has taken a huge toll on the African psyche and scholarship.

The New Diaspora: Voluntary Migrations and Transnationalism

The concept and framework of the diaspora has been extended to Africans who migrated after the abolition of the transatlantic slave trade and most especially those who did so in the twentieth and twenty-first centuries. In so doing, we connect the histories of different generations of Africans who maintain a connection with Africa irrespective of their era of migration. A common label of "diaspora" supplies a definition and a framework to allow us to understand the identity of Kenyans, Egyptians, Gabonese, and others who live outside of Africa. Located in other parts of the world, Africa creates a meaning for their existence as a cultural source to draw on in order to live and survive, or even merely as a point of reference to compare and contrast their new places of abode with their places of origins, their successes and failures, the meaning of life, and the understanding of their destinies.

There is an "alien" connotation to the meaning of the term "diaspora" to contemporary migrants who have left Africa. Like all diasporic people, they live outside of the homeland. However, unlike others who are rooted in their new countries within a long history, as in the case of African Americans or Afro-Brazilians, contemporary migrants may represent a cultural group in a host country. Thus, the Sudanese in Columbus, Ohio, or the Nigerians in Houston, Texas, are often seen as a cultural-cum-ethnic community. These communities, in many of their own self-characterizations, connect themselves to the idea of a diaspora:

1. When they talk about race, they link their experiences with the older form of black identity: African American. To the first generation of naturalized citizens among them, they are officially known as "black" or as "African American." A dual conception is formed: a public one that partakes of the uniformity of a label and a private identity linked to an original ethnic

group (as Yoruba) or country (as in Nigerian American). The second generation may think differently, delinking themselves from the reality of an original ethnic group.

2. Highlighting a distinct category of blackness, as in the label of Nigerian American, suggests that there are subsets among diaspora groups. Such an affirmation of difference connotes the fragmentation of one race into multiple components, indicating that values and interests may not be identical.

3. Diasporic identity can be part of the "condition" of living and surviving in other people's lands. The situation in a host country and the struggles to arrive and make a living become elements of their condition, which in turn is used to create linkages among people originally from the same country or ethnicity in Africa. Thus, not only do they define themselves as a community (e.g., Igbo or Yoruba), but they can also describe themselves as a "condition" (e.g., "struggling people," "strangers," "outsiders," "marginalized immigrants," and the like). The condition becomes the context for unity, thereby promoting unity over division.

4. By using the expansive and elastic labels of "diaspora" or "immigrants," as with Ghanaians or Nigerians in Austin, Texas, this community can include the members of different origins and identities—Ghanaian-born, Nigerian-born, illegal migrants, floating students, and the like.

5. A tiny section within the new diaspora regard themselves as political exiles, fleeing from oppressive regions in different parts of Africa. If political exiles engage in politics, their connections with their homeland are consistently interpreted as sabotage by their respective countries. As a tactic of creating relevance, political exiles mobilize fellow migrants to participate in politics. Seeing themselves as a diaspora of refugees, the members believe that they will return home to Africa. As in the case of Nigerian exiles under the brutal military dictatorship of General Sani Abacha (1993–98), political exiles encouraged a number of those less involved with politics to become active, and a number became political activists. And there were also a number of asylum seekers who were later to become permanent residents and who lost interest in politics.

6. Transnationalists are, in one way or another, connected with their countries and ethnicities. Their home countries are

aware of their existence in various ways: as migrants who can project a positive image abroad (if they do well in their various fields), as migrants who can damage their collective name (if they do badly, as in the case of African prostitutes in Europe or the 419 cyber crime associated with Nigerians), and as sources for obtaining resources for development and corruption.

7. Transnationalists seek to create relevance for themselves in their original homelands. Migrations have elevated many of them in terms of new opportunities, but have also brought many down in terms of loss of prestige and the inability to find good jobs. Whether successful or not, whether their lives have been ruptured or repaired, a large majority of transnationalists think of how to relate to their places of birth.

Modernity and Progress

Africa is in search of modernity without wanting to lose what it cherishes from its past traditions, cultures, and histories. People want progress, which could be defined as

- the creation of a diversified economy that does not favor the tiny elite, but rather the majority of the population in order to improve living standards;
- the promotion of stable politics, the rule of law, accountability, and the greater participation of the majority of the population in politics;
- the preservation of the sovereignty of the African continent and its countries such that they are able to take actions that benefit their economy and politics; and
- the expansion of educational and social services to lift people from poor living conditions, thereby granting them access to institutions of modernity.

Whether in Africa or outside of Africa, the predominant issue for discussion is development. The most articulate voices are those who define modernity in terms of advanced formal economies, technologies, infrastructures, and ideas that may be called Western. There are constant demands for democracy, good governance, accountability, and poverty eradication.[13] To the first generation of migrants, what

Figure I.7. Faces of the New Diaspora: Cherno and Fatou Njie of Austin, originally from Gambia, West Africa. They own their own business and routinely travel between Austin and Gambia, and have nuclear and extended families in both. Photograph courtesy of Cherno Njie.

is persistent in this discussion is how to bring about the modernization of Africans and eradicate poverty. The old and the new diasporas are connected: powerlessness in the past led to population loss; and underdevelopment in the present triggers large-scale migrations. Knowledge about the past often triggers hope. Those who are nostalgic about the past, whether from reading about it or from direct experience with lived cultures, are insistent about the values of indigenous traditions and how to bring some of these back to the contemporary moment.

The various conversations reveal paradoxes, contradictions, and ambiguities. Although they often present communities as crumbling, many want the restoration of African kinship, the extended families that provided the basis for economic survival and protected children and the elderly. Although urbanization and the population continue to grow, some praise the village setting of the past that was built on the cohesion of people and that offered peace and security. Although Christianity and Islam have spread widely, some still hope that the

Figure I.8. A Fusion of the Old and New Diaspora: Dr. Maurice Soremekun (Nigerian) and Professor Bessie House-Soremekun (American) united by marriage. They live in Ohio, but travel to Nigeria at various times, and hold chieftaincy titles in the Yoruba city of Abeokuta. Photograph courtesy of Professor Bessie House-Soremekun.

Figure I.9. Colemar Nichols and Bisola Falola, husband and wife, American and Nigerian American. Interracial and international marriages are common and facilitated by the large number of African migrations to the West. Photograph courtesy of Colemar Nichols.

ancient gods and goddesses can be recalled. Whereas Europeans valued land as the most important possession, a concept that was introduced to Africa in the twentieth century, Africans valued people above land and often measured wealth in terms of the family and kinship size. Today, many still seek to shift away from what can be commodified (such as land) to what can be appreciated as human values in people. The value placed on people over land is a statement on ideas of wealth and property perceived as different between Western and African cultures.

The contemporary discourse on progress and modernity is connected with the subject of this book in various ways. First, the migrations connect to issues of modernity. By the early modern period, Africa had developed viable economic and political institutions that were affected by its location in the Atlantic World. Whether Africa had the capacity to keep the modernity process going has become a debatable point. However, one fact stood out clearly: It had lost its ability to compete with Europe and the United States. Technological and resource differentials placed Europe and the Americas above Africa. By the nineteenth century, the encounter was so unequal that Europe conquered Africa and imposed its variant of modernity with consequences that last to this very day. Power conferred prestige on Europe, which it also converted into cultural domination, presenting itself as civilized and culturally unified while presenting Africans as backward and culturally fragmented. Europe turned itself into the center of civilization, with Africa as its backwater.

Second, Westernization became synonymous with modernization. For millenia, Africa developed independently of Europe, thanks largely to the inability to cross the Atlantic. Differences in cultures between Africa and Europe were able to develop over time. After the fifteenth century, the differences became one of the ways to understand the encounter and to analyze the impact of changes. In the use of slaves and land, we began to see how different notions of property and rights shaped the use of labor and the definition of land ownership. Land that Africans regarded as communal had become privatized by the twentieth century. Indigenous religions connected to ideas of land and people were later redefined as Islam and Christianity spread. Ideas around kingship and kinship were profoundly altered in the twentieth century, replaced by political authoritarianism, contested citizenship, and sovereignty.

Third, the root of black poverty is very often connected with the past history of slavery and colonization. Today, the brain drain is added as yet another obstacle. Thus, in a sense, Africa's underdevelopment has been linked to its location in the world economy, its role in the Atlantic World, its domination by Europe, and to the contemporary declining economies that forced thousands of people out of the continent in the last thirty years. While many in Africa talk about these broader connections, courses are hardly organized along that line. National histories (e.g., the history of Nigeria, the history of South Africa, and so on) are supreme from the elementary to the university levels. Regional and continental histories focus on transformations that are perceived as internal, often disconnected from that of the Atlantic. The various wars of the nineteenth century are often portrayed as power rivalries, with minimal attention paid to the global networks and forces that drove the interests of states and ambitious politicians. The arms and ammunitions used in the wars were imported; the tobacco and liquor enjoyed by the members of the political class were imported; and the captives, sold into slavery to generate revenues to purchase the imports, were exported. The extensive traffic in imports and exports was not just internal regional and long-distance trade within Africa, but was also connected to global networks across the Atlantic and the Indian Ocean.

The twelve chapters and postscript that follow elaborate in greater detail various aspects of the African diaspora. Chapters 1 and 2 examine the issues around slavery, not in terms of the historical evolution of the commerce and practices, but in terms of the consequences that survived well into the twentieth century. Chapter 1 connects the transatlantic slave trade to contemporary politics. It is not about the Atlantic slave trade itself—the literature on this subject is already extensive—but rather its linkage to contemporary politics and economy. The chapter also argues that there are still dependency practices that share a number of commonalities with the older ones. In making this connection, the chapter exposes the structures of global and regional economies and politics that maintain established patterns of domination.

Slavery is a process that has affected Africa for well over five hundred years. In particular, the transatlantic slave trade set up ideological structures that have had physical effects with implications today. Slavery is still actually practiced in places like Sudan and Mauritania, while in other places it is practiced de facto through the side effects of poverty and corruption. Furthermore, the results of the transatlantic slave trade and colonization, for which the West may owe a debt and certainly carries culpability, have partly created the conditions of African governance that allow slavery to continue. These must be eliminated to foster progress. The chapter's importance derives from its connection of past and present slavery, how we got from one form to the other, and the identification of the conditions that sustain these practices.

Slaves, as chapter 2 shows, were agents who sought to resist, rebel, and free themselves. Using the 1839 case study known as the Amistad rebellion, the chapter shows how events and the memory of those events can become misinterpreted in the attempts to sustain hegemonic power and ideas. People can be subjugated such that their spaces and history can be maligned, erased, and misinterpreted. By so doing, former slaves and colonial subjects suffered double victimization: they were subdued and conquered, and years later history presents them as willing collaborators who accepted their condition. The chapter focuses not necessarily on the history of what happened on the Amistad but what that history means and how it has been used. The chapter shows how resistance developed among those slaves who were lowest in the power hierarchy and how resistance later worked within political processes that were not determined by those individuals. The chapter further focuses on how this history has been monopolized by non-African or nondiaspora members. Many works on the Amistad rebellion tend to monopolize the historical narrative in a way that does not subvert the power structures. This shows that members of the diaspora must maintain a hold on their own historical narratives to ensure they are not manipulated and they must embody resistance within structures they can dictate.

In chapter 3, the relevance of Africa to the African diaspora is located in the context of slavery and migration. Africa holds a relevance to black people living outside of the continent—the connections in terms of origin, the emergence of their own identity, the way they frame the politics of their own insertion and exclusion in new societies, and the values and education they want to impact their own children. The chapter shows how, in writing and teaching about themselves, it is almost impossible to disregard the African connections. The core of the analysis is about the development of a black academia from several black intellectuals, the variation within the conceptions about blackness and black identity, and the struggles to place these theories and ideas on the same level as traditionally Western political, social, and economic narratives that presuppose conditionals that subjugate the black narrative. The chapter draws attention to the overwhelming importance of the development of black intellectualism as well as the very real modern conditions that threaten to push it back below the surface.

Chapter 4 points to more evidence of connections, that is, the events that historically bind Africans, Africa, and the diaspora together, despite various realities that separate them. It also documents the challenges represented by overnationalization and the limiting of Pan-African knowledge, as well as the continuous damage done by some institutions. It suggests the ways to strenghten the ties: the creation of a powerful media outlet to present the truth and reality about the black experience; the emergence of powerful integrationist, regional, and continental networks that will bring people together and promote a greater flow of ideas and goods;

the socialization of a new generation to older cultural values; better economic and political management to overcome poverty; the preservation of what history still remains; and, ultimately, the restoration of Africanness.

Chapters 5, 6, and 7 take a specific ethnicity, the Yoruba, to serve two purposes: to illustrate the general points made about the Old Diaspora and to make connections to the New Diaspora. Chapter 5 begins with a moral allusion to a historical Yoruba curse, as attributed to the Awole story in Johnson's *The History of the Yorubas*, in order to explicate the enslavement, fragmentation, and marginalization of an otherwise royal people. Far from dwelling on this mortal curse, it examines the aftermath of Atlantic Yoruba dispersal and the renovation and regeneration of the Yoruba ancestral diaspora, cultural diaspora, and continuities of "kingships" and kinships across the Atlantic World. From the discussion of history, memory, Yoruba identity, resistance and nationalism, regenerative religious traditions, new Yoruba diaspora cultures and complex modernity, to Yoruba immigrants and the role of Nollywood in the appropriation and critique of culture, the thesis remains cogent and consistent: an imagined Yoruba future must take cognizance of comparativism and contrasts as Yoruba *insiders and outsiders within cultures* formulate and foster a dialogue of minds in order to create a lasting legacy of Yoruba humanity and progress well beyond the confines of southwestern Nigeria, and even beyond such diasporic spaces as Cuba, Trinidad, Haiti, Brazil, and the United States, toward a new dispensation of engaging globalization with a viable Yoruba culture in the theorization of universal ideals.

If chapter 1 looks at the entire continent, chapter 5 deliberately chooses a more specific focus on the Yoruba, an ethnic group that was drawn into the Atlantic network and whose influence has remained enduring. The chapter relocates the center of analysis back to Africa itself, thus clearly showing that the legacy of slavery is not just limited to the Americas, as it is often suggested in many discussions, but is also within some specific ethnicities in Africa. In the Yoruba case study, domestic slavery survived the abolition of the Atlantic slave trade. However, as slavery ended in the first half of the twentieth century, individuals not only became free but also lost any enduring association with slavery as an institution. This chapter is about the ways colonial deconstruction of the system of slavery broke down barriers in the hierarchy between Yoruba people. Migrations of freed or runaway slaves to other cities also facilitated this end. Various subgroups within the Yoruba culture started to blur together as class distinctions became unclear under the slavery crackdown of British rule. This inevitably has led to the ability to construct a more unified Yoruba identity in the contemporary era. Both the history and memory of slavery have been lost in oral traditions. No one can find a family that traces its origins back to enslavement. This chapter has two particularly important aspects. First, it demonstrates that the reason why this unity has the potential to exist today is partly because of the massive loss of slave histories. It is nearly impossible to identify the descendants of previous slaves. Second, it lays the groundwork for the possible argument that many of those that are impoverished today, especially because of lack of access to land, may have some linkages to former Yoruba slaves.

Chapter 7 celebrates the survival of African indigenous religions in the contemporary world. The chapter shows how these traditions have navigated their way through the historical narrative, manifesting themselves in the practices of diaspora members all over the world. By recognizing this linkage, we can use the culture not only as a basis to understand diaspora history but also as a unifying commonality to which many diaspora members can look. Yoruba religion (Orisa) spread to the Americas during the Atlantic slave trade, but has been renewed over the years. In spreading beyond the shores of West Africa, Orisa traditions globalize African religion while creating new hybridization. Its survival promotes cultural stability and supplies creative imaginations to renew older practices. The legacies of Orisa traditions have become an integral part of contemporary modernity in both sacred and secular forms. The constituencies that keep the Orisa traditions alive remain part of a global collective heritage.

The five chapters in part 3 cover the history and experience of voluntary migrants in the twentieth and twenty-first centuries. Chapter 8 highlights the place of Western education in forging transnational migrations. It details a very contemporary problem. It also identifies the correlations between the American and African system as well as the ways in which "solutions," like affirmative action, might be detrimental. Western education is presented as a force of globalization. As Africans seek degrees in all fields, they relocate to various Western institutions. On completion, many return and many do not. Irrespective of the decision taken by various individuals, internationalism is strenghtened and cooperation is fostered. Lacking inheritance, education has provided the opportunity for millions of people to make a living, to become socially mobile, and to engage in politics. As the chapter argues, education should be a tool for emancipation rather than merely advancing the interest of a career. Africans and African Americans have fought within the American system for equal rights to education. From *Brown v. Board of Education* and affirmative action laws, there is huge divide on how to keep the forces of separate and unequal from continuing their push into pedagogical society. Among all this, the members of the diaspora are able to dabble in the American and African systems.

Chapter 9 indicates how diaspora communities imagine the realities of the homeland, form new communities in far-flung places, live in two spaces separated by long distances, and conduct exchanges across those spaces. Diaspora communities now constitute a permanent feature of contemporary geography and politics. In this extensive global village, the Internet serves a purpose to unite, to create nations without boundaries, to connect millions of people together to formulate new imaginations and futures, and even to protest existing conditions and create oppositional forces to power structures. The chapter details how the initial separation between members of the diaspora has been mended in the past few years through the use of the Internet. Although people fell either into African, African American, or African migrant groups based on location, members of the diaspora have been able to reconnect through options like online forums to discuss issues related to their homeland. This inevitably draws members of the diaspora back to their roots. The chapter details an option for reuniting the diaspora community. Although we should be cautious of the faults of the Internet, this is an opportunity that previous black intellectuals could not have ever imagined.

Chapter 10 points to a large number of contemporary African migrants whose history and identity are different from the older diaspora defined, in the case of the United States, by African American identity. The migration is recent (postcolonial in Africa), voluntary (although instigated by difficult economic and political circumstances in Africa), and includes new forms of politics (post–civil rights era in the United States) in their host societies. The chapter examines some of the reasons for migrations, the politics of adjustments, as well as issues around the role and relevance of migrants in Africa and the African diaspora (brain drain/gain/circulation). Using the work of the scholars among them, the chapter examines the contributions of two migrant scholars to African studies to point to how new ideas are being formulated and put to use. As the chapter argues, education remains the key to mobility. Knowledge must circulate, theories of power must be understood, and greater alliances have to be forged to put the ideas and theories to work. The chapter is significant in its portrayal of African history in the globalized world. It uses this portrayal as a basis for arguing how Africans can move beyond their initial position of subjugation and act successfully within the framework of globalization. The chapter also takes a step back from concepts of Pan-Africanism to help remediate the wounds inflicted by historical suffering, which many academics skip over.

Chapter 11 is about all the ways in which creativity has, can, and should be expressed in both a common and diverse diaspora practice. From art to movies to medicinal arts, diaspora members have created incredible works. Any one of them carries meanings that could make for much discussion. Ultimately, these works traverse the realm of art into the realm of what it means philosophically to be connected to Africa. The chapter unpacks the multitudes of meaning that seemingly simple works of African and diaspora art can have, and demonstrates their sheer power not only in fighting negative stereotypes, for example, but also in constructing the black narrative. It uses two examples drawn from movies and painting to illustrate how African cultural ideas are spreading to the Western world. It regards many contemporary African migrants as agents and couriers of cultures. They operate at the crossroads of change and innovations, generating hybrid knowledge in all aspects of life. They have succefully created spaces of cultural innovation and expression in scholarship, politics, inventions, music, dance, food, and various others. As they travel back and forth from Africa, they carry voices and beliefs across the Atlantic. As they practice African cultures outside of Africa, migrants serve as agents of communication and as innovators who produce new ideas. As they take Western cultures to Africa, they serve as agents of globalization.

Chapter 12 closes part 3 by pointing to elements that will strengthen, rather than weaken, the ongoing forces of migration and transnationalism. The mix of people and cultures will continue, but not without generating both opportunities and discontent. Differences in culture will create challenges, especially in competitive religions that inevitably produce conflict. Africans in the West will reimagine the African continent and their nation states, producing ideas in favor of greater secularization and development. This chapter encapsulates the significance of the book as a whole. It explains how culture (religion, cooking, and art, to name a few) is critical to shaping identity and history. That being said, the book resolves with the conclusion that we must as individuals and communities envision the current globalized world in such a way that there is full mutual respect for everyone and for their cultural heritage. Globalization is taken to be almost unstoppable. What we do have control over is the way in which that process continues and benefits peoples of different races and nationalities.

The postscript treats the rise of Barack Obama to the presidency of the United States as the context for contemporary politics and migrations. With Obama's presidency, African relations with the United States occupy a crucial spotlight not experienced before by citizens of these nations or other members of the diaspora. Within this premise, the chapter explores additional reasons that warrant the uniqueness of US and African relations in the international arena. A black president does have the power to alter the historical trend of relations, but whether or not Obama actually will remains to be seen, and what this may mean for race and race relations is even more ambiguous. Other reasons are not necessarily related to Obama, but rather to global geopolitics. The American pursuit of staunching terrorism as well as the recent Arab spring and other global social movements present circumstances absent from previous diplomatic interactions. Given these circumstances, it is critical that the United States reframes its stance on international aid. Development support must come in a form that is devoid of civilizing or exploitative themes, particularly ones that aggressively pursue Western globalization. The key is moving away from humanitarianism and toward investment. Second, African nations must adapt their policies to find answers to their problems within Africa. Help cannot be depended on from the outside world. It should only complement and empower responsible African policy goals. For America, understanding this is crucial because an independent Africa is still very much within US foreign policy interests, and how America frames its foreign policy from this point will determine American efficacy in the pursuit of its interests in Africa.

There are a number of emerging issues that should generate new inquiries in the years ahead. In this book, the old and new diasporas have been juxtaposed more than they have been fully synthesized. Certainly blackness connects the two, but future work will have to comment more on the current state of African American cultural politics in relation to the new diaspora. Thus far, the discussion of

Figure I.10. Africa's political divisions. Map by Sam Saverance.

the Old Diaspora terminates with Pan-Africanism, spotlighting the achievements of Du Bois and his generation. In the most recent period, the key issue is the extent to which African Americans are concerned with or implicated in Africa's current development debates and processes. As difficult as this may be, new scholarship has to address the collaboration and conflict between Africans and African Americans in the larger society, the academy, or elsewhere. More important, there is the generational question with regard to the new diaspora. To what extent would the second generation (e.g., my children) share the framework that I have laid out for the New Diaspora? Perhaps the most intriguing connections between the old and new diasporas will emerge from the second generation of new immigrants rather than from my own.

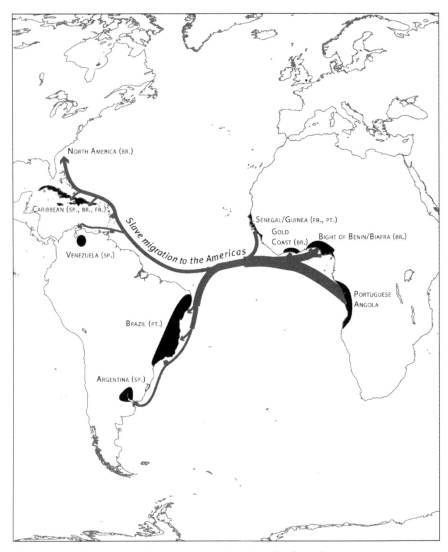

Figure I.11. The transatlantic slave trade. Map by Sam Saverance.

Part 1

The Old Diaspora

Slavery and Identity Politics

1

Africa and Slavery in a Transnational Context

No topic illustrates Africa's position in the international system better than slavery, both as an institution and as a system of commerce. While chattel slavery is virtually dead in most parts of the world, new categories and processes of exploitation have emerged displaying characteristics that defined slavery in the past. The Atlantic slave trade, colonialism, the Cold War, and the lingering economic status of Africa as a dependent continent are some of the most critical historical developments that tie Africa to the rest of the world. Of those ties, slavery and the slave trade remain the most significant; their effect linger to this day. A social institution connected with commerce produced a culture that highlighted the complexity and dangers of globalization. In any discussion of slavery, the transatlantic slave trade looms large. No other cases of human trafficking compare with the transatlantic slave trade in its magnitude and impact. Many will agree with David Northrup's summary of its centrality:

> First, it brought many millions of Africans to the Americas (four times the number of European immigrants who settled there down to about 1820), leaving a permanent cultural and genetic imprint on many parts of the New World. Second, the creation of slave labor systems in the New World was associated with the first phase of European expansion and the rise of capitalism. Third, the end of the slave trade was the subject of a massive abolitionist campaign that scholars widely have seen as one of the great turning points in Western moral consciousness. Finally, the Atlantic slave trade has been seen not only as affecting Africa during the four centuries of its existence but also as leading to the later European takeover of the continent and causing its present-day underdevelopment.[1]

The transatlantic slave trade and the experience of slavery in the Americas shape the way we look at the subject, and they dominate much of the space on writing about the African diaspora.

Working backward from the present to the past, the development of an Afrocentric paradigm in the United States, especially as advanced by Professor Molefi Kete Asante and his disciples, and the assertive demands for area studies are tied to a strong belief among blacks that the academy cares little about them and their concerns. If the academy does not develop alternatives to mainstream knowledge, topics such as slavery and the slave trade will either be ignored or treated with levity or duplicity. In his combative memoir, Asante even attributes the creation of an alternative PhD program at Temple University to the politics of race and what he sees as the deliberate undermining of issues relating to minorities in mainstream disciplines.[2] In this alternate program, Africa takes a center stage. As Asante closes his memoir, he exudes confidence: "The real work of this century is not going to be about race, color, or Black Studies but rather about the deep quest for African identity, liberated from mental enslavement on the continent and in the Diaspora, and gaining United Africa based on democratic power and founded on the realization of the dreams of Marcus Garvey, W. E. B. Du Bois, Kwame Nkrumah, Muammar Gaddafi, and Cheikh Anta Diop."[3] Asante's "quest for African identity" is hard to separate from race, color, and the very history of the slave trade that defined the Atlantic World for centuries. As he noted, until that legacy of "mental enslavement" is eradicated, moving forward may be too difficult. The names he invokes, all controversial figures, reveal his support for the kinds of struggles the men had that were all linked by a desire to create a powerful solidarity among blacks in different parts of the world.

Before the rise of the Afrocentric paradigm that Asante popularized, the Pan-Africanist movement developed as a diaspora organization by descendants of slaves who wanted to transcend the limitations of slavery and colonial exploitation, overcome dependence on other races, and create a new African world. Pan-Africanism responded to the earlier consolidation of racist ideologies and regimes that arose in part from the slave trade. By the nineteenth century, the West had imbibed an attitude of utter disrespect for Africa, and this has carried over to the present. Many argue that this lack of respect is attributable to the transatlantic slave trade, when the idea of racism was consolidated in ways that were very much tied to slavery. Various arguments over the era of the slave trade continue to be repackaged today, often disguised in elegant language and theories to mask the underlying ideologies: Africa remains the primitive "Other," the continent that requires rescue missions; and Africans are cast as a people without a worthy past or significant future. An "impending anarchy" is on the horizon, we have been told many times, and many pessimistic analysts have concluded that projects of colonization, similar to those of the nineteenth century, deserve to be pursued.

What the analysts forget to mention, not because they are ignorant but because it is convenient to forget, is that Africa's problems, in their many forms and ramifications, are due to both the inadequacies of its political leaders and the limited imagination of its planners on the one hand, and to Africa's role in the larger world on the other. Slavery represents one reason for underdevelopment. Africa is a huge continent, but in terms of total population, its one billion people is a rather small demographic comparatively. The slave trade is in part responsible for the low population. Unfortunately, the gains of the first half of the twentieth century that led to population increases are being wiped out in some places by the ravages of AIDS.

I hope I have mentioned a few points to indicate that the legacies of slavery do remain. I intend to explore this theme now, focusing on the globalization generated by slavery and its aftermath. We all know that the issues are many, the complications too countless to mention, and the controversies abound. I will focus on three major ideas: how slavery has impacted African history, the continued existence of slavery in the modern world, and new categories of exploitation.

The Past and Its Troubles

The starting point is how slavery created a diaspora and what this means to us today. European expansion after the fifteenth century was impressive, partially a consequence of the achievements of both the Renaissance and the industrial revolution. Technological improvements and the creation of nation-states empowered Europe in ways that devastated Africans, with the transatlantic slave trade as one major outcome. The early contacts established by the Portuguese were not sustained for long through trade in gold, raw products, and weapons, but came to depend on trade in humans following the heavy demand for labor in the New World. The establishment of small forts and the seizure of places along the coast to create trading colonies in the mid-fifteenth century established patterns that increased in scale and intensity over the years.[4] In later years, the trade in slaves became large, highly professionalized, and truly global in its operations.[5] The encounter was forceful and fatal, changing many aspects of the continent and its institutions in profound ways. It is now difficult, and nearly impossible in some cases, to comprehend African political and economic institutions before the rise of the transatlantic slavery. While Africans continued to keep some traditions of old, it was clear that many had to be adjusted to the needs of slavery and the global trade in slaves. At the same time, they had to accept new ideas from abroad and Africanize many of them in order to survive. Slavery became an established social institution in various parts of the world. Practices of enslavement acquired notions of racism in some places and contributed to laws and ideas that allowed one person to own, inherit, and sell fellow human beings. Ethical and moral codes arose to justify enslavement, wars were fought to enslave and sell, and rules were established to determine rights and duties between masters and slaves.

To be sure, Europe cannot claim to have pioneered all things connected with slavery. Arab slave traders and recruiters had been active for many years before the fifteenth century, moving Africans across the Indian Ocean and the Red Sea to different parts of Asia. We cannot accurately calculate the number of slaves that were also moved across the Sahara Desert to North Africa and the Middle East and from the Mediterranean Sea to southern Europe, especially during the eighth century. Arabs and Europeans sold Islam and Christianity to Africans, but not the belief that slavery was an assault on human rights. The Arabs connected the jihad with slavery, and the holy wars became an opportunity to turn war captives into slaves; consequently, the wars and captives multiplied in number as Islam spread into various parts of North, East, and West Africa. Africans in the savanna, in the eastern and central parts, and in the Horn suffered the most in what is now called by some the "oriental slave trade." Africans were used to serve in the army and state administrations and as domestics. Women and children were preferred. In the Horn, where the women were portrayed as obedient, honest, and beautiful, thousands of Oromo, Ethiopian, and Nilotic women suffered a great deal as they were relocated to other lands to become concubines and domestics. With respect to male slaves, Arab merchants who stayed within the continent, as with the plantation owners along the East African coast, needed them for intensive farm work. Raiding expeditions were many and devastated various areas.

The Arab slave dealers have been less scrutinized by African scholars.[6] For one thing, Islam is presented in many parts of Africa as an indigenous and pro-protest religion and Christianity as external and pro-Western. Elements of this historical presentation have led to the marginalization of oriental slavery, such that we talk more of the transatlantic than the trans-Saharan. The literature on the Indian Ocean slave trade is poorly connected to the larger body of the literature on slavery. Even assertive demands for reparations leave Islamic areas out of it. As if slavery and the slave trade had some redeeming values, oriental slavery is sometimes defended because it involved fewer victims (under five million compared to about thirteen million from the transatlantic slave trade) and emancipation was easier to obtain, thus promoting integration with society. While some of the comparisons are valid, the context of the economic systems must be borne in mind: Expansive economic systems did not emerge in most parts of the Arab world as intensely as in the American plantation economies. Neither did many slave communities emerge. But racism and exploitation were not foreign to the system. Today, Sudan represents the survival of elements of Islamic slavery. It was through the Arab connection that Africans found themselves in Arabia, India, and the Far East, traveling great distances as slaves carried across the Sahara Desert, the Red Sea, the Mediterranean Sea, and the Indian Ocean. Surviving as minorities, communities of descendants of African slaves can be found today in Iraq, Iran, India, and Pakistan.

Nothing, however, can compare to the heinous transatlantic slave trade. In attempting to underplay the damage and spread the blame, two issues have always been debated. One is the existing indigenous slavery before, during, and after the transatlantic slave trade. The other is the role of Africans within it. With respect to the nature of indigenous slavery, three points are relevant. It is abundantly clear that indigenous slavery in the nineteenth and twentieth century was a response to the external demands for raw materials on a large scale. Palm oil, palm kernel, peanuts, cocoa, and other crops were labor intensive. Thus, slavery during that era must be connected to a global economic system, with Africa playing the role allocated to it in the international division of labor.

Between the fifteenth and nineteenth centuries, what we call indigenous slavery was also transformed by the transatlantic slave trade.

The external trade injected violence into the system and relationships of power were sharply defined. A gap widened between those who managed the state and the poor producers. Definitions of social relationships increasingly responded to external pressures. As to the nature of slavery before the fifteenth century, we actually do not have substantial evidence on various practices, and some scholars such as Walter Rodney have denied that it existed in ways that we define for the nineteenth century.[7]

The definition of indigenous slavery continues to pose problems, as some are inclined to regard it as a mild form of servitude. Some scholars have warned that we may be confusing a slave with a serf. So too do the characteristics of slavery in Africa when they are compared and contrasted with transatlantic slavery; African practices were not similar to those of slavery in American plantation economies. No one denies that slavery was practiced in one form or another in various places or that it represented a major way to accumulate assets and expand the labor force.[8] The real issue that is always ignored is clear: domestic slavery did not instigate the external slave trade, nor did it establish the conditions for the transatlantic slave trade. Existing institutions of dependence could have been modified to take care of the external demand for slaves and, in the process, turn servants, political clients, and war captives into slaves.

As to the second issue of African complicity, one must make a distinction between people and states, between the poor and rich, strangers and citizens, the continent and ethnic units. Slavery and the slave trade involved the massive use of violence: in wars and military expeditions, markets protected by the state, and the power to make criminals and punish them. The tiny political class associated with the state saw benefits in the trade: the acquisition of resources to build and consolidate the state, self-enrichment and aggrandizement, and competition with fellow chiefs and neighboring states. This tiny political class collaborated with those who instigated and sustained the demands for slaves. When a greedy political class saw the opportunity to connect indigenous slavery with the external trade in slaves, the scale of brutality became boundless and wars—even those justified on the basis of state formation—converted innocent war victims into slaves. Economic gain motivated African chiefs, just as it motivated those who approached them for slaves. In a complex global economy, Africa was asked to supply the labor, Europe the capital, and the Americas the land to produce sugar cane, cotton, and tobacco. The African chiefs, no matter how much blame is apportioned to them, neither created this global economy nor served as its main financial managers.

Treating the slave trade as nothing but business tends to downgrade its human costs, that is, its far-reaching consequences. Philip Curtin calculated an estimated figure of 11.5 million as having left Africa, 9.5 million actually reaching the Americas.[9] His figures generated controversy. On the political side, some saw it as one effort to underplay the significance of the slave trade. Critics ignored Curtin's remark that a reduction in the estimate of the number of enslaved Africans did not lessen the harm caused by the trade. Statistics are one thing; their interpretation is another.

The overall impact on Africa's population has also been a subject of contention: While no one disputes the fact that the slave trade contributed to a population decrease, some point to other reasons such as wars, droughts, epidemics, and other forms of disaster. The enslavement of adult males negatively altered the population structure in some areas.[10] And millions of people suffered in the process of being captured, stored, transported, and exploited. More men than women left the continent as slaves, and the women left behind became intensely exploited for their productive labor, especially as farm workers.[11] Africa became the labor basket that sustained the economic enterprises of European settlers in the New World. The price it paid is incalculable. Violence spread, as slaves were obtained mainly through wars and raiding expeditions. The most devastated areas were Angola, areas north of the Congo River and the Gulf of Guinea, and large areas in their hinterlands. After the eighteenth century, southeastern Africa was drawn into the slave trade, thus spreading the devastation.

The slave trade scattered blacks to various parts of the world, in large part a consequence of centuries of slave trafficking. Thus, we have blacks in various continents, as part of both forced and voluntary migrations.[12] The origins of blacks in the diaspora approximate the main sources of the slave supply: West Africa supplied the majority, and others were drawn from southwest and Central Africa (areas of Cameroon, Congo, Angola, Gabon, and Zaire). Many slaves from East Africa went to the islands in the Indian Ocean and Brazilian plantations. So entrenched are blacks in these various places that many do not see the connections to Africa or understand its history, and some do not have clusters that are powerful enough to construct politics around those

Figure 1.1. Fort Metalen Kruis (Metal cross), Dixcove, Ghana, showing slave prison. Photograph courtesy of Professor Edmund Abaka.

Figure 1.2. São Jorge da Mina (Elmina castle), Ghana. Photograph courtesy of Professor Edmund Abaka.

connections. An articulate minority has always pointed to the connections in the diaspora, using it to build political movements.

Many have argued that the contributions of Africans and diasporic Africans to Western economies and civilization have been ignored, maligned, or underrepresented. Yet certain things are not at all controversial. Slavery made it possible for the New World to become part of a global economy, facilitated by the Europeans who recruited the slaves from Africa and sent them to the Western hemisphere, where they became the major labor force. Why Africans constituted the significant portion of the labor force has been a subject of contention. Economic reasons combined with racialist ones, and, as David Eltis argues, with the belief that Europeans should not enslave one another, thus making Africans the most desired slaves.[13]

Because of slavery, the Atlantic region became an active trading network that united four continents in the exchange of people, goods, and services. Credit and capital also developed as a result of

Figure 1.3. Fort Coenraadsburg, Ghana, showing Raviola and other defensive positions. Photograph courtesy of Professor Edmund Abaka.

slave trade. European merchants invested large sums of money in ships and goods; guns and other goods were produced in large quantities to sell in exchange for slaves. All participants were affected: The New World produced commodities that were traded to Europe in ways that affected the economies of such countries as Great Britain, the Netherlands, Portugal, and France.[14] Slaves contributed to the colonization and development of the Americas, enabled Brazil to become the leading producer of sugar, and made it possible for the Dutch to create successful sugar plantations in the West Indies, for the English in Jamaica and Barbados, and for the French in Saint Domingue to do the same. Slavery also shaped the identities of blacks . . . and whites and contributed to defining the character of European imperialism. The legacies of racism and contrasting identities remain in various parts of the world.[15]

Trying to show the varied impact of blacks on the creation of Western civilization has become a major academic industry that partly led to the emergence of the combative Afrocentric framework. The

Figure 1.4. Sâo Jorge da Mina, Ghana, showing the governor's quarter and drawbridge. Photograph courtesy of Professor Edmund Abaka.

gentle side of the paradigm looks at issues from the "African perspectives": writing history from the bottom up, focusing on issues of slave resistance and rebellion, African antiabolitionism, and the various contributions of Africans to the development of other places. The 1944 survey by Eric Williams lays the foundation. He shows the crucial role of the slave trade in building commercial capitalism, and he argues that the abolition of slavery in the nineteenth century also had to do with the emergence of a new generation of industrial capitalists who could profit by other means. Some of Williams's conclusions have been modified or rejected, but they remain widely influential. A major recent achievement of the historiography more aligned to the views of Williams is the brilliant book by Joseph E. Inikori who shows—with relentless energy, massive data, and mastery of the economic history of Britain—that the Atlantic commerce and the role of African labor in it contributed to the completion of the industrialization process between the mid-seventeenth and mid-nineteenth centuries.[16]

The contributions are not limited to the economies. Various studies have shown profound black imprints on American religions, music, and cuisines.[17] With cultural survival and adaptation at work, a spirit of "double consciousness" and cultural hybridity was put in place: African slaves and their successors would keep those elements of African cultures that were possible while integrating into new environments. Africa enabled them to create an identity while their host societies made possible the creation of new ways to live. Something new emerged in the process: the "modernity and double consciousness" that Paul Gilroy presents in *The Black Atlantic.*[18]

The less aggressive side of the Afrocentric paradigm sees the beginning of the decline of Africa from the slave trade era, an idea widely popularized by Walter Rodney.[19] In spite of the challenges offered to Rodney, most recently by John Thornton, Afrocentricists keep the argument alive.[20] To continue with Rodney's schema, the slave trade era was followed by colonialism, which incorporated the continent into a global economy in an exploitative manner. Decolonization did not bring about the much-anticipated changes, as the colonialists handed over power to a political class with values not different from theirs. The logic of exploitation was perpetuated, as the postcolonial leaders did not pursue a serious agenda of development. Rather, they merely facilitated neocolonial dependence, the marginalization of Africa, and the impoverishment of their own people. The failure to dismantle the institutions constructed around slavery and colonialism has created problems at a time when the technologies of global domination have become more efficient and more threatening.

Legacies and Lingering Problems

Slavery also has its recent history, a dirty aspect of the so-called modern twentieth century. Slavery and the slave trade survived the nineteenth century, as Brazil and Cuba did not enact laws to end slavery until the late 1880s. In the early nineteenth century, abolition of the transatlantic slave trade, however, did not translate into the abolition of slavery in Africa. In many parts of Africa, practices associated with slavery and other forms of servility continued well into the twentieth century.[21] While contributing to the abolition of slavery on the one hand, European colonial governments contributed to its survival on the other. The international demand for African products led to the extensive use of slave labor to produce and carry raw materials to the coastal cities. As a result, slavery had a slow death, surviving in some places until the 1930s.[22]

The need for labor to work on the creation of new infrastructures encouraged colonial officers to tap into various relations of servitude, notably forced labor. In the early decades of the colonial era, the need to sustain an economy based on cash crops allowed for the toleration of slavery.[23] The demand for raw materials also meant that many colonial officers overlooked abuses and cared less about the consolidation of social hierarchies. Many colonial governments also used labor in ways not different from slavery, such as forced labor, poorly remunerated labor, and semislave workers.[24] Pawnship consolidated itself in many areas, in ways not too different from slavery, largely to create cheap labor for cash crops.[25]

A fascinating case study has been done on the island of Fernando Po, which developed a plantation economy in the late nineteenth century. The migrant labor on which the economy of Fernando Po relied worked in conditions not much different from slavery. Ibrahim Sundiata shows how free and contract labor shared many things in common, concluding that free labor did not always triumph over slavery. As he concludes, "Far from collapsing, traditional slaving networks interdigitated with the new traffic in 'contract laborers.'"[26] In some other areas where raw materials were profitable, different methods were used to bind workers to the land in a way that benefited landlords and rich merchants. Wage labor could exist, but it did not necessarily mean that its conditions produced freedom and a higher standard of living. To return to the Fernando Po experience, the failure "to produce a self-replicating population created policies which made the distinction between slave and contract workers at times no more than nominal." Slavery was compatible with imperialism: "the triumph of British-imposed abolition and emancipation coincided with the increasing exploitation of the worker and the tying of the laborer to the plantation."[27] Women probably suffered more, staying much longer in socioeconomic conditions akin to slavery than men who could opt for wage-sector jobs.

In precolonial African formations where land was plentiful, the struggle was to obtain the means to obtain labor. In colonial economies, both land and labor became necessary to have in abundance in order to benefit from modern economies. Wealth had to be extracted from both land and labor. As slavery declined in importance, alternative forms of servitude were either invented or improved on, many in relation to debt. Pawnship of crops, of trees, and of the poor relied on indebtness to create access to cheap labor. Unlike slaves with outsider status, the new pawn could be an insider, even with well-known, visible kinship connections. A number of the aspects of the ideology that sustained slavery in the past are similar to those that maintain contemporary relations of dependence.[28] For instance, the apartheid system that existed in South Africa until the early 1990s was seen by many as the continuation of slavery by other means.

Mauritania and Sudan remain in the news as places where slavery continues in one form or another.[29] Both Mauritania and Sudan have complicated racial problems, although the government denies these problems, which are tied to the trade in slaves and the impact of Islam. In Mauritania, the French prohibited slavery in 1905, but it has continued nevertheless. Racial categories have been defined around slavery, land, and power. At the top are the *Beidan*, the Berber/Arab, called by some "white Moors," who own land, big businesses, power, and slaves. The *Beidan* construct themselves as superior to blacks and control the *Abid*, the black slaves either bought or born into slavery. The *Abid* are regarded as chattel slaves, owned by *Beidan* masters, exploited on land, and used to rear livestock.

The third category, sandwiched between the *Abid* and *Beidan*, are the *Haratin*, the descendants of local populations and freed slaves. They can use land given to them by the *Beidan*, own their own businesses, marry, and raise their children. The *Haratin* are not allowed to be equal to their former masters or to enjoy a similar social standing as the *Beidan*. The *Haratin* and *Abid* are collectively known as the "black Moors," and they regard themselves as an oppressed category. The droughts and economic decline of the 1970s and 1980s brought the interracial tension to a head with various conflicts over the rights to land and payment of tributes by slaves to their masters and landlords. In the 1970s, various protest movements by the black Moors to overcome their status were violently suppressed.

President Moussa Ould Sid'Ahmed declared in 1997 that opposition to slavery was against the spirit of his so-called democratic regime. Professor Cheikh Saad Bouh Kamara and four other leaders were arrested in the following year for so-called antigovernment activities that involved the internationalization of the problems of slavery and human rights abuses. The government argued that the universal declaration of human rights did not apply to the Islamic Republic of Mauritania. The argument came as a rude shock to political activists and many in the world community; after all, the country claimed to have abolished slavery in 1981 and inserted many liberal and democratic clauses in its 1991 democratic constitution.

Professor Kamara later received an award in 1998 from the United Nations for his activist role,[30] but his struggles and those of others have yet to transform Mauritania. The dominant class established its power through relations of dependence and justified itself by the force of history and traditions. The freed slaves (*Haratin*) do not believe that freedom has given them much economic and political power, although they are no longer slaves in legal terms. Many have been granted freedom but are still required to be part of former slave estates or pay dues to former masters. The *Abid* remain legally defined as slaves, and their masters enjoy their power.[31]

Turning to the Sudan, the external and internal slave trade has a long history in this country.[32] Current cases of slavery, which evoke conditions of violence reminiscent of the long-dead transatlantic and trans-Saharan slave trade, merit more space in the scholarship than most others. Slave raids to supply external markets began in some parts of the Sudan in the late eighteenth century, doing much damage to the society at large.[33] The wars associated with countless slave-raiding expeditions and other problems have created, according to Stephanie Beswick, a "memory of war and blood." Beswick has analyzed the dangerous psychology of this experience: "emotions . . . are attached to the memories of previous wars, killings, and misdeeds."[34] During the 1980s, an alliance of slave merchants and government officials conducted slave-raiding expeditions that were accompanied by the rape and abuse of women and children. In spite of various denials to the contrary, these expeditions have yet to end.[35] Even today, there are still cases of predatory attacks between groups, prompted by the fears associated with the domination of the south by the north, unending ethnic clashes, and slave raiding.

In 1990, the report by Human Rights Watch on Sudan was (and still is) highly disturbing.[36] In addition to detailing a variety of abuses committed in the conduct of wars, the report devoted attention to slavery, implicating both the army and the government in episodes where thousands of Dinka women and children were enslaved and dragged to other places to work as domestic and farm labor. The international exposure of the slavery cases put the Sudanese government on the defensive; it claimed that kidnapping was different from slavery and that taking captives was part of a long history of ethnic hostility between the Baggara and the Dinka. A government controlled by the north blamed the leaders of the south for trashing the name of the country. To the south, the Baggara and northerners of Arab descent have always exploited them, capturing their citizens and turning them into slaves.

In 1996, another report on Sudan concluded that slavery was still prevalent and linked to the ongoing war. To the compilers of the report, the Sudanese government could no longer call the widespread occurrence of slavery "hostage taking." Those who support it are most vocal in their denial, which is often expressed by government officials and soldiers who are known to have participated in kidnapping and selling people.[37] The situation in Sudan has energized more than a few organizations within the antislavery movements, such as the American Anti-Slavery Group (AASG) and Anti-Slavery International (ASI). In 2001, the AASG appeared before the US Congress to ask that trade in Arab-produced gum from the Sudan be stopped because the gum was being produced by slaves. It also asked Americans and others not to buy stocks linked to oil in Sudan. The AASG also took a freed slave, Francis Bok, to Congress. He testified about his sufferings and enslavement in ways that sounded eerily similar to the slave narratives Olaudah Equiano had written two centuries earlier:[38]

> I was born in southern Sudan near Nyamillel. When I was seven, my mother sent me to the market to sell eggs and beans. I never saw my mother again.
>
> At the market, the militia soldiers attacked. Hundreds of Arabs on horses came into market shouting. They shot people in the head. And they cut off heads with their swords. And the streets were a river of blood.
>
> They took me and many children as slaves. They put me in a big basket tied to a donkey, and they took us north.
>
> One girl had seen her parents killed, and she would not stop crying. So they shot her in the head. Her younger sister started crying. So they cut her foot off. I was quiet.

In the north, I was given as a slave to Giema Abdullah. He took me to his family, and he beat me with sticks. All of them—the women and children too—they called me "abeed, abeed" meaning black slave.

For ten years, they beat me every morning. They made me sleep with animals. And they gave me very bad food. They said I was an animal. For ten years I had no one to laugh with. For ten years nobody loved me. But every day I prayed to God.

One day I asked my master a question: "Why do you call me abeed? And why do you feed me bad food all the time and make me sleep with animals? Is it because I am black? My master was very angry. "Where did you learn to ask me this question?" he said. "Never ask me again." And he beat me and beat me.

When I was 17, I decided to escape. I would rather die than be a slave.

I ran away, and I came to a police station. "Please help me." I told the police. But they kept me as their slave and made me do work for them all day. After two months, I ran away. An Arab truck driver helped me escape. He hid me in his lorry, and he helped me to get to Khartoum, the capital.[39]

More suffering followed for Bok: The Sudanese secret police arrested him, and he spent five months in jail. He later escaped to Cairo where the United Nations Refugees Office arranged his relocation to Iowa in the United States. His story, packaged and popularized by antislavery groups, is one of many that have brought attention to the continuity of slavery in modern Africa.

ASI has also been relentless in popularizing the atrocities in the Sudan and pressuring its government to abolish slavery. The organization has noted that the Sudanese government is not sincere, and it has kept mounting international pressure to free those in bondage and prevent new enslavement.[40]

The cases of Sudan and Mauritania have long attracted international attention. The two countries and various cases of human rights abuse have led to the creation of many nongovernmental organizations (NGOs) to attack slavery and related forms of dependency and labor injustice. Also, within the United Nations a working group emerged in 1975 to address issues of slavery, pawnship (popularly known as debt bondage), various abuses to children (traffic in children, child pornography, child prostitution, involvement of children in warfare and criminal activities, sweatshops, and the like), various abuses to women (prostitution, genital mutilation), and the deliberate killing of people in order to sell their body parts.[41] It has had varying levels of success over the years. The new antislavery movements have given us a new definition of the institution of exploitation that includes not only the ownership and domination of a person but also cases of forced exploitation of labor, control of one person by another, and severe restrictions to individual freedom that deprive them of their liberty. In the process, indigenous people have been allowed to speak, and they have provided extensive data on a wide range of age-old abuses of forced labor, servitude, and debt bondage. Various governments have been forced to respond to criticisms and challenges offered by international organizations; not all have been sincere and some use all sorts of excuses, if not outright denial, to justify various practices. The more astute governments simply make promises or even send delegations to international meetings without necessarily reforming their societies.

While comparisons to chattel slavery of old may be misleading, and while it is certain that no country in the world now relies on slavery to sustain its economy, it is not wrong to emphasize contemporary relations of subservience and their connections to the slavery of old. It is also important to question the ideology of free labor and how poor wages affect millions of people in different parts of the world. The desire of those who seek labor and those who seek the means to survive converge in ways that create servile conditions. Modern forms of slavery exhibit three tendencies, according to Kevin Bales and Peter T. Robbins: "control by another person, the appropriation of labor power, and the use or threat of violence."[42] A few serious forms of contemporary slavery are identified below.

First, young African girls have been shipped to Europe to work as prostitutes; they are later abandoned by their madams or masters when they are no longer able to work efficiently or when they become independent in thought. An underworld economy, sometimes connected with crime and drugs, is hard to root out. Second, the rise of so-called illegal aliens in Western countries is often tied to bondage. Syndicates recruit migrants in order to exploit their labor. Afraid of the police and immigration authorities, illegal aliens cooperate with recruiters, making it difficult to arrest and punish the criminals. Third, within many African countries, young children, instead of going to school, can be found hawking goods or working as domestics in poor conditions and in exploitative situations. "UNICEF estimates that human trafficking is more lucrative than any other trade in West Africa except guns and drugs," declared Allan Little, a BBC correspondent who reported in 2004 the alarming trend in child trafficking in Nigeria. He added:

> The streets of Nigeria are teeming with trafficked children. Of the hundreds of thousands of street kids living rough in Nigeria's oil rich cities, perhaps 40 percent have been bought and sold at some time. The girls are most frequently sold into domestic service, or prostitution, the boys into labor in plantations, or to hawk fruit and vegetables for 12-hours a day in an open air market. Some work as washers of feet.[43]

Although we are not sure that his usage of the term "bought and sold" is correct, what is more common is the practice of parents collecting wages on behalf of their children. A way of socializing children to adulthood in the past has now become an avenue to make small amounts of money for parents to survive. In Madagascar, child traffic rings have emerged to steal new babies and sell them abroad for adoption. A few parents with many children have been accused of dumping the youngest ones on street corners because they have no resources to take care of them.

Fourth, the tradition of pawning continues in various ways. Poor people use themselves or children as collateral for loans, using their labor to pay off debts. The relationship between moneylenders and pawns is unequal and leads to gross abuses. Finally, cheap or poorly remunerated labor is a common feature in many parts of Africa.

Reparations and the Politics of Power

One of the main issues in recent years has been that of reparations, which in some ways revives some of the ideas of the Pan-Africanist ideology shaped by W. E. B. Du Bois. Since the nineteenth century, slavery and the diaspora have combined to create a black transnationalist ideology. For the greater part of the twentieth century, transnationalism was expressed in Pan-Africanism, a political movement that advocated the end of colonialism in Africa and the political and economic empowerment of all blacks irrespective of where they lived. Black transnationalism has enabled Africa to reassert its glory as the homeland and allowed blacks in various parts of the world to fashion their identity from African roots and the legacies of slavery, and to engage in multiple ways of survival in various places. The consciousness of Africa fuels the vigorous search for the creative means to move forward and solidify a non-Western way of living. Ideas such as those of Négritude represent ways of seeking new paths in a modern world. Pan-Africanism's connection to socialism was identifying a noncapitalist route to development, as capitalism was regarded as the source of slavery and colonialism.

The successors of slaves now demand compensation on various grounds. Some countries are being called on to start with an apology. In making the case, activists are exposing the ruthlessness and brutality of slavery. No one can deny the violence associated with slavery, the loss of relations and friends, the horrors of the Middle Passage, and the exploitation in the plantations. Suffering is grounds alone to justify an apology. However, apology is very much tied to domestic politics. Where racism persists, as in the United States, an apology is difficult for politicians looking for votes.

The aggressive demand for reparations is linked with black radicalism, most especially in the United States. African American scholars and politicians of the radical-nationalist persuasion have called on their members to calculate the debt—that is, the principal and accrued interest—and negotiate their collection from Western countries. Treating the slave trade as a case of war, robbery, and genocide against blacks, the radical-nationalists point to cases of compensation to Jews, American Indians, and Japanese for offenses committed against them in the past.[44] The various costs that advocates have demanded, calculated by different people using different criteria, are staggering.

In the late 1980s, Africans joined in the demands for reparations. A host of organizations emerged, and the Organization of African Unity (later known as the African Union) accepted the idea. Not only would African Americans receive compensation, but Africans too would receive a share. The late Chief M. K. O. Abiola, a prominent Nigerian businessman and politician, adopted the cause of reparations and donated time and money to it. Reparations can never do full justice to the victims, Abiola notes, but it is a principle that "wrongs must be righted, injuries compensated."[45] His arguments are similar to those expressed in the United States: Africa deserves to be compensated for the brutality and losses associated with the slave trade, colonialism, neocolonialism, and apartheid.

To Abiola, Africa suffered for five hundred years and continues to suffer because of "apartheid, debt burden and unequal exchange." As with African American advocates, Abiola sees reparations as crucial to Africa's development. "To a productive Africa," he concludes, "$250 billion in debt will be onerous but manageable. So, the solution being humbly proffered, is that reparations should take the form of massive infusions of investments in infrastructures, manufactures, machine-tools, power, telecommunications, education, health, advanced agricultural technology and support for political democracy in the motherland."[46]

The demands for reparations have to confront the Afro-pessimist views of a continent whose tragedy, it is erroneously thought, can disappear only with recolonization. It was when the movement for reparations was about to gather steam that some Western commentators began to call for the return of colonialism. Recolonization became the antithesis of reparations. While the view is not solely his, Paul Johnson, writing in the *New York Times Magazine,* doubted the capacity of many African countries to govern themselves and suggested recolonization in order to overcome problems of corruption, civil wars, ethnic conflicts, and famine.[47] In an imagined second round of colonization, independence would be off the table until the world is assured that a particular country is able to govern itself. This primitive suggestion undercuts the demands to transfer wealth to a so-called tragic continent.

Conclusion: Confronting the Legacy of Slavery

I would like to make a number of points here that tie the subject of slavery to contemporary realities in Africa. The connection between the past and present is not a stretch, at least not in this case. The thread is clear to see: the use of cheap labor has made it possible to build and manage states, centralize power, and accumulate wealth. Servitude is linked to power and accumulation. The slaves of old and the pawns of the present share a number of things in common: marginalization, poverty, ownership by a master, social domination, and the difficulty of redemption. The case of Sudan also shows that violence remains a defining characteristic of slavery even today.

First, the violence and criminality of the slave trade era bear a close resemblance to contemporary politics and warlordism. Violence underpins the exercise of political power in Africa. In the era of the slave trade, violence was used to capture people; now it is used to dominate and suppress the poor and the marginalized. Chiefs of old and warlords of the moment connect power with obtaining resources; whether it is slaves or diamonds, the two groups behave similarly. The political classes who supplied slaves are the predecessors of contemporary leaders who act as collaborators and compradors to bring together internal repressive forces and external profit seekers to prevent the state from pursuing an agenda of authentic development. Thus, as Africans complain about slavery and its legacies, we must also complain about the decadent and corrupt political leadership that promotes cultures of dependence and poverty. Those who want to help the oppressed and those in conditions resembling slavery may have to ignore the argument that the sovereignty of every nation is sacrosanct. Supranational institutions may have to acquire the power to deal with abusive political regimes.

Second, African governments, especially in Mauritania and Sudan, must stamp out slavery. Elsewhere, all the ways in which slavery affects democratic institutions or the growth of liberal politics must be reformed. Many governments will deny a connection between contemporary politics and past histories of social stratification. Some are clear to see, as in the case of gender relations or ethnicity. Many are more difficult to see and are disguised under so-called traditional practices, such as the male domination of women. Embedded in traditional practices may be relations of dependence such as slavery and pawnship, which affect the practice of politics. Traditional practices do affect what we define as political ideologies and do shape politics in ways that empower some established "traditional aristocracies" and disempower families related to the poor of old. Sudan and Mauritania show that established social hierarchies and the history of slavery affect political contests at the local and national levels. Even where the meanings of slaves and slavery are contested, there are attempts by those seeking power to manipulate the definitions to gain power and exclude others.

Third, conditions that resemble slavery must be eliminated. Today this includes practices such as child trafficking, child labor, and child prostitution, trafficking in women, debt bondage, and various coercive aspects of the sex industry. Such cases continue, sometimes on a staggering scale, as part of underground economies, leisure business, and the production of goods for an international market. Moral appeals to stop servile conditions will not work, just as moral appeals did not end slavery and the slave trade. Inducement in terms of cash payments for the enslaved to become free has been tried, but the success in both the short and long term has been limited.[48] Those who use cheap labor regard attacks on their practices as attempts to weaken them and destroy their privilege. Child labor, like slavery, may not be efficient, but it does work in terms of the ability of masters to maximally exploit labor, reduce maintenance costs, and operate without sanctions. The child or the displaced prostitute, like the slave of old, may be rootless, which makes them subject to a variety of abuses. Those who treat children or prostitutes as free agents miss the connection between poverty and servility and between servility and the ambiguous meaning of freedom in highly stratified and complex societies. Slaves were able to use force and resistance to negotiate power relations; in some cases they even created an independent power base and communities.[49] Children are unable to build alliances to free themselves, and prostitutes are not likely to be able to turn reproductive power to advantage. Governments and nongovernmental organizations have to intervene to protect the weak and to release the servile from their bondage. Access to credit and land will go a long way in preventing many people from surrendering their lives and futures to a greedy system.

Fourth, irrespective of the position one takes on reparations, I very much doubt that anyone can argue that the West owes no responsibility to Africa, if only to ensure that politics and economies develop in a sustainable manner. Involvement in the slave trade and ruthless colonial exploitation are more than enough justification for the obligation to be responsible now. Responsibility is not all about aid in the form of money. Just reducing the transfer of wealth from poor Africa to the developed West will go a long way in solving many problems. The strengthening of nongovernmental organizations and various social movements will contribute to the expanding democratic space, the training of leaders at various levels, and the empowerment of many people in positive ways. Africa is an integral part of the world, and its problems and promises must be included in global politics and the global economy. The continent has contributed to the development of other continents, gaining and suffering in the process.

Finally, the negative legacies of slavery and colonialism will disappear if Africa marches toward a better future. This is possible if conditions of democracy, good governance, sound economic management, and responsible political leadership are created in a sustainable manner.

2

The Slave Mutiny of 1839

The Colonization of Memory and Spaces

The 1839 mutiny now known as the Amistad rebellion is an important episode in the history of slave resistance. This chapter shows how that event transmuted into a permanent historical symbol and then into a template to understand race relations over time. I examine not the rebellion itself but how the interpretation of the events reveals our understanding of power and race relations.

The story is already so well known that I shall present only the basic details here.[1] On board the *Amistad* slave ship, traveling the high seas toward the northeast coast of America from Havana, Joseph Cinqué, one of the enslaved Africans, organized a bloody revolt against the Spanish crew. The temporarily liberated slaves hoped to sail the *Amistad* back to Africa. However, the Africans had no detailed knowledge of navigation and relied on one of the slave dealers, Montes, who had bought them. Perhaps Montes engaged in a deliberate trick. During the day, he steered the ship toward the east and at night toward the United States.

The ship was subsequently intercepted by the US Navy, which brought it to shore at Long Island, New York. The *Amistad* and its African cargo were then taken to New London, Connecticut. The Africans were jailed in New Haven, and a judicial hearing was set for August 1839. A trial ensued and exposed tensions between not only nations but also individuals in support of and against slavery. The *Amistad* episode energized abolitionists, who enlisted the services of John Quincy Adams, the famous lawyer and a former US president. A successful case of slave revolt galvanized the abolitionist movement, inserted itself into the American judicial system, and ended in freedom for the slaves. The legal issues included questions about who possessed rights to the cargo: Did it belong to Spain or the United States? The status of the Africans was also called into question: Were they slaves or freed people?

In September 1839, the initial criminal case was dismissed owing to a lack of jurisdiction. The following month, Professor Josiah Gibbs located an interpreter, James Covey, to speak with the Africans, teach them English, and introduce them to Christianity. Once they learned English, Cinqué and the other Africans filed cases against Montes and his fellow slave dealers for false imprisonment and assault.

The trial began in January 1840, and the district court judge ruled that the Africans should be turned over to the president of the United States, who should return them to Africa. An appeal followed in September 1840, but the circuit court upheld the decision of the lower court. The government took the case to the Supreme Court, where John Quincy Adams and Roger Baldwin argued the case. In March 1841, the Supreme Court ordered that the Africans should be freed immediately. Between March and November, the freed Africans learned more English and received a Christian education. In November 1841, they left for Africa as part of a missionary group. They arrived in Sierra Leone in January 1842, where they began evangelization work. Some of the Africans left the mission after a time. In 1879 Cinqué died and was buried in a cemetery dedicated to American missionaries.

My aim is not to revisit the narrative, which was the subject of a major motion picture directed by Steven Spielberg, but to comment on what the episode represents to Africans and people of African descent. The Amistad episode provides an opportunity to examine issues around slavery, race and power, domination and memory, conquest and nationalism. My analysis is limited to three broad interrelated themes: (1) the manipulation of historical memory for politics and for resistance to people of African descent who question or attempt to reinvent that false memory; (2) the transition from the control of people to the conquest of land; and (3) the response by dominated people to reclaim their own past and their struggle for inclusion. The Amistad revolt and the events before and after it reveal the difficulties that black people face in making their own histories in ways favorable to them. The conquest of Africa and the consequent disapora created by Western forces had cultural, political, and economic dimensions. This conquest, in its multifaceted forms, represents the colonization of spaces created by the African world. Its interpretation has also entailed the colonization of a people's memory.

The Colonization of Memory

Attempts have been made to erase the memory of the Amistad episode and related ones. For a long time, the standard narrative was that slaves accepted the condition of bondage for four hundred years and that many were unhappy with abolition and emancipation in the nineteenth century. Those who captured and used slaves were quick to write stories about slavery. In so doing, they sought to colonize memory regarding slavery. There were three rationalizations, which are sometimes repackaged even today. The first is the attempt to justify slavery on religious, ideological, and racial grounds. Motives can be disguised, putting the economic circumstances under the carpet and so-called humanitarian ideas on the table. Second, there is the flawed thesis that, in the long run, conditions of slavery were better than conditions of underdevelopment. Indeed, not a few blacks have even expressed the self-hating opinion that they were better off shipped out of Africa. Third, and arguably the most persistent, a clever intellectual approach is to treat the slave trade as a blame game, presenting a balance sheet between those who demanded and those who supplied. In this balance sheet presentation, the Africans who stayed on their continent and were forced to respond to a demand-side economy receive an equal share of blame. Those who have fallen to this balance sheet argument have been cleverly led to another problem: an attempt to divide black people into antagonistic blocs so that tensions can emerge between African Americans and continental Africans.

What also emerged from the colonization of Africa after 1885 was the shrewd attempt to colonize the African mind. The image of Africans as docile, eager to take punishment, and confident in bondage, since there was no better alternative for them, has deep roots. The presentation of Africans as passive and collaborators in the slave trade is also widespread in dominant circles even today, a notion that simply transfers the blame from hegemonic forces onto the victims of economic and political brutalities.

For a long time Western education became the tool of colonization. Consciousness of race inferiority was accepted and internalized by many black people. W. E. B. Du Bois spoke about double consciousness, defined as "this sense of always looking at one's self through the eyes of others, of measuring one's soul by the tape of the world that looks on in amused contempt and pity."[2] In his often-cited book, Carter Woodson spoke eloquently about what he called the "mis-education of the negro":

> The negro's mind has been brought under the control of his oppressor. The problem of holding the negro down, therefore, is easily solved. When you control a man's thinking, you do not have to worry about his actions. You do not have to tell him not to stand here or go yonder. He will find his "proper place" and will stay in it. You do not need to send him to the back door. He will go without being told. In fact, if there is no back door, he will cut one for his special benefit. His education makes it necessary.[3]

It took a while for new knowledge to replace old notions. Indeed, it was not until after the Second World War that the study of Africa received legitimacy in the majority of Western academic institutions.

The colonization of memory is based on the assumption that knowledge about events such as the Amistad rebellion, slavery, and imperialist domination can either be erased where possible or told from the point of view of the slave owners and conquerors. There is also the assumption that ignorance about the enslaved can be manufactured. The power of domination is turned into the power to construct memory. It is also the power to create silences when it was politically expedient to do so. The majority of Africans growing up in colonial Africa would never have been taught the history of slave resistance, particularly incidences such as the Amistad revolt. Until European colonial power on the continent neared its end, there was no academic project on the systematic study of Africa and its diaspora. African students were told that they had no history and that they did not make any significant contributions to world civilization.

The denial of a people's past does not mean that their past did not exist—all people have a past—rather it is a statement about power and the uses to which it has been put. When millions of people were enslaved and when their continent was forcefully conquered, it was a strategy both of justification and domination to deny the people a past, a memory. The maintenance of power also meant the creation of a new history to erase the previous one. The new history is of how domination has enabled the enslaved to benefit from their being in chains and how conquest has rewarded the colonized. Blacks were regarded as "the white man's burden": to prevent their extinction, they needed to be saved. To be saved, they needed to be civilized. To be civilized, they needed to be enslaved and conquered.

The colonization of memory is also based on the assumption that the colonizer was an effective teacher. The colonizer had become the ideal citizen, even in foreign lands. The colonized were transformed into subjects in their own spaces, and their land became a big classroom. Did not a notable British geographer, James MacQueen, arrogantly proclaim, "If we really wish to do good in Africa, we must teach her savage sons that white men are their superiors?"[4] He did. Policies followed that assumed the superiority of the slave masters and colonial officers and the inferiority of black people. Inferiors could not make claims to any credible knowledge. Their knowledge had to be colonized and taught back to them. The sources that sustained their epistemologies—orality, performances, arts, and the like—were delegitimized. They were told that to talk about the past, one needed written sources: not songs, oral narratives, or even their environments, which yields tremendous evidence. Egypt, Nubia, and Ethiopia were grudgingly excluded, since they had written evidence of history, but the forces of change and the evidence of the past were connected to a metanarrative that excluded black people as achievers and inventors. Even Hamites—a mythical horde of migrants from outside the continent—were invented as the creators of civilizations. Hamites were presented as Caucasians who joined other light-skinned people to create African civilization.

The colonization of memory has been clever in assaulting worldviews and religions. Many Christian missionaries aligned their views with those of slavery and imperialism. Turning themselves into agents to spread civilization, they were aggressive in their condemnation of indigenous worldviews and in their denigration of indigenous religions, which were mislabeled as paganism. The missionaries possessed a wide range of criticisms, carefully primitivizing indigenous creative endeavors in music, art, religions, languages, and cuisines. Attires were redefined as costumes, nations converted into "tribes," and legitimate state-building wars labeled as political anarchies. The violence of conquest was sanitized into legitimate wars of civilization;

the violence of resistance was presented as the activities of barbarians and cannibals.

The Amistad story reveals notions of memory. Technology, utilized by those in power, allowed for the acquisition of slaves and their transport across the sea. Manufactured guns and gunpowder generated the violence that conducted the slave trade, and plantations were places where slaves worked to produce sugar, tobacco, cotton, and other products. Owners perceived their slaves within a context framed by unequal power relations. Similarly, slaves resisted and tried to overcome their powerlessness. Slave masters, in relations with their slaves, relied on negative and limited knowledge about the uprooted men and women. Slaves were looked on not only as people in bondage but also as the representatives of primitive people.

Racism and evolutionism combined to generate stereotypes about black people in general. In the evolutionary tree, created by the Western idea of civilization, the most superior culture was Western and white. Others might be able to progress toward the ideals of this superiority. The black race was considered to be at the lowest stage of evolution, basically children who needed time before they become adults. Slaves were people with human anatomical features, but they were marked apart by race and evolution. Cultural evolutionism evolved partly out of slavery, was reinforced by colonization, and perpetuated by stereotypes. In this colonization of memory and experience, imagination ran wild—too wild.

The most positive image of the African would be that of a "different person," but never superior to anyone, only better behaved or exhibiting greater intelligence than other blacks. Rural lifestyles and the simplicity of slaves were seen as reminders of how the world used to be before progress came to the West. Universalism was invented from a premise of arrogance that one group knows and understands the truth, the only truth, which others must accept. Black people had to be invited to learn the truth, to move away from isolationism toward universalism. This is a form of control in which the claim of one truth becomes a strategy of domination—actually of total domination in the physical as well as epistemological sense.

The presentation of the Amistad resistors and of slaves in general has framed the meanings of Africa to Americans. They are meanings that show not merely the limitation of knowledge but also the deliberate creation of false images and memories. If Africa does not denote "tribes" and "natives," it can only mean the land of savages and cannibals. By extension, black people are poor, ignorant, erotic, and wild. A stereotypical canvass is painted: an exotic set of people living in primitive huts in the company of wild animals in the jungle. Language comes out of imagination, feeding ideas that are perpetually negative and supplying images of barbarism to entertain television audiences. Racism and exploitation are always coupled together and are very well accepted in the United States and elsewhere in the Western world.

For many years, the United States established a successful slavery and segregation system. Slavery and racism were practiced in a combination that ensured exploitation. In the years after the abolition of slavery, racist views persisted in one way or another. Today we find them in private discussions, exotic presentations, and the display of cultural arrogance. Animals, the jungle, and the primitive people who live there remain the most common themes of Africa, and they show that Africans are deprived and depraved.

The Amistad episode clearly reinforced the invention of Western images of Africa. The slave trade era redefined racial and political relations. From the eighteenth century onward, the Western construction of Africa united race and culture. A monogenist view of a world created by Adam and Eve gave way to a polygenist one in which God created separate races and gave power to one to control others.

The Amistad episode enables us to question the colonization of memory. It tells us about the fierceness of struggles for liberty and freedom. Moreover, we see hints and evidence of the value of heritage, the affirmation of culture, and the defense of humanity. It is important to consider how the slaves involved in the Amistad revolt formulated an identity of resistance during the Middle Passage. The struggles they produced led to a powerful representation beyond the symbolic: the representation of resistance as freedom and as politics, and of the culture of rebellion engrained in the experience of slavery itself.

Scholars have produced counternarratives to demonstrate the misleading nature of the colonization of memory. Today we have a long list of works on resistance to slavery that document various episodes and tendencies. Such studies demonstrate the failure of the attempts to silence or kill the slave narratives of resistance. On the African side, limited documented evidence reveals examples of people who tried to prevent the slave trade, such as Queen Nzinga of the Matamba in Angola, who from 1630 to 1648 fought the Portuguese who came to capture African slaves. In Dahomey, King Agaja Trudo attempted to end slavery between 1724 and 1726. The pressure on the demand side rendered these attempts feeble in the overall scale of the trade. Within Africa, the project of slave making was one of violence, made possible with imported guns and gunpowder. In the brutal Middle Passage, slaves had to be overwhelmed and shackled to prevent their jumping into the sea and killing themselves.

Individual experiences in the Middle Passage are not necessarily captured in the historical records. The Amistad was a revolt on a slave ship, one that we know best because of its prominence in the American legal historical records on slavery. But there were others as well. In 1730, ninety-six African slaves from the Guinea Coast staged a mutiny on board the *Little George*. They successfully confined the crew to the ship's cabin, reversed the direction of the ship toward the Sierra Leone River, abandoned the ship when they reached the river, and jumped inland as free citizens.

There was another case in 1740, in the same region, when a mutiny occurred on the *Jolly Bachelor* sailing on the Sierra Leone River. Free Africans attacked the *Jolly Bachelor* and set the slaves aboard free. Alexander Falconbridge, who had firsthand experience of the Middle Passage, recorded that the spirit and aspirations that shaped the minds of the fighters on the *Amistad* were widespread:

> As very few of the Negroes can so far brook the loss of their liberty and the hardships they endure, they are ever on the watch to take advantage of the least negligence in their oppressors. Insurrections are frequently the consequence; which are seldom expressed without much bloodshed. Sometimes these are successful and the whole ship's company is cut off. They are likewise always ready to seize every opportunity for committing some acts of desperation to free themselves from their miserable state and notwithstanding the restraints which are laid, they often succeed.[5]

Resistance within plantation economies was also common. Those with the ability to read and write and who took the opportunity to put their ideas in print composed slave narratives that have survived through today. Slavery was not simply about domination, as the narratives by slave owners tend to present it, but equally about resistance, as the activities of slaves clearly show.

Slave owners attempted to control the memory of slavery. Many of their successors have also attempted to appropriate the knowledge of slavery. This appropriation deliberately attempts to minimize the evils of slavery by blaming Africans for selling their own citizens and by making the demand-side economy less significant than the supply-side. Indeed, the continuity of poverty, in repackaged slavery conditions, is blamed on the poor. Alas, if only they can work harder! We have to reclaim the knowledge of slavery and of poverty in order to put events and actions in their proper context.

The Colonization of Spaces

The events that surrounded the Amistad rebellion were about the control of people. Around the same time, the control of spaces, manifested as colonization and direct occupation, was about to commence. The Atlantic slave trade was drawing to an end by the nineteenth century, but the forced movement of people from Africa was about to give way to a project of control of the entire continent and its people. Race supported the economic motive for colonization. Racist theories of the nineteenth century saw black people as inferior, as a race that could be destined for extinction. A number of studies conducted by pseudoscientists such as John Burgess provided a so-called explanation for black inferiority. With its enormous capacity to conquer others, Europe was confident in itself, its civilization, and its superiority. Europeans celebrated the industrial revolution, the progress in science, the Enlightenment, and their ability to travel worldwide. They used their own evidence to construct an arrogance of culture that saw others, notably Africans, as far below them. This was not the time to talk about the equality of races or of humanity, but rather of racial domination. A combination of politicians and businessmen saw the wealth that could come from Africa. Their vision was one of domination and maximum expropriation, not collaboration, and their ideas began to spread.

The colonization of the black space was a global project, the domination of Africa by Western forces, technology, and culture. The title of the famous poem by Rudyard Kipling, "The White Man's Burden," captures it all. The contents reveal a grandiose desire of greed:

Take up the White Man's burden—
Send forth the best ye breed—
Go bind your sons to exile
To serve your captives' need;
To wait in heavy harness,
On fluttered folk and wild—
Your new-caught, sullen peoples,
Half-devil and half-child.

Take up the White Man's burden—
Ye dare not stoop to less—
Nor call too loud on Freedom
To cloak your weariness;
By all ye cry or whisper,
By all ye leave or do,
The silent, sullen peoples
Shall weigh your Gods and you.[6]

Kipling gave us the clues. God and whiteness were constructed by Kipling as allies that would control others. These others were subordinate and childlike. Their subordination required an indefinite colonization of space because the transformation of the "half-devil and half-child" was a never-ending job.

The creation of the European empire in Africa after 1885 depended on the colonization of African space. Africa became an extension of Europe.[7] Colonial knowledge reflected this reality: The evidence of change, according to the colonizers, was produced by the colonization of space. The colonization of space, in combination with the transatlantic slave trade, led in the nineteenth century to the invention of Africa as the "dark continent." In justifying the violent conquest of Africa, the continent was presented as a place of strange customs: cannibalism, ritual murder, and warfare. European propaganda used to support the military invasions of other lands maintained that Europeans were dealing with people without civilizations. They presented their own public stories of Africans still grappling to learn languages, arts, and crafts.

Nineteenth-century science and philosophy also propagated evidence of racial difference to explain human diversity. In 1859 Charles Darwin published *The Origin of Species*, which showed how different species evolved in relation to biology and environment. Various interpreters racialized Darwin's conclusions to establish that one race invariably rose to the top of the hierarchy. Whites were on the top, followed by Asians, and then followed the inferior races—Africans, Native Americans, and Australian Aborigines.

The colonization of Africa became easier to justify in light of this hierarchy. Conversion—the introduction of Western ideas to civilize Africans—even became a secondary point. Africans were said to be too far behind to be easily uplifted. Rather, what the dark continent needed was a trusteeship; as inferiors, characterized as the lowest form of humanity, its inhabitants should be taken care of as if they were infants. The colonizers did not see evidence of achievement, only evidence of savagery and barbarism. Africans needed conquest as a form of assistance. Scientific race theory, now combined with imperialism, brought about the end of Africa's sovereignty, a condition from which it has yet to recover.

The colonization of space, like the colonization of memory, was based on lies—not ignorance, as many prefer to believe, but absolute, deliberate untruth. To start with, there was no foundation for their historical claims about the continent in relation to the European concept of progress and civilization. Second, the conquerors described African nations as violent, but Europeans conquered Africa with violence. Their rule also unleashed violence that subsequently became part of Africa's political culture. Africans were drawn into two world wars whose objectives did not concern them. Third, in converting Africans to Christianity, Europeans relied on a rather strange concept of love—God-appointed Europeans as prophets and saviors—that obscured the cultural damage inflicted by Europeans on Africans. Christianity became a gift. Former slaveholders and plantation owners were now condemning Africans for slavery. The transatlantic slave trade lingered until the mid-nineteenth century, but they were now the ones to control the moral agenda.

The colonization of space opened up avenues for the exploitation of people. Irrespective of the system of colonial governance—be it a policy of indirect rule, assimilation, association, paternalism, or various other categories of colonial relation, the objective was clearly the same: exploitation. A colonial dictatorship emerged with white officers on top, protected by the army and police. Africans paid taxes to finance the administration, and they produced crops and minerals that were shipped abroad. Established precolonial nations and their political structures were swept aside. Changes occurred in all aspects of African life, which produced anomie, confusion, and fractured modernity, elements of which have been captured in many literary and academic works.[8] The combination of slavery and colonialism laid the foundation of Africa's underdevelopment.[9]

Counter-Colonization Projects

Nationalism produced numerous forms of anticolonial resistance, including violence. Indeed, the fall of the European empire in Africa was made possible by the ability of Africans to make the enterprise unworkable. Similarly in the Americas, the emancipation of slaves led to various demands for inclusion in political and democratic spaces. The demands unleashed various struggles through the twentieth century, most notably the civil rights movement. Various forms of nationalist projects have survived until today.

Black people began to construct alternative forms of knowledge to counter the experience of domination.[10] Western-oriented universities emerged in different parts of Africa from the 1940s onward. A new generation of Africans acquired degrees and began to teach and hold positions of influence. In the United States, black-studies programs also emerged. As blacks contributed to scholarship, images of a lost past were re-created, and the narratives shifted from colonial condemnation to a more objective historical reality. New sources and methodologies produced new and rich histories. Nonwritten epistemologies emerged to describe the tragedies of the slave trade and the colonial encounters. When black people began to write, we see clearly the pain and anguish in the slave narratives. By the time we enter the twentieth century, academic writings developed as counterdiscourses. In Africa, nationalist historiographies developed to present Africa-centered histories. Cheikh Anta Diop became famous, supplying ideas that led to the creation of the Afrocentric movement in the United States, as popularized by Molefi Asante of Temple University.[11]

Black studies were created in the American academy despite opposition; some programs even confronted violence in the 1960s. African nationalist historiography successfully provided rich evidence on the African past, pointing to established institutions and structures. The contributions of Africa to other cultures have equally been acknowledged, while debate continues as to what the Greeks owed to Africans.[12]

Activist scholarship created new approaches, some non-Western in their orientation and others adopting the methodologies of so-called mainstream departments. The agenda of black studies is anticolonization. Combining intellectual with practical projects, black studies concentrates on the investigation of and the methods to end the oppression and exploitation of black people. Race and racialization should not just be seen as an epiphenomenal, as many social science disciplines tend to emphasize. Conceived as a distinct discipline, black studies is not shy in its actions and rhetoric, and it is clear about its investigation of the past, present, and future of black people to make various political and anticolonization statements and demands.

The knowledge of countercolonization dismisses the so-called neutrality of Western Cartesian models of knowing. Black studies contested the claim to historical objectivity by those in power, while it maintains that race, class, and gender must be at the center of historical and cultural presentations. As black studies matures, its emphases attain greater clarity: at the center of its epistemology is the promotion of an African ethos. Various writings fall on the structure of black communities and the language of liberation to address the omission of the black experience in the academy.

While the premise of black studies has been accepted in various quarters, its creation is a process of struggles against the colonization of memory and the colonization of spaces. In Africa, African studies was born in the era of decolonization in the 1940s and 1950s when scholarship was created by the political nationalism that saw the end of the European empire. In the United States, black studies struggled for inclusion in the universities as part of the black power and civil rights movement. From the mid-1950s to the mid-1970s, it created its form and content. It presented itself as innovative, a challenge to racism, and a methodology to understand the people of African descent. Moreover, many argued that black studies would provide a space for black students on campuses to learn about their history and interact with people of their race and ethnicity.

The creation of black studies was part of the general package of knowledge connected with political emancipation. Various anti-hegemonic discourses grew in nonacademic setting as well. As far back as the nineteenth century, Frederick Douglass and other abolitionists had called for the creation of new knowledge that would refuse to accept the racist view that black people were inferior to whites. Douglass was blessed with able successors, notables such as

W. E. B. Du Bois; Alexander Crumwell; Carter Woodson, founder of the *Journal of Negro History*; and Arthur Schumberg—all of whom supported the idea of reclaiming black history. In the 1920s and 1930s, Negro History Week and the Harlem Renaissance paid attention to black art, literature, and culture. Scholarship was broadly defined around the conception of blackness, an all-encompassing umbrella for Africans and people of African descent.

During the twentieth century, many activists argued that black history would generate racial pride among the youth and promote racial harmony. A number of black students on campuses in Africa and the United States said that they were not Europeans and saw no reason to study Shakespeare, Mozart, and Beethoven, and asserted that they preferred Langston Hughes. History became a relevant discipline to construct and defend nationalism, to repudiate the negatives about Africa, and to point to the achievements of black people throughout the world. An intellectual patrimony of disciplines began to reinforce the ideas of cultural patrimony. Blending oral with written sources and placing Africana at the center of discourse serves to prevent fragmented discourses on blackness, ones that would separate the history of slavery from European conquest or the history of the civil rights movement in the United States from that of decolonization in Africa.

The most sustained anticolonization project has been the use of culture—as an ideology, as a source of affirmation, as an agency of resistance. The ideas of Négritude[13] and cultural celebrations of the Harlem Renaissance were emphatic in stressing the cultural difference of black people, and in calling for the use of culture for political purposes. More important, culture was promoted as a critical source of identity. The connections between culture and politics have been hugely successful. With words eloquent, melodramatic, and combative, many writers have reclaimed the lost glories of the past. Not only have they revealed stories of achievements, but they also demolished the archives of Western domination. They redefined the notions and evidence of civilization, adopting the definitions that elevate people of African descent. They placed Africa at the intellectual center, projecting it as the center of the black world. Furthermore, the uses to which culture has been put created a mode of struggle against oppression. Aimé Césaire, Léopold Senghor, and others of the Négritude and Harlem school opened up a new library of African tradition and philosophy.[14] They used culture to create unity among blacks: an ideology of cultural patrimony that sustained the politics of

Pan-Africanism. Blackness was turned into beauty, the construction of racial pride. To be black was to be proud, drawing no references to affirmation from whiteness.

The use of culture as a tool of resistance is arguably now the most dominant. In the United States, it has become less common to deploy violent rhetoric, in particular since the success of the civil rights struggles of the 1960s. The combative black power movement of the 1960s has given way to a radicalized culturalist agenda of the Afrocentric movement. In Africa, violence is still part of a strategy to combat unjust power. However, black-on-black violence reveals stresses and tensions among the marginalized. Various governments deliberately opted for the use of culture for political purposes, some to shore up authoritarian regimes and some genuinely motivated by the need to stop the erosion of African cultures. Festivals of old are repackaged and represented to newer audiences, in large measure to entertain them. Technologies of presentation, notably television and the Internet, have made it much easier to popularize culture and to spread its nonpolitical manifestations. Various governments, with the support of the United Nations and UNESCO, formulated ways to preserve culture, making it illegal to take works of antiquity out of Africa. Cultural patrimony is also regarded as the bedrock of identity and, according to the UN, the "self-understanding of a people."[15]

By and large, the resort to culture has been successful in a number of ways. It provides the most effective politicizing tool to create black political solidarity. Cultural patrimony provides the opportunity to network at the level of international organizations and to build a series of ties between and within continents. More importantly, it allows people of African descent to mount challenges against mis-education, to reformulate damaged consciousness, and to assert mental autonomy as well as the independence of personality and the assertion of collective identities.[16]

Conclusion: The Amistad Legacy

An event as far back as 1839 continues to provide the opportunity to examine issues around history, race relations, and memory. The transatlantic slave trade is dead, the European empires in Africa have collapsed, and plantation slavery is no more. Yet there remains the subordination of Africans and the people of African descent to

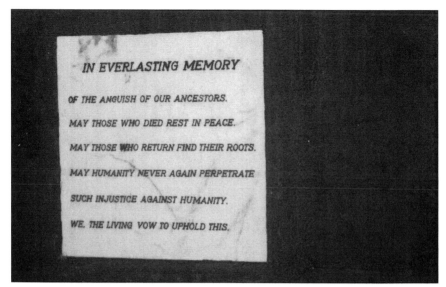

Figure 2.1. A memorial at Elmina fortress in Ghana. The president of Ghana had this created as a part of his formal apology for African participation in aiding slave traders. Photograph courtesy of Ben Weiss.

Western global forces. What, then, is the relevance of Amistad in today's circumstances?

First, there are the tensions between resistance and power. The connection is not hard to explain. What Africa lost to the Americas and the West is not just labor, but primarily power: the power to use its own labor and land for its own economies, the power to shape its own future and define itself, and the power to relate to the rest of the world on its own terms. How blacks have responded represents the politics of resistance. Those with power have struggled to silence the past and the memory of resistance. A celebration of the Amistad rebellion and related episodes of resistance is necessary to prevent the colonization of memory. If power wants to silence the past, it is our responsibility to keep the past alive, to bring back the ghosts to talk. This is the first major task, a rescue operation of the past. We have been successful in generating new knowledge and questioning many older assumptions. The so-called natives, as we can now tell, are not as dumb as the racialized images have presented them. They can see all the lies and present their own truths.

Second, in bringing back those ghosts, attention must be paid to the longer and larger legacy of the tradition of resistance and rebellion. We should not use limited resources and fragmented intellectual power to celebrate the domination of a group of people by another, notably imperialists and empire builders whose main goal is to exploit weak and marginalized nations and people. The enslavement that led to the Amistad revolt and the colonization of memory, and the imperial conquest that led to the colonization of spaces, have been shown to be ephemeral. In resisting the colonization of spaces, we have to pay attention to great moments and courageous leaders, patriots, and nationalists who fought in defense of their own people. Amistad is part of the tradition that must have a permanent stamp on our consciousness.

Third, Amistad is a preface to the narrative of rebellion and civil rights, all informed by nationalism, which questioned the Western model of suppression. Black intellectuals have challenged the racist idea of black inferiority. They have even moved further, as Du Bois did in *The Souls of Black Folk*, to reject the construction of the world into two: the civilized and the uncivilized. Black people cannot be at the margins of history.

Fourth, when moments of justice and fair play arise, even if it involves a few persons, they deserve the mobilization of our full support. The Amistad trial established precedence in American law: the ability to gain freedom through the courts. Law and the judiciary do favor the power elite, but they provide opportunities for the poor and marginalized to express their grievances.

Fifth, the judiciary and other institutions of power are not enough for liberation. We see the limitations in the case of Amistad. What is necessary is the acquisition of power, the distribution of key power to handle the negativity of the racial context. We have seen what happened to slaves without political power. And we can see what happens to free people without political power. Amistad has shown us the consequences of powerlessness. With sufficient power, there would have been no lynching, dispossession, and economic exploitation.

Sixth, Amistad shows us the beginning of the reparations and back-to-Africa movements. The resistors demonstrated the illegality of slavery, and they wanted to seek compensation for their sufferings and return to Africa. The two issues they raised continue to resonate today, and they assist us in framing the issues around reparation. Similarly, Amistad also connects us to the events and analysis around the Middle Passage that has been turned into a distinct subspecialization in slavery studies. We see the struggles on the high seas in the

Middle Passage. The Middle Passage has been a connector, bringing Africans to the Americas and Americans to Africa. Where new identities have been formed and shaped, they have become the subject of controversy, especially since the publication by Paul Gilroy of *The Black Atlantic*, which has been read as an attempt to erase Africa from the formation of African American identity. The desire by Cinqué and his colleagues to return to Africa has been manifested by many others through permanent relocation to Sierra Leone and Liberia, and until today by way of tourism by those of the African diaspora.[17]

Seventh, we must insert Amistad and all major forms of resistance into popular culture. There have been documentaries and films on the Amistad rebellion,[18] thus keeping the memory alive. This insertion into popular culture and the classroom is critical to keeping the memory of resistance alive. Popular culture must not be allowed to be part of the spaces of colonization but should instead occupy the spaces of resistance and nationalism. The academy must lend its full support to the creation of a just world in which the ideology that created Amistad will be crushed, and in which the system that produced inequities will no longer exist.

Finally, black people must be able to shape economic and political processes in order to assert themselves. Their ability to work turned them into slaves. The usefulness of their land and their ability to produce converted them from citizens into colonial subjects. Their ability to work and travel make them exploitable members in a globalized economy. It is not that black people do not work, which they do; rather it is the kind of work they do and who they work for that represent one source of trouble. While we should keep pointing to earlier, blatant racist discourses and formulations, we must also continue to specify the current neoimperialist forms and representations against which we have to struggle. Discourses around aid, development, security, democracy, and other issues present new challenges for resistance. We have to be alert to the dangers posed by seductive political propaganda that appeal to a sense of wanting to do good and imagining social justice while the actual intentions are disguised.

Black people have been successful in defining and using culture. However, the forces of global domination are getting stronger, and they cannot be fully tamed by ideas drawn solely from culture. Competitive technologies and economies have to be created and put to use. Amistad shows the dimensions of cultures—in the longing to go back home, in the use of language, and the like—but what produced results was action and resistance, that is, the ability to mobilize culture in the service of politics. The gap between the West and Africa, between whites and blacks, is not a gap about cultural difference or a gap structured by cultural peculiarities, but rather by access to resources, inequalities in global economies, and the political domination of one race by another. The African slaves who were part of the Amistad rebellion and millions of others were forcibly converted into slaves not only because of their skin color but also because there was an unequal economy in place. The colonization of Africa was made possible not only because one group was white and the other black, but also because one had in abundance the Gatling and Maxim guns and the other had outdated technology. Racism was justified on the grounds of political and economic interests, which is precisely how these interests were articulated to generate profit and maintain dominance. We have to close those crucial gaps in politics and economies. We have to construct power to remove black people from the very margins of politics itself. Self-assertion must transcend the patrimony of culture to embrace the patrimony of entrepreneurship, clearly guided by the patrimony of power.

3

The Centralization of Africa and the
Intellectualization of Blackness

Without question, the production of knowledge on race, slavery, colonization, and all forms of Western domination has been one of the most critical links between Africans and African Americans, and between Africa and most of the Western world. Of course, the movement of people from and to Africa provided the foundation for this mutual intellectual engagement and dialogue. The forced movement produced by slavery created the origins of African American identity. Voluntary migrations followed, with substantial increases since the 1980s, creating today a large number of black people in the United States whose ancestors have no connections whatsoever with American slavery. For over two hundred years, African Americans have been going to Africa as part of a mission of permanent settlements, semipermanent habitations, temporary visits, and heritage trips. The concept of "black" as a race and as a social, cultural, and political group has emerged concomitantly. African and African American scholars and the academy have recognized the concept of a black community as distinctive and have thus organized courses around and conducted research on it.

This chapter is about how knowledge has been generated around the black community. I will be dealing with how knowledge is constituted around the black experience (epistemology), how this knowledge is gathered and presented (methodology), and how it is put to use (activism). Aspects of this knowledge constitute a political manifesto: the use of knowledge to ensure the survival of the race, its emancipation from all forms of domination, and the generation of a proud future. We can identify a history to all these issues (process of knowledge production), a focus on the historical specificity of the black experience (focalization), as well as attacks on studies around blackness (hegemonic opposition).

Our scholars (amateurs and professionals) have insisted on restoring that which has been devalued, elevating a continent that has been ignored, and promoting knowledge that has been suppressed or underused. The knowledge process relates to power: how the long enduring structures of domination, racism, exploitation, and marginalization have defined the black experience; how the legacy of this experience shapes responses and actions in different eras; and how the psychology of black people has been affected by the experience, producing multiple reactions to the reality of their contemporary experience.

Countee Cullen's famous poem written in 1930, "Heritage," provides a window to the crux of this discussion. He starts with a question: "What is Africa to me?" He answered it in terms of imagination, using the imageries of copper sun, sea, star, lush environment, royalty, and more.[1] Cullen's question is both an intellectual and a practical one. With regard to the latter, there are various activities around the back-to-Africa movement whereby a number of African Americans saw emigration as an option during the nineteenth and early part of the twentieth centuries.[2] Even to those who did not emigrate, Africa had a relevant place in their discussions, dreams, and negotiations in relation to American society. Du Bois, the hero in black history, tries to answer Cullen's question in the conclusion to his major essay on race: "What is Africa to me? Once I should have answered the question simply: I should have said 'fatherland' or perhaps better 'motherland.'"[3] But the "fatherland" and "motherland" created, as Du Bois explains, a sense of "being a problem, that is being an American of African descent":

> The negro is a sort of seventh son, born with a veil, and gifted with second-sight, in this American world—a world which yields him no true self-consciousness, but only lets him see himself through the revelation of the other world. It is a peculiar sensation, this double-consciousness, this sense of always looking at one's self through the eyes of others, of measuring one's soul by the tape of a world that looks on it in amused contempt and pity. One ever feels his twoness—an American, a Negro; two souls, two thoughts, two unreconciled strivings; two warring ideals in one dark body, whose dogged strength alone keeps it from being torn asunder.[4]

There are also issues around identity. There is no single identity for all black people, since their location in different parts of the world shapes contents and practices, but there are some common elements in the bonding. Ronald W. Walters sums up the persistence of identity when he closes his book on this subject:

> Africans in the Diaspora are not a part of the daily particularities of African history and so cannot possess the identity which flows from these experiences. However, they do share certain aspects of this history, and the basis upon which they do so is (1) their affirmation of an African heritage; (2) their participation in the Diasporic aspects of pan African political struggles; (3) their continuing concern with the status of Africa and their efforts to improve it, and (4) their relationship to other hyphenated Africans in the Diaspora.[5]

What Walters itemizes has led to many practical cultural projects and cultural affirmations, including the practice of African religions and the emergence of an African American holiday of Kwanzaa.[6] There was also the construction of the Pan-Africanist movement, an idea that sought to create a universe of black politics and consciousness with Africa as the homeland; the organizing principle was to build political connections in all continents.[7]

The practical projects—whether political, economic, or cultural—have been undergirded by intellectual ideas around a set of interrelated issues: the generation of knowledge (utilitarian knowledge to be sure), the building of institutions to spread knowledge, the ideology to organize the facts and opinions, and the structures to use the knowledge. Both in Africa and the United States, the intellectualization of the black experience is one of the most successful academic achievements of the twentieth century. Indeed, these practical projects have also led to vigorous debates on a variety of options to emancipate black people.

In advancing this intellectual project, Africa forms the center of discourse. This is what I mean by the centralization of Africa, which is to say that Africa—as a continent, a people, a homeland—is put at the center of how ideas have been formulated, challenged, and packaged. The heritage of those whom we are dealing with is African, whether they live in New York or Dakar. The location of those who formulate the ideas does not necessarily matter, as they still have to deal with this centralization in which the continent is constructed as their genesis.

Returning to the poem, "What is Africa to me?" is a question that requires us to look at the past, the present, and the future framed within an enduring notion of the centralization of Africa.

The transatlantic slave trade and the European colonization of Africa resulted in the fragmentation of identities. Nationalities have multiplied so that we have Nigerians, Sudanese, and Americans, even if their color remains the same. However, encounters with the West, the slave trade, and the march of modernity have all created the need to talk about race. Talking about race links with conquest, domination, and exploitation, all of which represent a common experience for the black race. This experience has generated knowledge about blackness in Africa and its various diasporas.

The intellectualization of blackness is very much connected with the centralization of Africa. The creation of an epistemology on blackness derives from the African experience and encounters with the Western world. Thus, most studies deal with these experiences and their consequences for those in Africa and the Western hemisphere. The analyses focus on the African/black conditions, which cover the manifestations of living, struggle, and survival. As to be expected, the humanities and social sciences provide the lead, since it is much easier for those disciplines to "Africanize" the fields than it is for the sciences; to counter the pathologization of Africa with a set of both observable data and research; and to deconstruct the ideas of Western triumphalist and white supremacist discourses.

There is equally a strong desire on the part of African and African American scholars to conclude their discussions with a set of solutions to the challenges facing black people. Indeed, scholarship acquires relevance when it is able to articulate a set of ideas to solve specific problems. Advocacy theories become an integral part of talking about the black experience. A terminology of "activists" or "engaged scholars" has been coined to describe those who take strategic theories of change more seriously. In African studies, they are often labeled as "radicals." In the era before the fall of the Soviet Union, they could even be described as socialists or Marxists even if they were only marginally leftists. In the United States, many were described as communists in order to justify the encroachment on their privacy by the FBI and efforts to silence them. Thus, there are strong connections between the history of the black experience and those who reflect on its future. Black scholars respond to the historical reality of their black experience and to longstanding issues around race and freedom. While mindful of responding to the theories and canons in their disciplines, they seek relevance in the connections that these have with the black experience and with their own socialization within it.

Organic Intellectuals

The journey to reach our present point began not with scholars based in the universities but with community leaders, enlightened citizens, and engaged amateur analysts who generated a substantial body of knowledge to understand the black race. Oral narratives developed in virtually all black communities, together with the ability to transmit them from one generation to another. Similarly, slave narratives emerged when there were facilities and opportunities to write, and they constitute a distinct genre of their own.[8] In general, the ability to read and write was converted into an opportunity to record history and to reflect on the black experience.

In the United States, many blacks began to talk about Africa, their conditions, and the necessity of overcoming their marginalization. Their location in the United States created ambiguities in identity and relevance in a highly racialized society. After the American Civil War, black people faced a crisis of adjustment and emancipation, leading to vigorous debates on whether or not to stay in the United States. Martin Delany championed the cause of emigration, regarding it as an appropriate response to a policy of "political degradation" of the black population.[9] Frederick Douglass, the most famous intellectual of his era, was opposed to Delany's views on emigration, although not to his characterization of the brutality of the system. Thus, irrespective of the positions African Americans took during the nineteenth century, the centralization of Africa was dominant: to promote a return was to talk about Africa and to oppose emigration was to talk about Africa. Liberia and Sierra Leone became tied to the expressions of faith and fate among African Americans of this era. The majority chose to stay, leading to yet another set of vigorous debates on how to seek insertion into politics and negotiate issues around citizenship. The literature on black conditions in the United States reveals profound agonies and depression.[10]

The field of history served as the pioneer, as freed blacks spoke about their past, about Africa the homeland, and about their complicated contemporary conditions. History enabled them to situate their lives and conditions within and beyond the restrictions of race and slavery so that they could talk about a past when their people were free and a future that would bring freedom.

Black narratives of the nineteenth century and scholarly writings were emphatic about the celebration of blackness and of Africa. George Washington Williams celebrated black achievements in the United States in a well-received book published in 1883.[11] Williams and his contemporaries mounted evidence to show that blacks, wherever they were in the world, were great achievers. Alexander Crummell, one of the intellectual leaders of the time, was devoted to writing about black civilization. In 1897 he provided leadership for the establishment of the American Negro Academy, which asserted new historical interpretations on blackness.

As we entered the twentieth century, there developed a greater formalization of black knowledge. Carter G. Woodson, now known as the "father of black history," created a permanent legacy in the creation of the Association for the Study of African-American Life and History. In 1915 Woodson founded the Woodson's Association for the Study of Afro-American Life and History, and a year later, the *Journal of Negro History*. His objectives were to save the records relating to the black experience and to announce ideas and philosophies associated with black thinkers.

Going beyond the intellectual dimension, he went into public activism in 1926 when he established the Negro History Week (now Black History Month). Woodson and his contemporaries had to react to issues of racial segregation and the marginalization of the black experience in schools and colleges. Woodson and his associations denounced the ideas that represented the black race as primitive and degenerate. Calling for the rejection of the characterization of black people by whites, he deliberately sought to use history and culture to promote black pride.[12] Woodson's 1933 publication, *The Mis-Education of the Negro*, creates an enduring legacy for the totality of his ideas and scholarship.[13] This work, which is still in print today, dismissed the studies and teaching of the black experience by whites as no more than an attempt at a wrong presentation and misdefinition of his people. He also dismissed the education that blacks received, saying that it was of no service to them or others.

W. E. B. Du Bois stands in a class of his own, and his ideas remain relevant today. A liberal idealist with tremendous intellectual energy, his aims were to expand the democratic space and for blacks to have a share of economic power. A Pan-Africanist, his ideas crossed the Atlantic through activities that energized anticolonial leaders. The works of Du Bois and his contemporaries reveal the multiple tensions that they had to face. All recognized the relevance of Africa to their practical and intellectual projects. They rejected the academic presentations of blackness in their day, preferring instead to create new knowledge. Indeed, Du Bois almost advocated autonomy for black scholarship by providing revolutionary interpretations of the past and sociologizing the present. In a dense historical sociology, Du Bois presented the analysis of a fundamentally unequal and grossly unjust society, how the West profited from Africa, and how colonial domination must be ended.[14]

It is difficult to capture, in such limited space, the various strands and elements in the discourses about uplifting the black race. Suffice it to say that there were significant disagreements among them, which reveal and reaffirm the notion that scholarship and politics can never be homogenous. Marcus Garvey, W. E. B. Du Bois, Kwame Nkrumah, and Martin Luther King Jr., to mention a few examples, theorized about race issues and offered suggestions about emancipation, but they were not articulating the same positions. Labels and categorizations may exaggerate the orientations, but it is possible to see views that seek to reconcile with the system or to promote assimilation. In Africa, whether for survival or self-interest, there were those who collaborated with Europeans to make possible the conquest of their own people. In addition, there were those who collaborated with the colonial officers to ensure the success of the colonial administration. In the United States, an accommodationist view is associated with Booker T. Washington, who called for black entrepreneurship, education, and industrialism, while being disengaged from politics and eschewing aggressive, violent demands for civil rights. There were also the radicals, such as Marcus Garvey, who opted for black self-determination and sought the separation of races.[15] For Garvey, Africa should be at the very center of political and economic power for black people. Similar views have persisted, some pronounced by Islamic groups that turn to religion to organize a cultural separation. There is a difference in strategies as well—for instance, Martin Luther King Jr. was an advocate of nonviolence ("meeting physical force with soul force"), while others like Malcolm X were in support of self-defense and violence.[16] Many of the strategies and arguments about black liberation advanced by African American leaders and intellectuals have their equivalences in South Africa, where Africans also had to deal with racism, apartheid, and white domination.[17]

In Africa, organic intellectuals capitalized on their access to European languages and their own indigenous ones to write books, essays, almanacs, and features in the newspapers. There was no topic that they did not touch upon, from origin stories to the coming of the Europeans, all in order to announce and empower their identities, open new libraries on their people and histories, and affirm cultural glories. They generated a large body of work on origins, myths, beliefs, religions, customs, and various other aspects of life.[18] Anticipating the work of Diop and others, J. Africanus B. Horton saw Africa as the "nursery of science and literature" from which others borrowed.[19] Edward Wilmot Blyden was an encyclopedic figure, a major representative of nineteenth-century intellectuals, who wrote extensively on Islam, Christianity, economy, politics, and the future of Africa.[20] His vision of a great Africa inspired a generation of other writers. Three historical works from the period—written by Samuel Johnson, Christian Reindorf, and Appollo Kagwa—have endured to this day as classics to enjoy, as texts to understand the nineteenth century, and as sources to reconstruct histories.[21]

Creative and literary minds used ideas to create and connect a black universe. There were the apostles of Négritude, notably Aimé Césaire and Léopold Sédar Senghor, whose words, in powerful poetry, echoed black pride and resistance. Césaire celebrated African cultures, extolled their virtues, and pointed attention to African contributions to the Western world.

> We, vomited from slaveships.
> We, hunted by the Calebars.
> What? Stop on our ears?
> We, sotted to death from being rolled, mocked, jeered at,
> Stifled with fog![22]

Senghor, named one of the "immortals" by the Académie française, always pushed the frontiers of culture, with a mix of socialism, to create a new beginning for Africa.[23] Senghor enjoins us to be the bearers of a "unique message" powerful enough to create a universal civilization. A cast of highly talented, creative writers were to follow (e.g., C. L. R. James and James Baldwin), whose distinguished writings reflect a spirit of compassion and freedom, as well as a sense of urgency to fight for liberation.

The challenges that organic intellectuals faced were not those of building careers or pressuring universities to recognize their works and validate their scholarship. The challenges they faced were living in the shadow of the transatlantic slave trade, colonial domination, slavery, and racism. These challenges were not imaginary ones. As individuals and as a collective, the black race has been presented as inferior, pathologically lazy, mentally deficient, criminally oriented, and obsessed with women and liquor. The ultimate goals of the organic intellectuals were to prevent the death of the past by recovering evidence and data and analyzing them, to use this evidence to liberate the mind, and to motivate their generation to seek a better future. They sincerely believed that it was possible to infuse the knowledge of Africa and the black experience into homes (to train children) and into schools (to train people). The promotion of African values would enhance the worth of Africa, provide alternative reference points for African Americans, and build pride. They were quick to reject the notion of "universality" that privileged Western knowledge, offering instead a variety of new knowledge(s). As they offered something new, they questioned the notion of objectivity in mainstream studies that spoke about Africa and its diaspora. Organic intellectuals also articulated visions of leadership, since they recognized the need to have power in order to translate knowledge into action.[24]

African Studies–Black Studies: The Academic Connections

The insertion of the black experience into the academy has advanced the agenda of organic intellectuals. Indeed, in many ways organic intellectuals have written the prefaces for what scholars now write.[25] Their legacies include passion and enthusiasm, epistemologies, attention to the centrality of Africa, even debates and differences. Black scholars have consolidated teaching and research in colleges and schools, and they have, as a community of scholars, ensured the survival of many disciplines. They have also inserted themselves into many mainstream departments, courses, and curricula. The collective achievements since the middle of the twentieth century should be celebrated. The failures are clear to see, but they are sources of energy rather than of despair.

African studies as an academic discipline came into being in many parts of Africa after the Second World War.[26] It was a propitious moment, when the continent was undergoing the process of decolonization. Thus, the creation of all Africa-related disciplines was infused with nationalism. The humanities, to take an example, became decidedly anticolonial and succeeded in ensuring that all negative comments about Africa were corrected, that colonially derived syllabi were jettisoned, and that condescending attitudes about black people formed in the colonial milieu were ended. Africanists went beyond the archives of the colonial governments to tap into older sources—local, Arabic, foreign-derived (such as those of explorers, missionaries, and traders)—to reinterpret the past, thereby restoring history to Africans and Africa to history.

Africanists knew that they must promote a multidisciplinary perspective and approach (which explains the interactions between the various disciplines), they must redefine the field and take initiatives (which explains their choice of subjects), and they must validate nonwritten sources (which explains the stress on oral traditions). If colonialists had credited themselves for bringing about major changes in Africa, Africanists questioned this and examined evidence of the iron revolution, kingship, agriculture, and other developments that point to indigenous innovations.[27]

In addition, Africanists demolished the ideas of ethnocentrism, obsessive interest in so-called exotic and erotic societies, and an approach that treated societies as static.[28] Regional historiographies grew and reflected nationalist opinions. In North Africa, Maghrebian historians rejected the characterization of their people by the French as uncivilized, and revealed new understanding about Islamic and pastoral lives and societies. In South Africa, revisions and corrections had to await the dismantling of apartheid in the 1990s. Before then, black people were regarded as disposable items, a nonpopulation without a place in the historical record. In West and East Africa, so successful were the historical projects that nationalist schools emerged, known as Ibadan, Legon, and Makarere, with regard to the kind of ideas they generated, the students they trained, and the ideological orientation (called "schools") they established. The schools are associated with the works of notables such as K. O. Dike, Jacob Ade Ajayi, Adu Boahen, and Beth Ogot.[29]

In the United States, the creation of African American studies took place at the same time. Before and after the Second World

War, the context was that of the movement of black people into cities and urbanization, the growing influence of socialist ideas, and the beginning of the civil rights movement. Irrespective of the label, Africana studies, Afro-American and African studies, Black studies, and African American studies all intend a similar focus.[30] The Historically Black Colleges and Universities (HBCUs) were enthusiastic in creating courses on the black experience, as in the case of such concentrations at Fisk and Howard universities. The spread of such concentrations came in the 1950s and began to expand further in the 1960s after the death of Dr. Martin King Jr. and the various protests and demands that followed his assassination. Many black students became activists and demanded the creation of black-studies programs in their colleges. White universities joined the movement, and by the late 1990s there were about sixty African American studies departments and four hundred African American studies programs. New visions began to be espoused on race relations, and it became possible to earn degrees to the PhD level.

African studies in Africa and black studies in the United States are united by a set of theoretical and ideological questions on approaches, methodologies, and strategies. Essentially, the aim is to create a counterdiscourse to what has been regarded as antiblack knowledge and school curricula. To approach African and black studies, many think of alternative ways to expose the brutalities and continuing dangers of slavery and racism, economic exploitation, and Western domination.[31] Also, the approach focuses on the achievements of black peoples in all aspects of civilization. The pedagogy is infused with a notion of nationalism, an orientation that links scholarship of liberation, emancipation, and progress.

In Africa, the knowledge generated by colonial power was regarded as one-sided and demeaning.[32] In the United States, the knowledge generated by the mainstream on black people is regarded as flawed.[33] There is a constant claim that hegemonic knowledge is elitist and racist. The assumptions that have guided the works of many black scholars, irrespective of their locations, are that the acquired knowledge received from traditional sources excludes the black experience, undermines the achievements of blacks, and erases key elements in the development of a global economy that can equitably include black people. Similarly, the belief is that this knowledge is not objective simply because its methodology is flawed. It excludes black people, and when it does include them, its sources are limited and badly collected and its analysis is racist. African scholars successfully demonstrate the limitation of a discipline like anthropology in truly representing their people, and of history in accurately portraying the African past. African American scholars make related claims, arguing that racism is not always factored into scholarly analyses and that many conclusions from the traditional disciplines merely support capitalist interests and hegemonic power.

Black scholars have had to formulate methodologies to study the black experience. Those who pioneered the field were trained in methods that did not necessarily pay adequate attention to the black experience. The supervision of their theses was done by teachers without the requisite experience. Many had to rise to the challenges of reinventing themselves and the new Africana discipline. There is a consensus that all forms of nonwritten sources have to be validated and put to use. Oral traditions and oral histories became accepted as sources to counter the idea that people without written sources have no history. There is also a focus on history from below, looking at the theme of resistance, insurgency, and nationalism. Sociologists have made contributions in the areas of families, poverty, and inequalities.[34]

Studies on the black experience have acquired a professional intensity for over sixty years.[35] In the United States, most of the activities have taken place in the context of African American studies programs.[36] In this arrangement, faculty can belong to different departments. Students too are recruited by departments, and they take courses in African studies programs, enabling an interdisciplinary approach that gives students the opportunity to major in single subjects or to double and triple major. Where universities have created departments, these have survived much longer than programs. In a number of universities, resources in funding and faculty have enabled African American studies to grow in visibility. Today, many scholars have built successful careers in African American studies and have written major books.[37] Superstars have even emerged who command significant attention, including public intellectuals such as Molefi Asante, bell hooks, Henry Louis Gates Jr., and Cornel West.

The study of Africa and the black experience remains an arena of struggle and contestation. In Africa, the concern is the difficulty of connecting many academic degrees to the economic demands of the market. That is, most governments discouraged degrees and research in the humanities, preferring instead science and technology degrees. In the United States, internal struggles on campuses remain a never-ending problem. Recruitment of additional faculty with expertise in black studies can generate tensions, especially where the concerns of traditional departments clash with those of the programs. The structuring of electives is not always easy, as there are battles over the content and relevance of courses.

The intellectual challenges offered by the black reality to mainstream education have never been fully accepted. Indeed, many still question the legitimacy of the counterdiscourses on the black experience. In recent years, there has been a demand for the abolition of what is called "area studies programs." Some have urged the creation of transnational history as a discipline to replace courses on Africa and the African diaspora.

Africanist Perspective and Afrocentrism

The ideological underpinnings of the study of Africans and African Americans have merged into two concepts that are very similar. In Africa, the label is that of an "Africanist perspective," and in the United States that of "Afrocentrism" or "Afrocentricity." There is no consensus on the full meanings of these terms, as scholars have imposed different definitions on them. However, there is a consensus on the mission: the promotion of ideas relating to Africa and the black experience and the shift in the analysis of this experience from the periphery of scholarship to its very center. Irrespective of definition, the centralization of Africa in both ideologies challenges mainstream scholarship, the dominance of the West, and the monocausal explanation of world events as solely derived from the actions and activities of one dominant race. By refusing to accept some of the established canons, both ideologies create alternative ways of looking at the black experience and historical realities.

In Africa, the African perspective is simply dealing with the reality of Western domination and how it has been used to demean Africa's past. Since 1940, historians seriously questioned Eurocentric arguments, stereotypes, and images that have invalidated African history, misconstrued its philosophy and worldview, and deformed its entire universe. They demonstrated the antiquity of Africa, dating it back to the very beginning of humankind and providing a series of creation narratives. They analyzed African kingdoms, and North Africa, most notably Egypt, was brought into the orbit of African history. Hitherto, it had been disconnected and lumped with the Middle East.[38] The totality of the historiography shows the development of Africa before its encounter with the West, its destruction by the West, and the possibilities of restoration following the end of European rule.[39]

An often-repeated idea is that there is a cultural basis to sustain Africa's unity and development.[40] Various aspects of culture have been isolated for discussion in a way to affirm that, irrespective of location, Africans have many things in common. For example, John Mbiti analyzed the universe of African religions and philosophy, an approach that many others have duplicated; William E. Abraham of Ghana attempted the same for psychology.[41]

Those who seek endogenous development call for a return to traditional cultural foundations. This suggestion has further enhanced the centralization of Africa: Black people in different parts of the world see Africa as the source of culture, the primordial place. They point to an authentic Africa with ideas, institutions, and values so pristine that they could constitute the basis of a renaissance and revival. Regarded as anticapitalist and anti-imperialism, the belief is that Africa's humanity is so transparent and so real that it should be cultivated as a model of living. The stress on humanity is a clever way to expose all the elements that are "backward" and "primitive" in Western civilization, most especially alienation and acquisitive tendencies.

Afrocentricity in the United States and in Africa both deal with similar challenges, but the relationship of race to the black experience in the United States is a persistent issue. Race matters, as the title of Cornel West's book proclaims loudly and clearly.[42] West elaborates on the consequences of a color-coded society, following a long line of writers who have exposed the logic and atavism of a racially divided society. Molefi Asante celebrates black contributions to civilization and sees ideas drawn from ancient Egypt as necessary to transform black lives and behaviors.[43] To Asante and his ever-growing number of disciples, the starting point of scholarship is ancient Egypt. Borrowing from the work of his mentor, Cheikh Anta Diop, Asante accepts the claim that black people created Egyptian civilization. He then goes on to argue that Western civilization took its core ideas from Egypt. To him, the Afro-Asiatic origins of Western civilization that exist in religion, art, music, the sciences, and philosophy have been deliberately suppressed in order to deny black creativity. Others have followed Asante's mission to create black authenticity in culture and other aspects of society. Many have analyzed the age-long structures of domination in order to seek freedom, emancipation, and liberation. Like African scholars, African American scholars reject the scholarly attempts to marginalize black people and the organization of courses and instructions that exclude them.

Among Africans and African Americans, both ideologies have utilitarian goals as well, such as where to tap the sources of intellectual power and development. To Asante, there is no need to look to the West. To him, black people have the resources to use as their own model. They must seek the core of the knowledge generated by Egypt, center themselves as Africans, and promote indigenous religions and values to reclaim what they worship and honor as their own. Asante has generated a host of criticisms from several quarters, some misplaced to be sure because his critics are making a case for their own political constituencies, just as Asante is advancing the black agenda.

Against the background of modern conflicts and wars, following the European colonization of Africa in such places as Ethiopia and Kush, there are those who call for a return to the politics and society of old. The aggressive competition for power in the modern age is contrasted with the past to highlight institutions of cohesion and stability. In painting Africa's past as permanently peaceful (in spite of contrary evidence of wars and state formation), the idea is to show the damage of the colonial encounter and the brutal legacies of European rule.

In Africa, the insertion of African history, languages, and literature into all levels of the education system has been successful. This was a long-standing goal made possible by independence. In the United States, it has been a constant struggle, although significant successes have been recorded in revising world history textbooks and in introducing black studies-related courses even in high schools.

No race or group of people can be entirely united by a single set of beliefs. There are black Muslims, black Christians, and black neo-traditionalists, to mention a few. In addition, there are blacks who have assimilated to Western cultures and those who have refused to do so. Multiple identities abound among blacks. The diversity of opinion reflects the diversity of blackness. In Africa, there are those who have accepted the identities of the imposed colonial nations and boundaries, and those who have opted for identities derived from the precolonial nations. While all of these various identities still regard Africa as the basis of their cultural existence, they do not necessarily seek a complete disconnection from other cultural contexts or from

Western influences. They do respect the creation of black constituencies and black political communities, but they do not necessarily think that borrowing from the cultures of the past, as with Egypt, is necessary. There are also those who advocate assimilation and even integration into global cultures. They do complain about the marginalization of black people and the undermining of the collective interests of black people, but they see no solution in a return to Africa's past. Finally, there are black Afro-pessimists who see very little that is good or promising about the future of Africa.

When we cluster all these non-Afrocentric views, it is hard to conclude that they hate Africa or their own race. They simply offer an integrationist model of existence, seeing blacks as more a porridge in a melting pot. They can read about or visit Africa, but they are saying that others can do the same, that nonblacks are free to join in the discussion, that ideas of old are hard to reproduce. There are those who misread the postindependence instability, wars, and conflicts in Africa to mean the failure of Africans to even praise themselves for being descendants of slaves, now privileged African Americans.[44] As they write to celebrate themselves, they omit one compelling fact: Africa's problems, like the problems of African Americans, are located within the structures of economic and political domination.

Discovering the Past, Changing the Future

African and African American scholars have traveled a long way toward creating an established intellectual foundation and practices that have elevated the scholarship of blackness and enhanced political agendas. Various new facts have been presented and published, facts that would never have been known about Africa and African Americans. These facts have been put to good use in creating new courses that reject the claims of objectivity put forth by those who have studied black issues from their own perspectives. Facts and visions have combined to produce an autonomous reality about black issues that connect accurate representation of a race and its achievements with collective social and political aspirations. Within the academy, the insertion of new and different voices facilitated the building of diversity programs, the cultivation of multidisciplinarity and multiculturalism ideals, and the broadening of knowledge and epistemologies beyond Eurocentric models. Indeed, the totality and complexity of our contributions to the contents and orientations of education can be described as revolutionary.

There will always be challenges, even temporary crises that can set people back. In the United States, programs are not necessarily durable. Many have been abolished. Some programs struggle with internal politics, facing bitter attacks by traditional fields that dominate in recruiting faculty and students. Many African and African American programs are not even allowed to hire full-time faculty. Programs are dependent on elective enrollments in courses. As those enrollments fall or become harder to sustain, the programs can be eliminated or reduced.

Thus, the first task is to sustain the durability of these programs, to make their courses and roles enduring and influential. Building, sustaining, and reinventing institutional structures calls for hard work and maturity. These are compelling reasons to be anchored by the necessity of diversity and multiculturalism, as well as the benefits of interdisciplinary approaches for students. Perhaps it may be wiser to convert more programs into departments, since, historically, departments have endured much longer than programs. Cases of mergers and the abolition of departments have occurred, but they tend to occur less frequently. Departments have permanent lines and tenure power. Programs, on the other hand, rely on irregular funding, unpredictable staff funding, and the lack of core faculty who can maintain the integrity of the program.

The second task is to generate student enthusiasm. Indeed, in many cases pressure from students led to the creation of many of the programs and departments. Students are the best allies in the struggle to maintain the survival and credibility of courses on Africa and the black experience. Ground is being lost in elementary, middle, and high schools. In Africa, a generation of students exists who cannot speak or use their indigenous languages with any degree of proficiency or competence. In the United States, there are students who cannot recognize photographs of Martin Luther King Jr. or talk with any authority about the civil rights movement. The ideals and visions of Pan-Africanists such as Marcus Garvey and W. E. B. Du Bois have been compromised. Instead of building connections and speaking about a Pan-Africanist global vision, many are consumed with useless discussions on the tensions between African Americans and Africans. While students share some of the blame, the bulk of the responsibility has to be transferred to parents, the society at large, and representations in the media. In the United States, the insertion of the black experience into the curriculum is often considered a rude intervention. When the concept of Afrocentrism left college campuses, the worry was how its possible spread to high schools would be received. In Africa, globalization has brought in a variety of popular cultures that have undermined indigenous languages and knowledge.

The third task is to seek an agenda that promotes diversity on campuses. The politics of Afrocentrism and that of multiculturalism are not the same and should not be confused. The politics of multiculturalism blend very well with the aspirations of hegemonic power and traditional disciplines. Multiculturalism pursues its own ideas.[45] Many of us do not have problems with the ideas and ideals of multiculturalism. What is more difficult to handle is the politics of Afrocentrism, since certain segments of the public and universities are frightened by rhetoric they associate with radicalism. Some even see Afrocentricity as a race war, a battle that is not limited to campuses but rather fought in the pages of newspaper, courts, and Congress. Those in power seek the knowledge that reinforces power; those at the margins of power seek the knowledge for inclusion and centering. Multiculturalism, on the other hand, is not necessarily critical of hegemonic systems. Defined in a friendly manner, multiculturalism simply offers a tool to understand others in order to more clearly control the rules of engagement. We must continue to seek the truth about ourselves and use the truth to create a patrimony of collective interests.

The fourth task is to return to the vision of the founding fathers of Pan-Africanism, who fused the ideas of African and African American intellectual and political leaders into a powerful political project. The fragmentation of that vision from the 1960s has been one of the greatest mistakes made by black intellectuals. The challenge of this age is to restore this unity in order to generate strength in numbers. To do this, intellectuals cannot shy away from the label of activist-scholar. Traditional departments use the notion of objectivity to take activism out of scholarship. Yet the objectivity they sometimes claim is no more than the defense of capitalism, race domination, and Western hegemonic power. In too many cases, so-called objectivity is also activist scholarship in favor of capitalism, capitalist extension, and white supremacy. There is activism in defense of freedom, a far more noble goal than activism in defense of narrow interests. We also have to promote a notion of community, an amalgamation of scholars and community activists, that is, the cooperation and alliance of academic and organic intellectuals. The community has to be large to embrace diasporic connections between Africans in Africa, Africans in the United States, and African Americans. This is a powerful collective that is global and huge, but manageable.

Finally, irrespective of our ideological positions, we must seek, on a permanent and consistent basis, the means to harvest from our rich traditional values and histories. As we do, we shall see great wisdom in the activities and actions of our pioneers to centralize Africa, to create a diasporic network of ideas, and to come up with a global vision of responding to collective issues around racism and domination. We have discovered the past, now let us change the future.

4

Communalism, Africanism, and Pan-Africanism

Two sets of ideas serve as the preface to this chapter. The first revolves around a cluster of negative images about the continent of Africa in the Western media and various publications that focus excessively on wars, conflicts, coups, political instability, and their consequences.[1] Since the fifteenth century, the characterization of Africa as a so-called dark continent was meant to separate this so-called black Africa from North Africa, later to separate it from South Africa and then the rest of the world. You must have heard one or all of the following in the list of negative images generated by Afro-pessimists and Afro-cynicists: Africa's people had no history; they had no values beyond sex and gluttony; and they had no claim to justice, valuable land, religion, governance, or the ideas of state formation. Whether you add to or subtract from this list, there is a consensus around the reasons for these images: the need to exploit Africans (but at the same time to insult them); the need to enslave its people, basing the forced migrations of over thirteen million people on nonmarket rationality; the need to conquer them (and also to divide them in the process); and the need to prevent a unity that could generate anticolonial nationalism.

The current countries created by European conquest and violence have struggled to generate contested nationalities and nationalisms such that a Ghanaian may not have any sense of identification with a Zimbabwean, or a Nigerian may think that he or she has nothing in common with an Egyptian. Within the boundaries of modern nation-states, where precolonial nations were cobbled together, there are also competing nationalities such that in a country like Nigeria, the Hausa in the north may see themselves as different from the Igbo in the south.

Such contested nationalisms have provoked serious cases of political instability, warfare, genocide, and even the decline of the state. The depressing narratives of chaos and instability in Rwanda, Zaire (the DRC), Liberia, Sierra Leone, and Sudan dominate the media, giving the impression that communal violence, secession, and threats of secession are routine in Africa. Stories of conflicts presume that the ties that bind have been weakened or damaged beyond repair. Colonial boundaries tend to create the impression that the precolonial formations had very little in common and hardly interacted with one another.

The second set of ideas center on Africans themselves. The record of civilizations in Africa suggests a different reading of the past than what the pessimists focus on: stories of division, the common portrayal of the continent as fragmented, and the assumptions that Africans have little in common. We have deep roots in the commonalities of ideas and institutions that once united the majority of our people. Our history tells us something different; our routes and paths lead to crossroads and junctions, and to movements and interactions of people, goods, and ideas. Our spaces reveal that we are covered by big roofs that shape our perceptions and realities. In combination, our roots, routes, and roofs show ideas of unity, commonality, and interaction. It is these ideas and what they mean that form the basis of this chapter.

In spite of the aforementioned pessimists and their cumulative Afroskeptic orientation, many things unite Africans rather than divide them. Indeed, the sources of this unity and the positive consequences that come with it are far greater than the sources of division, even if those of unity have not been fully tapped to uplift the continent. Consider the early history of the interactions between humans and the environment, the peopling of the continent and the movements that led to state formations, and the institutions that emerged to create order and manage families and economies. These developments were not only similar, but they also indicate the success in the spread of ideas across the continent. Such prevailing ideologies as that of kinship and kingship reveal the commonality in the principles that guided the actions of Africans. The spread of Islam in North, East, and West Africa injected a set of ideas not just about God but also about different aspects of culture. Similarly, when Christianity spread it brought with it a new way of understanding the world.

The interactions between Africa and the world followed a similar historical pattern. Trade across the Sahara and the Indian Ocean originally dominated contact with the outside world. From the fifteenth to nineteenth centuries, the transatlantic slave trade revolved around the forced enslavement of Africans. In the nineteenth and twentieth centuries, Christianity was introduced to many places, and it spread with remarkable speed. In the last quarter of the nineteenth century, European conquest began, and the Europeans carved the majority of the continent into new territories governed by different European countries. Colonialism imposed its own ties and experiences. Anticolonial nationalism emerged, a defining moment for Africa, especially after the Second World War. As African countries struggled for their independence, the Cold War took shape, which left Africa with little or no choice other than to become part of global politics. By the middle of the twentieth century, while many countries were independent, those controlled by the Portuguese engaged in liberation wars in the 1960s and 1970s. Apartheid in South Africa did not crumble until the early 1990s, finally ending anticolonial struggles.

What the brief historical summary shows is that our people, nations, and societies, in spite of the various labels we give them, have interacted since the beginning of time. These interactions have been structured in at least four major ways:

1. The internal developments around building institutions and societies in Africa are comprised of military organization, diplomacy and statecraft, the emergence of dynastic groups, migrations and movements, and the creation of cultures (e.g., masks and masquerades, religions, artistic representation, and the like). The institutions and practices of the past now represent what the modern continent can invoke and use to establish national, regional, and continental organizations.

2. Contacts with the outside world have provided various ideas and institutions that have brought people together, as in the case of the spread and impact of Islam and Christianity that define the identities of millions of people.

3. The global network of regional and long-distance trade across the desert and sea led to multilateral relations, the integration of African hinterland markets with coastal ones, the extensive movements of goods and peoples within the continent, the circulation of ideas and ideologies over a wider region, and

the creation of the African diaspora in the Americas, Europe, and Asia.

4. The experience of colonization and domination, as well as the nationalism that emerged from it and contemporary events and sources that create common ground across imposed geo-political boundaries, are historical circumstances that have led to the emergence of various ideas on nationalism, neocolonialism, and modernity, the rise and spread of Western education, the creation of regional and continental organizations, and, perhaps most notably, the African Union.

I will elaborate on these four broad issues, and close the chapter with some suggestions on how to move forward.

Roots: Institutions and Cultural Foundations

The long history of precolonial Africa revealed the ability of the people to relate to the environment in order to create the basis of production and reproduction, which included the procurement of food for survival, shelter for protection, and security arrangements to prevent or overcome attacks. Ideas and institutions, whose logic and practices were similar over a wide region, clearly show a history of development and diffusion over time. There was a host of commonalities around how Africans lived, fed, housed, and clothed themselves; how they related within and between groups; and how they created beliefs about life and death. The human culture they invented, based on the relevance of land and agriculture, shared many things in common that can be grouped into three broad aspects.

First, the world, in spiritual and physical terms, had to be explained, which led to a body of ideas that can be characterized as *mental facts*. A series of works have shown how Africans, irrespective of their locations, shared philosophies and worldviews about God, gods, goddesses, witchcraft, destiny, human relationships (including respect for elders), explanations of death and disease in metaphysical terms, roles for divination and spirit mediums, the place of animals and forests, and of misfortunes.

Second, a body of ideas that can be called *social facts* dealt with the economic, social, and political institutions that evolved to manage society, distribute resources, and allocate rewards. For instance, the idea of divine or semidivine kingship was an element of *social facts* that explained the theory of power. Practices around rites of passage had to be justified. The distribution of land, cattle, and resources had to be based on commonly accepted values.

The third aspect, comprising tools and objects, creative works such as images, architecture, and other related activities can be called *artifacts*, which reflect the manifestations of *mental facts* and *social facts* in creativity and invention. Art historians, anthropologists, and archaeologists have concluded that many aspects of *artifacts* in Africa occurred over wide areas.

Evidence of similarity in aspects of *mental facts, social facts*, and *artifacts* lead to one conclusion: Africans interacted on the basis of ideology, religion, occupations, education, and other necessities of life. Ideas and practices were borrowed, transferred, adopted, and adapted between and among hundreds of groups and millions of people. For instance, cosmologies do explain technologies, as in mythologies around the use and spread of iron. Cosmologies and technologies also yield ideas about power—how men and women structured their gender roles, how resources were distributed, and how transformations in societies were justified and explained. The cosmology of power—how chiefs, men, and groups controlled the rest of their population—was a widespread ideology. There was a deep respect for elders and a strong belief in immortality. The respect for the elders promoted the belief that wisdom came with age, so that a reservoir of knowledge and wisdom was associated with old age. The belief in immortality promoted the belief in large family sizes. To purchase immortality, one had to acquire many children in order to extend the chain of kinship to an indefinite future generation.

The peopling of the continent itself is a story of migrations and movements from one place to another, many of which are now well documented in a variety of studies.[2] The Sahara Desert used to be well populated until desertification led to extensive relocation southward to the Sudan and northward to the Maghreb, such that we now have a recognizable "Saharan culture" in various places. The Bantu-speaking people are known to have spread from areas of the Cross River basin in modern Nigeria and Cameroon to various parts of Central and southern Africa: a massive migration in the first millennium A.D. that was also associated with the spread of iron, crops, and cattle. The Fulani spread widely in West Africa, the Oromo invaded Ethiopia in the sixteenth and seventeenth centuries, the Lwo migrated from the Nile Valley to Kenya and Uganda, and the Nguni warriors spread in southern and eastern Africa during the nineteenth century. These and other cases of migrations show the movements of people in different eras.

The development of agriculture over wide regions reflected the spread of metallurgy to the extent that tools of production made of iron were common. The adaptation within ecological zones shows clearly that the people engaged in similar practices, as in the production of grains in the savanna and root crops in the forest zone. The major occupations revolved around production (crop farming, animal husbandry, hunting and gathering, fishing, and craftsmanship), all of which showed regional continuities as well as variations. Some of the occupations, such as hunting and pastoralism, involved movements that brought places and peoples together. Ecological changes, state expansions, and natural disasters also necessitated movements, some even over greater distances away from previous places of habitation.

The creation of states and societies saw the emergence of both homogenous and heterogeneous societies organized into clans, villages, cities, kingdoms, and empires. The presentation of European colonialism as the unifying agency for thousands of disorganized "tribes" permanently engaged in destructive wars is no more than propaganda to justify the conquest as well as the violence that went with it. The cultural frontiers of precolonial nations merged into one another, uniting groups and neighbors who traded with one another, intermarried, and shared cultures. Everyone lived under one form of authority or another; people were organized into societies varying in size and scale and models of centralized (as in those with kings) or noncentralized (as in villages governed by elders) authority. The centralized states, by the nature of their size, scale, and concentration of power, reflected the ability to merge hundreds of places together into a meaningful political unit. Centralization was a process of intergroup relations; linguistic groupings were combined without fixed geographical boundaries. In states and societies, crossingcutting ties were established for social and cultural reasons, as in the case of membership in secret societies, age grade associations, and religious groups. Marriages between different kinships created an elaborate network of relations within large ethnic groups.

Cross-cultural collaborations and organizations were not only common, but they were also intense. One bit of evidence held in common by many societies is their origin stories; these stories reveal long journeys, multiple settlements before arriving at a final destination, interactions between migrant and autochthonous populations, struggles between different groups for power, and the like. The evolution of groups and group identities reflect extensive interactions with neighbors, participation in a complex network of trade, and the understanding of environment.

A crucial point is our collective memory of living anchored to the shared ethos of communalism. This is the ideology of unity at various levels—family and the village, and village and the land—all interlocked in ideas about production, exchange, and social payments that bound individuals into powerful interlocking webs of relationships. Cohabitation generated a group identity, which the European colonialists labeled as "tribalism," to primitivize a system that merged identity with plural politics to hold together millions of people. In holding people together, the key instruments were noncoercive, which privileged the hegemony of older men and women. The exercise of power ultimately involved control over people and resources, but the mechanism to do this in many places did not necessarily involve the use of violence, which explains why it was not the active young males who controlled power but the elders. Thus, age and gender supplied ideas that were commonly shared over a wide region, especially the belief that to be successful one must survive to old age and leave behind a large number of children as evidence of reproductive power. The power exercised by elders was tied to yet another idea: the possession of knowledge and secrets could generate cohesion and order.

The network of families (kinship) merging into the network of villages and then of towns were all integrated into a notion of group identity, a phenomenon that we label "ethnicity" in contemporary analyses. Ethnicity has acquired a negative meaning, especially in the context of rivalries and wars. What we now characterize as contemporary ethnic groups were autonomous nations in the past, products of state formation, culture, and identity. A group identified itself in linguistic and cultural terms, creating the basis for social formations that united people whom we now call various names such as the Yoruba, Kikuyu, or Ndebele. Such names could represent the inventions of the Western educated elite that emerged in the nineteenth century, as some cases have shown, but the people had already existed in their locations for a long time previously.

A nation created a sense of pride in itself, promoted a variety of customs to unite its members, and sought a set of beliefs to generate a strong identity. Belief systems regarding the gods and goddesses, spirits in objects, and roles of priests and priestesses were manifestations of how ideas could spread. The introduction of Islam was yet another agent that united millions of people along a set of common beliefs. Between the seventh and eleventh centuries, Arab groups invaded North Africa, spreading an Islamic and Arabic culture that ultimately gained a majority in various parts of the Nile Valley, North Africa, and the Sahara, from where it also spread to the savanna. Arabic and Islamic culture continues to provide unity in these places.

Production systems created the basis for extensive relations among individuals, groups, villages, and towns. All the great rivers were avenues to integrate hundreds of communities, as in the examples of the Nile and Niger, and these communities were established along the rivers. Communities were also dependent on the rivers to create habitable settlements, productive farming, and trade. The availability of water systems, which is related to development, was also an integrative mechanism. Thus, large settlements emerged along rivers and waterfronts or close to water bodies. The population density and distribution in different regions could reflect the quantity and quality of water resources and the ability to share them. Water transportation played a role in the establishment of extensive trading networks by a host of long-distance traders, as in the case of the use of the Niger. In the nineteenth century, the opening up of the hinterland to European activities was, in part, calculated on the knowledge of the rivers.

Iron made it possible to transform the landscape, build settlements, create states, and use brute force where necessary. The transformative processes made possible by iron have led to various books that show how the diffusion of iron and iron products linked the greater part of Africa. Where there were enough ores and fuels, metallurgy was practiced and led to related methods, various rituals, and the idea that a smith was a "culture hero."[3] Iron also generated various rituals around which there were gods (such as the Yoruba's Ogun), which in turn reveal beliefs about power and people.

Trade was an agency for connections as well, through the exchange of goods, the traders who sold and bought the goods, and the routes by which they traveled. Established trading communities emerged in various parts of Africa. The Soninke, who founded the famous empire of Ghana, created a formidable Soninke trading diaspora after the fall of Ghana. Located in various parts where they served as middle-men between the savanna and the Sahara Desert, they retained con-nections with their origins while assimilating local cultures. They received desert-side goods (livestock and salt) in exchange for savanna products (such as grain and cloth), and they took both sets of commodities further south for kola nuts, slaves, and gold, among other products.

Routes: Migrations and Africanisms

Movements within Africa and between Africa and the rest of the world have created continental and global connections. First, there are the internal migrations within Africa: extensive, widespread, and historically deep-rooted. Many cases of internal migrations consisted of movements between rural areas and cities, or cities to rural; and between one rural area and another, or urban to urban.[4] Second, there are the international migrations, notably the forced move-ments associated with the trans-Saharan and transatlantic slave trade. Both the first and the second types of migrations can be connected, sometimes blurring the distinction between the local, regional, and international movements. Boundaries were not clearly demarcated, and many migrations were so fluid that pastoralists and traders could actually cross areas in the course of their business. Economic activi-ties were complementary, thus promoting strong ties. In addition, there were cultural affinities that supported endless travels.[5]

The reasons why people move from one area to another demon-strate strong links among Africans. Some of these reasons include: population pressure that calls for relocation to create new econo-mies; droughts and wars, forcing people to look for alternative places of abode; declining agricultural production and overall changing economic fortunes; possibilities of better opportunities abroad; and the existence of social and cultural networks to serve as hosts.[6]

Migrations in the precolonial era date far back in history. Whole groups of people or entire villages were known to have relocated for ecological and economic reasons. The peopling of the continent has been connected with stories of migrations since the Stone Age. The assumption is also that population movement led to the dissemina-tion of Bantu languages throughout much of the continent.[7] During the colonial period, some groups migrated as a form of protest against the colonial power; some did so to look for jobs in areas with land in order to reduce crops or minerals available to the external markets, and some traveled as entrepreneurs. There were seasonal migrations by pastoralists, by farmers who moved to cocoa or peanut fields, and there were long-term migrations as well. Colonial economic changes promoted the movement of people to cities, mine centers, railway stations, and rural areas capable of producing cash crops. For instance, the peanut-producing villages in Senegal and the Gambia, the cocoa-producing ones in Ghana and Nigeria, and the plantations in Côte d'Ivoire attracted migrant labors from places where those opportunities were lacking. Disparities in incomes between villages and cities, and in development between one region and another, generated massive movements as well.

Both the reasons and the patterns of colonial migrations continue to be reproduced today. Where the colonial economic structure remains in place, they continue to affect the movements to cities, mining areas, and places with lucrative farms. A declining economy in one country triggers migration to others, as in the large number of migrations to South Africa and from Africa to Western countries.[8]

Connections with the outside world have been captured in three broad ways: the trans-Saharan, the Indian Ocean, and the transatlantic. These were forced migrations over many centuries that resulted in the displacement of Africans to Europe, Asia, and the Americas. Millions were taken across the Sahara Desert as slaves, although a number went voluntarily, as in the case of religious people who performed the pilgrimage to Mecca and Medina. Between the fifteenth and nineteenth centuries, the transatlantic slave trade saw the relocation of over twelve million people. The presence of Africans extended African cultures to the Americas, in such aspects as language, religions, and music. The routes taken—national, trans-Saharan, transatlantic, and others—have many consequences. That we can talk about Africa and the African disapora is a function of the creation and uses of hundreds of routes that connected one location to another within the context not just of a region but also of the world. An Igbo person in Nigeria may share origins with someone in the United States, and a Yoruba may have long-lost relations in Bahia, Brazil.

Regarding transatlantic migrations, which are the best studied in the literature, connections between Africa and the Americas were created in the sixteenth century and consolidated in the centuries that followed. The Portuguese incursion into the coastal cities of eastern Africa linked Africans to Europe,[9] while millions of slaves were taken from central and west Africa. The extensive making of slaves connected the African coasts with the hinterland to create a complicated logistical chain, which used not just the network of trade to deliver but also the network of violence to enslave.

The formations of black identities in Europe and Africa have widened the ties between and among peoples, nations, and nationalities. With respect to African Americans and Africa, Vincent Harding's remark in *The Other American Revolution* captured the history of a consciousness: "The roots we had in Africa continue to be important, necessary, life-affirming sources. But roots are ultimately for trees; and we must become new trees, striking out, reaching out, seeking new levels, new possibilities, here on these new shores."[10] The celebration of Africa and Africa's achievements became part of the source of bonding. From the pyramids of Egypt to the kings of Benin and Yoruba, the contributions of Africans to civilization became a source of pride. In documenting these contributions, one of the main aims was to dismiss the Eurocentric claim that black people did not contribute to civilization. Another purpose was also to say that the origins of those in the diaspora were not "dark" and "primitive" as claimed by those who enslaved them.

Contemporary migrations have solidified the African connections with the older diaspora. The Soninke mentioned above have been traveling to France since the 1950s, and labor migrants from other African groups joined their numbers starting in the 1960s.[11] During the same period, a small number of Africans went to Western countries to receive a higher education. Increasingly massive migrations to the West began in the 1980s, instigated by declining economies and political instability in many African countries. We now have millions of Africans in other continents, creating various migrant communities in the United States and Europe as well as smaller numbers in other parts of the world. Contemporary migrants have intensified the linkages in a global manner, evidenced in monetary remittances from the West to Africa, the movements of goods and peoples in various directions, the greater traffic in ideas, and the spread of popular cultures. Air travel between Africa and the West has increased markedly, carrying thousands of Africans as they moved from one part of the world to another.

Catering to the needs of migrants has led to the creation of stores (characterized as "ethnic" stores in many Western countries) that sell African products or Western products packaged to meet African tastes. Opportunities for cultural expressions are limitless, as stores market films and videos, music CDs, clothes, and other items that enable millions of people to enjoy products from various parts of Africa. The globalization of the African experience has led to cultural exchanges, intermingling of people, and the creation of Internet, radio, and television stations to cater to new generations drawn from various parts of the world.

Roofs: Colonialism and Nationalism

European conquest in the post-1885 period came with aspects of Western modernity that created sources of commonality and bondage. First, it brought together thousands of nationalities within about fifty countries. Although imperfect, the new boundaries created a new basis by which to define the nation-state. The discussions started during the nineteenth century by writers such as Edward Wilmot Blyden (1832–1912), James Africanus Beale Horton (1835–83), Rev. C. C. Reindorf (1834–1917), and John Mensah Sarbah (1864–1910), and extended into the twentieth century by political-cum-nationalist writers such as Kwame Nkrumah and Amilcar Cabral.[12] New notions of progress, Pan-Africanist visions, and the European partition of Africa emerging in the last quarter of the nineteenth century confronted these writers. Their ideas on nationalism, tradition, and modernity have served as a preface to a century-old set of ideas on how to reimagine Africa drawing from local and external knowledge. The encounter with the West has become a narrative that unites most African thinkers, irrespective of their location, in terms of how they—as the colonized, imperialized, and traumatized—have to analyze the West, the colonizing and imperializing agent. African scholars, within the homogenizing narratives of nationalism, have to borrow ideas from the West while at the same time taking ideas from their own roots. The combination of all these ideas reflects transatlantic visions, Pan-Africanist ideals, continental aspirations, and continental activism. We are united by knowledge production.

Modernity has been inscribed into the idea of being African. Moreover, being modern has been inscribed into the idea of being

Western. Reflections on the impact of the West on Africa, using the shorthand word "modernity," is one of the most discussed issues both in academic and nonacademic discussions about Africa. In these discussions, a small number of Western-educated African elite had to define Africa, African nationhood, and the modernity of the nation. The roots of the inscription of modernity into being Western lie in the colonial invasion and European governance of Africa in the first half of the twentieth century.

Institutions of modernity include the use of European languages, which for a long time created a dichotomy between those with access to English, French, Portuguese, and Spanish and those without access. The use of European languages was connected to formal economies, urban living, contacts with the outside world, and access to Western culture. Western education made it possible to teach the language, but it also began the process of teaching new skills in formal settings, generating occupations that defined prestige, income, and modernity. The responses to modernity have served to unite Africans and to define Africa in relation to others. There were those who sought access and benefits in modern institutions of health, economy, education, and the rest, and those who were denied.

However, modernity should not be seen as implying the end of African "tradition."[13] The dominant narrative in African history is that of change and continuity. Many of the precolonial institutions survived the colonial period. Those institutions have served as agents to unite the past of Africa with its present, and the bonds between the educated and the uneducated who participate in similar traditions. The older nations controlled by kings and chiefs commanded allegiance during the colonial period and after, serving as important forces for cohesion in villages and towns. Similarly, many of the cultural institutions survived the colonial period. The argument in the postcolonial states is that such institutions should even form the basis of contemporary development.

There are the common bonds of colonial exploitation and the neocolonial dependence that followed. The experience was the same in terms of the use of African labor to produce for external markets, the shift away from food production to cash crop production to sell abroad, the development of mining centers with profits going to external firms, and the use of migrant workers. In South Africa, Kenya, and other settler colonies, a large number of European settlers complicated land issues, changing land tenure regulations to privilege their acquisition of fertile places at the expense of native Africans.

If the changes of the colonial era created bonds among Africans, anticolonial resistance and nationalism also provided the politics and ideology that united them. The ferment and demand for independence united us in the first half of the twentieth century. Feelings of sympathy for liberation movements spread across Africa and the African diaspora. We could see the global black outrage against the Italian invasion of Ethiopia in 1935, and support for independence movements in various parts of Africa.

There was a common antiapartheid voice in the second half of the twentieth century. High expectations of what liberation and independence would bring were remarkably similar throughout Africa, a unity of hopes and wishes among the generality of our people. Everybody wanted to overcome the burdens of poverty and underdevelopment. The optimism about change expressed in the 1950s was the same all over Africa, a prevailing mood based on the strong desire for a new beginning. Regional and Pan-African organizations have emerged not only as manifestations of common ties but also as an affirmation to present a common front.

There is the common bond of neocolonialism. The legal sovereignty brought by independence did not end the domination of Western forces, the intervention of the West in the affairs of Africa, or the control of African economies by external powers. During the Cold War years, two ideological forces in fierce opposition extended their politics to Africa, France maintained a tight grip on its former colonies, and the West used a combination of financial and military strategies to reward their friends and to punish their enemies. Such international institutions as the World Bank, the International Monetary Fund, and the World Trade Organization do not always operate in ways beneficial to Africa's interests.

In the management of postcolonial politics, there is the common experience of ethnicity. The rise of ethnic politics during the twentieth century, creating the problems mentioned previously, has checked the growth of nationalism and Pan-Africanism. Ethnic groups that feel marginalized in contemporary nation-states have asserted their rights to self-determination, sometimes leading to ethnic conflicts, the use of violence to separate people or to force them to live together within the same national boundaries. With internal differences and distances from earlier Pan-Africanist aspirations, identity politics have become fragmented. "Almost everyone thinks of themselves as a Nigerian or a Tanzanian first," wrote President Julius Nyerere in a lecture delivered in Lagos in 1987, "and as an African second. In a few cases, regrettably, one thinks of oneself as a tribalist first, as a nationalist second, and as an African third."[14]

A collective response to colonial and postcolonial challenges was the formation of all-African organizations, notably the Organization of African Unity, subsequently replaced with the African Union in 1999. The aim was for the countries to work together to plan a better future for the continent and its peoples. It was correct to hold the view that stronger ties between African countries would provide opportunities to exchange ideas, goods, and people. As Nyerere remarked in his 1987 lecture:

> For each of our nations now deals with its problems alone. Whether or not it is trying to serve the interests of the masses, and whether it has majority support, each Government is therefore vulnerable to destabilisation. This can come either from the power hunger of strategically placed groups, or from the intrigues of a foreign state which feels that a different government more sympathetic to its interests could be established with the help of local dissidents. Greater African unity and co-operation is particularly vital for dealing with severe economic problems of our countries and our continent. It is these which are exploited by those who wish to seize power, for it is the fashion to attribute them solely to the incompetence and venality of African Governments. (9)

For Africa to attain political and economic liberation, Nyerere affirmed the consensus among African political thinkers that it is difficult to negotiate with the West, attain equity in world trade, and overcome domination while acting as individual countries. The various economies and politics have to be coordinated. Nyerere continued:

> Even in the short-term, however, firm co-operation and united action by African states could make us stronger in our dealings with the Economic North. At present in order to get essential economic help, each of us can be—and sometimes is—forced to pay a price which we know is inappropriate for our long-term development, or incompatible with Africa's policy of non-alignment. Together we could more effectively resist making such concessions. There is no salvation for Africa without Unity. (12)

A respected politician, he was aware of the difficulty that faced a continent whose leaders were not ready for a strong political union:

> Without question, political unity would be the best way of achieving the coordinated economic and political action which Africa needs. But the political unity of Africa is not a realistic possibility in the near future. It was unacceptable to the majority of national leaders in 1963, and since then African nationalism has grown stronger and more jealous. Even Regional political unity has proved very difficult to achieve. The Founding Fathers of independent Africa . . . have failed our people in this important respect. (12)

Nyerere did not see the situation as hopeless, suggesting "intra-African cooperation," in particular economic cooperation, which he did not regard as an alternative to political unity, but which he saw as "a method of action not a replacement of action" (12). As the history of the Organisation of African Unity (OAU) shows, such cooperation was much stronger in rhetoric than action.[15] Nevertheless, the idea of continental and regional organizations remains important, as in the examples of the African Development Bank and the Economic Community of West African States.

A Bigger Roof: Pan-Africanism

The migrations instigated by slavery generated the creation of a global black identity that became a political movement in the twentieth century. Black politics in Europe and the Americas began to connect in many ways to those of Africa. The African diaspora produced consequences that served as agents for ties across and within the Atlantic.[16] The rejection of the negative images associated with blackness became both an individual and a collective project. One of the tasks of educated black persons, whether in Africa or the United States, has been to fight and attack the negative images about them, write their own histories, and present their own culture. For blacks based outside of Africa, creating their identities and histories inevitably reveals ties with Africa. Although born and raised in Europe or the Americas, they could not claim the genesis of their histories in those lands, but rather in Africa. They had to develop a black nationalism embedded in multiple histories and experiences—of forced relocation, slavery, suffering, discrimination, and exploitation. Black nationalism had to fight alienation—of rejection in the Western world, of the stigma of identification with a so-called primitive Africa, and of lies about the irrelevance of the existence of black people. Racism and slavery have become the two powerful ties that bind Africa with its diaspora.

Racism in South Africa and the entrenchment of apartheid during the twentieth century provided enduring sources of unity. Black intellectuals were united in condemning South Africa. As early as the first Pan-African Congress in 1900, they pointed attention to the suffering of black people and the atrocities of the government of Jan Christian Smuts. The criticism continued in later years, leading to the formation of activist organizations such as the Council on African Affairs (CAA), established in 1937 by Paul Robeson and the sociology professor Max Yergan. The CAA brought to the attention of the public the racial crises in South Africa and the contributions of the United States government to the maintenance of apartheid. In the 1940s, the CAA organized lectures and rallies in support of black liberation. The United States government persecuted the CAA and labeled it a subversive organization. It folded in 1955, yet antiapartheid movements and criticisms continued to grow, becoming part of the civil rights movement in the United States. Numerous campaigns were organized until the fall of apartheid,[17] and struggles for emancipation from European domination strengthened the transatlantic ties between Africa and the African diaspora.[18] All the major Pan-Africanist leaders invested in the project of African decolonization, as reflected in their speeches, activism, and campaigns. The price was high: in the assassinations of Martin Luther King Jr. and Malcolm X, in career ruination for Paul Robeson, and in the allegation of communism for W. E. B. Du Bois.

The horizontal integration of the black world also received its expression and validation in literary and cultural production, leading to the emergence of great thinkers and enduring works of scholarship. Aimé Césaire, a poet of global significance, celebrated Africa in its premodern essence, turning that which the Eurocentrists characterized as "primitive" into romantic power by praising the civilization that never invented or discovered anything, but had the abundance of joy and happiness. Poetry and politics became connected in advancing the Pan-Africanist agenda of black solidarity, attaining mental and political decolonization, securing freedom from oppression, and seeking the means to attain economic and political power.[19]

Figure 4.1. Tomb of Kwame Nkrumah, Accra, Ghana. Photograph courtesy of Ben Weiss.

Future Ties

I have identified a number of the leading causes, events, and consequences of the ties that bind Africans, Africa, and the African disapora. Let me bring this chapter to a close by offering a number of suggestions on how these ties can be managed, maintained, strengthened, and used to bring about positive and rapid changes in Africa and to the people of African descent. There are adequate lessons to draw from past historical experiences and contemporary historical realities.

The starting point is to create the media that will reveal enduring truths about Africa, the extensive stories of hardworking people, energetic migrants, and talented householders. Knowledge about one part of Africa is generated not within, but rather from the outside. What people in South Africa know about Nigeria may come by way of the British Broadcasting Corporation in Britain and Cable News Network in the United States. The bias of Western media is long-standing and

Figure 4.2. Monument to Dr. Nkrumah, Accra, Ghana. Photograph courtesy of Ben Weiss.

Figure 4.3. Memorial statue of Dr. Nkrumah. Photograph courtesy of
Ben Weiss.

Figure 4.4. Pool surrounding Dr. Nkrumah's mausoleum. Photograph courtesy of Ben Weiss.

Figure 4.5. Dr. Nkrumah's mausoleum. Photograph courtesy of Ben Weiss.

Figure 4.6. Kwame Nkrumah Memorial Park, Accra, Ghana. Photograph courtesy of Ben Weiss.

legendary, and it needs to be corrected. The creation of regional and Pan-African news agencies should be a top priority and must be properly coordinated and managed. The creation of an all-African media is not for propaganda to replace the truth or for bad leadership to be defended, but rather to highlight the achievements of millions of people who have been denied voices. The negative images of divisions and chaos have to change to the positive reality on the ground: extensive human interactions, transborder commerce, movements of pastoralists, smart long-distance traders, energetic youth, productive women, honest farmers, and the like. As the media presents better information, the values and aspirations of our people and the solidarity among them will reveal what define us as a continent and as a people.

The divisions instigated by colonial boundaries have to be overcome by creating regional and continental networks to facilitate greater contacts, promote economic exchanges, and ensure the free movement of labor. What this means is that all the existing regional and continental organizations must function in line with their clearly stated objectives. A powerful media in combination with a united continent will give power to the opinions of Africans and enable black people all over the world to assert themselves and build greater pride in themselves and their achievements.

We must overcome cultural amnesia and transmit what remains of our positive cultures to a new generation so that we can affirm our heritage, our collective living styles, and the generosity of our kinship. The road to success, as it has been said many times, is always under construction. As we reconstruct the road to the success of Africa, we surely have to look back in order to look forward. Our life-affirming values of the past can work for the present: ideas and values that cherish women, adore elders, venerate ancestors, protect children, and honor hard work. As part of ideas around culture, we have to protect African languages so that they do not die or remain second place to European languages. Not only is the dependence on external languages limiting creative capacities, but it also reduces opportunities for the majority of Africans to communicate across ethnic and national divides.

There have been suggestions regarding the possibility of promoting Hausa and Kiswahili, both languages with enormous regional power, the former in West Africa and the latter in East Africa. Advocates of the use of Kiswahili say that at least one hundred million people are able to speak or understand it. Let me add the even greater possibility of the use of a nonelitist pidgin, a combination of African languages with European ones.[20] It is widespread in West Africa, where English and another language are combined, leading to a language with a regional and national spread, one that meets the demands of plural societies and has the enormous capacity to facilitate education and communication in schools and media.

Whether it is about the choice of language, the use of pidgin, or the promotion of culture, the overall mission is to turn culture into an agency of development and integration. Whether citizens and locals are poor or rich, what they have in abundance is the reservoir of culture. African politicians have been clever in the manipulation of culture to stay in power and to justify excesses, which suggests that it is not that they do not know what to do but that they are doing the wrong things. Liberation movements in South Africa and Lusophone Africa successfully used culture to fight the forces of domination and to unite their peoples against colonial forces.

We have to manage politics in a creative manner to attain positive goals. The danger that instrumentalized ethnicity has played must be minimized. As we struggle to attain democracy and equal rights, we also have to struggle to respect the rights and status of constituent nationalities in each country. Most African countries are multiethnic, plural societies. Peoples and groups have to relate. Granted that war is a form of intergroup relations, but this is not the tie we desire. Peace and cooperation are our goals. Leadership is critical to develop visions that are transformative, agendas that are liberating, strategies that cut across ties and peoples, and tactics that strengthen the bonds of peoples and communities. Political instability tears people and states apart. Insecurity generated by politics leads to parochial identities. Where the state itself generates violence—as in the case of Sudan and Rwanda—the bloodletting, genocide, ethnic cleansing, and killings force groups to hate one another and to minimize the use of civic institutions for survival and prosperity. Wars linked to ethnicities and leadership struggles are great sources of divisions, and they can lead to regional warfare, as in the case of Central Africa.[21] Military dictatorships and authoritarian civilian regimes unleash prolonged crises of power struggles and ethnic rivalries.

We have to manage our economies to benefit from our size, our number, and our diasporic communities. The resources of the great rivers such as the Zambezi, Niger, and Nile must be managed to generate greater intraregional integration. As water resources become scarcer because of environmental and human factors, so too must we devise greater political and management skills.[22] The elimination of poverty should take priority over all other issues. War and conflicts will wreck our economies and create divisions and turmoil. Better economies will lead to greater integration within and between countries. Africans are developing consumer cultures, a commonality that will make millions of people demand resources to secure economic benefits. Opportunities to make a good living and enjoy luxuries will lead to greater travel and less use of repressive methods of governance. Mismanaged economies will promote xenophobic feelings and minimize crosscutting ties.

Finally, we have to restore the feeling of being African, the strings of thoughts and ideas that created pride in "Africanness," which sustained the spirit of Pan-Africanism for the greater part of the first half of the twentieth century. The actions of men like W. E. B. Du Bois and Kwame Nkrumah were based on the notion that Africans were one large family, that the continent was one large place, that hope in one corner of the continent could be felt in others. The use of culture, expressed in the power of poetry and stories, can promote commonality. Pan-Africanism, based on the positive politicization of identity and culture, has an enormous capability to create unity, the horizontal integration of cultural producers and political elite. The organization of a huge cultural event such as the Second World African Festival of Arts and Culture (FESTAC) in Nigeria in 1977 has shown that "cultural integration" is possible. The experience of the military command of the Economic Community of West African Monitoring Group (ECOMOG) under the Economic Community of West African States (ECOWAS), in spite of its many limitations and failures, provides an institution to improve upon to organize regional intervention in crisis management. The possibility of "military integration" has been demonstrated by ECOMOG, the building of a regional force whose structure can be reworked and expanded. The replacement of the OAU with the African Union and redefined objectives point to the possibility of political integration. The unifying force of Islam in North Africa, accompanied by the use of the Arabic language, points to the possibility of religious integration. Removing the sources of conflict between Islam and Christianity will go a long way in turning these two religions into sources of unity. The economic cooperation in the creation of ECOWAS and the Southern African Development Community (SADC) shows the possibility of economic integration. Economic cooperation between nations and their people will be accompanied by movements and exchanges of cultures. For instance, the movements from Nigeria to Ghana have in turn made Nigerian movies arguably the most popular in Ghana, a successful example of economic and cultural integration.

With all the projects of integration already formulated and some already in place, it shows that we do not lack ideas to unite ourselves. Indeed, we have ideas in abundance. What we lack is the translation of great ideas into practice. It is the role of political leadership to translate the ideas of scholars and policymakers into practice. Let me give the final words to Mwalimu Julius Nyerere by repeating a line in one of his statements cited above: "There is no salvation for Africa without Unity."[23]

Part 2

An African Case Study

Yoruba Ethnicity in the Diaspora

5

Atlantic Yoruba and the Expanding Frontiers of Yoruba Culture and Politics

The Yoruba have become truly global in their locations in different parts of the world; the representations of various aspects of their culture (including religion, philosophy, worldview, economic practices like the "esusu," art, music, dress, and cuisine) in their new locations; the distinctive Yoruba Orisa traditions in the Americas; their physical presence in various parts of the world, either as the descendants of Yoruba people taken as slaves between the seventeenth and nineteenth centuries or as Yoruba voluntary migrants in the contemporary era; and the integration of Yoruba into academic fields such as African, Diaspora, Black Atlantic, and Atlantic History Studies.

The geographic location of this chapter is the Atlantic, a site that unites the Yoruba in Nigeria with the coastal areas of West Africa, Europe, and the Americas. Within this Atlantic unit, the Yoruba are located far and wide, not just along the coastlines but in the hinterland as well. The Yoruba in diaspora reveal to us profound imaginations of diasporic movements and connections; processes and outcomes of cultural hybridization and identity formation; and strategies of adaptation and social integration in diverse locations in different historical formations.

Yoruba oral narratives have actually privileged diasporic events and episodes. Our early mythologies are actually inaugurated by a diaspora: stories of princes leaving Ile-Ife to establish kingdoms, settlements, and towns are narratives of a diaspora in formation. As the scattered princes of Ile-Ife were linked to an ancestor—Oduduwa—the unity in diversity was inscribed through and reinforced by ceremonies and festivals. Thus a notion of ancestral diaspora was created that also connected to a cultural diaspora, as, for example, in the spread of the ideas of kingship and political centralization. Primary migrations fueled secondary ones: If Oranmiyan is credited with founding Oyo-Ile, so too did many leave Oyo-Ile to create new settlements, and those internal movements created a larger network from Ile-Ife to Ife-Aana in Togo.

The mythological origin of the diaspora became further reinforced by a historic event, a violent power struggle, and a mortal curse. Samuel Johnson locates the struggles in the post-*Alaafin* Abiodun era (1780s), as the dividing period between peace and war, prosperity and poverty, success and failure. Abiodun's cousin Awole succeeded him (1789–c. 1796) and was beset by the problems of power rivalries with and among his chiefs, growing traffic in the sale of slaves abroad, the chiefs' ambitions to profit from the trade, and political miscalculations over the competitive struggles for high-ranking titles. A disloyal faction of the army mutinied and sent an empty, covered calabash to the king, indicating its rejection of Awole's authority and prompting him to commit ritual suicide. In most dramatic language, Johnson brings his impressive but depressing narrative of Awole to a close:

> There being no alternative His Majesty set his house in order; but before he committed suicide, he stepped out into the palace quadrangle with face stern and resolute, carrying in his hands an earthenware dish and three arrows. He shot one to the North, one to the South, and one to the West uttering those ever-memorable imprecations, "My curse be on you for your disloyalty and disobedience, so let your children disobey you. If you send them on an errand, let them never return to bring you word again. To all the points I shot my arrows will ye be carried as slaves. My curse will carry you to the sea and beyond the seas, slaves will rule over you, and you their masters will become slaves."
>
> With this he raised and dashed the earthenware dish on the ground smashing it into pieces, saying "Igba la iso a ki iso awo, beheni ki oro mi o se to!" (a broken calabash can be mended, but not a broken dish; so let my words be—irrevocable!)[1]

I fully understand Johnson's mindset, grounded as it was in a theological way of thinking. Indeed, we cannot conflate myth with history. However, human beings make sense of their experience using

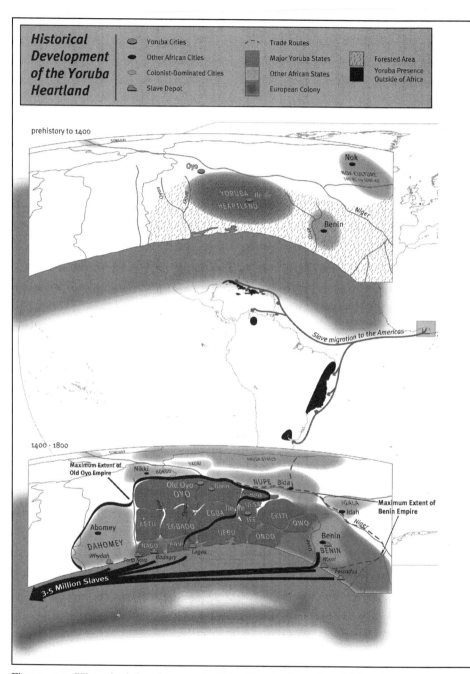

Figure 5.1. Historical development of the Yoruba heartland. Map by
Sam Saverance.

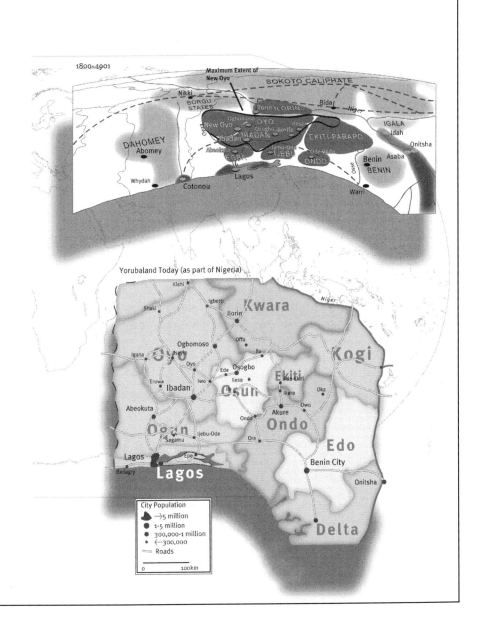

mythic frameworks, just as Johnson did as he witnessed events that produced wars and resulted in captives who were sold abroad. His account, therefore, is a sensible presentation of a violent foundation for a diaspora, in this case manifested as a greater number of Yoruba entering the traffic of the slave trade than ever before. Many found themselves in Cuba. The sale of Yoruba into slavery increased dramatically in the post-Awole years and reached its peak around the mid-1820s, a trend that was sustained until about 1850, when the trade began to decline, and ended in the late 1860s. Though the trade ended, enslavement continued and was integrated into domestic economies. Recent estimates put the total export at about 1.12 million, and about 80 percent taken between 1750 and 1850. The number cumulatively represented about 9 percent of the African population sold into slavery.[2]

The core of the activities and struggles of Yoruba lives abroad has actually been, to retain Awole's metaphor, to mend a broken calabash; and to reinvent the wheel to make new earthenware, since, as Awole reminded us, the broken dish cannot be put together. Like the broken calabash and pots, lives in exile are fragmented and spirits broken, but restorative and redemptive efforts are equally as powerful.

There was equally a third force associated with trade and other economic opportunities that enabled the Yoruba to spread within West Africa. Nineteenth-century data are clear that the Yoruba were long-distance traders; both men and women traveled over wide distances to buy and sell among the Kanuri, Hausa, and Nupe, their near neighbors, and in far-flung places in the north. They went east to Benin and much further to the Congo valley. Westward, they were noted in almost all Aja towns and moved further to the Senegal valley.

As the Yoruba moved into the twentieth century, the traffic intensified. By the 1920s, large numbers were reported in the Gold Coast (now Ghana), and their trading network spread as far as the Gambia. They penetrated both the cities and the rural areas and, according to J. S. Eades' case study of the Gold Coast, emerged as the largest and most successful trading network, which linked prominent citizens, rich merchants, and Yoruba colonies.[3] The network shared information and distributed capital to consolidate its economic power. Yoruba culture spread with them, and they were even able to invite guests and musicians from Western Nigeria to Togo, Republic of Benin, Ghana, and the Ivory Coast to join them in major celebrations such as marriages and funerals. Disaster struck in 1969: a mass expulsion forced thousands to return home to Nigeria from Ghana.

As the Yoruba moved to other parts of West Africa and to faraway lands in the Americas and Europe, they continued to maintain and create mythical, genetic, and cultural ties to their homeland. They have become intercultural and transnational, claiming to be both ethnic and transethnic. Yoruba culture has fragmented and reproduced in new forms in different Atlantic locations, along the seacoasts and coastal hinterlands. To connect the Yoruba in Abeokuta in Nigeria with those in London, cultural heritages as well as genetics become markers. Colonial politics lumped the Yoruba in Nigeria into what became the Western Region, creating a colonial marker that became a unit of political formation and competition for power. Postcolonial experience has consolidated Yoruba ethnicity within the politics of Nigeria. Those who were forced to migrate in the years of the Atlantic slave trade fell on Yoruba culture to create new identities. Contemporary migrants chose the tropes of modernization and globalization to affirm their Yorubaness. Whether as members of old or new migrations, Yoruba habits can be identified, expressed forcefully in some places, and invoked through ideas on communities and worldview, as well as practices around Yoruba food (even of Orisa food), rituals, kinship cultures, and the like. Whether in the clothes they wear or the food they eat, Yoruba culture is daily restaged in different parts of the world. This restaging forms the core of this chapter.

Various notions and labels now describe the Yoruba as a nation, if the reference is to their location in West Africa; as a language, if the reference is to linguistic group; as an identity, if Yorubaness is defined in terms of some common unifying characteristics; as a religion and spirituality for those who venerate any of the gods and goddesses in the Orisa tradition; and as a culture, if those who practice elements of the culture identify themselves as Yoruba, regardless of whether they live and practice in West Africa, New Zealand, or Australia.

Yoruba has become a consciousness of being. This consciousness has a regional dimension, such as being born in Iwo or Ede, but it has a diasporic connection, such as being a native of Bahia in Brazil, as well as a transnational dimension, as in the case of Toyin Falola of Austin, Texas. The consciousness can also be ethnic, as in characterizing Yoruba as an ethnicity in modern Nigeria, but it can be inherited, as in the case of Afro-Cubans of Oyo descent. It can be dual or multiple, as in cases of intermarriages. It can be historic, as in the case of millions of people whose original ancestry is Yoruba but who now live in Haiti or Jamaica. And it can be philosophical and scholarly, as there are scholars of Yoruba cosmology who are Caucasians: William Bascom was perhaps the first to highlight for the world the literary, philosophical, and scientific interconnectedness of Ifa divination. A slew of Yoruba scholars, including Justine Cordwell, William Fagg, Frank Willett, Robert Farris Thompson, Henry Drewal, and Andrew Apter facilitated, we might argue, the intellectualization of the Yoruba diaspora.

From this consciousness has emerged a notion of political awareness and political aspirations by ambitious individuals. Within Nigeria, it translates as competition for power in the national center, struggles for positions and access to power, discussions of revenue allocations, and the belief that the pace of modernization and progress would have been accelerated if the Yoruba had constituted an autonomous political unit. Outside of Nigeria, political awareness takes multiple forms. In the older diaspora of slavery, it was used to construct cultural communities. For contemporary migrants, it forms the basis to establish associations, hometown networks, and the like.

Consciousness may be used to strengthen political awareness. Political awareness, in turn, may be used to promote consciousness. Both may combine to produce the equivalent of an ideology. There are many people in the Americas who use the word "Yoruba" in ideological terms, as a way to live without appropriating Western traditions, to combat Western values with Yoruba ones, or to preserve and use alternative social and cultural mores. When constructed as an ideology, the assumptions are that elements of Yoruba culture are sufficient to live an orderly life, to engage the reality of existence, and to confront the obstacles of life.

This chapter is about the Yoruba as a diaspora at two main levels: the diaspora of slavery and the contemporary diaspora in the age of globalization. The older and newer diasporas are connected by ideas of Yoruba ethnicity and nationality, by how the diaspora of slavery created enduring legacies that survive to date, and how these legacies are being extended by the contemporary generation of Yoruba migrants. The diaspora of slavery tapped into an African Yoruba past to adjust and survive in a milieu of slavery. Although attempts were made to erase ethnicities and call all Africans "black," Yoruba ethnicity existed long-term, as the enslaved retained their sense of history and culture in order to hang on to an identity. On the other hand, the Yoruba related with other African slaves, and they used associations and culture to come together.

The contemporary Yoruba abroad are transnationalists who maintain contacts with the Yoruba at home. The Yoruba diaspora has globalized Yoruba culture and developed Yoruba consciousness. Whether in the older or more recent migrations, the Yoruba needed to create effective organizational strategies to cope with new locations. The details of these strategies show elements of the Yoruba method of mobility. Social practices such as respect for elders, naming ceremonies, celebrations, and funerals have been understood in the context of Yoruba culture.

Yoruba culture, of course, is not static in any particular era. The Atlantic Yoruba, in creating processes of self-definition and identity construction, understood the necessity of change. Thus, we can even speak of Yoruba identities in the multiple senses of time, space, and individuality. Identity ascription, a process that also occurred, meant that individuals could borrow and create, thereby blending with other ethnicities or nationalities such that we can speak of Yoruba-Brazilian or Yoruba-American. As the Yoruba homeland has also always been divided into multiple subgroups such as Ekiti, Ijesa, Oyo, Igbomina, and the like, the Atlantic Yoruba also combine the ideas of the Yoruba nation with those of Yoruba towns and cities, suggesting that the understanding of ethnicity is more elastic than immutable. The individual could claim to be part of a larger Yoruba collective when that identity creates a set of advantages or confers nationalistic prestige. In that collective sense, myths of origins can be shared, references to Oduduwa can be made, and events that lend themselves to group memory can be emphasized.

However, as the case of contemporary transnationalists shows, they can also be organized on the basis of their specific cities, as in the case of Egbe Omo Ibadan of Chicago or the Ilawe Progressive Association in New York. The Eko Club in Houston is one of the strongest examples of such organizaions. This level of organizing also occurred in previous eras. In the nineteenth century, the wars between groups affected how various Yoruba cities and subgroups solidified their identities and plotted their politics. Collaboration and socialization can occur at the level of being Yoruba, but also of being Egba, Ekiti, or Ijebu.

Religions also supply differences that lead to subordinate or specific Yoruba identities, such as Yoruba Muslims, Yoruba Christians, Yoruba Santeria, and the like, which in turn lead to arguments over culture, power, representation, and politics. Religion intersects with issues of networking, self-definition, expectations, and sociability.

Thus, in speaking of the Yoruba, there can be no single story or single definition, nor even an attempt to construct and impose a pure identity onto others in far-flung places such as Rio de Janeiro in Brazil and Birmingham in England. To take a random example, a Yoruba may eat pork but another Yoruba may not eat pork if his religion forbids it, but neither will use pork consumption to erase their sense of a "nation," notwithstanding religious differences. There are equally generational differences in taste and preferences. Using the case of the Mahi of Dahomey in Brazil as a case study, Mariza De Carvalho Soares has made an observation that can be applied to the Yoruba as well; incidentally Mahi's neighbors in West Africa were coslaves in Brazil:

> The meanings, markers, and discourses that identified a given nation could not be gathered and passed down, like a bag of valuables, to the later generations of African descendants born in Brazil. Only Africans brought to Brazil could belong to a nation, because the whole premise of the nation—which was an aspect of Portuguese Imperial power—depended on one's place of birth in the colonial universe, not on lineage. At the same time, as we saw with the term *naturalidade*, the colonial concept of "nation" carried the built-in implication that something, some inherent ethnic quality linked to the homeland, could be inherited. But the argument for an unchanging ethnic heritage is complicated, both theoretically and historically, by the emergence of African-descended creoles in Brazil who developed other social practices.[4]

As we can see from many cases of diaspora, the experience and identity of those who left as slaves are different from those of contemporary migrants. Thus, the Afro-Brazilians of Yoruba descent in Bahia and recent Yoruba migrants to the same city do not necessarily blend well, just as African Americans and "continental Africans" (the label for new migrants) in the United States also do not blend and their interaction can actually manifest conflicts. Nevertheless, "the base of shared identity," to use Soares's phrase,[5] has created a permanent sense of common expression of history and labeling.

Migrations

The massive expansion of the Yoruba occurred in the context of the Atlantic World, defined as the four continents united by the Atlantic Ocean. The Yoruba were among the African slaves drawn from Central and West Africa and tragically relocated to the Americas. Slaves were funneled to the Atlantic. After the abolition of the transatlantic slave trade, secondary migrations occurred as freed slaves returned to West Africa, and thousands migrated within various countries in the Atlantic World.[6]

In my coedited book *The Yoruba Diaspora in the Atlantic World*,[7] the contributors examine the history of the Yoruba in different countries. The slave trade violently took the Yoruba to several places in the Americas: Brazil, Cuba, Uruguay, Argentina, Haiti, Venezuela, Trinidad and Tobago, and the United States. Characteristic patterns emerged, the first being location: (1) in an extensive land mass from Rio de la Plata in South America to the Chesapeake Bay in North America and small islands in the West Indies; (2) in North America, areas of concentrations were in Virginia, Georgia, Florida, South Carolina, and North Carolina; (3) in Central America, Costa Rica, Panama, and Nicaragua; (4) in South America, Brazil, Suriname, Guyana, and Venezuela; and (5) in the West Indies, Cuba, St. Lucia, Saint-Domingo (Haiti), Barbados, Guadeloupe, Martinique, Jamaica, and Trinidad and Tobago.

A second relevant aspect is concentration; the Yoruba were concentrated in three places in sizeable numbers in relation to the totality of African slaves: Bahia in Brazil, Cuba, and Saint-Domingue. In these places, their value was mainly in their labor. They worked on plantations and processing firms that produced sugarcane, sugar, tobacco, cotton, and other profitable crops; in mines; as domestic servants; as itinerant semiliberated urban laborers organized in *cantos* (street corners), as was the case in Brazil; and in such other economic sectors as ports and commerce.

While Yoruba cultural influences were strongest in Cuba, Bahia, and Saint-Domingue, they equally had a noticeable impact in other places where their numbers were smaller. Some cultural influences were Yoruba-based, that is, based on elements that we can define primarily as Yoruba. Other newer influences were part of the creolization of cultures as the Yoruba interacted with slaves from other African ethnicities and with European-derived cultures and institutions such as the church and family. Creole cultures, with Yoruba elements in them, have emerged over time. Davis Eltis, in his contribution to *The Yoruba Diaspora*, points to the disproportionate contribution of the Yoruba to cumulative African creolization and hybridity:

> Within coerced African migration, the Yoruba were among the latest to arrive but were neither the most numerous nor the least scattered over the Americas. Reasonably precise estimates for other groups will eventually become available; but it is probable that Igbo and some

West-Central African peoples were larger and more heavily concentrated than the Yoruba—the Igbo in parts of the British Caribbean and some of what have been termed the Congo groups in southeast Brazil. Yet the impact of the Yoruba speakers on Creole societies that emerged in many parts of the Americas appears to modern scholars to have been strong and, in the light of the evidence presented here, out of proportion to the relative size of Yoruba arrivals.[8]

Attempts to find explanations for Eltis's observations are ongoing; tentative suggestions include the strength, richness, and durability of the Yoruba culture in its homeland; the Yoruba people's skill in cultural retention; as well as their cultural domination of West Africa before and during the period of their enslavement.

The Yoruba extended themselves in West Africa and gained tremendous influence in various parts, notably along the coastal areas. This remarkable influence, characterized by John Thornton as "cultural intercommunications," owes a debt to two forces: migrations by the Yoruba within the region as well as migrations to the region by those who returned back from the Americas. By the seventeenth century, Yoruba language and various aspects of its culture had become widespread along the West African coast. The impact of Yoruba language on the Aja and Edo languages is uncontested. So too are the elements of Yoruba religion and kingship, ideas of state formation, and mythological origins in these and some other places in West Africa. In far away Gambia, Yoruba cuisine, including *eko* and *olele*, became well-known, while the *egungun* (masquerade) was adopted and integrated into indigenous cultural practices. The empire of Oyo contributed to this regional dominance as Oyo exerted its power to create an extensive trading network and adopted the expansion of Yoruba culture as a strategy of colonization and of soft diplomacy to link subdued areas to the metropole. Professor S. A. Adebanji Akintoye has used one example to link the impact of Oyo on another West African group with Yoruba cultural dominance in the Atlantic World:

> Founded and led by a mixture of Yoruba and Aja elements, the kingdom of Dahomey minutely mirrored Yoruba cultural institutions and traditions, all of which were later reinforced by Oyo conquest and overlordship. In particular through the Dahomey and other Aja people taken as slaves across the Atlantic, the influence of Yoruba culture was already significant in a number of places, for instance, Saint-Domingue

(Haiti), long before the arrival of Yoruba slaves, and considerably assisted the growth of Yoruba cultural influence after that point.[9]

The reverse diaspora of enslaved Yoruba returning to West Africa, in combination with intraregional migrations within West Africa, contributed enormously to the spread of Yoruba over a wider region, which also strengthened connections between the West Africa and the Atlantic. The returning émigrés, known as Aku in Sierra Leone, contributed to the widespread nature of Yoruba culture. Not only did they spread the notion of the Yoruba as a nation, fusing the various Yoruba subethnic groups under one umbrella, a number of them acquired the modernity of literacy and Christianity, which became the vehicle of transforming the Yoruba in the nineteenth century and gave them enormous educational and social advantages in the twentieth century.

Atlantic ideas of politics and economy spread to West Africa through the Aku, who in turn served as agents of dissemination. Their imaginations of modernity were rich and deep, embedded in notions of race, nation, and ethnicity. The Aku constructed ideas of Yoruba nationhood and cultural nationalism, pointing to common origins and cultural similarities. So too were the Aguda and Anago, émigrés from Cuba and Brazil who also brought back new ideas and transformed the culture space.[10] Yoruba cultural nationalism and self-assertion emerged in the nineteenth century, later to be transformed in the 1940s as political nationalism, most clearly manifested in the formation of the Egbe Omo Oduduwa.

Yorubaism

Presence is one thing; impact is another. Be it in Brazil or the United States, the diversity of those countries, even when not recognized, is grounded in the multiple histories and experiences of different groups and ethnicities from various countries. Among the citizens in these places are people with Yoruba roots. Where the roots are denied, unappreciated, or simply not known, alienation develops. This consciousness has been expressed repeatedly in various poems, essays, and texts to underscore how diaspora groups seek recognition, self-depiction, collective affirmation, and cultural authenticity.

Where a strong demographic presence made it possible, the Yoruba formed communities and reinvented a new "nation" with their own kings, chiefs, and rules. They formed an identity that others recognized and defined as Yoruba, which meant that the Yoruba were able to transfer and negotiate identities for themselves. In Brazil, the Nago, and in Cuba, the Lucumi have had a considerable impact on religion, orality, families, and social institutions. The Nago built various communities linked by elements of Yoruba culture—language, facial marks, celebrations, names, origin mythologies, drums, songs, music, culinary traditions, and more. The Yoruba gods and goddesses became defined as Pan-Yoruba and migrated into an overarching religion of Candomblé, which in turn was used to reinforce Yoruba ethnicity.

Whether by orality or literacy, the Yoruba have contributed to developments and discussions of religion, culture, ethnicity, gender, and other issues that define migrations, globalization, and multiculturalism. These discussions foreground the reality of culture as a mosaic. Thus, on the one hand, they adopted cultural elements from their hosts and demonstrated the dictum "when in Rome, do as the Romans do." By so doing, they respected other peoples and their cultures and knew what to take from them. There was no desire to pursue a project of ethnic absolutism. On the other hand, they sought to promote and protect what they regarded as the core values of their cultures. In combining those two options—borrowing and maintaining—the Yoruba affirmed the principles of assimilation and cultural retention that are part of creolization.

They migrated Yoruba words, using them to create new words or new meanings. Images, an aspect that is often ignored in the literature, were created to embody a wide range of ideas. Even without the facility of literacy in the Euro-American tradition, they composed ideas with images, using symbols and dislocated alphabets to generate new meanings, produce new calligraphies, and make statements on autographies.

As with other African slaves, the Yoruba were given new names and many were converted to Christianity. They redefined a number of practices in Catholicism, as we see in the examples of Vodun, Candomblé, Santería, or even in the Orisha Baptist of Trinidad. When they became free, adaptations to economic circumstances dictated learning new trades and crafts. Thus, in Cuba and Brazil, we had Yoruba as shoemakers, tailors, barbers, hawkers, and the like. They formed guilds and constructed economic networks, such as the Esusu method that enabled them to save and invest. They respected the successful among themselves. In the case of Bahia, a number of streets were named after the Yoruba, while freedmen and women who clustered together lived in such places as Nagotedo ("Nago-established"), a way of claiming their own autonomous space.

The Orisa tradition is one of the most visible aspects of Yorubaism with the Candomblé practices in Brazil, made visible by devotees and the activities of Babalorixás and Iyalorixás. In Cuba, the Lucumi (the name for Yoruba) practice Santeria or Regia de Ocha.[11] In Haiti, there is Vodun, an integral part of Nago culture. Egungun and Gelede have spread in Latin America and the Caribbean, even in such places as Trinidad and Tobago. In the United States, many variants of Yoruba religion have survived, especially in Louisiana and South Carolina.

The survival of these religious practices has exposed other aspects of culture: the use of language, food habits, expressive traditions, activities of diviners, priests, drummers, medicine, and the like. Each and all show the richness of culture, including its use in creating nationalism and self-assertion, allowing for the conquest of new spaces (as in the Yoruba domination of Bahia, Brazil). Various studies have pointed to the use of Yoruba language in Brazil and Cuba. Pierre Verge wrote extensively on Yoruba medicinal plants and the incantations that made them work.[12] Studies on music have indicated the use of Yoruba drums, words, and mythologies in Afoxés and Axé music.

Yoruba/African Medicine

Healing, medicine, and religion are intertwined. Recent literature and various examples are beginning to bring out the contributions of the Yoruba and other Africans in the diaspora to the field of medicine and knowledge of plants. To draw attention to this important topic and the emerging scholarship, some non-Yoruba examples are included, although it must be pointed out that practices were similar. Healing practices, including ideas and the uses of plants, were part of what African slaves brought with them, as well as divination and incantation, to make them work. Various studies have shown how Africans carried their cultural ideas to the Americas. A recent book by James Sweet uses the case of Domingos Álvares, a prominent healer and diviner, to illustrate how many African ideas of healing survived and spread during the era of the Atlantic slave trade.[13] Álvares was originally from Benin in West Africa. Forced into slavery in 1730, he worked on a sugar plantation in Pernambuco and was later exiled into Portugal as a prisoner. In various locations until his death in 1750, Álvares converted his spiritual and healing power as a vodun priest into service to the needy, thus acquiring fame and prestige in the process. Curing illnesses and diseases, Álvares also made speeches and remarks attacking imperialism and the capitalist system that upset slave owners. Although Sweet's study is located in the Lusophone world, Álvares's experiences were not peculiar to this part of the world. As Sweet shows, Álvares's knowledge and practices were acquired in Africa. In the Atlantic World he had an audience made up of those who subscribed to his faith and worldview.

In the United States many similar practices have been noted in different parts of Louisiana, South Carolina, and Virginia. For example, reference has been made to Caesar's cure for poison published in the *South Carolina Gazette* on May 9, 1750, recorded by the wealthy slave owner Richard Jordan and his successors from about 1620 to 1687.[14] The remedy gained widespread fame, and its inventor, an African slave, was able to use his medical knowledge and healing power to attain freedom.

We cannot know how many Álvareses and Caesars existed in different parts of the African Diaspora, bringing various ideas from Africa and introducing them in new lands, not just in medicine but also in all aspects of culture. The nameless enabled the transfer of various aspects of African cultures to different parts of the world.[15] During the era of the transatlantic slave trade, migrations moved people and their knowledge, ideas, skills, and mindsets. They were also able to reproduce their knowledge, using socialization within families to transfer what they knew to their children. As Linda M. Heywood and John K. Thornton show, as early as the first hundred years of the Atlantic slave trade, slaves from Central Africa laid the basis of an African American identity, one that included aspects of religion, languages, and material culture.[16] As Marie Jenkins Schwartz also shows, children born into slavery had opportunities, even in cruel plantation settings, to learn useful ideas from their parents, enabling cultural retention.[17] Various aspects of Africans' contributions to science, technology, and medicine have not been fully explored. Botanical and food ideas were developed and transmitted from one generation to another.[18] For instance, with respect to medicine, we see creativity in adapting African herbs and knowledge to new situations not just at the time of Álvares and Caesar but even today.

Healing in Africa and its re-creation in the African diaspora reveal several issues: knowledge of plants and animals, poetic incantations to manipulate symbolism to prevent and cure disease, and divination and magic. No disease escapes the imagination to find an answer to cure it. Where the original plant used in Africa could not be found, new ones were sought, as in the case of Brazil and Chesapeake plantations during slavery. Without knowledge of science and pharmacology, there could be no medicine. Kay Moss, who examined some of the documents relating to the eighteenth and nineteenth centuries, points to the combination of herbs, incantations, and witchcraft to cure many diseases.[19] Whereas these are often wrongly presented as "primitive," they demonstrate incredible knowledge, great insight into people and the forces that shape their lives, and prescriptions for many health problems as complicated as smallpox and barrenness to simpler ones such as cough. Different scholars of the African diaspora have written about these healers' authority and relevance, which suggests that Caesar of Virginia was not alone—nor was he unique.[20]

As for medicine itself, studies have confirmed the impressive knowledge contained in indigenous practices. In Brazil, where African medicine and religions are more intermeshed, research has shown that the Yoruba have a profound knowledge of the uses of plants and animals to cure various ailments, minor and major. Pierre Fatumbi Verger has done the most comprehensive study ever conducted on the use of plants among the Yoruba.[21] A scholar and a practitioner, his book of well over seven hundred pages describes over 2,000 remedies and practices, 3,529 Yoruba plant names, and the Yoruba equivalences for 1,086 scientific names. A careful observer, Verger provides dense elaboration in five forms: (1) parts of plants that are used for medication, that is, the leaves, bark, and roots; (2) how the leaves are prepared, that is, boiled, burnt into ashes, or pounded; (3) how they are used internally and externally; (4) the Ifa divination sign that makes the remedy work; and (5) the incantations that give power to the plants.[22]

Verger collected his recipes from established practitioners who combined knowledge of herbs with divination, "based on 256 signs called *odu* under which traditional medical practices are classified. These 256 *odu Ifa* are double signs derived from sixteen single ones and paired, either with themselves to form sixteen primary *odu*, or with one of the fifteen other single signs to form the 24 secondary ones."[23] Spoken words expressed in the *odu* acquire power (*ase*) that makes the plant work. Knowledge of plants and signs becomes the "creative force" that can heal and cure. Verger demonstrates the plants used in various remedies, linking specific ones to medicine, magical formulas, and pharmacology. "The medicinal virtues and values of a plant," he concludes, "are not easy to find out, because rarely is a plant used on its own. In general, formulae are made up of three to six different plants. . . . A plant may be compared to a letter of a word. On its own it is insignificant, but when joined with other letters it contributes to the meaning of the word." His recipes, numbering thousands, are classified into six categories:

1. 237 formulae for medicinal remedies (*oogun*) which tally, to some extent, with similar ideas in western medicine
2. 32 formulae for remedies relating to pregnancy and birth (*ibimo*)
3. 33 formulae for "magical works" relating to the worshipping of Yoruba deities (*orisa*)
4. 91 formulae for "beneficent works" (*awure*)
5. 32 formulae for "evil works" (*abilu*)
6. 41 formulae for "protective works" (*idaabobo*)[24]

Verger points to the difficulty of demarcating the difference between magic and scientific knowledge: "This stems from the importance . . . given to the notion of an incantation (*ofo*) spoken during the preparation or application of the medicinal formulae (*oogun*)." As he further explains:

> If Western medicine prioritizes a plant's scientific name and its pharmacological characteristics, then traditional societies prioritize the knowledge of ofo. Countless remedies from around the world were originally extracted from plants and later replaced by chemically reconstituted drugs, which had the same curative effects on the human body. But in traditional societies, it is the knowledge of the ofo (incantation) which is essential, as it contains the "power-to-alter" the formula's pharmacological effect.[25]

From the *ofo*, the medicinal effect of the plant is revealed. When an *ofo* changes, the action of the plant may also change. Verger considers *ofo* as definitions: "The incantations are often based on a particular reasoning being used for a particular situation or remedy. They also serve as evidence of the continuity in the traditional archive of data transmitted from one generation of babalawo to the next."[26]

Examining the thousands of entries in *Ewe* and their *ofo*, it is clear that there is an established knowledge of pathology. Diseases are named in various ways. Some are merely descriptive, as in diarrhea (*igbe gburu*) and dysentery (*igbe orin*), with the use of medicine that requires no *ofo*, rituals, or reference to any supernatural forces.

No society can have this rich, extensive, and expansive knowledge without an understanding of chemistry, biology, and related sciences. The knowledge cannot be accumulated and transmitted without education and socialization processes in place. The consumption of the products of the knowledge requires that social and political institutions be in place to mediate interpersonal and intergroup relations. Indeed, without the means for a class to extract resources, it would be much harder for politics to function and to sustain social stratification where it does exist.

Different forms of creativity and knowledge reveal the nature of society with regard to power and control, relationships among individuals, and work and leisure. References made to magic and poison may also allude to fear by those in power that those under them can kill them. Connections have been made between magic and resistance,[27] and between slave medicine and social control.[28] If Álvares and many other diviners had power in Africa (and they still do), we can imagine that Africans with the knowledge to heal and create new meanings from new plants and other resources would also have power. If Caesar had the power to invent an antidote for poison, we should also assume that he had the power to make poison to kill. Thus, in combining both powers, to enhance and destroy life, we see how his status among his peers and slave owners would be enhanced.

The ability to create music, dance, and acquire spiritual relevance is to convert low status into social status and produce political agency within the community. A contemporary of Álvares, Caesar was able to obtain his freedom in 1750 through his discoveries, the testimonies they generated, and his consent to reveal the elements of his work. He was given a moderate stipend for the rest of his life. He converted his knowledge into freedom. That whites sought the means to neutralize poison was not new by 1750. In earlier years, seeking bezoar (organic materials found in ungulate animals) and Goa stones (substances of herbal medicine) to neutralize poison was not uncommon, drawing not a few to Africa and parts of the Indian Ocean region.

New forms of knowledge were created in many aspects of human endeavor. Knowledge circulated over a wide region, and it was carried from Africa to Europe and the Americas, as in the examples of healing and plant species, knowledge of divination and herbs, and food cultivation.[29] Spirituality and religions have received prominent treatment in books on Candomblé and Santeria by scholars and practitioners.[30] Healing and praying were connected in religious beliefs. What they created and repackaged have served as the basis of new identities.[31] These identities and their meanings are different from those of other races with regard to aspects of living, interactions with others, and even death. Álvares and Caesar would be confused if their remedies were dismissed as irrelevant or not real medicine, or if the knowledge to cure was separated from that of killing. As Sweet points out, preaching and healing were also political statements that had the capacity to rupture society.

While Álvares and Ceasar were two remarkable men, they probably were not alone in the knowledge they possessed, and their skills and ideas were grounded in communal traditions that originated from Africa. Today, such traditions are being revived and extended in different parts of the Western world where a new generation of African priests, healers, and diviners practice non-Western medicine in the context of African religious traditions.

Resistance and Nationalism

Countless Yoruba women and men of courage imagined freedom and sought new spaces and a world of independence from slavery and the plantation system. Resistance and nationalism took various forms, covert and overt, spiritual and secular. Using Yoruba culture, they engaged in processes of cultural rebirth and collective affirmation. As stifling and crippling as the plantation systems were, a number of Yoruba people demonstrated enormous courage in rebelling against enslavement and domination. The condition of slavery gave birth to cultural expressions that tapped into Yoruba ideas, practices, and history, which resulted in resilient language and religious practices in the face of powerful attacks. These expressions were in turn nurtured by a sense of nostalgia and the search for liberation. Those in power interpreted worshipping a Yoruba god as an expression of militancy. Mythologies became very powerful devices of remembering, of reenacting aspects of the past, of formulating practices for the future, and of aesthetic imagination. Mythologies supplied the basis for creating ideologies of acculturation to Yoruba identity outside of the Yoruba homeland.

Enslaved communities, as with colonized subjects, were ridiculed by those in power. To fight back, the Yoruba turned to their mythologies to indict slave masters and colonizers and to ridicule the culture imposed on them. In turning to Yoruba gods, they subverted repressive forces and actors. In creating hybrid religious forms, they borrowed clandestinely to accept a culture and then to reinvent it strategically. Turning Yoruba gods into the equivalent of Catholic saints was not an affirmation of the inferiority of their own heritage or dependency on a borrowed one, but rather recognition of their own gods in a way that relocates them to the center of worship. They were not making a plea for Sango or Yemoja to be recognized by repressive forces, but rather that such forces were powerless to destroy their own heritage. By turning to their own history and drawing from it to construct a cultural presence, they created the legitimacy for Yoruba practices to spread globally. Indeed, the Yoruba were critical of themselves as they sought new ways to practice culture and debate issues surrounding authenticity and orthodoxy, but in the process they legitimized their presence and successfully reproduced their culture for over five hundred years. Outsiders to the culture ultimately accepted Yoruba practices, and by the twentieth century they became part of legitimate academic fields.

The aesthetics that shaped cultural practices were aggressive: The template of slavery experiences called for dehumanizing and disempowering the enslaved. Combative aesthetics sought redemption and cleansing. The new mythologies, songs, and dances had the unmistakable mark of combat, even of violence, as all were invoked to attain liberation. Yoruba supplied many resources to counter the imposition of Euro-American culture and values. When acculturation took place, which was expected in new lands, resources were available to fight its absurd elements. More important, Yoruba resources prevented imposed acculturation from becoming an acceptable mythology. Yoruba mythologies were powerful enough to counter Euro-American mythologies. Euro-American acculturation strategies, whether in slave systems in America or colonized Africa were based on the same premise: slaves and subjects were inferior and the conquerors superior. Inferior culture, so goes the assumption, would ultimately be "civilized," a belief, once described by a literary critic as an "absurd nationalistic mythology,"[32] that was even at the root of concrete political and bureaucratic policies.

Cultural manifestations translated into a myriad of concrete actions, most notably of slave revolts. The Yoruba were among those agile and free blacks who played leadership roles in a number of revolutionary actions in and around the Americas. Violent insurrections involved the ability of the leaders to mobilize other slaves and to build alliances with free people of color. Jane Landers described these revolutionaries as "Atlantic creoles," and provided evidence from the eighteenth century of how, among others, Yoruba royalists, maroons, and counterrevolutionaries fought against the slave system, gained freedom, and even established autonomy for themselves.[33] Among them were José Antonio Aponte, a famous Yoruba who led the 1812 revolt against slavery in Havana, Cuba, and Juan Nepomeceno Prieto, the well-known leader of a Yoruba brotherhood called the Cabildo Lucumi, also in Cuba.

In the 1830s, Prieto greeted incoming Yoruba slaves at the dock and served as their patron. Ira Berlin, whom Landers quotes, described the cast as possessing "linguistic dexterity, cultural plasticity, and social agility."[34] This was at a very difficult moment, when slavery was firmly entrenched. This hidden history, related by Landers using examples from multiple locations, shows courage, political sagacity, and wisdom:

> Because Atlantic Creoles were so often on the front lines of these contests—European and American revolutions, Indian wars, slave revolts, and the international efforts to abolish slavery—they were keenly attuned to shifting political currents. These African and African-descended actors had access to a wide range of political information, both printed and oral, and they made reasoned and informed choices in their attempt to win and maintain liberty. They were often critical to the balance of power and soon became adept at interpreting political events and manipulating them, when possible, to achieve freedom. Their initiative and agency—their acts of resistance, flight, and marronage (the formation of fugitive slave communities in the wild), and their shifting relationships to various European, American, and Native American powers—shaped the course of international events, as well as local responses to them.[35]

They understood multiple cultures, plantation regimes, and European languages. They formed families where they impacted African-derived cultures. They were products of their age, able to factor political exigencies into the reality of living and use political skills to forge fluid identities. "Atlantic creoles," Landers concludes, "were extraordinarily mobile, both geographically and socially, and their horizons had few limits."[36]

A linkage has been established between conflicts in Africa, enslavement, and migration patterns. A link has also been established between the military and cultural background of slaves and major slave revolts, as in the 1739 Stono revolt in South Carolina, the Haitian revolution of 1804, the Aponte rebellion in Cuba in 1812, and the 1835 Malê revolt in Brazil. We can see the role of the Yoruba in some of these. The 1812 rebellion in Cuba was connected to the Yoruba. During the eighteenth century, the Oyo Empire made thousands of people captives who were then sold as slaves in the Atlantic slave trade. Slaves were also sold in the first three decades of the nineteenth century, and they were mostly captives from the wars that led to the fall of Oyo and the struggles by its successor states for dominance, notably Ibadan and Ijaye. Many of these slaves made it to Cuba. Matt D. Childs, who has written a brilliant book on the 1812 Aponte rebellion, summarized the direct linkage with the Yoruba:

> Given the high influx of Africans into Cuba as a result of the collapse of the Oyo Empire, and the ability of Yoruba culture to have "an impact out of all proportions to its relative demographic weight," according to historian David Eltis, the military background of slaves may have likely contributed to a proclivity for rebellion. The marked increase in revolts during the decades of 1790 and 1800 testifies to a heightened commitment to resistance by Africans in Cuba. Political events in the Atlantic world, from revolution in Europe to independence in the Americas to civil wars in Africa, all exerted an influence in Cuba that polarized society by strengthening a commitment to racial slavery for masters, while cracking the foundations upon which Spanish rule rested.[37]

As in Cuba and elsewhere, the Yoruba were able to come together in associations that were then converted to a variety of uses: to assist one another or, as in the case of the Aponte rebellion, to unite and fight. As the Aponte demonstrated, they had access to current information and strategies from elsewhere. The rebels understood their immediate environment, even if they sometimes underestimated the level of betrayal by fellow slaves and free blacks, and they knew how to use African cultures and certain commonalities to unite themselves. One common organization was the "brotherhood" in Cuba and Brazil. Called the *cabildos* in Cuba, and *confrarias* or *irmandades* in Brazil, members formed fraternities to discuss and promote common interests. Variants of Yoruba Ogboni society, sometimes organized in secrecy by men, found their ways to the Americas. Unlike in Oyo or Abeokuta, where the Ogboni could advise kings, the members advised one another and plotted survival strategies. Being Yoruba made those associations possible, but the associations also reinforced an even wider Yoruba identity (as with the Lucumi in Cuba and Nago in Brazil) in ways that were more visible than in other places. Childs writes,

> Cuba (along with Brazil) represents something of an anomaly for African identity transformation in the Americas during the late eighteenth and nineteenth centuries. In other parts of the New World, a broad-based racial identity began to eclipse African ethnicities with the ending of the slave trade, the growth of a Creole slave population, and the gradual abolition of slavery. In Cuba, however, African ethnic identity remained strong due to the dramatic increase in slave imports.[38]

Not only were the Yoruba able to maintain their self-definition as Yoruba, but there were also cases when some other ethnicities accepted Yoruba dominance and shared in their culture. There were also cases of accretion in which two ethnicities merged, as in Nago-Jeje in Candomblé houses in Brazil.

In moments of protest and violence, the consequences were drastic, but they more often ended in displays of courage and resoluteness. In the Aponte rebellion in Cuba as well as in the Malê revolt in Brazil, the authorities executed the twelve leaders and whipped many insurgents and threw them into prison. These actions did not quell aspirations for freedom and justice in Cuba, Brazil, or the United States. On the day the Aponte leaders were killed, the authorities granted freedom to the collaborators who betrayed their colleagues and friends, if only to make the statement, notes Childs, that "the most effective strategy for gaining freedom was not armed rebellion but allegiance to masters and the Spanish Empire."[39] To make his point, the authorities executed 34 protesters, publicly humiliated 78 by whipping, and put 170 in prison. Masters rewarded loyal slaves with freedom, although colonial authorities, judicial officials, and some citizens donated money to reimburse those masters who did so.

However, the rewards did not stop the acts of resistance. In 1835 the Yoruba again revolted in Havana to seek an end to slavery and overthrow the government. Fearful of more uprisings, some slave masters called on Spain to end slavery while others called for greater vigilance. Childs notes the fear that gripped the authorities, and concludes, "The Aponte Rebellion illustrated in bold strokes the dangers of expanding slavery and plantation agriculture throughout the island."[40] Slave owners and the authorities, in fear and to protect their property, imposed stricter rules and regulated the movements of slaves.

Slave rebellions occurred in other places during the nineteenth century, aided by widespread thoughts of freedom and the necessity of not just fighting slave owners but also the governments that supported them. The slave revolt that began in Haiti in August 1791 led to the country's independence in 1804, creating the only free black republic in the Western Hemisphere. Three years later in 1807, Yoruba and other African slaves began a series of over twenty insurrections;[41] the biggest one, the Malê rebellion, occurred in 1835.[42]

Malê (from "imale") is a Yoruba word for Muslims. Thousands of enslaved Yoruba were taken to Bahia in Brazil in the eighteenth and nineteenth centuries. Brought together in one location, Yoruba culture supplied a strong identity with manifestations that are still there today. The practice of Islam also provided a unifying point; the Yoruba came together to pray and listen to sermons, and they used their prayer meetings to discuss their depressing conditions and how to overcome them. The Yoruba strategized as to the timing of actions, including plans to capture arms from police barracks in order to attack plantation owners. As João José Reis, the Bahia-based scholar who has written a distinguished book on this subject, notes, Yoruba and Islam constitute the two main ingredients that supplied the energy and synergy. Childs summarizes João José Reis:

> When Africans went into battle to end their enslavement, they wore amulets that contained folded Koranic verses written in Arabic containing fiery and revolutionary messages. Moreover, Muslims figured prominently among the rebels' leadership. Like the Aponte Rebellion and Gabriels's Conspiracy, mastery of the written word and the power of literacy served to structure the movement. And as in Cuba, free and enslaved urban artisans played a prominent role in the 1835 Malê Rebellion. In summary, the overwhelming African background of the rebellion, and in particular its identity as Muslim, displayed the specific Atlantic cultural dynamics of the Bahian revolt, while the methods

slaves and free people of color utilized in the urban environment to resist slavery highlighted how they drew the local circumstances in executing their plans.[43]

The power of Islam is reflected more broadly in protest politics, nationalism, and grassroots politics.[44]

Many Yoruba also used legal and political means to protest slavery and to fight for abolition, as in the case of the Afro-Brazilian Luiz Goma, a politician, lawyer, and poet who died in 1882, six years before the proclamation of abolition. The activities of Goma have even been compared with those of Frederick Douglass in the United States.[45] Furthermore, radical politics continued in the postslavery years, expressed in various forms during the twentieth century.[46] The expression of "Africanity" has generated both political and cultural movements in all countries where the Yoruba can be found.

Memory

Forced relocation brought about by the Atlantic slave trade and the colonial subjugation by European powers imposed a certain kind of history on slaves and colonial subjects. It is a history of domination, one that attempts to erase the history of slaves and subjects by destroying their archives and trivializing their subjectivity as agents of change. Exploited and dominated people were presented as primitive, foolish, lazy, and incompetent, which created a damaged image that was then used as a justification for domination and exploitation. Irrespective of where they came from in Africa, the generic descriptor "black" was imposed on them, and it became a way of asking them to forget where they came from and to accept a homogenous, debased identity. In rejecting a blanket racial category, the Yoruba opted for a nation instead, one in which they defined themselves in specific terms and were accepted as such by slaves from other African groups. In this definition, history and memory played a significant role: They retained their sense of geographical place of origin, specific culture, and of course language. As the Yoruba formulated new bonding strategies in the diaspora, as Paul Christopher Johnson shows in his study of Carib religion in New York, they had to plot "itineraries of spatial memory that at once recover and remold their histories."[47] Even with the minimal material objects they carried with them in support of their religion and worldview, they had memory to support their belief system: the memories of their practices, rites, and rituals; myths, tales, and proverbs; lyrics and rhythms; architecture and sculptures; and other vectors of religious philosophy.

In the diaspora, the Yoruba reconstituted themselves by drawing from mythologies to create their own history. They used myths not only to talk about the past but also to build the consciousness of traditions based on their past. They converted memory into celebration, and they carnivalized mythologies to create bonds in communities and to socialize children. They combined play and recreation in historical reenactments in ways that enabled the Yoruba to overcome efforts to dehumanize them. The experience of exploitation and dehumanization was converted into the memory of rebirth, turning the survival of past freedom and struggles into positive regenerative memory. It is not a case of trying to forget the past, its pain, its brutalities, but of remembering it to regain control and to assert collective identity.

The enslaved Yoruba, cognizant of the value of their past and the link between that past and nationalism, kept their memories alive, identified with Yorubaness, told stories of origin, and used their ethnicity to forge an identity. The formation of associations, savings clubs, and mobilization for resistance vividly reveal their groundings in identity. Within the various associations, the people kept memory alive. They discussed their past, and also their present condition of enslavement, racial inequality, and more. In the Aponte rebellion, the connections between the past of the people, the formation of associations, and uses to which such associations were put showed a great deal of intentionality. Writes Johnson:

> By providing a network of alliances and an institutional structure that offered a limited sense of familiarity for Africans in Cuba, *cabildos* helped their members survive in a society based upon racial oppression. The process by which *cabildos* could address the specific needs of their organization and also serve the common interests of all people of African ancestry became apparent in the Aponte Rebellion. *Cabildo* houses offered security to organize and plan the revolts. The Aponte Rebellion revealed the flexibility and innovative nature of African identity in Cuba. Africans in Cuba could define themselves by simultaneously emphasizing both their Old World ethnicity and their New World racial identity.[48]

Distorted histories of the enslaved were strategies used to perpetuate slavery and postslavery racial hierarchies and differences. The memory of Yorubaness and the history emerging from it restores a sense of "correctness" that make what is reconstructed about the past a form of therapy to heal the damage done to souls and bodies. Displacement and relocation removed the Yoruba from their cultural mainstream to an Anglo-American milieu where assimilation to privilege and power was difficult. They found themselves in situations that were new, strange, and different, and they lacked memoirs and blueprints to order their lives. However, what they did have were their inheritances—their own stories and past. Memory ensured that, although they were perceived as physically weak and powerless, they could construct themselves as mentally powerful by using the past as a resource. They manifested their rebellion in written texts and oral narratives that stressed the power of opposition to exploitation and antagonism to racialized power.

In the exploitative and discriminatory context of the enslaved and free black people, the Yoruba developed what W. E. B. Du Bois characterized as a sense of double consciousness or a bifocal mindset of living—thinking of their Yoruba homeland and adjusting to a strange new land. The Yoruba became part of what Du Bois called "a sort of seventh son, born with a veil, and gifted with second-sight in this American world—a world which yields him no true self-consciousness, but only lets him see himself through the revelation of the other world."[49] Yet they could find true self-consciousness by recourse to Yoruba history.

Double identities emerged to deal with oppression and racism: the identity of being Yoruba on the one hand and of being a slave, a free black, or a hyphenated subject on the other hand. Located far away from their homeland, a Yoruba man or woman became the recipient of the cultural practices and values of others, becoming a mixed breed, in the words of Du Bois, "looking at one's self through the eyes of others, of measuring one's soul by the tape of the world that looks on in amused contempt and pity."[50] To lift the burden of race and marginalization, the Yoruba utilized the memory of being Yoruba—their history, their ancestors, their values—to understand what options and choices they had to live in hostile spaces.

Aroba, the Yoruba word for memory, is distinguished in some ways from *itan*, or history telling. *Aroba* transforms *itan* into remembrances and preserves *itan*, putting the past to use as a consciousness of self, others, and community. *Aroba* connects with the multiple dimensions of and contradictions in Du Bois's paradigm of double consciousness. To arrive at this consciousness, the *itan* was the lived experience and its legacies in the continuity of poverty, materialism, and racism. Being part Yoruba and part something else (Brazilian, Cuban, or American), they were confronted with the ambiguities of being nowhere and being some place, of being rendered in a state of permanent transition. They were being asked to receive the histories and cultures of others while struggling to retain theirs; they were asked to be multicultural and bilingual, temporarily or permanently.

Articulating history, memory, and the realities of contemporary living have become literary projects. Professor Omoniyi Afolabi, a Yoruba scholar who specializes in Lusophone literature, has written extensively on Afro-Brazilian writings. His works bring out how creative scholarship has captured the past and present of people of African descent. He works specifically on some Yoruba aspects of the Ile Aye in Bahia.[51] Afolabi's work is part of a genre by writers who promote cultural heritage (as in the case of Abdias Nascimento)[52] and who tap into the Orisa tradition to find new meanings. As a Yoruba, Afolabi is able to see continuity in the texts, to see a past that is being called to the service of the present, the constant reawakening of culture and the reinvention of traditions.

Felix Ayoh' Omidire, another Yoruba who followed Afolabi in a similar intellectual trajectory of moving from Ile-Ife to Bahia, has pursued similar themes, uncovering Yorubaness in a wide range of practices. He stresses language and music. Like Afolabi, he highlights texts with Yoruba centrality, as in the case of Mestre Didi, the son of Iyalorisa Ile Ase Opo Afonja Omidire, who has reinterpreted some aspects of Samba music, pushing the argument further that some introductory lines are adaptations of Yoruba *ayajo/ogede* incantations. What Brazilian listeners will think of as supplication to Catholic saints, Omidire sees as an *ofo* (incantation) that the Yoruba use to seek the protection of their gods. He invokes and translates one example, poetic and incantatory, recited in one piece of Samba music in Portuguese:

I am clothed in the armours of George[53]
That my enemies may have hands, but never touch me
That my enemies may have legs, but never catch up with me
That my enemies may have eyes, but never see me
That, not even in their thoughts may they ever be able to see me, nor do me harm.[54]

The wording, without the context, will sound like a song put together by a Juju band in Lagos or Ibadan. But, as Omidire explains:

> The incantation is part of a song rendered by Brazilian singer Jorge Ben or as an "epigraph" to one of his tracks. It was also used by my compadre Jota Velloso in his 2004 album called "Aboio para um Rhinoceronte" in which I participated with an oriki for Osoosi. The incantation is originally a verse from the chants to the orisa Osoosi in Brazilian Candomblé. Being from such a religious source, it is considered in Brazil as belonging to the public domain, so it can be cited freely.[55]

Omidire's incantation suggests how older ideas can be adapted through secularization, synthesis, and syncretism; continuity and change; rupture and rebirth. Perhaps in the mouth of a priest able to add herbs the incantation acquires both magical and medicinal power, as Verger has shown, elaborated with further examples by Obafemi Jegede, drawing on the Nigerian-Yoruba data.[56]

In both the works of Afolabi and Omidire are the tropes of revival and regeneration, which are two powerful forms of empowering oral traditions that serve as collective memory and the motivation for contemporary literary texts. Indeed, the trope of regeneration that forms the central theme in Afolabi's first major book, *The Golden Cage*,[57] has a greater application beyond the postcolonial that shapes its interpretations.

Regenerative Religious Traditions

Regenerative projects are the conquest of humiliation and tragic histories, displaying how the Yoruba who survived the trauma of the Atlantic slave trade and the racism that followed have emerged triumphant. Enslaved subjects in the Americas saw in Yoruba mythologies and religions the resources necessary to escape degeneration. To make that escape, they needed to preserve Yoruba inheritances, using various elements as combative instruments.

These inheritances manifest in various forms and manners, defined by descendants of Yoruba people in different eras and locations. They require us to understand history in multiple ways. First, we must understand Yoruba history in terms of not only the "pastness of the past, but of its presence."[58] The past is invoked to create a meaning for the present. Inheritances become tools to mobilize against power; one draws from them to create combative approaches to organize resistance, shape identity, and invent nationalism. Socialization strategies reinvented associations among the Yoruba, as in the case of *Ogboni*, but also of *esusu, aro,* and *owe* that enabled considerable interactions in neighborhoods, community building, and extensive networking, all of which made it possible to engage in recreations, celebrations, and savings. The measure of success revolved around the memory of past institutions, shared ethnicity, mutual understanding of codes of behavior, and respect for community leaders.

Regeneration is not just about affirming past heritage, but it is also about new inventions and creativities. The Yoruba in the diapora have redefined and expanded the boundaries of Yorubaness. By taking Sango and Ogun abroad, they globalized the gods. They are no longer gods localized in fixed towns like Oyo and Ire that have mythical origins; they have been redefined in regionalist and Atlantic terms as religions of the Yoruba in Havana and Miami. The cults of Osun and Yemoja[59] have also traveled far and wide, doubling as part of the Orisa, and also as the radical politics of using gendered religion to advance feminist and liberational politics.

The reimagining of the gods and goddesses outside of the Yoruba homeland creates many new practices for worshiping, making sacrifices, and communicating with the spiritual world. What the gods and goddesses can do for devotees has become endless as it has adjusted to meet the demands of the contemporary moment. As enunciated by various Yoruba religious leaders, among other beliefs the Yoruba believe in the Orisa, divination, magic, the use of herbs, a supreme being, ritual song and dance, and the power of the ancestors.

In Brazil, Candomblé reflects elements of Yoruba religion expressed in divination, healing, music, spirit possession, and sacrifice. As if in awe of this powerful Afro-Brazilian religion, J. Lorand Matory, in his fine study, praises it for its complexity and beauty, its ability to penetrate rural and urban areas to meet the needs of both the poor and the rich:

> Believers attribute miraculous powers and exemplary flaws to gods known variously as *orixás, voduns, inquices,* and *caboclos,* depending on the Candomblé denomination. The adventures, personalities, and kinship relations of these superhuman beings are described in an extensive mythology and body of oracular wisdom, which also serve

to explain the personalities and fates of their human worshippers, as well as the worldly relations among those worshippers. Through blood sacrifice and lavish ceremonies of spirit possession, the gods are persuaded to intervene beneficently in the lives of their worshippers and to keep the foes of those worshippers at bay.[60]

As Matory elaborates, it is clear that Candomblé extends itself to the economic and political spheres of networking in small and big ways:

> The Candomblé temple, or "house," also serves the social and economic needs of its class-diverse and largely urban membership. It is usually the primary residence of the chief priest, some of his or her lieutenants, and their wards, as well as a temporary shelter for fugitives from police persecution, domestic crises, and poverty. The temple is also often a conduit of bourgeois largesse, a source of job contacts, an employer in its own right, and a major port of call for politicians.[61]

In Cuba, Santeria is also a continuity of Yoruba religion, and it shares a number of elements with Candomblé. According to Umi Vaughan, a scholar and performer, and Carlos Aldama, a distinguished Bata drummer, Santeria serves as "an important element of cohesion, strength, identification, and pride, and has also become a theoretical and philosophical base for black Cubans in their resistance against slavery and then in their later struggle against racism."[62] One powerful commonality is the use of musical instruments to praise the gods and goddesses. Distinctive ensembles have developed for such powerful divinities as Esu, Ogun, and Sango. In Cuba, the set of three bata drums (known as *iyá*, *itótele*, and *okónkolo*) are the most visible and powerful symbols of Yoruba religious continuity. Bata, cylindrically shaped and by-membranous, is one of the most famous drums. Its origins have been associated with the historical Sango, who is credited with having introduced it to the empire in his role as the *Alaafin* of Oyo. Batá spread to Cuba, Brazil, and other places as part of the transatlantic slave trade. Vaugh and Aldama recognize it as "one of the richest cultural legacies that enslaved Yoruba people brought with them into the New World . . . [with rhythms that] have helped maintain religious and cultural practices shared by millions of people who are spread far and wide." They point to both continuity and adaptation in the use of this drum:

In Nigeria, musicians stand to play the four drums that are included in the typical batá ensemble. In Cuba, however, just three batá complete the set and the drums are played while seated. The largest and lead drum is called the iyá (mother). The middle-size drum is called the itótele (the one that follows). The smallest drum is called the okónkolo (the stutterer). All together, the tones of the drums recreate language to praise and tease or "call down" the spirits, known as oricha or santos in the Yoruba-derived Afro-Cuban religion called Santeria. Whereas in the Oyo area of Yorubaland the batá had saluted only ancestor spirits and Chango himself, king of the drum and dance, in Cuba they were reoriented to address an entire pantheon of oricha.[63]

The spirit animates the drums, and those possessed of the spirit, the *omo Ayan* (the chosen ones), are not only versatile in the creative sense, but they also manifest spirituality. The drummers are also community leaders who are skillful in dance, music, and ritual performance. They are not just drummers but are also religiously empowered to lead their communities in morality and ethics. The drummers are part of the social actions that regularly take place; these social actions are integral to the complexity of diaspora communities. Bata and the drummers are intertwined with Orisa worship and ancestor veneration, both of which define and unite communities.

Regeneration has continued until today. For example, a strong link between the past and present exists in the case of the Oyotunji Village, a semiautonomous religious community with its own king and chiefs. Founded in the village of Sheldon, Beaufort County, South Carolina, in 1970, Oyotunji Village has attempted to recreate Yoruba religions in the context of Yoruba politics and social institutions. Oyotunji rejected the two Western dominant religions of Islam and Christianity, opting instead for the Yoruba Orisa tradition.[64] In turning to a Yoruba world religion, the village is not returning to an alternative religion but rather to what it regards as the central religion. The choice of Yoruba religion rejects both the humiliation associated with accepting the alternative religions of Christianity and Islam and the cruel pathology of living in a capitalist-structured environment. In terms of when it was created, Oyotunji is postslavery, but its founders and members are very cognizant of the history of slavery and race relations. Oyotunji has generated impressive scholarly attention, and the cultural space has been grafted into African religions now taught in academia in the contemporary period.[65]

If Oyotunji Village represents the translation of an idea into practice, countless oral and written texts exist that embody the notion of cultural regeneration. Even bàtá drumming is now part of secularist music as the drummers create new meanings for performances while not abandoning its ritual essence, which they invoke when necessary.[66] Oral and written texts that subvert hegemonic power, reassert Yorubaness, and celebrate hybridity and creolization exist in many mythologies, stories, proverbs, songs, and dance. The survival of Yoruba words in Brazil and Cuba, the attempts to sustain Vodun in Haiti, and the search for origins in each of these places reveal how history, mythologies, and language are embodiments of power. Rich Yoruba heritage has been retained and transferred orally, through drums and songs, and through various cultural practices. Oyotunji emerged within the context of Islam and Christianity, just as in previous generations Candomblé and Santeria flourished under hostile conditions. Surviving traditions reveal the Yoruba creative imagination, and its ability to "substitute elements and adjust philosophical values to new social situations with great improvisational virtuosity."[67] Orisa traditions are now being fully reworked into contemporary lifestyles; there are even manuals explaining how to tap into the power of gods and goddesses.[68]

New Yoruba Diaspora Cultures and Complex Modernity

The Yoruba are *outsiders within* various other cultures in different parts of the world. The narratives of existence have become so diverse and so complex that mythologies that sustain the Yoruba as *insiders within* cultures such as the Oduduwa origin story may not be sufficient or always useful with Yoruba who live in multiracial, multiethnic, and transnational spaces; these individuals can proclaim that *other civilizations are of me and are mine.*

The historical layers are many, as the older diaspora has demonstrated. The new Yoruba in the West are recent, mainly first-generation immigrants. They are transnationalists who talk about both their Yoruba homeland and their new adopted homeland. Some present narratives tend to imply that they carry multiple personalities of transnationalism in one body, sometimes manifesting what Du Bois noted for an earlier generation: "two souls, two thoughts, two unreconciled strivings; two warring ideals in one dark body, whose dogged strength alone keeps it from being torn asunder."[69] The reconciliation of the multiple personalities entails a host of different strategies by various individuals, although globalization has provided limitless opportunities to recreate "home" in multiple locations. A new body of work, the most recent by Toyin Falola and others, is emerging on this new generation of immigrants.[70]

As *outsiders within cultures*, they can be regarded as the *Other*, that is, converted into exotic objects to gaze at and subjects of study who generate conversations about their identity, their spaces, and their very being. When they are made into the *Other* in the academy, they fall into a division of knowledge that Immanuel Wallerstein has captured as follows:

> The fact that the study of Africa was thus limited of course reflected the division of intellectual labour that had been carved out in the late nineteenth century, among whose features was the division of the world into three geographical zones: modern European and European-settler states, which were studied by economists, historians, political scientists, and sociologists; non-Western areas with a long-standing written culture and a preferable so-called "world religion," which were studied by so-called Orientalists; and backward peoples, which were studied by anthropologists.[71]

The Yoruba have certainly been excessively anthropologized and equally overanthologized! The Yoruba need not rejoice at this statement, which is a critical claim: The misguided implication, which is not intended here, is that the anthropologization of the Yoruba is indicative that they are perhaps the most important of the "backward peoples" who are the favorites of anthropologists!

The economic model of neoliberalism shapes the contemporary world, but it does not sustain the older Yoruba values of communal sharing and generosity with land and money. New forms of knowledge, notably in computers and technology, have replaced older knowledge. Where knowledge is connected with careers and mobility, age is not necessarily an advantage, as technical education may count more.

Globalization, in turn, connects with neoliberalism. Indeed, some will make the argument that the agenda of globalization is to extend neoliberalism. The Yoruba benefit from the global forces in terms of the ability to migrate, travel, and move their goods and ideas.

Figure 5.2. Yoruba in traditional attire made with modern fabric. Photograph courtesy of author.

Figure 5.3. Professor Akinwumi Isola, playwright and filmmaker.
Photograph courtesy of author.

Figure 5.4. Egba chiefs with speaker. J. F. Odunjo Lecture, 2012, Ibadan, Nigeria. Photograph courtesy of author.

However, they also suffer in terms of the undermining of their language and various aspects of their cultures as they lose some of it to the spread of Western ones.

An Imagined Future

The Yoruba have dispersed all over the world and are part of a trend that will not abate, as the forces of modernization and globalization are inevitably unleashed through travel, movement, migration, and relocation undertaken for a host of reasons. Large numbers have moved out of the Yoruba homeland as exiles and immigrants—some are forced to leave and others move voluntarily. As they leave, they carry with them elements and ideas of Yoruba culture so that we can also talk of the migrations of culture. The diaspora belongs to different historical eras from the slave trade to the present. Whether from the old or new diasporas, the Yoruba who find themselves in multiple places have contributed to the ideas and reality of cultural diversity and multiculturalism. Tolerance is a core element in the Yoruba character, a point made by David Laitin in his book on the adoption of Islam and Christianity by the Yoruba and the coexistence of people of different religions in Yorubaland itself.[72] Thus the Yoruba do not seek cultural insularity, but rather cultural inclusion. They do not reject globalization, but do not allow the death of their own culture. This affirmation of culture operates at different levels: whether it relates to individuals and the food they eat and the clothes they wear, or to the group in terms of shared religious practices, festivals, and celebrations. Omidire has used the survival of culture to argue that the Yoruba have successfully challenged the imperative of globalization; their actions and behavior question the hegemonic presentation of the West as universal:

> In Cuba and Brazil, as well as in every other part of the Yoruba Atlantic Diaspora, this challenge to "dehegemonize" the cultural globalized scene has been taken up and a vibrant alternative achieved through the proud adoption and expansion of the Yoruba cultural epistemology via Cuban-lucumí, Afro-Brazilian nagô, Afro-Venezuelan and even contemporary indigenous Yoruba-African networks (Orisaworld, Yorubaworld, etc.). These confront, on a daily basis, the canonic values of globalization with options of cultural diversity that offer subjects all over these metropolises another way to live with themselves, live with the others, and interact in a less predatory way with nature and the environment itself.[73]

The dispersal comes with all of the consequences that I have highlighted, including the elevation of a homeland to the status of a cultural and genetic marker and the use the homeland to create a sense of identity in distant places. For this identity to be formed and then reproduced, it must formulate consciousness and powerful forces of solidarity and collectivity. As migrants—forced or voluntary—struggle in new places, the diaspora can become an experience of marginalization, discrimination, and exploitation. The experience itself leads to struggles for survival, which in turn calls for strategies to formulate an identity, to create memory, to structure history, and to invent a past and reinvent new traditions, which is done with the homeland in mind. Thus there are connections between the Yoruba at home and abroad, the same way that there are also discontinuities. At the same time, contacts with other cultures and nationalities mean that borrowings will occur, that distances will be created from the original homeland (sometimes too far to bridge again), and that new sources of labels and identification will emerge.

Yoruba studies have acquired legitimacy in different countries around the world, making the Yoruba one of the best-studied groups in Africa. Precolonial Yoruba history has been validated, colonial understanding has been enriched, and postcolonial conditions have been analyzed. The scholarship on the Yoruba is inserted into many of the debates on African studies: What is the best language to teach at an early age: indigenous or foreign? What is the role of scholars and critics in society? Can culture serve as a platform for development? Did colonialism halt modernity? Did colonialism produce alienation? Are the gods gendered enough? Is there a concept of women in Yoruba language and other parts of the culture? Irrespective of the arguments and their resolutions, the insertion of Yoruba data and the involvement of Yoruba scholars have all cumulatively added up to advancing a visibility within global research, from Tokyo in Japan, to the School of African and Oriental Studies in London, to the University of Texas in Austin. Yoruba scholarship is not an appendix to African studies and forms, but, in various ways, it is a critical component of its center, particularly in the case of history, literature, sociology, African languages, and anthropology. In combination with African studies, Yoruba has contributed to the framing of multiculturalism: how diversity in knowledge advances the quality of education; how focusing on nonempires minimizes the dominance of Europe in world history; and how focusing on the themes of ethnicity, race, gender, and culture expands the frontiers of knowledge.

Studies on the Yoruba diaspora are equally extensive and refined. The language is flourishing. Its values and traditions have supplied the basis for regenerative politics. Yoruba mythologies have led to a vibrant literature by writers such as J. F. Odunjo, D. O. Fagunwa, Ademola Dasylva, Toyin Falola, Wole Soyinka, Ola Rotimi, and Femi Osofisan. Yoruba healing systems have found new expressions. Yoruba spirituality is a source for maintaining emotional balance. Memory and regenerative projects have attacked the hegemonic narratives and realities of power and conquest. The scattering of Yoruba people has spread their worldview and belief systems, and, consequently, various aspects of culture have survived. Nollywood is powerful, challenging its viewers in multiple places to understand and interpret Yoruba culture, to decode the middle ground between tradition and modernity, to grapple with the paradoxes of change, to question degeneracy, and to contemplate regeneration. Countless literary texts have attributed the woes of the Yoruba to the duplicity among the Yoruba themselves, the role of slavery, and European colonizers. In attempting to resolve these woes, texts have placed their emphasis on rediscovering and promoting Yoruba culture, rebuilding fractured networks, and engendering reconciliation where conflicts exist.

Let me close with some ideas to further empower the Yoruba as well as the studies about them. First, the scholarship on the Yoruba in different parts of the world is yet to be fused; scholars and works are not fully in dialogue with one another. Many areas of commonality do exist: the conditions of slavery and post slavery, of colonial conquest and domination, and of migrations. Liberation texts are virtually everywhere, as in overcoming slavery, wars, and exploitation, but analyses tend to take specific places or nation-states as their context. Hundreds of specific texts exist on various subjects, but reflections of a comparative nature are rare. In merging the disparate works divided by space and time, crosscutting themes in comparativist perspectives will yield greater insights and unite the disciplines in more creative ways. Diversity and diaspora are connected, and their multi-faceted nature needs to be fully understood so that the Yoruba in various locations may begin a process of creating convergences. Even the contrasts that emerge will create greater understanding of cultural affinities and sources of difference and departure. The traffic of ideas would be clearer and more clarified. To compare and contrast is to understand multiple contexts and understand how events are shaped by individuals who need to relate to their own specific milieus.

We always tend to assume that ideas move in one direction: from the Yoruba homeland to other places. On the contrary, ideas also move in the opposite direction. The case of the Brazilian returnees is well known in terms of how they transformed language, architecture, and city life in the nineteenth century. Formerly enslaved and modernizing Yoruba agents of Christianity contributed to the spread of Christianity and notions of modernity during the nineteenth century.

Second, rather than using the Yoruba to test so-called universal ideas, we should use the Yoruba to universalize scholarship, that is, to turn our own data into theories with universal applications. Thus far, the Yoruba are more on the receiving end. If we are able to use the Yoruba data to make theoretical points, we will extend scholarship to better understand human conditions in universalist terms. Without the ability to formulate larger theories or a unique body of ideas, we will be pushed to the marginalized, so-called ethnic or area studies with minimal connections to the mainstreams.

Third, there must be vibrant discussions on change and modernity in the future. Such discussions are usually elite projects, whereby a small group of individuals construct the future for their own people. Today, the vanguards lack a voice and coherence. In the nineteenth century, men such as Reverend Samuel Ajayi Crowther and Samuel Johnson, who were ahead of their time, prepared the Yoruba for the first half of the twentieth century. They combined the desire for modernity with Yoruba unity, an idea that a politician like Chief Obafemi Awolowo was able to turn into practical and political projects. Modernity is not just about culture, it is also about economic expansion. Wealth has to be created and then used to expand productivity, which in turn will generate more wealth. A cultural group is also a market.

Fourth, the fragmentation of the Yoruba into various states within the Nigerian federation and dispersals in various countries should be treated as a political device to bring progress to the poor and the majority of the people. To prevent fragmentation from doing damage to a collective sense of identity, cultural projects have to be created and strengthened in ways that will ignore boundaries of states and nations. There should be a Yoruba Day marked all over the world with a set of cultural ideas, perhaps carnivals that borrow from the annual masquerade festivals. Principles around dress, greeting codes, and food for that day can be formulated.

Fifth, the rich cultural resources should be converted to opportunities to promote pilgrimages from other parts of the world to Yorubaland. There are rich and diverse places to meet various interests. The beach- and sea-oriented have their slot, complemented by lagoon routes. The hill- and forest-driven have their places. There are historic sites, some of which are underdeveloped, such as the location where Sango, the god of thunder, is said to have ended his life; the Yoruba frontier; zones of cultures; religious sites; and many more. More museums have to be created; various customs have to be festivalized, that is, revived and inserted into modern celebratory functions; and artifacts have to be collected and celebrated. Pilgrimages are homecomings, combining tourism with cultural immersion, connections to kinship, and a careful blending of the search for authenticity with aesthetic imagination.

Osogbo, with its annualized Osun Festival, becomes the exemplar in this regard. In the process, those in the homeland are able to bond with those outside. In moments of need or crises, there are people at both ends who can be mobilized for action. Resources and energies for development are increased. The ties that bind, as the linkages between Africa and African Americans have shown in the past,[74] can be revived within larger political networks, intellectual engagements,[75] and entrepreneurship. The ideals and debate on repatriation from the Americas to Africa,[76] that even saw Martin Delany choosing Yorubaland as one location, are no more. However, the ideals of connections, pilgrimages, tourism, study-abroad programs, language immersion, and Orisa networks are still alive, and they can be promoted to build strong bridges and fuel cultural and economic development.

Sixth, the Yoruba within Nigeria have to return to the idea of cultural competition, such as those in the 1950s and 1960s that I participated in when schools competed for awards in drama, language, literary creations, and many more. The competitions engendered a strong ability to read and use the Yoruba language, to promote Yoruba values, and to socialize in the young a respect for the values of *omoluwabi*. The *omoluwabi* concept raises the issue of the responsibility and accountability of leadership, a leadership that should be conscious of a tomorrow, which, though it is the child of today, is yet greater than yesterday. *Jegudujera, ajenigbolagbe* (greedy thieves) among our people may destroy themselves along with us. The potent force of the god, Esu ("Esu laalu, ogiri oko") as warning against *ibaje* (corrupt practices) is a trope for us to utilize in the classrooms and in layers of dialogue.

Today, the Yoruba world is dominated by the young, who are our future. Unfortunately, the young are decreasingly active in Yoruba culture and are far more exposed to Western culture, which serves to disconnect their intellectual interests from indigenous ideas. Yoruba history and culture must be integrated into major studies irrespective of the future careers of students. Play is politics when it translates words and action into knowledge—self-knowledge in which students are further embedded and inserted into their own environments and aesthetics is turned into culture.

The process of cultural immersion advances the project of cultural reproduction, enabling playful and critical engagement with stories, legends, mythologies, proverbs, and rituals to affirm the value of the past and to minimize the burden of modernity. Expressions of cultural identity cannot be neutral in the context of globalization and Western cultural hegemony. Neither can they be neutral in the context of a growing generation of parents in cities who are disconnected from speaking the Yoruba language and reproducing its values. Cultural competitions can close the gap between generations (as youth engage with adults as their audience) and also between creativity, thought, and fragmented human lives. They can bring back forgotten voices of the past, thereby raising consciousness about the past and the present. We will certainly discover excellence in youth and creativity in ways that will advance our lives and thoughts.

We have to culturalize ourselves before we can culturalize others. The past must always have a useful function. Places that the Yoruba call "home" have expanded far beyond the geographic space of southwestern Nigeria. Those within the original homeland who invented the *Isese* (original traditions) have to find lasting values in them. Those abroad have to find value in their hybridity, in the combining of Yoruba with elements of the culture where they live. All have to find values in continuity and change and develop techniques to accept contradictions and ambiguities in the evolution of new cultures, popular cultures, and youth behavior. Changes will come, but locality remains as well. Modernist theories that posit that older traditions and religions will just fade away have been proven wrong by the resilience of culture. Globalization theories that predicted the disappearance of the local are not correct either. Cultures and ethnicities remain powerful; nationalisms have been formulated around them. How people understand themselves and their heritage shapes how they understand others.

The vision of modernity must remain expansive, accommodating, receptive to change, and progressive. As the Yoruba at home and abroad see themselves in the framework of a "nation," they should continue to learn from one another, interact on the basis of common interest, share ideas to promote development and innovations, and minimize divisive conflicts—all while promoting competition. The Yoruba live within national, regional, continental, and global universes as members of diverse spaces that are transethnic, transnational, transcultural, and even transracial. All these spaces have to be managed, but they also have to be crossed to benefit each other, promote peace, and minimize conflicts.

The final remarks are directed to the Atlantic Yoruba, irrespective of where they live. Tokunbo[77] is Yoruba—whether she stays put in the land across the ocean where she is born or whether she returns home! And when Tokunbo becomes Toks, Tosin becomes Tosyne, and Toyin becomes Toyen, we do forgive the transgressions, bearing in mind that *omi leniyan, oruko to ba wu ni la je lehin odi.*[78] Surely, in the spirit of tolerance, we must live by this proverb. However, as you conduct the transgressions, bear the following three ideas in mind:

1. With regard to language: Frantz Fanon's view on the phenomenon of language is apt, I think, in relation to the efforts by the Yoruba in the diaspora to cling to their culture. For sure, they were assimilated into the host culture in the Americas. However, they inserted themselves through their various Orisa into the controlling religious syntax. The strategy has become very effective in allowing for a multitude of cultural events and religious ceremonies.

2. Still considering language, keeping the Yoruba language alive, especially at home and abroad, is crucial to cultural sustenance. The tribute to J. F. Odunjo, the author who popularized the teaching of Yoruba language in elementary schools in the 1950s and 1960s, is important; he is a man whose name has become for many in my generation synonymous with culture, although we probably were not that discerning at that time. Our literature should flourish through an invigorated Yoruba language. Nollywood has taken the lead here. There may come a day when many colleges in the West are sufficiently convinced about the preeminence of Yoruba culture to make the study of Yoruba language a required or even an elective course. When that occurs, the potential of tourism will be fulfilled: when Western scholars are enthused enough about Yoruba that they do not consider themselves fulfilled until they have visited Oyo Ile, Osogbo, Idanre, and several other potential tourist destinations.

3. An essential aspect of culture is its adaptability. However, for the Yoruba in the diaspora, names are an important marker of ancestry and locality. Names are among the major ways in which the Yoruba will essentialize themselves in the diaspora. For sure, *Oruko to ba wuni la je lehin odi.*[79] However, the idea is

probably more applicable to those who are on a sojourn, *ajo*, who are intent on returning home to enjoy the labor of their haul as sojourners. The Yoruba in the diaspora have a responsibility to contribute to world civilization by holding on to their Yorubaness, which we first confront through their names. In the United States in particular, this is what has made it easy for the Yoruba to identify easily with other ethnic Americans. Their names are a perpetual reminder of their nationalities and ethnicities. In the age of Facebook, we should impress on our wards the importance of respecting themselves by asserting their individuality. And what better way to do that than to learn to write their names properly, rather than the Facebook gibberish that seems to have become a fad?

We must rework the relationships between the Yoruba *insiders within cultures* and the Yoruba *outsiders within cultures* so that we can merge our interests in all the locations, centers, and margins in order to create a genuine dialog in the promotion of Yoruba humanity and progress.

6

Politics, Slavery, Servitude, and the Construction of Yoruba Identity

Slavery and freedom operate within a social milieu, an economic system, and political structures. In the nineteenth century, Yoruba warriors who responded to external demands to produce palm oil and palm kernels dominated politics and thus looked for labor to work on their farms. In the first half of the twentieth century, the colonial government in Nigeria began the process of creating formal economies. In the postcolonial phase, the Yoruba developed a much stronger sense of ethnicity in order to compete with other groups in a complicated Nigerian federal system. In the more recent period, political turmoil has created new ideas of ethnicity, a hundred years after the Yoruba ended their long wars of the nineteenth century. The Yoruba's past connects to its present in visible ways.

In the context of my discussion of the role of slavery in the formation of contemporary identity and politics, I will limit myself to four issues:

1. How the Yoruba confronted the issues of slavery, servitude, pawnship, and the like after the wars of the nineteenth century. Slaves were absorbed into the social mechanisms in place and there was a conversation on the role of domestic slavery in society. However, defining the Yoruba nation, articulating policies to put ideas in practice, and negotiating with British colonial power and with representatives of other ethnicities were bigger projects of politics and nationalism than the specific issues of slavery and freedom.

2. What happened to slavery after the Yoruba wars and the British imposition of colonial rule.

3. The alternatives that were put in place as slavery declined, and how institutions of credit—or arrangements to raise loans with far-reaching implications on dependency, labor relations, and economics—led to the emergence of a professional class of lenders.

4. Finally, how the slaves adjusted to new conditions and experiences.

All these connected issues enable us to understand events after the end of the Yoruba wars and to understand the impact of British colonization on slavery and servitude.

On June 12, 1993, the wealthy Yoruba businessman and politician Chief M. K. O. Abiola, a well-known advocate of reparations, won the election to become the president of Nigeria. He acquired a large number of votes from among his fellow Yoruba and also from different parts of the country. A notable Muslim and philanthropist, he made an impressive inroad into the northern part of the country and broke the age-old opposition to Yoruba politicians. His success in the north was credited to his being a Muslim; perhaps his victory was more a result of his generosity than his religion, or perhaps it was a combination of both. Alhaji Tofa, his main contender from the north, was also a Muslim, but he lost. In the east, Abiola had a respectable showing as well, although he was not the leading candidate. His victory suggests a rethinking of the role of ethnicity in politics.

A Yoruba had emerged as a national leader. The ethnic nationalism that originally propelled him might as well have instigated Abiola to contribute to a Nigerian national identity. It was not to be. The military government, under the leadership of General Ibrahim Babangida, annulled the elections that brought Abiola close to the main seat of government at Abuja. Abiola protested, prodemocracy movements activated, and violence erupted in several parts of Yorubaland. In the crises that followed, an interim government was installed. It lasted for a few weeks, and the military dictatorship of General Sanni Abacha followed.[1]

The Yoruba felt betrayed: The optimism of creating a national identity died. However, Yoruba nationalism was revived with the talk of secession. As the crisis deepened, the Oduduwa People's Congress (OPC) was established with the aim of fighting for the political rights of the Yoruba. Some among them even wanted a secession to create a new country, the Oduduwa Republic. Opinions were divided on what the political future of the Yoruba should be. A number of Yoruba leaders called for a "restructured federation," with autonomy granted to various units within the union. The youthful leadership in the OPC became like the restless pseudo-Jama or "Ogo were" of the nineteenth century who went about with war implements to empower themselves and destabilize the political order.

The political crisis that followed the presidential election was now approaching an imminent collapse of the country. Events began to read like the nineteenth century, when power rivalries led to the fall of the Oyo Empire and the fragmentation of the Yoruba into new city-states such as Ibadan, Abeokuta, Ogbomoso, Ilorin, and others. In the post-1993 era, the retelling of Yoruba history acquired greater significance. In this retelling, the Yoruba became citizens of one nation, the Yoruba nation, and sought one goal: development and progress as members of one sovereign nation. Many Yoruba began to talk as if they were strangers within Nigeria, redefining the meaning of citizenship.

Arriving at 1993 required a long journey that began when the Yoruba ended their long wars of the nineteenth century in 1893 and comprises a substantial history. The interval between 1893 and 1993, part of the period covered by this chapter, reveals various attempts to construct the idea of the Yoruba nation and to talk about notions of citizenship that included issues pertaining to servitude and freedom. Just as Yoruba dialogue and practical actions of the 1990s were initiated in the context of political crises and military rule, those of the post-1890 era were done in the context of a prolonged warfare that was ending and the imposition of a colonial power. Slavery and servitude operated in a political and economic context of power relations between individuals and among competing groups.

The conditions for change in the twentieth century were laid in the nineteenth century. The Yoruba states fought for most of the nineteenth century until a peace treaty was signed in 1893.[2] The famous Oyo Empire fell, and the Ibadan that succeeded it was unable to sustain majority power among the cluster of competing states. The wars created enormous opportunities for warriors and merchants to put slaves to use in large numbers, and also for entrepreneurs to establish large-scale farms and trading networks. European incursions brought missionaries, traders, and colonizers, notably in the second half of the century. The missionaries set up various stations in such Yoruba cities as Badagry, Lagos, Ibadan, Abeokuta, and Ijaye; and their activities, a combination of spreading Christianity along with Western education, progressed slowly during the nineteenth century. A large number of former Yoruba captives and their families also began to return from 1839 onward: they contributed to the activities of the missionaries, and advocated the strengthening of an agricultural and commercial economy in order to sustain a new generation.[3] The British opened a consular post in Lagos in 1851, and the beginnings of a colonial administration was later extended to the Yoruba hinterland in the 1890s.[4] Between 1892 and 1893, the Yoruba states lost their sovereignty and were incorporated into part of the British colony and administered as a protectorate. In 1906, Lagos and the rest of Yorubaland were amalgamated into the Nigeria Coast Protectorate, which was, in turn, amalgamated with the Protectorate of Northern Nigeria in 1914 to form a country now known as Nigeria.

Initial administrators, known as traveling commissioners, governed after 1892. They were later renamed or replaced by residents and district officers who operated the Lugardian system of indirect rule in a way that allowed many of the kings to retain their power and for the nineteenth-century states to maintain their identities. At the same time, new conditions allowed the Yoruba to create a new set of ideas on Yorubaness: ideas that emphasized the unity of race and culture. As the political unit of Nigeria became imposed on them, they needed the unity of a Yoruba "nation" to engage in anticolonial politics and to fashion ways to compete in a multiplural federation.

Race and Its Hierarchies

The conversation about defining the modern Yoruba identity began well before the nineteenth century, although much of the contemporary written evidence from the Yoruba themselves dates to the nineteenth century. Sudanese Muslims discussed "Yorubaness" at least as early as the sixteenth century, as in the work of Ahmad Baba; his writings influenced dan Fodio, Mohammed Bello, and Sokoto jihadists in justifying the attack on Oyo. There were also the Nago Lucumi discourses in the Americas and Alladah/Dahomey in the seventeenth and eighteenth centuries. These discourses continued well into the twentieth century.

Many intellectual ideas were articulated into cultural projects during the nineteenth century. Those who began the conversation were, in one way or the other, connected with the transatlantic slave trade or with domestic slavery in Yorubaland. The written material that began to appear from the nineteenth century, and on which most of what we know about the nineteenth century are based, are partly associated with the missionaries, their Yoruba agents, and repatriates based in Lagos and Abeokuta.[5] Although the point is not well discussed, Yoruba Muslims were not excluded from the conversation. Some would even argue that the acceptance of "Yoruba" as a name, rather than Aku, Nago, or Lucumi in Sierra Leone, owed largely to the works of the Yoruba Ulama. Not only were the writers of the nineteenth century activist observers of politics and wars of the era, but they were also committed to changing the Yoruba as a people and as a nation.

In 1843 one of those liberated slaves, Samuel Crowther, wrote an introduction to the Yoruba language, providing the foundation for a Yoruba orthography.[6] In 1859 the first newspaper, *Iwe Irohin*, was established at Abeokuta by the Church Missionary Society (CMS). In 1863 the *Anglo-African* newspaper appeared in Lagos. Ideas of Yorubaness began to emerge in written articulations. These new voices were opposed to the transatlantic slave trade, and they supported the penetration of the missionaries to the Yorubaland. Crowther was sent to London in the 1840s to argue that the British should take over Lagos in order to end the slave trade and control commerce. The promissionary Yoruba wanted the spread of trade, education, and commerce, partly in the hope that the combination would terminate the slave trade and the institution of slavery.

The characteristics of the Yoruba people and race were clearly mapped out, as if to convince themselves of their uniqueness and difference from others. Three features stood out very prominently in this articulation. First, the Yoruba had a history; some presented it as if it was uniquely theirs. Myths of origins, already in circulation, were put into print during the nineteenth century. Some of these myths were even told to visiting Europeans, such as the Clapperton and Landers expedition, who then recorded short traditions collected at Oyo and Sokoto. More stories of origins were collected during the twentieth century and published in various books.[7] The ideas of origins centered on the city of Ile-Ife (Richard Lander mentioned Ile-Ife in his 1830–32 work)[8] and on a progenitor founder, Oduduwa. Both the city and progenitor founder had a series of mythologies of affirmation and legitimization: they are the sources of the Yoruba cultural identity, the foundation of their institutions, the beginning of their civilization.

Second, there was a culture of power and hierarchies of social relations. At the very top was the king, operating within a complicated set of ideas on kingship. There were different monarchs and dynasties, and the Yoruba successfully carried many ideas on both to the present. The kings remain, in spite of losses in power, at the top of the hierarchies in their cities.[9] Even today, they still enjoy prestige and influence based on tradition and individual personality.[10]

Kingship, as an aspect of the political system, was tied with the legal system and the culture that sustained it. A concept of *iwa* (good behavior) was necessary to maintain social hierarchies. Just as the king manifested good *iwa* by being a leader, so too was it expected of a slave or pawn to manifest a good *iwa* by being obedient. As to the supreme exercise of legal authority, there can be no question that it was a monopoly of kingship:

Eni boba jiyan ni npe l'Afin.

[To argue with the king is to be kept long at the palace.]

It could safely be assumed that if the post-1893 conversation and subsequent policy validated the role of the kings and their chiefs, it could not have, at the same time, redrawn the boundaries of power with regard to slaves. The king and his chiefs were lawmakers and law enforcers. The gap between them and slaves was too wide. This judicial system was carried forward to the twentieth century, and the British not only accepted it but also created a patriarchal judicial system of their own. Thus slaves, ex-slaves, and pawns had a limited judicial system to protect them, though there were opportunities. British courts allowed manumission and forcefully freed some slaves, and the colonial government banned human sacrifice (although some priests carried this out secretly). Some slaves joined the Hausa constabulary as a way of gaining freedom.

However, the courts at all levels were administered by those who subscribed to prevailing notions about social institutions and labor practices. At the most basic level of the compound, cases were administered by a *Baale* (an elder with authority), and at levels beyond those by chiefs and kings. All court administrators were members of the political class that had vested interests in land, production, and accumulation. These interests involved the use of labor. Profits from trade and production formed the economic basis of power in a highly stratified and urban culture.

Third, the Yoruba have a set of ethnocultural features that include the use of idioms, proverbs, songs, and performances, all of which have notions of slavery and freedom embedded in them. In various sayings, idioms,[11] and proverbs, slavery was translated into a set of abuses: disempowerment, suffering, exploitation, marginalization, and torture. The Yoruba were socially stratified, as reflected in its entire oral literature and performance. They sought wealth and power, and both the means to gain and to use them could undermine the esteem of the lowly placed. In general, poverty was regarded as a sort of disease:

> Akisa a ba eni rere je
> Aje a gbeni ga.

> [Rags demean the illustrious person
> Wealth can catapult one to higher status.]

> Aje saluga
> O fi eni iwaju sile se eni ehin ni pele.

> [Wealth the almighty
> It skips the person in front to celebrate the person at the back.]

Slavery, as a condition of poverty, can be equated with foolery:

> Won se bi otosi o gbon bi oloro;
> Won ni i ba gbon i ba lowo lowo.

> [People tend to think that the poor person lacks the wisdom the
>   wealthy person has;
> They say if one had wisdom, one would be rich.]

The space to compete, while it existed, was already diminished by poverty.

Intellectualizing Slavery: Conversation and Debate

Those who participated in defining the Yoruba identity also engaged in conversation on slavery. Opinions were divided between those who supported the institution of slavery and those opposed to it. The arguments of those for were based on the premise of culture

Figure 6.1. The king of Oke-Ila, Orangun Adedokun O. Abolarin, at a university function. Photograph courtesy of author.

(it was presented as an aspect of the social institution, age-old, and well ingrained), and justified on the basis of the economy (labor was needed to generate a productive economy).

There is a small body of knowledge associated with the Christian missions that allows us to elaborate on the opposing views.[12] The CMS staked out a position in 1880: "We venture to maintain that slavery in any shape or form, as distinguished from voluntary hiring and service, is thoroughly alien from the spirit of the Gospel . . . the spirit of the Word of God has eliminated slavery from Christianity."[13] As many of the CMS priests were ex-slaves or descendants of slaves, their statements amounted to "victim impact" testimony. The missionaries saw moral decadence in such institutions as polygyny and slavery. The hope, as they expressed repeatedly, was that conversion to Christianity would create a new society and a Christian middle class.

Several agents of the Anglican Church, including many of their Yoruba converts, associated slavery with negativity. In the middle of the nineteenth century, they linked domestic slavery with the transatlantic slave trade. The argument was that the institution of domestic slavery made slaves available to European buyers.[14] However, the historical evidence suggested otherwise: the demand for so-called legitimate products—what the missionaries wanted the Yoruba to produce more of—encouraged domestic slavery.

The missionaries linked what they saw as a state of underdevelopment to slavery, which had kept the "native population in a perpetual state of calamitous excitement, fomenting bad passions." Slavery, as they argued, interfered "with all industrial effort, preventing the development of African capabilities, the productive powers of the soil, and the intellectual powers of the people."[15] As long as there was slavery, argued the missionaries, there would be limited room for agricultural and industrial growth.

Slavery was linked by the missionaries to warfare. Indeed, they believed that the principal cause of the wars was to obtain slaves: "The slaves for export, with few exceptions, are obtained by war, and most of the wars in Africa are for this object."[16] The evidence clearly shows that slavery and war were connected, but, for slavery, the motives were much larger and the politics much deeper. To press home their point, the missionaries exaggerated the consequences of the wars, sometimes concluding that life was at a standstill. They ignored the enormous expansion in production of commodities for exports, for local economies, and for the sustenance of wars.

As to be expected, the missionaries emphasized the evil represented in the institution of slavery. Writing in 1886, James Johnson, one of the most influential missionary opponents of domestic slavery, concluded thus:

All able-bodied slaves have some care, but the sickly and infirm have little or none, and may sometimes be found dying, neglected in the streets, from starvation and disease—passers by, or those about whose doors they lie, dying, and women amongst them, manifesting stolid indifference and unconcern. The number of such unfortunate is often large when expeditions are very successful and have just returned home. Instances of individual cruelty and barbarity to slaves are not wanting. Slave holding mistresses have been known to be guilty of them. Slave-wives may sometimes be found by the side of their dead mothers, thrown out on the muddy bank of some river. . . . Their carcasses are often thrown into some rivers, in groves, and other fields to be food for wolves and vultures, which sometimes surfeit on them.[17]

This and similar views were repeated throughout the nineteenth century to strengthen the antislavery position of the missions.

As much as the missionaries engaged in conversations on this subject, they lacked the power to abolish slavery. They admitted slaveowning converts to their churches. The Rev. Henry Townsend, the pioneer missionary at Abeokuta, concluded that a full-scale attack on slavery would affect the work of evangelization: "I cannot admit the principle that everyone holding a slave is an idol worshipper, an adulterer etc. for possessing a slave is not among the works of the flesh enumerated by St. Paul."[18] As Christianity attempted to spread, its agents toned down their antislavery rhetoric. However, by the late 1870s a powerful antislavery group began to criticize fellow missionaries for their tolerance, such that the camp was divided between "idealists" and "realists." At a meeting in Lagos in 1879, the CMS reached a decision that "no Christian should purchase or sell a slave, and those who possessed slaves before their conversion, should afford them time and opportunity to buy out their freedom, and in the meantime should provide for their Christian instruction."[19] The CMS decided to impose a sanction after January 1880 on any of its agents who held slaves or pawns by excommunicating them.

In the 1880s and 1890s, a number of church agents implemented the decision of 1879. They preached against it, they bought the freedom of a number of slaves, they encouraged desertion, and they hoped that the intensification of evangelization would have a long-term beneficial effect. Although slavery survived the nineteenth century, a vigorous dialogue emerged within the churches and among their agents about the institution; the dominant voices were opposed to it.

From Slaves to Citizens: Freedom and Emancipation in the Late Nineteenth Century

The Yoruba wars of the nineteenth century were responsible for the dramatic increase in the number of domestic slaves. There were notable members of the political and merchant class with large holdings. For example, the *Balogun* of Ikorodu had no less than four hundred slaves in 1892, and John Augustus Otunba Payne, an Ijebu prince, had over eight hundred during the same time.[20] These slaves were needed to work on large farms, serve as domestics, and even fight in wars. The wars were linked to production of goods (the generation of surpluses to feed large populations, make money, and live affluently), to the export of goods (the sale of produce, notably palm oil and palm kernel), to the desire for firearms (the need to obtain resources to buy muskets, and later on in the nineteenth century, rifles), and to the maintenance of prestige (the ability to count wealth and support in numbers of people). The more wars fought, the more captives who became slaves. There were incentives for the large private armies and professional soldiers to fight. The various city-states struggled for political dominance, and war captives met the increasing demand for slaves: first to feed the transatlantic slave trade and later for the reasons mentioned above.

When the wars ended in the early 1890s, dramatic consequences also followed, which involved dialogue among slaves, dialogue between slaves and their masters, and dialogue among various masters and government officials. These conversations have not been fully reported or analyzed because of lack of evidence. The period also coincided with the beginning of extensive cultural and political transformations of the Yoruba. In referring to the late nineteenth century and beyond, the Yoruba would describe the period in two ways in a kind of shorthand for capturing the complicated and diverse changes of a rather turbulent period. The first is *aye olaju*, that is, "the modern world" or "the age of modernity." The expression either explains, understands, accepts, or rejects the rapid rush of changes associated with Christianity, Western education, the emergence of a new elite, and colonial rule. The second is *aye Oyinbo*, that is, "the age of whiteness," which is a way of explaining the colonial period and the changes associated with new technology and foreign impact.

While decadent values are associated with the age, there is a general belief that people either had to become reconciled to changes that they were unable to resist or had to adapt to new circumstances. The history of slavery after the 1890s would appear to have been captured by the belief in *aye Oyinbo*—that the age was controlled by white men, and in *aye olaju*—the "age of modernity." This belief was shaped not exclusively by local history or forces but by the integration of Yoruba society into modern Nigeria within the colonial context, which generated conversations on power and power relations. The Reverend James Johnson, for example, declared, "I think before slaves should be free, there should be an interregnum—the slaves in their own interests as well as of their masters might serve a time, say five years."[21] Consequently, the process included the partition system and then a colonial system that lasted until October 1, 1960.

If the institution of slavery was accepted for most of the nineteenth century, the foundation for its eventual end was laid in the last quarter of the nineteenth century. The wars came to an end, which put an end to the supply of fresh captives. As the hinterland became stable, hundreds of former slaves could flee to their former homes. Colonial rule unleashed the conditions that eventually terminated slavery in the first half of the twentieth century.

The imposition of colonial rule involved, in the language of the humanitarian justification for the exercise, the emancipation of slaves. As is well known, the abolition of the transatlantic slave trade did not lead to the abolition of slavery among the Yoruba. Indeed, the production of palm oil and palm kernel for export during the nineteenth century led to an expansion in the use of slaves, while the wars of the nineteenth century created a regular supply. The combination of the end of the war and British imposition of colonial rule led to the emancipation of thousands of slaves who reintegrated themselves back into the definition of free citizens as Yoruba.

Such concerns for emancipation became part of the justification for the attack on some Yoruba states opposed to the British. A most notable example was the attack on the Ijebu in May 1892. The attack was based on the allegations that they were opposed to free trade and supported slavery.[22] Couched in the language of humanitarianism, Governor Carter authorized the attack and claimed that his desire to end slavery was his paramount reason. Indeed, between 1892 and 1895, Carter believed that colonial expansion and the use of force would lead to the abolition of slavery. A number of missionaries, intent on evangelization, were supportive of colonial conquest, and they also believed that abolition of slavery would be part of a package of "civilization."[23]

A major impact on ending the wars and colonial imposition was the liberation of thousands of slaves. This was anticipated as early as the 1890s, when some missionaries warned that the British invasion of the hinterland would encourage slave resistance and escape. As one missionary put it 1892, slaves would "rejoice to see the Union Jack waving above their masters."[24] While we do not know whether the antislavery conversation among some missionaries and officials reached the ears of slaves, we do know that the weakening of military power, the end of the wars, and the attack of the British on the Ijebu created opportunities to escape. If, for most of the nineteenth century, slave rebellion or massive flights did not occur in most Yoruba towns, the survival of the slave system was undermined in the 1890s as thousands were able to abandon their masters. In the case of the Ijebu expedition of 1892, the number of slaves who fled was so high that Samuel Johnson, our leading eyewitness observer of the era, predicted the end of domestic slavery.[25] Those who left slavery behind numbered in the thousands. Captain Campbell was stationed at Ijebu Ode in May 1892 and was its first resident. Supported by an army unit of one hundred soldiers, his temporary abode and office became a destination for runaway slaves. He arrogated to himself the power to grant freedom to slaves. In Abeokuta, where stories of the war and the flight of slaves from Ijebu had spread like bushfire, hundreds of slaves ran in the direction of Lagos. They took advantage of the feeling of safety they felt there.

Ibadan and other towns in the hinterland were concerned that the slaves among them would become fugitives. Pioneer colonial officers were posted in a number of towns, which led to a belief that the colonial government would interfere with slavery and some other institutions that Africans were not happy with. In 1891 Ibadan refused to accept a British resident, in part because it feared interference in the slave trade. Fearing a possible war, it presented a set of conditions, one of which was that a British resident could not liberate his slaves or use his residence as a refuge for fugitive slaves. Acting Governor George Denton assured the chiefs that the Lagos government would not "interfere with the domestic slavery so long as it is conducted on humane principles." He insisted that slaves would not obtain their freedom "by running to the Resident."[26]

However, Captain Robert Bower, the first resident and traveling commissioner placed at Ibadan in 1893, ignored the agreement regarding slaves. No sooner did he arrive than his residence actually became a center of freedom. To the slaves, Bower became "the good man."[27] Without the wars that had supplied Ibadan with slaves, the increasing number of fugitives added to the woes of slave owners. Bower's encounter with the chiefs outside of Ibadan was based on the use of his power to humiliate them or to curtail what he regarded as their excesses. In 1894 he arrested the leading war hero of the Ijesa, Ogedemgbe, who had kept slaves numbered in the thousands. The arrest led to the disbandment of Ogedemgbe's private army, which included hundreds of slaves. A large number of slaves belonging to different masters also seized the opportunity to regain their freedom. A year later, Captain Tucker, the traveling commissioner at Ilesa, arrested Fabunmi, the notable Ekiti war leader. This led to the disbandment of his private army and the release of hundreds more slaves.

There was a fall in prices in the 1890s, as many slave traders sold at a discount. Slave clearance sales were reported in the same decade. Two related events brought this about. The first was the war against the Ijebu in 1892 and what slave dealers saw as the great losses to the Ijebu merchants and chiefs who lost hundreds of slaves. The other was the possible use of force to liberate the slaves. A number of Yoruba chiefs were cowed by the threat of force. Carter understood the linkage too well, by traveling with his army and guns to the Yoruba hinterland in 1893. As Johnson remarked, "a display of force offered far more convincing weight of argument than volumes of treaties."[28] A number of slaveholders read the move not only as an expansionist bid, but also as an antislavery one.

In November 1895, Oyo suffered a similar fate to Ijebu's. Under the pretext that the Alaafin disobeyed his instruction, Captain Bower attacked the city and razed one-fifth of the houses to the ground. Thousands of people fled the city. About fifty "shackled slaves" belonging to the Alaafin showed up in the Baptist mission house, where their chains were cut free and about a thousand slaves released.[29] Bower acquired considerable fame among slaves for taking measures to ensure their freedom, while he generated considerable resentment from kings and chiefs for creating ruptures.

A final force in producing emancipation was the collateral impact of placing a set of colonial soldiers and police power among the Yoruba. Far different from the direct exercise of power by such residents as Captain Bower, those who worked for the new colonial government had some impact on the institution of slavery. The most notable were members of the colonial army, known as the Hausa soldiers. The narratives of the 1890s and early twentieth century presented sad stories about the sadistic behavior of low-level agents of the colonial state. Not only were they accused of rape and theft, but they also aided in granting freedom and safe passages to fugitive slaves. Hausa soldiers were recruited by the colonial government in part because many of them were socially uprooted. Those recruited in Lagos were fugitive slaves. As they transited from slaves to privileged soldiers, they had little sympathy for merchants and chiefs who enslaved their kindred. As they moved from one Yoruba town to another, they provided opportunities for slaves of northern origins (also labeled as Hausa, even when they were from the Middle Belt) to escape.

As historical narratives portray, the barracks served as places of protection. I. B. Akinyele, describing the Ibadan experience of this era, portrayed the soldiers and other minor colonial workers as thugs.[30] Akinyele's testimony and those of his contemporaries provide glimpses of an entire Yoruba society in a state of chaotic transition: husbands lost control of their wives, children disobeyed their fathers, and wives eloped with slaves. Most of the blame was placed on those who exercised new power, such as the Hausa soldiers. The records are indeed clear that Hausa soldiers did encourage slave desertion. In addition, the soldiers forcefully recruited people as labor to work on the construction of roads and railways. As they "disturbed the peace of the town," to use Akinyele's phrase with respect to Ibadan, a disturbance that was also observed in other areas, the soldiers introduced a new power element that reshaped the social order.

Slavery and the Conditions of Colonialism

Slavery survived the nineteenth century.[31] Not all slaves could escape. Slaveholders' attempts to maintain their hold were equally vigorous. A number of leading chiefs and kings openly expressed their opposition to the end of domestic slavery. The Egba chiefs of Abeokuta advised Governor Carter not to talk about abolition, as he did not understand it.[32] The Alaafin of Oyo was very hostile to Carter's visit in 1891, on the ground that he would encourage slave desertion and rebellion. The Alaafin presented the face of contented slaves: "These slaves are perfectly free to eat and sleep, to come and go at their pleasure, and are content to stay with us on these terms."[33] In the Ijesa and Ekiti areas, the warlords who participated in the Sixteen Years War (as in the case of Ogedemgbe) continued to use slaves. Thus the evidence was clear for the last decade of the nineteenth century that there was an entrenched interest in keeping and using slaves.

There was an equal traffic in slaves within the various towns. New supplies came from Ilorin, the frontier city-state to the north, and the rest of the Yoruba country. Ilorin was fed by markets north of the rivers Niger and Benue. The centrality of Ilorin in the exchange of slaves continued into the early decades of the twentieth century. The Yoruba towns that benefited from Ilorin lent it support in continuing with the trade by pressuring the British and the missionaries to delay their contacts. In 1897 the Royal Niger Company, the first to control this part of what became Nigeria before it was appropriated by the British, was able to assert its control on Ilorin. This enabled a large number of slaves to take to flight in ways similar to what had happened at Ijebu and Ibadan four years earlier.

The traditional uses of slaves continued for many years after the 1890s. To those who were able to maintain their large farms, slaves provided labor. Slaves were still connected with kingship as part of the palace staff. While new slaves could not be obtained from war booty, there were transactions in the older ones, and inheritance probably occurred until the early decade of the twentieth century. The disbanding of private armies and the cessation of wars meant that there were no more slave soldiers, one of the most privileged roles in the war years. Long-distance bulking of goods continued, and human porterage was common between towns and villages until lorries and railways made it redundant for greater distances.

Slavery and other forms of dependency operated within the colonial milieu and a set of new economic conditions. The politics of indirect rule that privileged the kings and chiefs encouraged the use of labor to do farm work and maintain royalty. As Lord Frederick Lugard, the architect of indirect rule, explained, the system would lead to the development of British colonies while bringing financial gains to Britain. While this was a clever rationalization of imperialism, it also served to justify practices such as the use of labor that sustained the colonial economy.

The Yoruba region was part of the colonial regime for the production of raw materials based on the use of land and labor to cultivate cocoa, cotton, corn, rubber, palm oil, and palm kernel, and to exploit timberlands. The creation of an infrastructure, such as harbor, roads, and railways in Lagos, involved the use of labor. Railway construction began in 1895, and the railroad reached Ota in 1897, Abeokuta in 1899, and Ibadan in 1901. Thereafter, the lines went into the hinterland of Ede, Osogbo, Ikirun, and Ilorin and connected them with northern Nigeria. Roads connected the rest of the region to the railway. The building projects diverted labor from farm work to construction. As a formal sector economy developed, and new ways to recruit labor to work on farms emerged, slavery began to decline as an institution and was phased out by the 1930s.

Post Slavery Adjustments: Labor and Credit

In responding to the end of slavery, the Yoruba had to seek alternative ways to provide and use labor and to organize credit. New uses of labor were promoted by the creation of new economic activities such as banking and trading firms (notably subsidiaries of European firms such as the United Africa Company, UAC).

Ultimately, all the new economic ventures required agricultural production to thrive and survive. Agriculture was the core of the economy, the engine that drove everything else. More land was put into cultivation, which generated the need for more labor. Export crops such as cocoa and cotton were lucrative, and established products such as kola nuts generated more revenues. As the increase in production was not dependent on the use of technologies, labor was needed to do virtually all aspects of farm work. The goods had to be moved from the villages to the cities. Labor was needed to process the products so that they could be consumed or transported. A class of merchants known as produce buyers moved from farms and villages to cities to buy in smaller quantities goods that were resold to foreign firms.

Economic changes impacted labor. The formal sector of the economy used wage labor, as in the case of working for the colonial government or European firms. Building roads and railways required forced and communal labor. The cooperative use of labor in reciprocal arrangement of *owe* and *aaro* was on the decline; this was true in the cities but not in the countryside.

Cash crops made it possible to use paid tenants. Those who were able to create extensive farms, especially cocoa cultivation and rubber tapping, had to use extra labor. A large number of temporary farm workers, known as the *alagbaro*, began to replace slaves as farm labor and made it possible to deal with the consequences of slavery. Pawnship—the use of labor as collateral for loans—was a form of labor dependency that survived the colonial period, and was a way to transition from slavery to another form of labor. Obtaining credit for personal and business uses was connected with production, especially of cocoa. Trees could be pawned, often replacing the pawnship of people, as a way of raising credit.

Providing credit was institutionalized into a profession as part of the legacy of slavery. Mobile and itinerant professional moneylenders, known as the *Osomalo*, approached borrowers in scattered locations to advance and collect loans in a most brutal manner. If the economic and political success of the merchants and political class of the nineteenth century rested on the use of slaves, the success of those connected with land in the twentieth century depended on the control of the poor, the landless and powerless, who served as tenants and pawns. The poor would include the slaves of the nineteenth century, although now working as free agents. As Ann O'Hear shows in the case of Ilorin, slave resistance and emancipation was one thing, what the free would do thereafter was another. A colonial economy that focused on export production required the use of labor and the control of landowning farmers to produce cash crops. With limited economic alternatives, O'Hear concludes that "resistance proved ineffectual, and the rurally based ex-slaves and peasants were subjected to harassment and deprivations." Through an impressive amount of evidence, she isolates the parts of Ilorin to its west and north (the "metropolitan districts") with the greatest concentration of peasants, most of whom were former slaves. Here, she observes, they suffered privation "and were largely forced to accommodate to their overlords."[34] The peasants resisted in various ways, including converting to Islam, but in the 1950s they took to an open rebellion made possible by temporary political union and agitation.

Postslavery Integration

There are no remnants of the large farms sustained by slave labor of the nineteenth century. The Yoruba have been intensely urbanized, and many cities, such as Ibadan, have now expanded into the villages and farms of the nineteenth century. There are stories—oral and written—of many of the warriors and kings who owned the large farms of the nineteenth century. As Dare Oguntomisin and I have shown in *Yoruba Warlords*, the praise poems (*oriki*) of those prominent men and women have survived, and they all contain information on how they used slaves on a large scale.[35] Thus the memory is carried forward, if not the physical evidence of their farms, big compounds, horses, and slaves.

However, the memory of slaves and slavery is limited. To start with, the memory of the transatlantic slave trade exists only in a few locations such as the port cities of Lagos and Badagry. I have yet to come across any research on contemporary Yoruba lineages whose ancestors were sold into slavery, with the exception of the limited slave narratives of the nineteenth century, as in the case of Samuel Ajayi Crowther and Samuel Johnson. Obtaining evidence from women would prove even harder. Women slaves who had been forced to marry the freeborn had access to freedom, although not always. When colonial rule was imposed, the new climate enabled women in forced relationships to rethink their relationship: either to stay in it or divorce. This rethinking explains the increasing divorce rate in the contemporary conversation, as the women were presented as exercising more rights to leave bad men. In retaliation, a number of men raised the manumission fee for those women in bondage who wanted to pay for their freedom.

Evidence of domestic slavery exists in the contemporary literature as well as the various writings of the first three decades of the twentieth century. The memory of it in oral narratives is rather meager. When I conducted fieldwork in the 1980s, I could locate a number of people who owned slaves but not the slaves themselves. By the 1990s, no individuals or families admitted to ever being slaves.

Thus the question is whether the silence was deliberate or whether complete integration to full citizenship had been attained; this issue comes up frequently during land and chieftaincy contests. I want to approach the issue in various ways. We no longer have the data on non-Yoruba slaves who fled to their places of origin. A large number of slaves came from the areas north of Ilorin. As they returned, they probably adjusted to their old lives. A number of slaves fled to Lagos, where they lived as free citizens and sought new opportunities. It was among this group that the British recruited soldiers who fought the wars of conquest in different parts of Nigeria. Some probably served as daily workers in various construction jobs, especially the building of new roads and railways. A large number relocated within the Yoruba region as well. The success of the Ibadan empire led to the capture of many war captives in the east and northeast who were converted into slaves. In the 1890s, many Ekiti and Ijesa fled back to their homelands.

There would have been other movements from other places to Ibadan as well. In the places where slaves circulated, the best way to understand integration would certainly be through the *ebi* system (kinship or clan). No one could be a stranger where he or she had a clan. In a patrilineal kinship system, a member only had to trace a relationship to any living or dead male or female relatives. Individual memory could facilitate a process of integration, but even when such memory was lost, the slightest connection to a male ancestor was enough. There was no one, even those who were former slaves or *iwofa*, who had no *idile* (kinship). Thus a relocating slave need not even remember the name of his long-dead ancestor, but would certainly have a memory of names, a compound, some taboos or identity markers. An *idile* had an identity of its own that most members understood. A slave (*eru*) in another town was an *omo ile* (clan member) in another. "The origin might be far," declared a famous proverb, but "a slave had a father." What the flights after the early 1890s did for the slaves was to reconnect them with their "fathers."

As with all members of a clan, a history of previous enslavement would not prevent access to land, space in one of the clan's compounds in different parts of the town, and reciprocal rights and obligations. In addition, previous enslavement did not disqualify one from attaining titles. Relocation also widened the number of contacts, as the number of blood relatives tended to increase. Blood relatives would provide immediate support for survival and would also assist in the long-term plans for marriage and occupational choices and achievements. Immediate acceptance into a clan along with support from a large network assured integration, and the memory of enslavement might last no longer than a first generation.

Clan membership translated into power. A former slave was connected to structures of power and political responsibility not only within the clan but also in the town itself. Thus it was not inconceivable that a number of former slaves later became heads of compounds (*bale*), lineage chiefs (*ijoye*), and even kings (*oba*). To outsiders, members of a clan could be viewed as enjoying a certain level of parity, but to insiders they were stratified by gender, seniority, and status. A slave could regain his lost prestige through age and ultimately become the head of the clan corporate unit as its *bale*, one who performed judicial functions, administered oaths, and assigned land. Seniority determined the position of *baale*, and a previous history of enslavement was not a disqualification. Possibilities to attain mobility and prestige through priesthood in a religious cult also existed. Seniority rule would confer immediate advantage on any slave. Seniority in terms of age generated respect and deference. A clan organized on the basis of seniority made it easier to identify the bachelors (*omo ile*), the young adults with their own responsibilities, and the elderly (*agba ile*). A former slave could fit into any of the categories within days after his arrival.

There were other mechanisms of integration within the traditional social structures. One was membership in age-grade associations, where they existed, as among the Ekiti and Ijesa.[36] Except when one had a serious criminal record, age-grade associations did not establish restrictive admission rules. Thus former slaves could possibly use such associations as entry points to the entire social network of a whole city. The other was through the social unit of friendship. Association through friendship was important, and it would be most unlikely that previous experience of slavery would be a factor in establishing friendships. Assuming it did not, friendship would be a rewarding source of extending network connections, tapping into small resources, obtaining advice, and even establishing roots in new areas.

Adjustments and integration were ultimately connected with social stratification. Former slaves had to operate within existing structures and cultural paradigms of success and failure. A major opening to former slaves was Western education, one of the best paths to attaining mobility in the first half of the twentieth century. We do know that a number of slaves went to school, because the recruitment strategies of missionaries favored members of the lower class. However, we do not have a way of knowing the long-term consequences of Western education on specific individuals.

The unsuccessful (not necessarily slaves) were identifiable among the Yoruba. Known as the *mekunnu* or *talaka*, they occupied the lowest rung of the ladder as commoners without money, power, or influence. The worldview of *ayanmo* (destiny) explained their fate, just as it explained that of the *olowo* (the rich) and the man of honor (*olola*). In cherishing wealth, the Yoruba saw it as the best form of control over people (children, wives, pawns, slaves, clients), so that the *olowo* and *olola* were regarded as ultimately superior. Wealth was to be reflected in behavior as one became an *enia pataki* who possessed the ability to display upper-class character and culture. The display had to be reciprocated by the *mekunnu* through hero worship. In turn, the wealthy man showed generosity while lavishing the rest of his money on consumption. Former slaves, irrespective of their location, had to respect the boundaries of social status. Thus the ultimate aspiration was not just to be free but also to move up the social ladder from *mekunnu* to *olola*, which was a difficult and long process.

Colonial and postcolonial economies created huge gaps in income and social status.[37] Those with Western education and skills earned respectable incomes. Laborers, rural farmers, and small-scale farmers earned small incomes. Thus former slaves connected with rural economies and with unskilled labor were likely to have remained poor. On the whole, sectoral imbalances in the economy marginalized those who depended on the land and who lived in rural areas. There was also a large number of urban poor working in the informal economies. Even those among the urban poor who worked for wages were poorly paid and their jobs were insecure.

The ability to build a large house (usually more than one) demonstrated success, as did spending lavishly on social events, acquiring titles, displaying generosity, and sending one's children to school. To the poor, life meant indebtedness to moneylenders. Poverty led to occasional outbursts of rural violence.[38] Perhaps a large number of former slaves became members of the urban poor and rural talents, in which case they would have sustained the tradition of resistance developed in years of slavery.

Connecting Slavery with the Present

The economic and political circumstances that produced slavery and related forms of servitude are no more. Modern banking has replaced a variety of credit institutions, even if such older forms as *esusu* (rotatory savings) remain at the community level. Modern Yoruba identity is no longer defined through distinctions between freeborn and slaves, pawns with limited freedom, and citizens without restrictions.

There are various connections between past slavery and the present. In the structures of indigenous power and institutions, those families with clearly established slave origins are excluded from royalty. In a number of places, the institutionalization of "royal families" in written documentation ensured that families created by slaves would be excluded. Where palace organizations were established and managed by slave officials of the past, as in cities such as Oyo, their lineages are still recognizable today.

Yoruba town histories and identities do show the connections of one place to another, as in the dynastic connections with older cities such as Ile-Ife. Pockets of people from Oyo exist among the Ekiti and Ijesa, as well as pockets of people from Ijesa and Ekiti in Ibadan, who have histories dating back to the nineteenth century. The praise names of individuals reveal the connections. An example from Ilesa states:

> Owaluse, your father is from Oyo
> Yours is not the wretched, pitiable looking Oyo man.
>
> He is the Oyo who wears the gorgeous dress
> Who gave birth to you.

This is the *oriki* of a prominent man of Ijesa origin but with historic connections to the citizens of the Oyo Empire. He was not peculiar in his origin; similar poems show connections to various cities. Such histories are now narrated in the framework of voluntary migrations and settlements. Evidence of slave origins, if any, has been elided.

If all have attained citizenship as Yoruba, what we deal with in contemporary identity is no longer markers of freedom and servitude but rather of social and political hierarchies associated with honor, privilege, and poverty. The old language of slavery has become the new language of poverty. The Yoruba have put behind them a history of slavery, and the memory of slavery is dim but now replaced with the reality of the poor. The gap widens between the rich and the poor and the politician and the ordinary citizen, who is often treated as a mere subject. So insensitive have the politicians become that a contemporary song, accompanied by dancing and drumming, summarizes it all:

> Ba mu ba mu layo
> Awa o mo pebi npa omo enikokan
> Ba mu ba mu layo.
>
> [We are fulfilled, with a full stomach
> We care not if others are hungry.]

Many are hungry in this land of plenty. Slave terminologies, dating back to the nineteenth century, remain in circulation to indicate poverty, exploitation of one person by another, human rights violations, and insults.

When the great Chief M. K. O. Abiola was denied the presidency of Nigeria, a denial that provoked a crisis that in turn generated conversations on identity, the Yoruba invoked the language of slavery to describe themselves and their ethnicity as one nation that had been thrown into a cage occupied by a ferocious lion, as a people enslaved by northerners. Abiola engaged in struggles that landed him in prison and ended with his death. A metaphor used to capture his efforts was that he was struggling against slave masters who tried to prevent his ascension to power and that of his race. Language is powerful, as reflected in the usage of the word "slavery," which will surely remain in our vocabulary even if the practices associated with enslavements of one individual by another have become history.

7

Orisa Music, Dance, and Modernity

Music and dance present both the public and private faces of African gods and goddesses. They create limitless opportunities to express emotions and aspirations in diverse settings and scattered locations. They have served as agencies of resistance and cultural nationalism during slavery, colonial domination, and thereafter in all places where the black experience has been shaped by domination, oppression, and exploitation. Orisa music and dance assault the entangling indignities brought on by commerce and mammon. In racialized contexts, most notably in the Americas and Europe, they add to how the boundaries of race are created and negotiated—indeed, they even create a moral order for blackness and for castigating oppression and those who participate in it. Through music and dance, Africans have been able to reinscribe their Africanness and identity in hostile, racialized environments, and women have particularly found a source of power to reinscribe their femininity in patriarchal spaces.

Whether in Africa, the Americas, or other places where Orisa traditions have spread, we have a deeply rooted ethnography that depicts the minds of black beings: recording and performing lived experiences, capturing the mental milieu in which they exist, and verbalizing the texts of their inner feelings. Renditions and performances expose the activities of human beings, the character of nature, and the relationships between human beings and the spiritual forces that shape their minds and actions. We use music and dance to publicize the confrontations within us, confrontations between us and others, and our ongoing dialogue with the universe.

We owe to the Orisa traditions the portrait of our emotions and thoughts, the coloration of words and actions with that which is authentic, located within African/black imaginative and cultural spaces. Orisa music and dance archive our collective experience on a wide number of subjects, including our orality, etymology, mythologies, order, sexuality, feminism, personal histories, as well as our luxuriant insights on local and global structure; our personal narratives on individuality and community; our social histories; and much more. Orisa dance and music affirm the intensity of our universe as communicated through our worldviews and metaphysics and within the milieu of our existential being and cosmos, revealing our inherited and reshaped ideas on a variety of subjects (divinities, destinies, sin, sacrifice, life, death, after life, and the like).[1] Music and dance elevate our insights, transforming our interior awareness to an open arena where the worldview merges with the landscape.

Orisa music and dance have become part of our collective global mimesis that reflects the richness of our imaginations in different locales; a reminder of the permanence of African worldviews, the achievements to broaden the definitions and uses of cosmogonies and cosmologies; the merger of histories with creativity; and the ability to maintain communities, define nationhood, and create alliances between globalization and hybridity without losing focus. Orisa music and dance have become pervasive and embedded in various other genres that are secularized. It is not possible to understand the artistic creations of such geniuses as King Sunny Ade and Fela Anikulapo-Kuti of Nigeria, Babatunde Olatunji (Yoruba drummer located in the United States), Mongo Santamaria and Art Blakey (Caribbean and New York), and various others without acknowledging what they owe to the Orisa traditions.

In unpacking these opening statements, I want to limit myself to four major themes. The first is how the origins of Orisa traditions themselves provide ideas for globalizing the Orisa and making them open to hybridization. Human beings, as instigators and agents of cultural change and retention, need ideas to work with. Orisa traditions have given us the template to maintain culture stability over time, but they have not inhibited our creative imaginations to generate new meanings out of ruptures. The second is how our imaginations have been globalized in multiple centers all over the world such that great distances from original and secondary centers have not created damage but rather affirmation and renewal. The third is how the legacies of Orisa traditions, along with the music and dance that they promote, remain part of our contemporary modernity in both sacred and secular forms. The fourth is how knowledge generation and reproduction

Figure 7.1. H. E. Oloye Aina Olomo at an Orisa celebration. Photograph courtesy of author.

in the academy must recognize the various constituencies and their contributions to a global collective heritage.

Isese's Mythography

The Orisa have a homeland, with a history about the origins of gods and goddesses, practices, music, and dance, all encompassed in a notion of *isese*, meaning a pristine moment when ideas and practices were created. The Yoruba geographic area in West Africa serves as the homeland, the place of birth. *Isese* encapsulates organic stories and practices but does not insist on rigidity. *Isese* provides a reference point but does not freeze actions, ideas, and time. *Isese* is not an obstacle to creativity, expansion, growth, voluntary initiation, or even revolutionary transformation. *Isese* must have anticipated modernity and transnationalism, as various elements in its mythography indicate. Space allows me to make only three general broad statements on *isese* mythography.

First, and the most commonly acknowledged characteristic of *isese*, is that the universe is composed of both the spiritual and physical, and the Orisa live in both. Their symbols can be seen, their stories can be heard, their essence can be imagined, and their power can be felt. Orisa music and dance reflect cosmologies in various layers. The realms of spirit and ancestors, representing the past, have their music and dance anchored to a set of clear beliefs. The ancestors are with us, representing our past and framing our identities. The future is here, represented in ideas, music, and dance with images of productivity and femininity. The metaphysical space of the ancestor and the unborn are united, and Orisa traditions unite the vision so effectively in performance and representation. We create music and dance to celebrate the ancestors, a belief in the afterlife, but we celebrate birth as well, a belief in the future. We are "humanized" by the gods and goddesses.

When we move to the clusters of gods and goddesses, that eternal realm that is pervasive and powerful, we see a dense ontological map, loudly articulated voices and performances that range from the mild to the ecstatic. Will Sango, the god of thunder, allow inaudible voices and snail steps? Drumming, songs, and dance steps reveal the various characters and idionsyncracies of each god and goddess, each ancestral spirit, which is why we speak of Ogun music as different from that of Obatala. Rhythms, songs, and dance movements by devotees of a specific god or goddess tell us about the theology of the Orisa. In a clear manner, performance and the divinities are united, as one tries to represent the other. Indeed, the function of songs and drumming are related to the nature of the god or goddess. Offerings to the gods and goddesses, which include feasting, are accompanied with songs and dancing.

Second, if each eternal voice has different requirements, tastes, and preferences, we see how *isese* has created a limitless zone of creative imagination. In honoring Ogun, to take the example of the god of creativity and one of the most popular gods, different localities can impose their stamp on forms and worship that may affect the composition and rendition of songs. A popular oral Ijala chant remarks on the ability to translate Ogun in multiple domains:

Ogun meje l'Ogun mi:
Ogun Alara ni gba aja;
Ogun Onire a gba agbo;
Ogun Ikola a gba gbin;

T'Elomona ni gba esun isu.
Ogun Akirin a gba iwo agbo;
Ogun gbena gbena eran ahun lo ma je.
Ogun Makinde to Ogun lehin odi
Bi oun ko gba Tapa, a gba Aboki
A gba Uku-uku, a gba Kemberi.

[There are seven Ogun who belong to me:
Ogun of Alara it is who takes the dog;
Ogun of Onire takes a ram;
Ogun of surgery cherishes the snail;
That of Elomona wants roasted yam.
Ogun of Akinrin desires the ram's horns;
Ogun of the artisans devours the flesh of tortoise.
Ogun of Makinde, located outside the city walls
Wants a human being: either a Tapa, or an Aboki
An Uku-uku, or a Kemberi.]

There are now more than seven designations for Ogun and more than seven offerings, as this god has become truly diasporic. Ogun, the god of creativity, embodies a limitless energy to create and destroy, to seek new meanings in life and move on after discovering an answer. One Ogun has mutated into seven, demanding sacrifices and songs with various versions. Ogun has mutated further and is now found in far-flung places outside of Ire, his temporary place of residence where he relishes palm wine, producing new names, songs, and performances in the Americas.[2] This mutation is by itself an engagement with modernity: In the restless spirit of Ogun, a world has no end. If a world has no end, tradition provides the relevance needed to create order as society reinvents itself to regenerate its tradition.

In defining the eternal forces in relation to unseen and seen forces, in relation to ourselves and the wide range of physical forces, we are compelled to undertake a host of musical and dance inventions, to keep expanding our notions of the ontology of the Orisa tradition. What others label as theater for entertainment, we see as rituals to affirm life.[3] Orisa costumes, music, dance, and dialogue speak to larger issues of healing, gratitude to the gods and goddesses, and requests for favor and prosperity. There are odes to great women and men, plants and animals, nature, and the like. There is even a genre of vulgar jokes. Orisa music and dance do serve ritual purposes—as worship and entertainment for a god or goddess—but they also serve to entertain people and, in the process, give them blessings. Thus songs and dance can take place during religious festivals, but they are also associated with death and funerals, marriage celebrations, name giving, and honors. Celebrations, although they appear as entertainment, are connected to the Orisa. Songs ask for abundance of everything that is good (health, children, money, and the like), for long life, happiness, and many other blessings. Praises to cities, big men and women, and chiefs and kings not only invoke the Orisa but may also borrow forms and content from Orisa songs and dance. For instance, royal poetry, using the genre of Ijala associated with Ogun, is adaptable to the praises of a king.[4]

Artistic creations empower music and dance. The Elegun Sango not only exhibits spirit possession but artistic hairstyles and dress. The priest wears colorful clothes. Dancers might wear masks that reflect the genius of wood carving. The masquerade, in mask and full regalia, displays various creative aspects in complex paraphernalia while the voices, sometimes in disguised tones, communicate multiple meanings. When the masquerade appears, there is singing, performance, and even elaborate poetry in praise of the masquerade and the ancestors. The drums are many, as each god demands his or her own family of drums: the Igbin drum for Obatala, Bata for Sango, Ogidan for Ogun, and Ipesi for Ifa. The gods and goddesses now allow the manipulation of the Dundun in various other regions as a complement or as a substitute. The great variety generated the rise of professionalism and specialization in singing and performance; performers have to learn through a process of apprenticeship and initiation. If Ogidan, Igbin, and Ipesi stand in an upright position and are barrel-shaped, the Bata and Dundun are carried from the shoulders, suspended by a strip attached to the drum. Shapes, timbre, and playing techniques are different, and some attempts have been made to use Western musical notes and techniques to understand them.[5] We should add that hand clapping, gourds (the *sekere* and *agbe* gourd-rattles), hand drums, and percussion instruments (the *eporo* made from bamboo sticks) are also utilized. Songs and drums have their histories, linked to events and gods and goddesses. For instance, the history of Bata is linked with that of Sango, who, according to a version of Oyo mythology, introduced the Bata to boost his prestige and frighten his opponents. Songs have many versions and dances are varied, as the Orisa make room for a host of differences and localization in dialects, languages, instrumentation, song tunes, dance presentation, and rhythm. The genres are many. Even within one genre, there are various forms and versions, while some are even gendered. For instance, there are male and female Ijala chanters who use different falsetto voices to praise Ogun, the god of iron.

The third and final point on the relevance of *isese* mythography is that there is a diasporic notion embedded in the story: Orisa spread within the Yoruba space and from there to other places. Views are diasporic, but historical events, notably the transatlantic slave trade, concretized the spread. The spread of people led to the spread of the Orisa, creating new genres in multiple centers that are linked to how religions and rituals have been adapted. As Orisa traditions spread to various parts of the world, they are domesticated and translated so that modernity reforms tradition, tradition reforms itself, and new hybrids emerge. The outcome is a dialectic capacity for a people to act upon themselves, upon their existential makeup, and upon their interactions with others. The creative focus in music and dance revives African social and religious phenomena and reflects various aspects of *isese*'s mythography. The diasporic adaptation and extension into postcolonial modernity are also clear to see. Creativity transcends Yoruba origins and cultivates productions and presentations of global relevance. As J. Lorand Matory has convincingly argued, the spread of the Orisa tradition revealed the power of tradition, the longevity of transnationalism as a global phenomenon, and the relevance of African ideas in several spaces and among diverse social classes.[6]

Many reconfigured elements in performance practices have emerged, all connected to the inventions of new modernities, the outcome of encounters of various peoples in various places, and the larger consequences of large-scale movements of peoples and ideas. Orisa music and dance are rich, containing emotional and human motions and actions drawn from diverse historical origins and experiences. The depth is unfathomable: it is a well whose waters cannot dry up, and millions of performers create compact renditions that portray millions of imaginations.

The diversity of imaginations leads us to a web of dense expressive thoughts and of holistic texts of self-fashioning and sensemaking. Orisa music and dance give black history a forceful potency and affirm the rather expansive imaginations of organic intellectuals and their skills at adaptation and creative versatility. The existential relevance of human beings is made manifest, as their universe is revealed even in moments of tension where imaginations create a conflict

Figure 7.2. Singing for the gods. Photograph courtesy of Ben Weiss.

Figure 7.3. Performance with Yoruba talking drums. Photograph courtesy of author.

Figure 7.4. Dancing to Yoruba drums and music. Photograph courtesy of author.

with humanity itself. If Orisa traditions gave birth to their music and dance, the music and dance have in turn extended the currency of the Orisa through vibrant renditions and performances that sustain the visibility of gods and goddesses. These renditions and performances also lubricate the engine that sustains the relevance of Orisa traditions in the public, secular arena. There, the engagement is less with religion and more with entertainment and the search for happiness and emotional stability. The search for happiness may be misguided or temporary, but the thirst for music and dance is hard to quench: Orisa traditions expand the scope and the creative ambient of the arts.

Creativity without Boundaries

The dispersal of Orisa traditions outside of Africa has multiplied its creative power. We are no longer dealing with that which is only Yoruba but rather with repackaged inventions and reforms in the context of new landscapes and culturescapes. The political structure that shaped the Orisa traditions and the belief systems in West Africa is different from the political system in the Americas, where the institutions of politics have their roots in Europe and were shaped in many ways by Native Americans.[7] Power was crucial in shaping the American economy and in promoting leisure and creative expressions. Thus, as to be expected, Anglo standards became the norm in many places and also imposed their stamp on various aspects of creative expression, including music and dance. Anglo influence also spread to Africa with the imposition of colonial rule. Christianity also spread, most notably during the twentieth century.

The impact of Anglo structures and worldviews in the Americas and in Africa, notably after the nineteenth century, have introduced both practical and theoretical notions of "Euroculturalism," that is, the aggressive influence (even the transplantation) of Western/ Eurocentric ideas on black culture in music, dance, drama, literature, and other art forms. Where the impact is obvious, we see the characterization of black responses as xenophobic. As black performers fight back, either to reclaim authenticity or for recognition of their contributions, they sometimes draw from Orisa traditions, and their activities and actions are often labelled "Afrocentric." Thus, in trying to capture the essence of the legacies of the Orisa in music, dance, and drama, we have seen the application of the contradictory theoretical tools of Eurocentric evolutionism or Afrocentric relativism.

African music and dance, sport, orality, and a host of other creative expressions created a space of influence. Orisa traditions filled some of these spaces, as religion and the appendages to express it revealed human nature in its complicated forms. Music and dance make statements on society and politics; performances reveal joy and tragedies, dramatic ironies, and even depressing soliloquies. Elements drawn from Africa become embedded in religious practices in various parts of the Americas. Premonitions and dreams, as well as signs from the ancestors, are represented in performance. Orisa songs show the ultimate power of supernatural forces. Songs can warn a community of the dangers ahead, lampoon bad leadership, and critique the social order. The extraordinary generosity of nature receives praise, the productivity of women is celebrated, and there is even a distinctive musical genre for twins.[8] They can warn witches and sorcerers or even threaten them to leave people alone. Composers can use animals, plants, and a host of natural objects to project positive or ominous outcomes, predict the future, or even announce impending chaos. Virtually all important occasions are accompanied by poetry and songs, an integration of oral literature into the daily reality of living.

Transculturation is inevitable. Orisa music and dance appropriated elements from host societies, as various examples in the Americas have shown in their aesthetics and forms. However, they also rejected many influences as well as created a logic of aesthetics and performance. Where we find cases of appropriation, it was done by amalgamating various traditions. Performances have undergone a nativization process in various places and examples, as in the case of Vodoun or Lukumi dance and music. Dance steps, some revealing elaborate plots and drama, can be eclectic in their combinations. The arena stage, with audience involvement, is the most common, revealing ancient African roots, but we also find evidence of transculturation in stage performances. Musical words, then and now, can be saddled with social commentary. Orisa songs could become politically charged, as we see in moments of political crisis in Africa.

The overall historical experience since the fifteenth century shows that the musical and dance genres of the Orisa have been reinvented to create new modernities and to adjust to the myriad impact of international forced and voluntary migrations. The process of reviving and reforming Orisa music and dance, well documented since the time of slavery, will not come to an end, at least not in our generation. Some elements of this process are now clearly understood. Ideas are transplanted from one area to another, as in the case of the *isese* to the New World. Ifa divination, for instance, spread, but not without modifications. William Bascom's book on the use of sixteen cowries for divination shows how the inherited Yoruba Ifa was simplified and allowed women to be involved as diviners in various locations.[9]

Within the New World, ideas about Orisa worship, like its spread, moved from one location to another. The transplanted ideas took root. As they took root, they underwent transformations. Some practices were discarded to give birth to new ones; as contexts changed, new meanings were created for older practices. New crops of leaders and interpreters emerged on the scene, creating new ethos, new language, new codes, even a new idiom. We also find situations where a combination of people, representing different ethnicities, created new packages, as in the coming together (but also in their disagreements) of people from Africa, the Caribbean, and North America to recreate various elements of the Orisa traditions in New York after the 1950s, which in turn led to fresh creativity in music and dance.

Even today, the traditions adapt to the currencies and language of globalization. On the latter, the Internet has been put to good use. The template of the Orisa traditions in the modern world is consistent in creating crosscultural correspondence between the Yoruba and their diaspora: intertextuality and philosophical ideas tend to use the *isese* mythography as foundational. Thus, we find the Oba in the Oyotunji village and the music and dance of kingship, a representation of the idea of monarchy.[10] Monarchy is translated in the Candomblé experience in the way power is vested in a Baba. The Yoruba Oba, which is an idea of the monarchy in the *isese*, invested enormous power in the person who was also linked to the spiritual forces as an Ekeji Orisa, that is, the deputy to the supreme deity. This royalty generated its own music and dance, which have been carried elsewhere to become the representation of power and leadership. Conflict is embedded in the notions of monarchy and patriarchy: power can generate competition to attain it and opposition to tame it. Violence, war, and conflict are managed by various gods such as Ogun and Esu, leading to extensive musical renditions and warlike dances. Reenactment ceremonies may capture the histories of state formation, territorial expansion, and intergroup wars. Today, we have war songs as part of the Orisa traditions that engage in prewar and war boasting, war drama, and mock violent encounters with the use of machetes, knives, and swords. The warrior ethos can be seen in dress and stern look, choreographed reenactments of conflicts among enemies, and their resolutions in ways that affirm the power of a specific Orisa. Evil forces have to be conquered, and conquered they are by the power of music and dance, some of loaded curses that turn evil into the image of an outcast, a leper, a bastard.

Divinations intertwine with songs and performances in praise of Orunmila (the god of divination) and even in unraveling the meanings of life. Musical chanting is an element of divination itself. Orunmila has its own codes and can be indexed via performance and poetry.[11] Divinatory codes can be communicated through music, and character songs that identify human behavior can be coded in dance. When divination communicates a piece of good news, it can be greeted with singing and dancing.

Figure 7.5. Osun Odunde. Members of Ile Olokun Sanya dance in celebration of Osun. (2003). Photograph courtesy of Omi Osun Joni L. Jones.

Contemporary Legacies

What can we learn from Orisa music and dance over time? A multitude of things. We have seen their connection to ethnicities and race. Orisa music strengthened the idea of the Yoruba race in the diaspora, so that we could point to Yoruba bata drums or Yoruba Sango dance. The music allowed for the creation of what can be labeled as "Yoruba fundamentalism." Since music also became connected with resistance and nationalism, Orisa music and dance became a way to fight racial oppression and discrimination. Western cultural imperialism means that music and dance have had to confront how creativity is measured with the so-called assumptions of universalism. Where music and dance have experienced severe persecution and attack, they have had to challenge the aggression of universalism and work out the mechanisms of survival. In doing so, Orisa music and dance exhibit the African worldview that has been shaped by insertion into

Figure 7.6. Members of Ile Olokun Sanya Awopeju and guests dance in the groves in honor of Ifa, 2004. Photograph courtesy of Omi Osun Joni L. Jones.

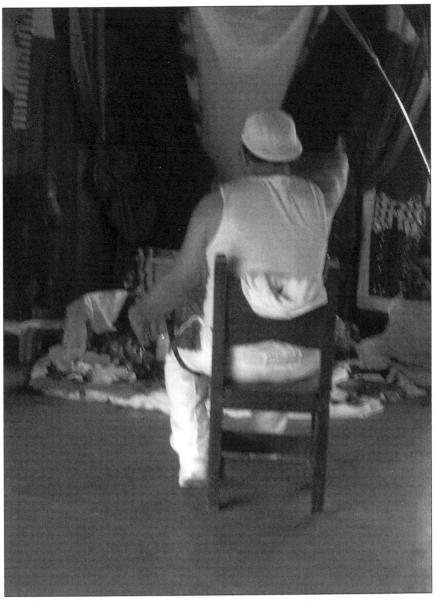

Figure 7.7. Master Drummer performs the traditional Anya service that acknowledges the sacredness of the drum at Bastrop State Park, 2005. Photograph courtesy of Omi Osun Joni L. Jones.

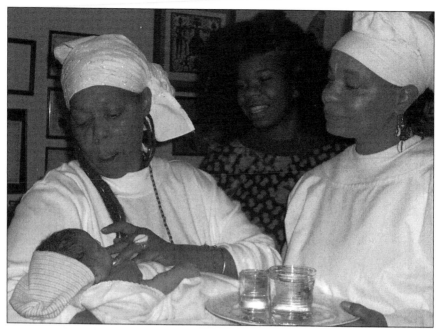

Figure 7.8. Oloye Ajidakin (*left*) presides over the naming ceremony for Omoniyi while his mother (Akilah, *center*) and Iya Yemi assist, 2004. Photograph courtesy of Omi Osun Joni L. Jones.

Figure 7.9. Led by Iya Olu, members of Ile Olokun Sanya Awopeju of Cedar Creek, Texas, process through the groves wearing blue and white of the ocean, playing instruments, and singing Olokun's praises, 2005. Photograph courtesy of Omi Osun Joni L. Jones.

Figure 7.10. Oriki. Baba Ojedele sings passionately for Sango, 2005.
Photograph courtesy of Omi Osun Joni L. Jones.

multiple geographical spaces and locations, and responses to historical and global processes since the fifteenth century. They project African realities in a focused manner, and their preoccupation with culture and histories is unambiguous. They are clearly grounded in an ethnographic consciousness that projects the ideas and vitality associated with the Orisa.

Orisa music and dance reveal the power of identity and nationalism. Indeed, some mechanisms have led to a ritualization that insists on the rigidity of steps and words so as not to lose identity and compromise nationalism. Yet, they are transcultural in nature as they borrow from other cultures. Western instruments can be used to express indigenous ideas. Performances, texts, and related dramatic effects do reveal a great deal of openness to innovations and ideas. Those who create them are not just cultural agents fixed in their ways, but they are also adaptive. Thus, on the African side, one cannot help but see the impact of Western forces, modern Western education, Islam, Christianity, and globalization. Even specificities in performance can encode the consequences of global interactions, as in the impact of the transatlantic slave trade.

Orisa music and dance have also reshaped the practices of Islam and Christianity in various ways. Thus common Christian choruses have, as their foundation, Orisa practices. The Yoruba *ijala* (hunters' songs)[12] have been used by Christians to formulate new praise songs. The traffic is not one-sided, revealing various cases of alterity. Orisa music and dance are receptive to new ideas, and we see how they have appropriated elements from other cultures and religious practices. In such appropriations, art cleverly reworks new elements into a template that is remarkably enduring. Where Islam and Christianity have benefited from borrowing, it has not prevented both from assaulting Orisa music and dance and condemning them as "paganism." Exchanges are well documented, showing an intertextual correspondence that deserves respect, especially by Christians and Muslims, who could acknowledge what they owe to Orisa music and dance. The dance steps and rhythms of Orisa music have been repackaged into popular forms, as in the song "Bahia" by Angélique Kidjo.

Through Orisa dance and music, we see the affirmation of history, the endurance of tradition, and the extensive archives of a people with a traumatized past. It may be a small performance given only here and there, but there is a cumulative impact. It is true that a localized context, an identifiable local milieu, may frame a song or dance, but it can feed larger communities beyond its boundaries, and it can transcend its local ambient. Such has been the power of the Orisa traditions to instigate imaginations that connect to the world. Imageries and metaphors can arise from specific locales, but they can be consumed on a global scale. Orisa music and dance have widened imaginary spaces far beyond their initial sources of creation. While Ogun was originally a Yoruba invention in Africa, it has been inserted into various other countries, extending its space and creating fresh autonomies in definition and practice that we find today. Ogun, like other Orisas, has been transformed. Ogun's music and dance are now delimited, as they have been reinvented, restructured, and repackaged to meet new needs and to respond to racial taxonomies.

That Orisa music and dance are connected with racial categories is not in dispute. However, we must note two important issues around this linkage. First, the very fact that production draws from racial or ethnic insights does not mean that it cannot be accessed by others, just as the Bible is now accessed independently of the racial category that gave birth to it. Human conditions that lead to production can be global, and reflections on such productions can equally be global. Second, the intellectual labeling of some practices as "local" and others as "universal" tends to undermine how the human experience produces content that combines what is local with what is universal. Tagging Orisa music and dance as "local" or "ethnic" without examining their contents and forms and what they have to say to the human experience is no more than a project of Western cultural imperialism. Western categorizations have "universalized" their own local experiences while parochializing those of others. In creating the canons, which are almost always Western, established practices with long histories such as Orisa music and dance are being projected as inferior, being forced to validate themselves, and being sanctioned for deviating from so-called canonical norms and forms. We, as scholars, should not contribute to these paralyzing efforts, which insist that our own traditions must be validated by others who have to discover us, create a provenance for us, and sell us as we pray to have a market value.

The linkage between slavery, music, and dance did not just end with abolition and emancipation. Orisa traditions and what define and sustain them have continued through today. Freedom and the transition to new inequities supplied the context since the mid-nineteenth century. Rather, the problem of what to do with freedom and how to negotiate the restrictive conditions of citizenship generated new adaptations, new responses, and new creative outbursts. The music listened to and the responses to it were shaped by questions about how to define life itself, how to relate to life, and what to do with life. Much more, how would blacks learn to express their identity to themselves and to nonblacks?

Yoruba are used to cultural renewal and cultural reaffirmation, which means that they are able to respond to new processes. New skills and international migrations have further inserted us into new societies, new markets, and new metropolitan spaces to create new forms of music and dance. A combination of new geospatial settings now define for us a "homeland heritage" that will continue to transform our individual and collective experiences, enabling new interpreters of Orisa traditions to create new autonomous spaces and genres.[13] In the contemporary world, we now have people drawing from different sources and heritages. Established identities now live side-by-side with newer ones created by migrants who are transnationalists. These migrants bring new experiences to and create new encounters with established practices. Located in various places, transnationalists offer new intellectual and practical formations that instigate new forms of creativity and hybridity, they connect the global with the local, and they exhibit the cosmopolitanism of living in different cultures and different spaces. The boundaries of aesthetics and textual arrangements are being redrawn, as new themes of migrations enlarge contents and as the Yoruba cultural universe becomes embedded in multiple locales.

Today, the various genres of modern music presented as secularized owe a lot to the Orisa traditions. Juju, apala, sakara, and fuji music[14] among the Yoruba borrow many ideas from the Orisa worldview, notably the concept of destiny, character, moderation, and the need to balance the good life with the fear of death. Sometimes, we see how direct they are, as in Sunny Ade's famous song in praise of Ogun. Some have used their voices to critique the privileging of Islam and Christianity over Orisa, as in several pro-Orisa songs of Fela Anikulapo-Kuti in which he lampoons the Imam, the pope, and the archbishop for contributing to the devastation of blackness. There are so many more examples, as in the case of Babatunde Olatunji, where the template of Orisa music and dance is reworked into a new presentation to appeal to contemporary taste. The words of Ifa have been secularized into the lyrics of popular music. A countless number of singers and dancers have enlivened a host of other musical genres (for example, jazz) by borrowing from Orisa philosophy, dance movements, vocabulary, and more. Sometimes so-called secular performances that people enjoy are derivative of Orisa choreography and cosmology. Countless contemporary movies, stage dramas, and music dramas from Nigeria draw extensively from Orisa traditions. If Duro Ladipo derived his fame as a playwright from Oba Koso's music dramas on Sango, so too does Wale Ogunyemi derive his fame as an author from *Obaluaye*,[15] a music drama based on the Yoruba god of smallpox (Sanponna). Many of our singers and performers are embedded in our culture[16] and participate in the selections of those indexes and metrics of experience that encode our histories, our imageries, even our judgments.

Orisa Traditions and Knowledge Articulation

Orisa traditions now constitute part of the body of knowledge that we research and teach in various disciplines, and they cut across the humanities and social sciences. The referential markers are distinguishable, giving us the content to create syllabi on multiple subjects and identities. Even the professor standing before a class—for example, as a Yoruba, Nigerian, immigrant, and spiritual—embodies subjectivity and reflexivity. Orisa traditions and their representations enable us to create a framework to study other traditions, to use our own social framework to understand others, and to further enrich ethnographies. This understanding is essential to broaden people's minds, to create a peaceful coexistence, to question the validity of canons, and to promote different forms of knowledge.

By fusing religious and cultural practices, manifested in music, dance, and various performance genres, the Orisa traditions open multiple windows to view the humanities and deconstruct knowledge. The grammar of existence of believers and the syntax of actions of those who subscribe to the worldview cannot be dismissed. Orisa music and dance, and the bodies and language that are used to express them, teach us about nations, hybridity, translocalism, and transnationalism. Whether in Miami or Bahia, the bodies that convey the spirit of the Orisa carry multiple histories and identities that reveal interconnected nations and communities. Orisa music and dance give us the evidence to create sustainable knowledge around an Afro-Atlantic World.

Orisa traditions have allowed us to undertake transnational and comparative projects by linking disciplines, interfacing multiple ideas, and working across continents and various regions of the world. Such notions as the diaspora and the Atlantic World are trans-border, transnational projects. Without the power of retention, the ability to rework tradition into new practices, such diasporic projects would not have been possible. We as scholars, in collaboration with contemporary immigrants, can serve as the interpreters of culture, even the arrowheads of cultural nationalism.

The global relevance of the Yoruba has been affirmed and its impact revealed in West Africa; North, Central, and South America; and the West Indies and Caribbean. Orisa music and dance have contributed enormously to this global outreach. Contemporary migrations have further expanded the relevance of the Yoruba in various countries in Europe and the United States. As scholars, our commitment should include advancing the project of globalizing the Yoruba language, which can then convey the Orisa traditions in their various genres. Music, dance, and other creative productions elevate the linguistic prominence of any language, which means that the Orisa traditions, if properly presented, can enhance the visibility of the Yoruba as a language, culture, and people. Orisa music and dance have enormous power to sustain interest in Yoruba cultural elements: We have seen, for example, how they have enriched the cultural repertoire of modern Brazilian society. This achievement can be further extended to other places and has the possibility to promote new forms of modern and transnational Africanisms. Orisa music and dance offer the opportunities to preserve language and culture, and to confront the hegemonic dominance of other languages and religions. Yoruba is a rich language, and what we do with it can further globalize the language and validate various cultural practices.

The cultural power that blacks have had over the years derives in part from maintaining elements of the Orisa traditions or from borrowing from them. Where such power exists today, it is possible because the people have been able to work out a successful resistance strategy against racism, cultural domination by other groups, and the influence of other religions.

As scholars, we can extend the interest and agenda of Orisa practitioners to the classrooms and textbooks. Our motive is to seek ways to create an upsurge in academic pursuits, bearing in mind their impact on communities outside the academy. No one can deny our ability to shape the production of knowledge and influence artistic production. Moreover, there is something for us, a promise that, through good deeds and purposeful contributions, we too can be transformed, as a stanza from Okànràanadàsàéé affirms:

Òrúnmilà wi èèyàn ni dòrìsà
Emi náà wì; èèyàn ni dòrìsà
Oní Ogun te ri n ni
Èèyàn ni nìgbà o gbón to ni Agbara
Ohun ni won fi nbo o
Oní Oòsála te ri n ni
Oni èèyàn ni
Nigbà ogbón to ni Agbara
Ohun ni won fi nbo o
Njé e . . . eni tó gbon ni won
nbo o èèyàn ni dòrìsà

[Orunmila said,
Human beings become Orisa
I said, human beings become Orisa.
He said don't you see Ogun
He was a human being when he was brave and wise
He became Orisa
He said, Don't you see Oosala,
He was a human being
When he was brave and wise
He became Orisa
They only worship those knowledgeable
It is the human being that become Orisa.][17]

Yet so few become Orisa—this is the daily challenge of divinity.

Let us become knowledgeable, hoping that we can become an Orisa and inspire an abundance of new creative music and dance. In closing this chapter, I want to borrow from the ancient template of the *isese* tradition that ends a discussion not with arguments or ambigous conclusions but with a definitive spritual command that the Orisa must receive and act on:

Irawo yin o ni womi
Irawo yin o ni wo'kun-kun
Enikan kii dowo bo ogo osupa
Beeni, a kii dowo bo ogo oorun

Enikeni ko ni le dowo bo ogo yin o
Ase, Ase, Ase.

[May your stars not become drowned
May your stars not be eclipsed
No one covers the glory of the moon
No one can cover the glory of the sun
No one will ever cover your glory
The command is sealed.]

Part 3

The New Diaspora

Transnationalism and Globalization

8

Western Education and
Transatlantic Connections

I want to start with an emerging set of data drawn from three valuable colleagues. The first is a Senegalese-born professor of computer science who teaches at Humboldt State University in a beautiful and heavily wooded part of California. Married to a Togolese woman of cosmopolitan background, their first language is the West African Fon, their second is French, and their third is English. They use Fon at home to structure family interactions and socialize their adorable children into their indigenous culture, they use French for correspondence with relations and friends in Africa, and they use English to earn a living in the West and to prepare their children for adult life. The couple started their education in the Republic of Benin, completed their graduate training in France, and moved to the United States for work.

The second is an American who specializes in the history of the American Northwest and who secured a Fulbright to teach at the University of Lagos in Nigeria. After a while he left, moving temporarily to South Africa before returning back home to the United States.

The third is a polyglot literary critic who started his education at Ile-Ife, Nigeria, where he received his first degree from the University of Ife in French and Portuguese, and later went on to the University of Wisconsin to earn his doctorate in Lusophone Africa. After teaching at Tulane and the University of Massachusetts at Amherst, he moved to the University of Texas at Austin where he is popularizing the study of Yoruba language, teaching Portuguese, and writing on Afro-Brazilians.

These scholars and many more like them represent the faces of education in its transnational essence, consisting of a history and containing a future hard to fathom. In exploring the topic of education, my idea is to cover aspects of interest to Africans and black people in general. In stressing the global dimension of this topic, a larger picture emerges at the intersection between education and transnationalism. Thus I will underscore a history of training students and of building schools and cultures across nations. These transnational connections raise various issues around

1. internationalism in education—in what we know, how we know it, how what we know shapes how we think, how knowledge is packaged, and how it reflects the interconnectedness of the world;
2. transnationalism in education as a force of globalization, creating powerful vehicles of dialogue, migrations, and limitless networks of ideas and relationships;
3. the politics of education and international education; and
4. the future of Africa and the world.

However, there is more to the above. Many black leaders have emerged, hundreds of ideas have been propounded, and many of them have been tested on various aspects of life and society. Linked to culture, economy, and politics, education has consistently been regarded as the key to success. Indeed, it is the cheapest investment for the benefits that accrue. It brings power and mobility, which begs the question: how and with what limitations?

It is surely unproductive to discuss what education can do for people, especially marginalized people and communities. However, I must point out that the values of education can be presented in a rather simple and naïve manner. People can be miseducated and we have abundant evidence to show this. A number of scholars who study the colonial education system in various parts of Africa have reached the depressing conclusion that there were multiple cases of miseducation, limited education, and content that did not necessarily reflect local traditions and the long-term needs of underdeveloped countries. In addition, there are various studies reaching the same conclusion with respect to the education of blacks in the United States during the nineteenth and twentieth centuries.

Also, people can be educated and marginalized at the same time. Education and oppression can go hand-in-hand. Thus, to discuss education, we have to talk about politics, emancipation, affirmative action, structured inequalities, rivalries, and competition for resources. Individuals receive education in the context of politics and the economy.

The Relevance of Education

The modern history of blacks can be summarized in one phrase: the struggles to liberate the race from exploitation and domination by other races and devastating economic systems. Whether in the United States or Africa, the struggles have focused on this same concern, and whether it was in the eighteenth or twenty-first century, the dominant issues have remained the same. Many leaders have emerged, hundreds of ideas have been propounded, and many of them have been tested. No idea has been as persistent as the need to use education to uplift the race. Linked to culture, economy, and politics, education has consistently been regarded as the key to success.

The results of education have always been a subject of debate. Where a black elite has emerged, which thinks like the race or class that once dominated it, debates have focused on the miseducation of blacks and the dangers posed by assimilation. Frantz Fanon became a famous scholar by exposing the ideologies of black assimilation and elitism. Where globalization is pervasive in its power and products, the education of blacks has been seen as a way to extend the market to the race, turning them into consumers who would enrich a few industrialists and capitalists. Where Christianity spread, sometimes along with commerce, as in various countries in Africa and Latin America, education is often regarded as the handmaiden of capitalism. The middle class that emerged out of it, Christian and educated, has cleverly used the opportunity for class consolidation and corruption. In spite of these troubles, no one has ever argued that education is not important or that fewer schools should be created. Rather, people want more schools and greater power to shape the curricula. In areas once under imperial control, blacks immediately used their new power to decolonize the syllabi and to place black issues at the core of the school curricula.

I have started with statements that sound like concluding remarks just to indicate one point: Blacks have historically been interested in education, even in conditions of segregation in the United States or under apartheid in South Africa. It is absolutely not true that blacks have a self-perception of inferiority or that they avoid schools or the challenges associated with learning. What is true is that those with power have rationed education to blacks on the basis of their own needs rather than the needs of blacks. The examples of missionaries in Africa and colonial educators wanting to limit black education to an elementary level are well-known. Similarly, one cannot deny the original pattern that emerged in the United States to prevent the education of blacks. When it was allowed, policies of segregated education took many years to dismantle.

As a historian, I want to demonstrate yet another point. The concern for education is not recent; it cannot be dated to the civil rights era in the United States or even to a so-called period when blacks became less fearful of a presumed belief in white superiority. The struggles of blacks have been long and bitter.[1] Education can be understood in the context of the struggles for racial emancipation. No one needs to be reminded that the oldest context for education was slavery and the transatlantic slave trade that created the black diaspora. In the United States, emancipation came with struggles and became part of the reason for the Civil War of the nineteenth century. Which appropriate strategy to take in a deeply divided society divided black leaders in the nineteenth century. Men like Martin Delany, Alexander Crummell, and Henry Garnet argued for emancipation and the emigration of blacks to Africa. According to these pioneer civil rights leaders, blacks should not hope for equality or dignity in the United States and should move to Africa or other places where they would be in a position to establish autonomy and implement educational and other policies for their liberation.

On the opposing side was yet another staunch abolitionist, Frederick Douglass, who maintained that blacks should stay in the United States, a country that was theirs, to struggle and uplift themselves. Like others, Douglass was opposed to slavery, but his civil rights advocacy did not see emigration as a solution. As if anticipating Martin Luther King Jr., he believed in forming alliances between blacks and whites to realize the goal of empowerment. Booker T.

Washington was a staunch supporter of education, adopting the strategy of accommodation.

Delany and Douglass did not live long enough to see the outcome of their protests: the end to legal segregation in the South. Winning the franchise came later, and it was regarded by many as the ultimate achievement of the civil rights movement. Using the power of education, blacks succeeded in moving into the middle class during the twentieth century. For those who need to be reminded, the struggles to attain education preceded the first law relating to affirmative action. Even when it was illegal to do so, many black parents taught their children to read and write. Whether in Africa or the United States, many people overcame the barriers to educate themselves. The opportunities were few, and the doors of success and mobility were closed by hegemonic powers and races, but many blacks were able to force the door open and to use education to challenge a caste system that had been set up to destroy them.

Entering the twentieth century, the tensions between emigrationists and antiemigrationists remained. The radical Marcus Garvey was for black empowerment based on the promotion of business, education, and the development of Africa. Garvey and some of his successors also argued that the content of education must contain moral instruction and a strong attitude of self-help. Highly talented and educated, W. E. B. Du Bois stood for revolutionary changes in education. Irrespective of the ideologies they espoused or the strategies to which they were committed, all the black leaders of the twentieth century were opposed to racism and injustice, and they wanted a new society to be defined along equal lines.

Rising radicalism also worked tirelessly to demand positive changes in laws to ensure access to education. In fighting for the civil rights and equality that they had long been denied, black leaders became better organized in mobilizing protests and taking their case to the appropriate places. Political support, by way of backing candidates for elections, yielded some rewards. The use of the judicial system and legal interpretations brought their successes as well. The political leaders in power, sensing the changing climate, made executive decisions to initiate some changes.

Black leadership has expanded in recent times, including persons associated with the various civil rights organizations, university activists, labor union leaders, and the congressional black caucus. Current leaders link education and black empowerment with white racism, which regards blacks as inferiors. They advocate equality, fair practices, and respect for civil rights. Throughout the twentieth century, black leaders have successfully forced the society to change old laws and use executive power to correct the problems of segregation and promote equality. Those who presented their case in *Brown v. Board of Education* highlighted the place of education in ways that even people divided by ideologies have come to accept:

> Education is perhaps the most important function of state and local governments. Compulsory school attendance laws and the great expenditure for education both demonstrate our recognition of the importance of education to our democratic society. It is required in the performance of our most basic public responsibilities, even service in the armed forces. It is the very foundation of good citizenship. Today it is a principal instrument in awakening the child to cultural values, in preparing him for later professional training, and in helping him to adjust normally to his environment. In these days it is doubtful that any child may reasonably be expected to succeed in life if he is denied the opportunity of an education.[2]

Initiating changes, building public opinion to initiate change, or just capitalizing on law, Thurgood Marshall was an effective legal advocate while Martin Luther King Jr. focused on social aspects. The above-quoted statement on education has relevance to what these and other leaders said, and they merely sought its implementation.

The opinions of black leaders can be lumped into two categories, both of which are hard to integrate, although the aspirations that lead to disagreements are often similar. On the one hand are those who believe in a philosophy of assimilation. On the other hand are the nationalists (also separatists) who advocate more radical ideas. Both positions are aimed at dealing with the issues of education and inequality and oppression. In expressing their strong positions, there are elements who think that it is possible to pursue the republican ideals of a just society, and those who think that oppression will be hard to overcome. Black leaders and the movements they have created respond to two contradictory impulses of working either with the possibility that American positive ideals can be pursued or that the country is so venal that daily struggles are inevitable.[3]

My third point is about the value of education. It is misleading to say that groups and individuals do not know or appreciate the value of education. Many negative comments have been made on black values relating to education and the family, many of which are divorced from the context and the social structures of society. When we review the history of education and race relations, we cannot but celebrate the achievements of blacks at various historical eras. Many Africans who obtained higher degrees before the 1930s lacked support and struggled on their own. In the United States, a review of the history of people such as Delany during slavery must praise the efforts of his mother to educate him though it meant running afoul of the law. The generation after Delany lived under the Jim Crow laws in the American South, which relegated blacks to the lowest rungs of the ladder. Those who struggled to attend schools generated a long list of frustrations that many scholars have cataloged. To quote one example from the East Baton Rouge Parish school district in Lousiana:

Oath of all white Teachers and Principals

All white high schools will write up as many suspensions on Negroes as they occur, small or large.

All white high schools will bring about the suspensions of 25 Negroes who are supposed to graduate (15 boys and 10 girls).

All white high schools will send Negroes home for any little thing they do so that we may have on record their lack of interest in school.

Nigger is not a bad word to call Negroes, so use the name at will.

Be aware that all maids and yard boys will do as we tell them because in their eye-sight white is still the best thing they have ever seen.

All white school board members are with us (except one).

K.K.K. are doing a thing too, so together we will have Niggers in a turmoil.

Junior high is the area where we get Niggers prepared for 12th and 14th grades.

This paper is not to get in the hands of any negro mothers (don't worry about the fathers, they don't show up for nothing) or Negro children.

> The good we are doing for the reading of this nature should be read and burned up before it gets in the hands of your maids or yard boys.
> Reappointment of the School Board (one man one vote to a single member district vote went like white supremacy is supposed to go?).
> Anyway, we feel that Negroes are getting more education now than they will ever use.
> Our goal is to average 240 Negroes suspended per month to aid drop out inferior education.[4]

Whoever endured such a system deserves praise. It should be added that this was part of Jim Crow culture. Permanently subordinated, blacks were forced to obey segregationist laws in public places and prevented from realizing their potential. Then and after, a large number struggled to receive education.[5]

It is fair to say that most human beings understand the role of the family, at the minimum as an institution to reproduce and protect its members. The real problem that the majority of black families has faced has been the inadequacies of wealth and cultural capital to bequeath to the next generation. The ancestors of the present generation came as slaves without luggage; the majority that followed lacked land and capital to invest. For many years thereafter, the characterization of blacks as inferior prevented the rise of a large number into prestigious occupations. The inheritance and ascribed status that a child carries at birth can serve as strong factors in succeeding in a competitive society. As the Yoruba say, the son of a cow is bigger than that of a goat from the very first day of birth, and if both sons grow in the same climate and milieu, one does not have to guess the future consequences by way of opportunities and energies. Biological genes can be complicated by the "genes" of family wealth and inheritance.

Realizing the difficulty of using the family to build a network to parachute them to influence and power, the majority of blacks all over the world have looked to education as the main vehicle. The poor who struggle to become professors and doctors have used the power of education to leverage and to overcome the circumstances and limitations of birth. Even in the best of circumstances, everyone cannot become a member of the higher professions or be mobile enough to become part of the small elite, but most realize that through education they can at least uplift themselves and have access to important services and desirable goods. A modern society like the United States has contributed to the belief in the value of education as the primary means to enhance the mobility of the individual in a meritocratic society. Despite the avowed claims about the importance of education, the dilemma is that a capitalist society requires a large number of people to exploit. The dreams of black families for an education may be negated by the logic of the market and globalization.

Hegemonic Power and Education

If blacks have struggled over the years and if their long history of problems was not caused by God, as some say in frustration, how then do we understand a system that has marginalized them? To understand blacks, one has to go elsewhere: to discover how a capitalist system based on race has constructed privileges for the race in power. White privilege has historically been constructed on a notion of black inferiority. Whether in colonial Africa, apartheid South Africa, or the United States, the evidence is abundant to show that white privilege was constructed on an ideology of racial superiority for the purpose of obtaining maximum advantages in virtually all sectors: in the laws and institutions that empower them, in the use of force to sustain those laws and institutions, and in the control of power by vested interest groups. The use of power to maintain class and racial privileges runs through the history of the United States, though with significant changes since the second half of the twentieth century.

During slavery, power relations were clear-cut and the roles assigned to blacks did not require education. Thereafter, and for a long time, the white race used its power to maintain the structure of dominance by means of a firm control on the economic system and lucrative occupations. Stratification carries forward to recent history, and it manifests itself in income differentials, control of power, ownership of businesses, and entries into major occupations. Many blacks realized that education could open up the economic and power arenas, but they had to struggle for access and overcome the stigma of inferiority. A stratified society is cost effective: The inferior group accepts poorly paid and low-status jobs, and the superior group the lucrative positions, creating a social order in the process. As the poor struggle to overcome, the superior uses power to consolidate its privileges. It is not unusual for a group in power to resist changes that threaten its privileges.

The pursuit of self-interest by those in power may bring its own positive outcome to the marginalized. Many Africans went to school because the missionaries, committed to spreading Christianity, sent them to school in order for them to read the Bible. Once they were able to read and write, Africans redefined their interest more broadly, moving beyond the initial goals of the missionaries' rudimentary, limited education. In the United States, the demands of capitalism have resulted in the spread of some opportunities to migrants and the poor. One of the most significant phases in the emergence of a black middle class was in the 1940s, during the Second World War. Many jobs opened up in the military and defense sector, some of which necessitated the recruitment of blacks. A. Philip Randolph seized the moment to pressure President Franklin Roosevelt to open access to jobs to more blacks, leading to Executive Order 8802, which forced industries that secured government contracts not to discriminate on the basis of race or national origin. As the army discharged men and women, the need to reeducate a large number of veterans opened up opportunities for blacks to go to college. The "G.I. Bill of Rights," the popular name by which the Servicemen's Readjustment Act of 1944 came to be known, not only made loans available to veterans who wanted to buy houses but also offered a free college education in addition to job training.

The G.I. Bill of Rights was one of the biggest boons to blacks, considering the unintended consequences that followed. In northern states, white colleges opened their doors, since they could take educational vouchers from anyone, irrespective of race. Some level of race integration began to occur. Black colleges, taking advantage of the opportunity to receive vouchers, expanded quickly. With funding and college admissions, many blacks experienced their first major opportunity for higher education. Many were able to go to school. Even those who were ill-prepared benefited from remedial courses offered by various colleges for blacks and whites alike.

The next major change was associated with the aftermath of *Brown v. Board of Education* (1954), which had effectively challenged the doctrine of "separate but equal," thus bringing about integration in elementary and secondary schools. Colleges and universities also responded. Among the notable changes after 1954 were the establishment of special education, bilingual education, employment opportunities for minorities, access by blacks to higher education, more attention to talented and gifted children, and the education of women.

Empowering Black Studies

Those in power control the school curricula. Students in colonial Africa had to learn European rather than African history. Colonized subjects were usually exposed to knowledge and ideas that would minimize their resentment of racism and legitimize authoritarian power. For a long time, the school system and other educational institutions socialized blacks into a world of inferiority.

One of the remarkable advances of the increasing education of blacks has been the "decolonization" of the syllabus and the validation of studying black issues. The study of black experience has grown rapidly and has acquired tremendous respect in a number of places. The process of acquiring respect has been long and full of struggle. Before the 1960s, before currently recognized curricula were yet to emerge, the exploration of the black experience was pursued by a long list of intellectuals, including black scholars like George Washington Williams, Carter G. Woodson, W. E. B. Du Bois, Anna Julia Cooper, Arthur A. Schomburg, E. Franklin Frazier, Harold Cruse, John Henrik Clarke, and John Hope Franklin, as well as white scholars, notably Melville Herskovits, Herbert J. Aptheker, and Robert E. Park. The works of a number of successive scholars such as Nathan Hare, Martin Kilson, John Blassingame, Nick Aaron Ford, Charles V. Hamilton, Ron (Maulana) Karenga, Jimmy Garrett, and St. Clair Drake moved black studies into the curricula of white universities. Between 1900 and 1930, Du Bois pioneered a series to reconstruct black history, Schomburg and Woodson began projects on history, and Woodson established the *Journal of Negro History*.[6]

A number of schools began to teach black studies after 1930, although the most rapid and prolific expansion came after 1965, following the civil rights and black power movements. As more black students entered college, they demanded courses about their peoples and history. Great debates ensued, relating to making black studies more relevant and applying various theories. A major study that reviewed the scholarship until the early 1980s underscored the needs that led to black studies, namely, the search for identity, political pressure, and the need for academic relevance.[7] Various courses cover aspects of history, culture, and society, and the skills necessary to cope with modernity.

In its radical manifestation, black studies can be presented as Afrocentric and regarded as a challenge to mainstream scholarship. It is interdisciplinary, connects the academy with the public, and promotes the ideology of self-knowledge and social action.[8] This and some other related expressions argue that scholarship must not only attack existing views and present alternatives, but it must also be useful. Black studies has given voice to black positions, offered alternative views on many issues, and radicalized the demand for access to education at all levels. Among the issues that have been addressed with rich data and profound insights include those relating to the history of injustice against blacks, black resistance, black nationalist thought, and strategies to improve the present and future conditions of all minorities. According to James Stewart, the contributions of black studies have been the

1. destruction of the myth of the passive acceptance of subjugation by blacks; peoples of African descent have always attempted to shape their own destinies;
2. documentation of the critical role of collective self-help in laying the foundations for black progress;
3. restoration of the record of ancient and modern civilizations of blacks in developing high technology and establishing early civilizations in North and South America;
4. exploration of the contemporary implications of psychic duality, building on Du Bois's classic formulation of the concept of Afrocentricity as a guiding principle; and
5. explication of the critical role played by black women in shaping the black experience.[9]

The pressure is still on to make black studies more relevant and practically oriented. Activists argue that students and their teachers should always be concerned with providing solutions that affect blacks and encourage political movements fighting for positive changes.

The Politics of Affirmative Action

It is no longer a matter of choice to discuss affirmative action in higher education. Many are likely to argue not only that the struggles over access to higher education have been intense but also that the resolution of issues around equality have affected other tiers. The dismantling of the segregated system of higher education has involved the use of affirmative action. *Brown v. Board of Education* and various legal cases, including the *Hopwood* case at the University of Texas at Austin, have failed to resolve the controversies over admissions to higher institutions. Criteria and policies have been contested. Those who use the law to back affirmative action point to the Fifth, Thirteenth, and Fourteenth amendments and the Civil Rights Act of 1964. The Higher Education Act prohibits discrimination on the base of race, sex, and national origin in all educational activities and programs funded by the federal government.

Established privileges have clashed with public interests, and the judiciary has been brought in to resolve race issues. Affirmative action has been attacked as a quota system that rewards minorities at the expense of whites.[10] Those denied admissions have gone to court; notable cases include those directed against the University of Washington Law School, the University of Texas at Austin Law School, the Board of Regents of the University of California, and, more recently, the University of Michigan. The argument has been that affirmative action violates the individual rights of others.

One reason for the uproar over affirmative action is that the concept has never been clearly defined or articulated. One thing is clear: each time there is a national debate about it, the wounds of racism are reopened. Indeed, various scholars have argued that the root motive of affirmative action was not to seek race equality but rather to create divisions. For example, in a widely quoted study, Andrew Hacker summarized the politics behind affirmative action in its early years:

> The first coherent affirmative action measure was Nixon's "Philadelphia Plan" of 1969, which required federal contractors to show that they were hiring blacks. The plan arose from mixed motives. The Republicans needed to make some response to the rioting of the 1960s, and jobs were clearly an issue. But Nixon, who won the 1968 election by less than one percentage point, was also looking for a long-term strategy to undercut the Democrats. Affirmative action was useful to him ... since it "placed on the table something to help African-Americans at the expense of unions, producing discontent and factional rivalry in two of the liberal establishment's major supporters," Nixon gambled that white workers would direct their anger at those

taking "their" jobs, and overlook those who had put the plan in place. The strategy paid off in 1972 and he won reelection by a large majority, including white blue-collar voters who would later be dubbed "Reagan Democrats." A quarter of a century later, Republicans are still betting that affirmative action will stir racial resentments in their favor.[11]

Some would apply Hacker's conclusion to the policy of the Republican Party under George Bush, that is, a strategy of using affirmative action to mobilize white hostility against blacks. The Bush administration's 2003 amicus brief used affirmative action to consolidate its conservative base. Politicians have cleverly manipulated affirmative action for votes, especially among white male voters in the South. The courts have issued only contradictory judgments, case-by-case adjudications that have confused issues. If in the past the courts had contributed to the promotion of equal opportunity, as in the *Brown* case, they can also work in the opposite direction to create barriers. Affirmative action is yet to receive wide legislative support and approval, and its implementation has been subject to the whims and caprices of those in power. In 1996, *Texas v. Hopwood* dealt a severe blow to affirmative action. The case challenged the use of race in admission policies, blaming affirmative action for halting the progress of whites who were more qualified than blacks. A 2003 *Newsweek* poll estimated that as much as 73 percent of the white population opposes affirmative action.[12]

Conservative forces have cleverly moved public opinion against affirmative action. There have been occasions when the Republican Party in power (as in the case of the Reagan-Bush years) actually drafted executive orders to abolish it, but withheld the announcement and passage of the order because of early leakage to the press. If the spirit of the intent of affirmative action is to redress age-old inequality, astute politicians opposed to it have turned opinions around, making whites the victims of the system.

Balancing the interests of those who use established privileges to seek upward mobility with those who are part of neglected communities pursuing aspirations of equality and empowerment are some of the key issues around the politics of affirmative action. Admission preferences are not popular, even among blacks who point to other criteria (such as legacies) that have been used against them. However, affirmative action, defined as increasing the enrollment of minorities in colleges, is popular among minorities. Blacks opposed to affirmative action base their arguments on the need to reward hard work and individual talent; they believe that being victims of past injustice is not sufficient reason to use quotas for an indefinite period, and that middle- and upper-class blacks have no claim to special preference at the expense of poorer black people.

What about diversity, celebrated as desirable even by conservatives, in the attack on affirmative action? A modern and successful university must be comprised of students from various backgrounds, defined by class, race, ethnicity, and nationality. Students coming from segregated cities and high schools receive their first experience of interracial interactions on college campuses. An end to affirmative action will hurt not only blacks but also other minorities, white women, immigrants, and the disabled.

Structured Inequality and the Future

Today, various contradictions surround the issue of black education; evidence of both success and failure exists. Let us start with some cases of success. First, millions of blacks have become part of the social, political, and economic mainstreams of their countries. In Africa, majority governments have been in power since the middle of the twentieth century, although their control of power has been constrained by the politics of the Cold War and globalization. Power has brought with it prestige. In many other countries, black faces in power no longer seem strange. Similarly, it has become normal to see black faces everywhere—again one of the achievements of education and political struggles. Superstar black intellectuals have emerged, even in the most respected white colleges, and there are many black students and faculty in most colleges of the world. Thus the evidence is clear that opportunities have been created for equality and education.

Second, the school system has massively expanded in all countries with black populations. In addition, most countries no longer have segregated education laws in place. In the United States, the older laws based on a philosophy of "separate but equal" have given way to integrationist laws, as in *Brown*. One can point to the impressive performance by historically black colleges and universities (HBCUs), some of which have witnessed expansion as many more blacks pursue quality higher education or simply want to avoid some of the hostility associated with white colleges. In public schools, parents and communities cooperate to improve school conditions. An increasing number of black suburban families pay serious attention to the education of their children, and many send their children to private schools. Publically and socially conscious urbanites and suburbanites cooperate with city councils to bring about change in schools and embark on scholarship programs.

In spite of these achievements, many problems remain. In the case of Africa, it is clear that educational changes have not translated into widespread economic development and political stability. In the United States, the problems are equally abundant. There is a consensus on the worsening social conditions of blacks in the inner cities, the devastation of housing projects, and the poor quality of schools. The large numbers of youth without education has, in part, contributed to rising violence, drug use, teenage pregnancy, and other problems. There is data to conclude that a large number of blacks believe that a caste system still exists, which keeps them down and denies them educational opportunities and sources of mobility. If a number of HBCUs are doing well, there are many others devastated by declining resources and declining enrollments. While blacks are found in white colleges, many have reported experiencing hostile environments, including racially motivated brawls, ghetto themes, insulting graffiti, and other incidents to suggest that they are not wanted.[13]

When we turn to urban public schools, the results are disappointing. No law supports segregation, but in practice elements of segregation remain. Various lawsuits, debates over voucher programs, and widespread discussions on the decline of public education reflect the lingering problems of segregation. Without question, the long-held view of white superiority is yet to be completely vanquished. *The Bell Curve*, the much-publicized 1994 book by Richard Herrnstein and Charles Murray, confirms racial perceptions of white superiority.[14] The use of standardized tests, some based on cultural preferences, has become an indicator of intelligence. No amount of evidence of the success of blacks can erode the agenda of the ideology of superiority.[15] On the one hand, it seeks to hang onto established privileges. On the other hand, it argues against integration in schools and cities. A number of cities have segregated schools. There is even a disturbing trend in some parts of the South to have segregated classes in integrated schools, putting white students in college preparatory classes with better facilities and teachers and black students in remedial classes.

After 1970 a number of cities witnessed the massive relocation of whites from the inner cities to the suburbs, in part to escape racial minorities and school integration. As blacks attained legal victories to end school and neighborhood segregation, some whites cleverly resorted to relocation, moving not only their valuable assets and wealth but also tax bases. As municipal tax revenues diminished, the quality of schools and neighborhoods declined. Middle-class blacks followed, creating "slurbs"—all-black areas—or they simply moved to predominately white suburbs.

Data reveal that established privileges favor the race in power. Even when segregationist laws have been ended or a caste system dismantled, established privileges can be retained for many years. Political opponents of change are not defeated overnight, and the politics of segregationists could resurface at any time. Those who criticize others of ineptitude and laziness forget the power of custom and tradition in the service of maintaining their own unearned privileges, the conventions associated with the status quo that often stand in the way of needed reform and revolution, and the incremental accumulation of assets and knowledge that can be manipulated for greater success. Blacks constitute a minority with limited power who lack the judicial and political power to shape society in the ways they want, particularly to use education for equality.[16]

The politics of race affects access to education. Laws and regulations no longer exist to prevent any university from hiring black faculty or recruiting black students, an achievement that took a long time to attain. Nevertheless, race remains a factor and a context that shapes recruitment. So-called race bashers hide under extreme conservatism to attack blacks, such as the most publicized works by Dinesh D'Souza.[17] In spite of programs to promote diversity, one cannot help but note the segregationist tendencies on many campuses. In some classrooms, students may even choose where they sit on the basis of race.

As much as people might deny it, race affects education as a privilege to secure mobility and opportunities. If one race can define itself as superior and human, and others as inferior and subhuman, inequality is already built into the system. The histories of the United States, colonial Africa, and South Africa confirm the linkage between race and education. In South Africa apartheid was a system of racism fully committed to promote injustice and oppression. Colonial Africa rationed education, and some countries like the Belgian Congo had only a handful of African college graduates by the 1960s. In the

United States, the entire period of slavery was based on the maximum exploitation of labor. When slavery ended, followed by emancipation and then Jim Crow, the laws were clearly constructed to deny blacks access to education.

Even after the legal abolition of segregation, there still remained many instances of discrimination. The problems of elementary and public education that I have mentioned reflect racial divisions in the cities. There is as yet no end to discrimination in employment. Those who violate the laws in schools and private companies are not always punished, and there are many people willing to circumvent *Brown*. Political parties struggle to appoint judges who will interpret the laws in their favor, thus using the court system in pursuit of political ideologies and to consolidate established racial prejudices.

Politicians manipulate the politics of race and education for party and personal agendas. Even when no one advocates racial quotas, demand for educational equality can be presented as another way to demonize race. To many politicians, democracy can be easily reconciled with black inequality. Blacks can be treated as exceptional, that is, as a race different from others because of their limited intelligence. To a number of politicians, "good blacks" can be assimilated through education, since politicians claim it socializes them to democratic ideals, principles of capitalism, and the cultural values of the market. It also creates an avenue for social mobility. If the assimilated can enjoy parts of the culture of the nation, the rest can be segregated in a ghetto, separated from others by poverty and prevented by the police from causing havoc.

The overall economic ideology as well as the distribution of power have always affected access to education. Not a few have argued in tandem with Beverly J. Anderson that "inequality is necessary to motivate those at the bottom to strive to improve their lot. Inequality serves to make available the necessary cheap labor for menial jobs. Furthermore, some work requires long and difficult training, and to motivate the most talented to undergo such preparation, they have to be able to look forward to being differentially rewarded."[18]

Africa and America: Diasporic Bridges

Let me close by returning to one of the early agendas of pioneer black intellectuals. Scholars such as Delany, Garvey, and Du Bois were

Figure 8.1. Participants from Africa at the annual conference on Africa, the University of Texas at Austin, 2012. Photograph courtesy of author.

Figure 8.2. Main entrance, Lead City University, Ibadan, Nigeria. Photograph courtesy of author.

Figure 8.3. Main entrance, University of Ibadan, Nigeria. Photograph courtesy of author, 1996.

Figure 8.4. With Professor Isaac F. Adewole, the president of the University of Ibadan, Nigeria (*third from right*). Photograph courtesy of author.

able to think in terms of Pan-Africanism, or the unity of all black people. They factored education and liberation into their Pan-Africanist consciousness, a theme that African leaders such as Kwame Nkrumah and Nelson Mandela also adopted. The developments in Africa and the United States regarding education and the fight against white supremacy were so close that ideologies and leadership looked very much alike.[19] We need to sustain this Pan-Africanist consciousness. Africans need to know more about African American history and issues, and vice versa. Increasingly, Americans are beginning to appreciate the fact that African history is dynamic and unfolding, far different from the static history that many learn from outdated encyclopedias. As Du Bois and others clearly demonstrated, Africa has always played an important role in the popular consciousness, identity formation, and visions of African Americans.[20]

The desire to contribute to the development and education of Africans has always been intense among a number of African Americans. African American churches have contributed their share to the development of education in Africa, while many Africans have attended HBCUs in the United States. The development of education has been successful, as witness the keen competition among young Africans to enter colleges in America. African Americans may learn from the African experience in the way that youth on the continent compete for scarce resources and limited college spaces.

Today, the links between African and African American education continue. We are now witnessing a new African diaspora, consisting of migrants to the United States in the last twenty-five years. Not only will recent migrants affect African American or black culture in the United States, as in cuisine, attire, and music, but there is also a greater likelihood that students might study African history with an African scholar. African migrants, too, will study with African Americans and regard black leaders as heroes. All black people are now connected in a so-called global world, one dominated by popular culture and market forces. Many blacks know who Michael Jackson and Michael Jordan are. In fighting the excesses of globalization, diasporic connections are necessary, and the response to such issues as AIDS, reparations, and cultural imperialism requires cooperative efforts. Whether in Africa or the United States, many continue to search for leaders of the caliber of King and Du Bois who will combine the power of education with vision to liberate their people.[21]

As we work together in a new century, we should cooperate to make education one of the instruments to attain equality. To deny any individual or group access to education is to prevent the emergence of a system based on equal opportunity. We should not simply regard education as a passport to stability and (upper) middle-class success, but we should also see it as the weapon to liberate the individual and group.

9

Africa in the Diaspora
and the Diaspora in Africa

Toward an Integrated Body of Knowledge

This chapter intends to complicate the motivations for writing about the African diaspora in order to suggest ways to integrate African and African diasporic histories and communities. Two bodies of knowledge that are treated as distinct and separate will be connected on the basis of themes around the notion of a diaspora connected with Africa. Some scholars regard the study of the African diaspora as a political project, an attempt to use knowledge for the purpose of uniting Africa with the black people scattered in Asia, Europe, and the Americas. From this perspective, the dominant issues relate to the marginalization of black people and the need to overcome it; Marcus Garvey and Kwame Nkrumah fall into this category.[1] To these two and others, Africa has a relevance to the African diaspora, and the African diaspora has a relevance to Africa. They are twins, and knowledge about them can be integrated to achieve political purposes such as dismantling the colonial powers in Africa and attaining racial equality in the Americas.

Some intellectuals look at this subject strictly from an academic point of view. To this category of scholars, teaching diaspora history is similar to teaching world history, with the underlying assumption that Western civilization should not be the only or dominant point of interest. Among this second category are those who believe that an insertion of Africa and the slave trade into the long narrative of world history is enough, a sort of intellectual tokenism. Without being dismissive of this approach, it can be argued that diaspora history should not be equated with world history and world history should not be limited to teaching about the diaspora.

I will combine the aforementioned approaches and suggest additional ways to bring together various issues and themes to connect Africa with its diaspora in the production of knowledge. An integration will suggest that what we characterize as a diaspora cannot be limited to one event or an episode (as in that of slavery), to ties created by the transatlantic slave trade, and to a time in the past. Scholars of the African diaspora deal with movements in various eras up until today, the creation and continuity of cultures, the survival and repackaging of traditions to meet new challenges, the creation of identities that do not respect boundaries, the linkages between power and representation, and the sources of conflicts and cooperation between and within diasporic identities. My intervention will include my own project of using the Internet to empower Africa and its diaspora.

The chapter's multidimensional focus includes the following: (1) an understanding of how displaced people think about a "homeland," what Stéphane Dufoix calls the "reference origin";[2] (2) how the connections to a far-removed place of origin are intellectualized and acted on in practice; (3) the formation of contemporary migrants into a transnationalist diaspora with one foot in Africa and the other in their host society; and (4) the deliberate creation of exchanges and suggestions on concrete actions by diasporic communities to talk about "self" and the "other," that is, other races (such as, for example, the projects on the African side to connect the continent with its diaspora). The chapter recognizes two distinctive clusters: the diaspora created by the slave trade (as in Afro-Brazilian or African American), and those that belong to the more recent voluntary migrations, whom I label the "transnationalist diaspora."

The Starting Point: Slavery

The role of slavery as an institution in Africa must be integrated into the larger framework of the diaspora. Paul Lovejoy contends that slavery was far more pervasive and widespread in Africa than we tend to factor into our analysis.[3] He has added that slavery practices were more brutal than often assumed, and that in some societies slaves experienced conditions similar to their counterparts in the American plantations in exploitation and difficult working conditions. To be sure, there were economies in Africa that made use of slavery. While many operated within small-scale peasant production, there were cases of large-scale farming in the nineteenth century on such large states as Ibadan and Sokoto in West Africa. At Sokoto, the use of slaves was part of the institutionalized method to facilitate production. Slavery actually became a central part of the production process. Some of these assumptions, whether right or wrong, mean that slavery should be studied in a comparativist perspective.

To understand slavery in Africa, we may have to insert the Americas into the narrative. There was a connection between the transatlantic economies and African slavery. Capitalism transformed domestic institutions of slavery, particularly in terms of the profitability of feeding the external markets with labor. Demand for labor drove practices at the supply end. Even during the nineteenth century when the transatlantic slave trade had ended, the rise of domestic slavery partly had to do with increased production of palm oil, palm kernel, peanut, cotton, and cocoa for external markets. Internal demands for slaves were instigated by the necessity of generating production for external markets. In turn, such demands provoked the use of violence as states and communities competed with one another for captives. The relevance of the use of labor was more and more consolidated as slaves became well connected to power and economy, the wars that produced them, and the economies that they had to service.

There are also definitional and conceptual issues. The data that speak to slavery and the transatlantic economies, mainly in written forms, have been generated by outsiders. The records were created and stationed outside of Africa. In the critical fifteenth through nineteenth centuries, when the Atlantic economies were conducted, African nations lacked the facilities to record and keep written documentation. Recent ambitious data collection, like the Du Bois database on twenty-seven thousand voyages, reveal the lopsided nature of this documentation.

To revisit slavery, it is important to evaluate Africa-based sources where available, to understand what they speak to in terms of slavery as an institution, and to understand how the conclusions from such analysis can be set within an Atlantic framework. The merit of an Atlantic perspective has been demonstrated in such works as John Thornton's *Africa and Africans*, which uses the Atlantic basin as one unit (the Atlantic coast of Africa, Europe, and the Americas).[4] Such an approach offers the possibility to create linkages as well as to integrate various narratives on different sides. The risk is that of distraction, which may marginalize the African hinterland, or the difficulty of managing large historical regions, which may then suppress local data of value. More important, other regions may be marginalized. Thus we have to be careful not to exclude the interactions between Africa and Asia, the Islamic world, and the Indian Ocean societies.

There are societies with historic roots in slave societies: Cuba, Brazil, and Haiti. The structures of economy, politics, and culture that they evolved emerged out of relations based on sugar production. Up until now, the understanding of identity and the nation-state reflects this historic foundation. If we study ethnicity in Africa and we study race in the Americas, it should be possible to compare and contrast. Of importance has been the attempt in a place like Cuba to talk about the "nation for all," as Jose Marti did in the 1890s. Cuba has attempted to present the face of a "raceless" society, although many of the assumptions on equality have been questioned.[5] Similarly in Brazil, attempts have been made to create a "racial democracy," although expressions of Afro-Brazilian identity reveal the past role of slavery and the societies created by plantation economies. The lingering impact of slavery in Africa and the African diaspora is a subject that can be attempted in ways that advance the scholarship on all sides of the Atlantic.

The Politics of Location

Diasporic Africans live in multiple locations as natives and hosts, citizens and strangers. It is not uncommon for them to talk as sojourners in "this" and "that" place. The physical spaces tend to define the spiritual spaces as many talk about the connections between heaven and earth and the joining together of traditions drawn from multiple places, as in the case of Candomblé.

Multiple locations mean that we can see the diaspora as representing many things at the same time: a geography where people can be defined in spatial terms, an identity where the meanings of life have to be defined and lived, and a notion of citizenship where "belonging" becomes both a political and identity question. The various meanings may be connected to (1) points of origins; (2) the complexities of journeys and migrations; (3) the interactions in host societies; (4)

the conversion of exiles into new beginnings, creating new roots that produce new societies; and (5) the creation of historical mythologies and histories.

In the aforementioned, Africa becomes embedded in various ways. The seeds were originally scattered from there by the forced migrations associated with the slave trade across the Sahara, the Atlantic, and the Indian Ocean. Millions were displaced, dislocated from hundreds of nations with hundreds of languages. The creation of the African diaspora was a global phenomenon, in many ways unprecedented in world history by its sheer size and scale. A large number was displaced across the Sahel to North Africa and the Mediterranean world. Then followed the transatlantic trade from the fifteenth to the nineteenth centuries that saw twelve million forcibly relocated to South and North America and the Caribbean to work where slave labor was central to the economy. Millions of others have joined since the nineteenth century, not forced, but as migrants, temporary workers, and permanent exiles.

Africa has to be studied in terms of points of origination. The details of what we define as "African history" should not, therefore, exist in isolation of the global phenomenon of the African diaspora. It is clear that African history has not always been interpreted with diaspora history outside the mainstream of studies on the slave trade. What many of the studies on the slave trade privilege are issues around regional and ethnic origins of slaves and migrants (that is, geography) connected to crises of relocation, and to economic and political circumstances (dislocation). In African history, the analysis, for the most part, tends to end at the departure points, meaning that the histories of where people relocate to—continent, countries, nations-states, etc., are not reworked back into the understanding of African history. It is rare to find in African history the insertion of the experiences of slaves and exiles into national or local histories, suggesting that those who have left have been disconnected from those who remain behind. The narratives of both deserve to be integrated.

The Two Tropes: Migration and the Homeland

When Africa looks outward, the dominant narrative is that of migrations. When those in the diaspora look outward, the main issue is that of homeland. Both are connected, although we tend to treat them as separate subjects. Research should fuse migration with nostalgia to integrate our knowledge. The expanding African diaspora, marked by recent relentless migrations to the West, is creating a set of linkages and new ways to rethink the field: (1) why are Africans leaving? (2) if they are leaving, should Africans who do migrate see the place as a homeland? and (3) are the contemporary migrants creating a diaspora different from that of the diaspora of slavery?

Since the time of slavery, first-generation migrants usually think of the homeland and have a dream to return. The dream became actualized in some physical relocations, now labeled as the "back-to-Africa movements," from the United States to Liberia and Sierra Leone, from Brazil to Ghana, and other such migrations. Where physical relocations were not possible, the idea of a homeland became embedded in memory, which in turn was expressed as poetry, songs, mythologies, and ceremonies.

In recent years the return is much easier, temporarily as visit of renewal and permanently as a wish to return to the place of birth. The daily reality of survival or of thriving makes it difficult for the majority to embark on a permanent relocation, and there may be more corpses being sent for the final burial rites and interment than those who return to live their dream of comfortable life after decades of toil. Such is life!

Nostalgia for the homeland is both real and imagined. What the nostalgia signifies is important and should be part of academic and public knowledge on both sides of the Atlantic. Diaspora location and nostalgia complicate our notions of identity. There are unresolved tensions. Those who blame Africans for participating in the slave trade—even the reckless blaming of contemporary generations who do not know the history of this cruel trade—tend to hold a sort of a grudge. Their own feeling may be that of a homeland that betrayed them. The dimension of this blame perspective needs to be integrated into African history.

Africans who have been prevented from pursuing their lifestyles, as in the case of gays and lesbians, see living in the West as a better option, while at the same time they are eager to change the situation in their homeland. Reconciling the queer communities with Africa is an important project, as many individuals feel that the culture in Africa is hostile to them. Similarly, political exiles may also have a sense of ambivalence. They want to fight for a variety of causes but they need to protect their lives.

The homeland can compete with new societies in which people have planted their roots. Sources of identification with the homeland may diminish over time, thereby generating a need for discovery (as in the case of Alex Haley's investigation into his historical roots), nostalgia (as in making trips to Africa in search of one's origins), or ambivalence to the notion of home. The subject of nostalgia and the homeland has to be pursued in a variety of new ways: in the context of different subjectivities who think about a homeland but are afraid to go there, of transnationalists who see themselves as being "here" and "there" at the same time, and of those already assimilated into Western cultures who see Africa as unsafe and insecure.

Africa has been romanticized by those in search of a homeland and those with strong feelings of nostalgia. The traditions of the past are presented in eulogistic terms, feeding the positive portrayal of values, the merit of communal living, society's cohesion, and limited stress levels. Such a characterization has led to a Diopian Afrocentricity in which scholars in this tradition see the hope of Africa and black people in what this characterization can offer, instead of borrowing from the West. Those who study African precolonial societies and those who study diaspora history from the Afrocentric perspective need to work out a creative dialogue to reflect on the meanings of the past in relation to the present.

Contemporary Transnationalists and Africa

Black people can locate themselves in their countries of birth or citizenship and claim the privileges that come with it. At the same time, their history has enabled the creation of a diaspora, a nonterritorialized identity based on connections with Africa. Modern technology has made it much easier to create a sense of proximity and zones of interactions between members of the diaspora in a global world. Within this diaspora, we have a rich variety: the national (as in the case of Nigerians abroad), the religious (as in the devotees of Ogun, the Yoruba god of iron), and the continental (as in Africa and Pan-Africanists).

There are mutual desires and benefits for interactions between transnationalists and Africa. On the side of the African states, their citizens abroad represent a community that can advance the national agenda of development in terms of fundraising to support a variety of causes, the hosting of fresh migrants, the diffusion of knowledge, and much more. Thus when African politicians, administrators, and business leaders visit the West, their goal is not just to meet with their foreign counterparts but also with the citizens of their countries. In Austin, Texas, for instance, it has become routine for Nigerian families to host state governors and cabinet members.

To the transnationalist migrants, Africa represents the place to seek self-esteem, influence politics, participate in the development of their towns and villages, and sell the alternative voices on modernization. Emigration and actions regarding the homeland are connected, as migrants seek ways to change politics and policies, improve living standards, and expose the limitations of the government.

Immigrants can also become the sources in host societies that provide knowledge about Africa, to teach school children about their people, and even to act as consultants to host governments. International financial institutions such as the World Bank and the International Monetary Fund recognize the need to factor the presence and views of immigrants into institutional strategies, if only to prevent immigrants from initiating moves that would generate violence, but more so to draft them in seeking ways to improve the economies so that the volume of migration can be reduced.

Multiple Blackness, Diverse Africa

While the presentation of Africa in the diaspora may lack the notion of difference, the presentation on the diaspora in Africa ignores heterogeneity. In essentializing one another, issues around difference and division are either ignored or poorly done. In creating an integrated body of knowledge, the study of diversity and difference should be a key component. On the Africa side, there are scholars who project the continent to the diaspora as a unit. On the diaspora side, the presentation can be that minorities and immigrants form a homogeneous community that is familial. In both presentations, people think and act alike, culture is static, institutions of society are transmitted from one age to another with limited changes, and the differences in class and gender can be erased.

There are many ways in which the diaspora and the African continent are diverse: ethnicity, race, culture, and economy. The recognition of this diversity is not to undermine the crucial work to unite us, to construct a collective identity, to solidify the ties that bind us. Rather, it is to understand historical and contemporary realities so that we may relate the differences to our statements on identity, on strategies of building alliances within and across boundaries, on the explanation of conflicts and wars (in the case of Africa), on tensions among immigrant groups (in the case of the diaspora), and on the challenges in generating unity across the Atlantic.

Afro-Brazilians and African Americans share many differences (to take two examples of two identities in the diaspora). African immigrants in the United States are not alike (to take the example of minorities in the United States). In both examples, the historical context that creates the groups shapes certain outcomes. The politics of exclusion and inclusion are not the same. Generational differences in cultures are marked. Views and behaviors may be affected by gender, language, class, and religion. Be it in Africa or in the diaspora, traditional practices have been disrupted by the forces of change, the spread of Western ideas, and the insertion of different rules and codes of behavior from other cultures and societies. An African coming from a patriarchal setting to the United States, which has different gender roles, will be confronted with the necessity to adapt. This migrant may experience a sense of loss and manifest a nostalgia for the homeland. If one thing has been lost, another has been gained: American culture.

Once we factor diversity into our crosscontinental analysis and relations, we are able to deal with the practical consequences. African migrants in the Americas are fond of complaining that they do not always share in the African American experience. Among statements that have been publicized include the characterization of Africans as outsiders, as inferiors coming out of a continent that is primitive, tribal, and destitute. African migrants feel offended when they are asked questions about living conditions in Africa. It is not uncommon to accuse contemporary migrants of benefiting from the changes brought about by civil rights struggles without having contributed to those struggles, particularly the accusation that they come to America and take jobs away from citizens. In addition to this allegation, the success of African immigrants is being used by the media to spite the African American population. African immigrants, too, have been uncharitable in what they say, portraying African Americans as violent, lacking a sense of family, dependent on welfare, and unreliable as workers. While intermarriages are common, there are families that discourage their children from marrying outside of their groups.

Within the community itself, the monolithic presentation of migrants creates problems, as many confuse West Indians with Nigerians or when both groups use nationality and culture rather than skin color to identify themselves. In cities where many of the black population are foreign-born, as in Miami, New York, and Boston, the monolithic presentation troubles the various nationalities, more so when media narratives criminalize all of them. There is evidence that both native-born and foreign-born blacks, like other races, tend to have differences based on aspirations, education, culture, and social status. There has been competition for power among different groups, as when group representatives competed for the post of mayor in North Miami or for a city council seat in Brooklyn, New York.

We need not avoid the reality that there are different communities and different definitions of their peculiarities. The understanding of cultures and identity can be messy, and their reality in concrete relationships can produce conflicts and challenges. Definitions of particular identities may clash, and some definitions have the capacity to complicate interactions. Even the naming of specific segments and actions, such as "Négritude" and "mestizaje," may produce their own disagreements. Such differences need not be dismissed as irrelevant.

Heterogeneity does not make the quest for unity an impossible one. What it does is to call for a different kind of strategy, which may be that several units of Africa and the diaspora will forge alliances, as in those among scholars or those organized on the basis of interests (e.g., practitioners of indigenous religions), or those based on politics (Pan-Africanism) or on gender. Indeed, the intellectual project of uniting blacks irrespective of their locations predated the twentieth century. Such projects, aspects of which follow, show that we can unite in spite of our diversity.

Antihegemonic Impulses and Actions

The most common expression of oneness in Africa and the African diaspora is that of uplifting the race by resistance and nationalism. Slave rebellions, anticolonial resistance, black protests, and global black nationalism can be seen as a unit of analysis in spite of the multiple narratives. Underlying the discourse, especially since the late nineteenth century, is the contradiction between the expression and propaganda of Western ideals of freedom and liberty and that of colonial exploitation in Africa and racial injustice in Europe and the Americas. In relation to the experience of race and colonialism, black responses have been conditioned by the culture of accommodation, assimilation, resistance, and nationalism. Ideas on the various strands of responses have circulated globally, and projects of black solidarity have revolved around some of them.

There were tendencies to seek entry into white-privileged identities, be it in South Africa or Bahia, a sort of assimilationist strategy. Just as there were Senegalese who sought to become French citizens during colonial rule, so too there were blacks in the Americas who sought identification with the values and ideals of whiteness. In Africa and the African diaspora, many developed ideas of liberal consciousness and sought the promotion of a capitalist ethos and the benefits that modernity offered.

Similarly, black identities have been formed around issues of resistance. The use of music and religion for the purpose of resistance is common in Africa, Brazil, and elsewhere. On slave plantations, for example, resistance took the form of protest and flight, practices that colonized Africans were later to replicate. Strategies of resistance ultimately became the bedrock of identity formation.

Historical parallels are many: resistance to slavery in Europe and the Americas, and anticolonial resistance in Africa. In all these places, we see how black people developed coping mechanisms (cultural, political, and social) to survive exploitation and assaults on their freedom and humanity. There were calls for reforms and emancipation in Africa and the African diaspora to free people from bondage.[6] The belief in the use of violence was common in most places, and turning to religion (both Islam and Christianity) as a vehicle to express radicalism and organize radical politics was also widespread. Participation in both world wars produced similar consequences in terms of instigating demands for reforms and freedom, the mobilization of the masses in cities, and even the increasing urbanization as more and more people relocated to the cities.

Mass black political movements have been predicated on similar reasons, whether in Haiti or New York. The experience of racism and suffering has served as the most powerful unifying factor among blacks in the diaspora. It was this experience that promoted a culture of respect for blackness, gestures of brotherhood expressed openly, energized radical nationalism in Africa, and instigated the civil rights movement in the United States in the 1950s.

Practical projects have been created. Marcus Garvey founded the Universal Negro Improvement Association to create a political platform for black solidarity. His ideas of creating a successful entrepreneurship to generate wealth instigated various ideas on black economic empowerment. TransAfrica, founded by Randall Robinson in 1977, has promoted the cause of unity between Africa and the United States.

To date, the most successful global project is that of Pan-Africanism, about which a lot has been written. While the possibility of its revival, in the ways advocated by W. E. B. Du Bois and Kwame Nkrumah, may no longer be possible, the idea that it offered provides one of the key elements to globalize blackness. The heroes of the movement should be rescued from the history books and written into the centers of the metanarratives in Africa and the diaspora as a way of rejecting the trivialization of black heroes in the grand historical narratives. If the end of Jim Crow laws in the United States and of European rule in Africa contributed to the decline of the relevance of Pan-Africanism, the conclusion that has to be questioned and challenged is that the struggles in various locations are different and need to be coordinated.

The spirit of Pan-Africanism is revivable, even at the level of an elite project that is able to bring intellectuals together as a form of unity, and create a bank for their ideas as a form of knowledge that is accessible to policymakers. Pan-Africanism is also revivable via the agency of religion, as in the case of Islam. The priests and priestesses of indigenous religions (as in Santeria) are developing both regional and global connections that are Pan-Afrianist in nature, indicating that cultural and religious connections are actually far more achievable than the political ones.

The Religious Connection: Islam

Islam has provided one of the sources of antihegemonic ideologies in Africa and the African diaspora. In addition, Islam connects with Africa and the African diaspora in so many ways that it can serve as a theme around which to organize studies. Through the trans-Saharan trade, Islamic societies in North Africa and the Middle East recruited slaves from Africa. Within Africa, the expansion of Islam and the various jihads led to the making of captives who were converted into slaves. Islamic jihads led to the expansion of production systems that

Figure 9.1. An open market in Bahia, Brazil, with practices and items that unite Africa and Brazil. The author holding a tuber of yam, the "king of crop," with his host, Professor João José Reis, the distinguished scholar of Africans in Brazil. Photograph courtesy of author.

used slaves in large numbers. Connections with the Atlantic World were equally deep.

Various black muslim movements emerged during the twentieth century in various parts of the Americas and the West. Many were formed as resistance movements against domination and marginalization and slavery. As members of a minority religion, they feel a double jeopardy—as blacks and as Muslims. Feeling constrained, they sometimes become radicalized and take melodramatic action to make their point. A minority character exposes them; a marginalized status traumatizes them.

Blackness and the practice of Islam can present serious complications. Combining black maleness with Islamic devotion can be read as an expression of anger. At once, the combination can lead to criticism of manifesting the most extreme form of radicalism, or the most intense form of black nationalism. Black Muslim males tend to be constructed as outsiders, an independent segment of the black population.

Black Muslim radicalism has a connection with slavery, imperialism, and racism, manifesting itself in various forms of nationalism—whether in Africa, Europe, or the Americas. Combined with black protest radicalism, Muslims often get painted as "extremists," anti-West and antiwhite. To a large extent, Islam has had to respond to a power structure created by slavery and Western domination.

Irrespective of the negative construction of Islam in the West, Africa cannot distance itself from this world religion. Many parts of Africa are part of the Pan-Islamic tradition. Building regional and pan-continental unity requires embracing Muslims and Islamic areas. Building diasporic connections requires transcending the religious affiliations of members. Indeed, Islam and other religions have to be used as part of the cultural assembly to unify black peoples and build cohesion among people divided by geopolitical boundaries.

Some of the most important issues that must be negotiated are how to respond to anti-Muslim sentiment in the West, the characterizations of Muslims in the Western media and by African Christian fundamentalists as violent, tensions in identity politics in the Sudan between the North and the South (now divided into two countries), tensions between black Muslims and Arab Muslims, and the deep conflicts between Arab Muslims and Jews. Overall, the relationship between race, politics, and religion will pose a challenge to building bridges between Africa and its diaspora.

USA-Africa Dialogue and Diasporic Interfacing

In 2000, following the disputed election results in Florida that brought President George W. Bush to power in divisive and controversial circumstances, I was inundated with questions from many Africans to explain why the fight over votes in Florida should not be interpreted as "election rigging" the way we define this practice in African politics. After a brief introduction of the subject, I invited debates over the Internet.[7] It became an instant success. A global diasporic community emerged. Within a few weeks, the membership of the USA-Africa Dialogue reached a high number, with over a thousand subcribers, and thousands of readers. Listserves representing other interests joined in, and the membership became truly Pan-African as most African countries were represented. It also became global; membership was drawn from all the countries and regions traditionally defined as the African diaspora. Nongovernmental organizations (NGOs) and some governments began to see it as an avenue to publicize their activities. Current news was circulated and analyzed. Events of global relevance, as in the plight of African migrants in the West or the rise of Barack Obama, became popular. Thanks to the Internet, a global African diaspora was created, connecting Africa with its diaspora and the diaspora with Africa.

The massive volume of the USA-Africa Dialogue indicates new meanings about the diaspora and the regeneration of a global network across the Atlantic and beyond. My own reading of this vibrant space of interactions shows the insertion of Africa into the diaspora and the intellectual penetration of Africa by the diaspora, especially the representation of Western educated migrants to the West in the last decades. The diaspora, in the process, acquires a series of new meanings. Those in Africa are constructing the diaspora, and those in the diaspora are constructing Africa and the African nations. The interactions between both are mediated by the large issues of blackness. The boundaries between both groups are fluid, as locations may or may not affect intellectual orientations.

The USA-Africa Dialogue is part of the larger reality of living in an age of technospheric space where a virtual community can be imagined, a nation can be invented, democracy can be constructed, boundaries can be erased, and patriarchy can be challenged. Online bulletin boards have demonstrated a tremendous capability to bring what appears to be disconnected people together, to merge areas that are separated by great distances, to unite those who live in dislocated spaces, to turn the world into a village. Infosphere is married to geosphere, creating fresh paradigms for the diaspora to interface with Africa in order for Africans to inform and deform the diaspora (and vice versa). As ideas circulate, penetration and counterpenetration acquire an intensity in which boundaries interact more routinely than ever before.

Maintaining daily contact between the diaspora and Africa is as simple as pressing a button. When rampant use of cell phones and satellite television transmissions are added, one can be based in Houston or Bahia and enjoy communication in Yoruba and enjoy Yoruba movies in the original language. Activities in Africa can be shared, and cybertechnology enables instant viewing of sports and entertainment programs.

Facilities for border crossings—diverse, multiple, aggressive—are limit-less, and with the Internet blackness provides a solidarity that Marcus Garvey could not have imagined or anticipated a hundred years ago. The convergence is blackness, the source is Africa, and the strands are transnational, connecting a Gambian with a Senegalese, both based in New York City. Loneliness is cured, for the World Wide Web keeps communication and contacts alive. To be sure, certain memories have to be discarded, but not those of a place—the place of birth, the place of migrations, the place of childhood, the place where the making of history begins. To me, it is Africa, as it is to many of us. What the USA-Africa Dialogue has done is to legitimize this place as a memory to those in the diaspora and as an ongoing passion for those interested in the upliftment of their people.

I can only hope that the fact is not lost that thanks to the power of the Internet, new diasporas have been created, as in relabelling the USA-Africa Dialogue as the "Toyin Falola Family." The USA-Africa Dialogue can be described as the formation of a new diaspora. This family spins its web, producing strong, passionate affiliations around sets of issues concerning the development of Africa, the trauma of migration, and the necessity of transferring power from a privileged group to the marginalized. The Internet has ensured that memory will not become ossified. To those in the diaspora, the web is the memory of Africa, of their place within it, and of a time important to them. It is much easier to bring people together around com-mon interests (as in the various associations, such as the Yoruba Progressive Club), or old schools (alumni associations), countries (Organization of Nigerian Nationals), and professions (Association of Nigerian Medical Practitioners). Many of these institutions serve as points of linkages between the diaspora and Africa and as avenues to share information and to mobilize for fundraising.

Chat rooms and message boards generate a spontaneous feeling of nearness, even when the individuals have never met or when they live in two different continents. They also create a liberatory space that allows for a more open discussion about themselves, individual aspi-rations, the agenda of the nation-state, and relations among blacks. The cumulative impact is a serious intervention to critique how the nation-state is managed and to mobilize various movements for posi-tive actions.

However, cyberspace alliances have their pitfalls. They can be used to spread falsehoods about people and the constituencies they represent or defend, in some cases damaging them so badly that restoration of goodwill becomes a difficult process. The most dangerous has been the circulation of stereotypes about blacks in Europe and the Americas; they are defamed as lazy, welfare dependent, and lacking the ability to tap into the opportunities made available to them for advancement. Similarly, blacks in the diaspora have accused Africans of selling their ancestors into slavery, of being used as foils to deny jobs and privileges to them, and of being insensitive to issues of race.

Technospace politics may also fragment nations. In plural societies divided by ethnicity, race, or religion, activitists defending any of these identities have used technospace to promote not just the strengthening of their group identities but also the conflicts between them and others. The continent, the diaspora, and the nation are fragmented. Diasporic cyberspace can turn into the endorsement of separatist identities. A notion of Yorubaness and Igboness has been fostered by the Internet, rather than that of Nigerianness or Africanness. While the promotion of ethnic affiliations in the diaspora is good as part of developing a culture of fictional kinship and communal identity, attacks and criticisms of the other groups can create frictions that severely damage continental and black solidarity.

Conclusion: A Future World

Africa and its diaspora face a crossroads and new paths. The global economy is interlocked, and Africa and the diaspora are very much embedded in it. We want to be active within this global economy, not as suppliers of slaves and labor or as producers of cash crops, domestic servants, and other exploitable categories, but as creators, inventors, managers, leaders, and entrepreneurs in control of the economic forces that shape our lives. The integration of Africa with its diaspora—in knowledge production and policies—has to reinforce ideas of empowerment within the global economy. Powerful global forces may try to impose limits on us, just as they have done for centuries in the creation of Atlantic and colonial economies; we have to fashion a new beginning in which we constitute the center and not the periphery. There are several ways to strengthen the connections between Africa and its diaspora and vice versa.

I am proposing the practical and academic integration of Africa with its diaspora so that ideas, goods, and people can freely circulate for the upliftment of all and so that we can move to the center of world history. In this integration, the message is not that of the abusive use of the forces of globalization in the service of Western domination or the never-ending penetration of competitive global capitalism. I am advocating the merger of dislocated geographical units so that ideas can spread with frequency to pollinate any degrading part. The continent and its diaspora can disintegrate their boundaries to allow for culture and capital to circulate with ease and efficiency. The World Wide Web and cyberspace have shown that imaginary nations can be constructed, that "liminal" communities can be invented, communities that are neither in the diaspora nor in Africa.

Digital and cyberspaces will continue to mediate the relationship between Africa and the diaspora. As more and more people obtain access to the Internet, thereby reducing the digital divide, greater ties will be fostered among people who will never meet but who can share ideas and information. The expansion of technospheres will enable a new generation to develop connections across the globe. However, staying connected requires access to computers and Internet facilities. In many parts of Africa, access to digital technology is still a problem that needs be corrected with time and resources.

We live in diasporic spaces that will continue to expand. Many of us may be able to answer the question, where are you from? but not all can answer in any definitive manner, given the boundaries they have traversed, the places they have lived, and the sources of the knowledge and ideas that shape their lives. The question, where do you come from? can become an entry to an identity marker that is misleading. Even if the question can be answered, it is far more complicated to respond to the questions where are you going? or where do you retire to? The African and diaspora world are constantly being reimagined.

The dream of returning to Africa has to be balanced with the historical reality of its difficulty, nay, impossibility for the majority. The dream has to be kept alive, as a way of creating a feeling and nostalgia for Africa. The reality of its difficulty has to be accepted as a way of affirming our extension to new frontiers. It is possible to advance the agenda of the cyberinterfacing that USA-Africa Dialogue has created and expanded, making it possible for the diasporas of the different ages and eras to converge, to share their passion for the advancement of common interests, the promotion of enduring values, and the lessons that rational intellect will remake a world created by violence.

The worlds of cyberscapes and technospheres are linked to the world economy, politics, and popular culture. A new so-called Generation D has emerged, one that is readily attributed to the electronic age and its social media—Facebook, Twitter, E-mail, etc.—by which millions can connect with one another without knowing one another. The assumption is that this Generation D includes all of us. We are all targets of the marketing of products and ideas that will shape our minds to control our pockets. This calls for a recognition of how to define our collective interests as Africans and diasporic Africans in such a way that niche marketing is not taking from us but rather in a way that we become agents with the power to determine the market and popular cultures. If Generation D thinks globally, its identity may not be fully grounded in an ethnicity of blackness. We cannot exclude blacks from membership in this Generation D, but we have to wish that their color-free, race-free embracement of global digital economies and cyberspaces will not destroy the idea of "national belonging" in Africa, of Africa as a "home," of black solidarity, and of the development of Africa and all Africans in the diaspora.

Forging zones of interactions between Africa and the African diaspora on the one hand, and within the diaspora on the other, is a necessity at various levels: the strengthening of transcontinental political views that have been shared for over a hundred years; the advancement of practical projects such as acadamic exchanges and the training of a new generation of youth in various fields; and the generation of new knowledge on crossingcutting issues and the organization of conferences to exchange ideas and promote new knowledge. The virtual community of the Web will definitely grow stronger and play an increasingly greater role in merging the boundaries of Africa with those of the African diaspora. As the core of the influential USA-Africa Dialogue shows, this virtual community will confront the nation-state without respect for patriarchy and hierarchy. It will respect the interests of marginalized groups based on class, gender, and social orientation. Diaspora communities, as they create zones of alliance, will reconfigure the nation-state as well as social and political movements. Their activities and actions will ultimately lead to the integration of knowledge on blackness in general and on the permanent relationship between Africa and its diaspora in particular.

It should be possible to fuse the various interests: practical, scholarly, and pedagogical. Scholars with an activist goal can keep examining the human side of the diaspora, focusing on the long-term consequences of slavery, sexism, racism, and class as they affect black people, and coming up with important suggestions on how to move forward. Blame should be assigned where necessary and apologies should be offered and demanded, for it is moral to atone for the sins of the past. Lingering cases of abuses of labor, in whatever name or disguise, should be condemned. We all have a responsibility to end a prolonged crisis in a place like Darfur, as it perpetuates slavery and the legacies of colonial and postcolonial exploitation. Cases have been reported in the Sudan where poor people are captured and forced to work, part of the legacy of ethnic and racial prejudice that must be exposed, attacked, and abolished.

With respect to pedagogical issues, research and teaching should move forward to elaborate more on what the diaspora can teach us about non-Africans in relation to themselves in the context of global interactions about fragmentation within black identities, and how to rebuild stronger communities, solidarity, and cultural and political networks. An African "global tribe"[8] has been created, sustainable by the affinities of history and culture. We live within a world diaspora both by force and by choice, a reality created by the circumstances of history.

10

Tanure Ojaide and Akin Ogundiran

Knowledge Circulation and the Diasporic Interface

The New African Diaspora

A distinctive category of African has emerged in the United States, Europe, and elsewhere. The label "new African diaspora"[1] encompasses the era of migrations (postcolonial in Africa), instigating factors for migration (voluntary, but in the context of constrained or straightened circumstances in Africa), new forms of politics (post–civil rights era in the United States), new identities (transnational, dual/multiple citizenship), and issues around the role and relevance of migrants in Africa and the African diaspora (brain drain/gain/circulation). The label can also be considered synonymous with, as I use it, the terms "transnationalists" and "immigrants." Some even refer to the groups of the new diaspora as "continental Africans" to mark them apart from African Americans. Among Africans in the United States, various identities are also emerging, such as Nigerian Americans, Senegalese Americans, and many more. Within each, there are also identities defined by religion, as with members of the broadly defined Islamic community or of the Nigeria-based Redeemed Christian Church of God.

The new African diaspora is transforming the American landscape. Its members are everywhere as migrant workers in diverse professions, including nurses, doctors, and pharmacists in hospitals and clinics; professors in universities; and engineers and researchers. They are everywhere as low-paid labor, including cab drivers, janitors, and maids. They are part of the commercial landscape as storeowners, hairdressers, and barbers. They are part of the physical landscape in all of the major cities, and can be found in airports, hotels, and other service industries. They are a visible part of the cultural landscape. The majority of them speak English with an accent and use multiple languages that connect them to their African ethnicities and identities while their occupations, locations, and interactions occur in the context of a globalized world.

The two interrelated themes of migration and transnationalism are defining elements in the understanding of this new African diaspora. The constant movements of people, goods, ideas, services, and money connect the homeland and host societies. The migrants live in a way that disregards the fixed categories of maps; nationality and citizenship can be dual and multiple, social relations can be conducted across borders, and one can live in one country and consume the culture and products of another. Africa and the United States, to use the examples that shape this chapter, are united by transnationalists as a single space of action in which economic, political, cultural, and familial transactions are conducted across borders. A husband may be living in Chicago and his wife in Accra, Ghana. Their children may be in school in London. The savings accumulated by the husband in Chicago can be used to build a house in Accra, which he defines as his "home." This example can be multiplied by millions of practices in transnational networks. Realizing that thousands of migrants live in clusters in specific cities—Gambians in Providence, Rhode Island; Senegalese in New York; Sudanese in Columbus, Ohio; and Nigerians in Chicago, Baltimore, Houston, Dallas, and Atlanta—one notes the emergence of communities of the new African diaspora: transnationalist villages. These villages are, even now, governed by rules; some have their titled chiefs exercise a great deal of moral authority over members. The state has its own laws, and transnationalist villages can also have their own laws, enforceable in the context of powerful codes of informal authority. These transnationalist villages are connected back to Africa in several ways: exchanges of ideas, the remittance of money to Africa, the circulation of cultures (as in the case of Nollywood films), and projects aimed at changing politics in Africa, including participation by some in the government and administration of their home countries.

Members of the new African diaspora manifest habits that may mark them apart from the far more established African American communities. They tend to pursue two strategies simultaneously: a set of African-oriented and African-driven practices and integration into the host societies. In other words, as they develop new ties in new lands, they do not sever ties with their former lands. The reference to "home" is ambiguous, as it may mean where they originated rather than where they now live. Many host society citizens, understanding Africa as underdeveloped and insecure, always wonder why immigrants are not contented, grateful to God, and thankful for new opportunities. This is a misreading of a rather complex reality. Immigrants use a language of contradictions and comparisons, depending on the topic and theme. They may praise American technology and praise African culture, both within the same hour. They may criticize African underdevelopment and American individualism in a string of related sentences.

The answers to the apparent contradictions in the conversations are rooted in the ideologies of the relations between individuals and society. Americans are acculturated to an individualist ethos, while Africans are socialized into a kinship ethos. What Americans call philanthropy will translate into elaborate kinship projects for Africans; as Americans seek out the Red Cross, Africans seek members related to them by blood in the "kinship Salvation Army." Kinship ideology ultimately imposes not only a notion of "dual citizenship," in which one belongs to separate and multiple concentric rings of actual and imagined communities, old, new, and emerging, but also to leading dual or multiple lives. Leaving Senegal for New York means leaving behind parents, siblings, and friends; taking one's entire kinship group is simply not feasible. Yet communication is never suspended, and the greater the immigrant's success, the greater the intensity of communication with those left behind. Ties of kinship and ties of affection make for a powerful glue that ensures that transnationalists continue to see Africa as "home." Thus it is not unusual for people to speak of returning to their homeland.

The politics of incorporation into host societies are complex, unpredictable, and time-consuming. The politics are even preceded by the stressful process of leaving a country behind and entering another one.[2] Seeking full acceptance in any society is always a hard task, and one cannot but note the resilience among immigrants. Competing for well-paying jobs and obtaining economic security is much harder still. Attaining political power is an impossibility for the majority. It is not uncommon to have extensive dialogues on difficulties. It is also not unusual for some immigrants to see themselves as victims of race and worse off than African Americans.

To be sure, we are not in the postracial society that Obama's victory signaled. Discrimination will take a long time to be completely eradicated in any society. In Africa itself, discrimination exists based on ethnicity, religion, and gender. It is also difficult to fully understand the lingering impact of racism in the United States, but there is no doubt that people can still be discriminated against on the basis of externals: accent, gender, color, age, religion, and sexual orientation. Even in a country such as Brazil where race mixture is more widespread, the fair-skinned have more privileges.[3] Images are equally powerful, as films and media denigrate immigrants.[4]

Race is about exclusion, and it is misguided thinking for someone from Kenya to land in Washington, DC, with the hope of an immediate inclusion in politics and the economy. Those who fail may present a falsified image and vision of their host societies to their friends and family back in Africa. Migrants have to pursue strategies of incorporation that require an intellectual understanding of host societies, an enormous amount of networking among fellow migrants, and an awareness of practical measures including legal means of gaining permanent residency and citizenship.

The strategies may point to contradictions, confusion, ambiguity, and the difficulty of defining morality with precision. In dealing with the complications of adjusting to a new country, certainty, truth, and reality are not always easy to define and defend. Individuals deal with experiences that lead them toward what I see as ambiguity and confusion in relation to understanding themselves and the fast-changing historical events of Africa and their host societies. The problem is that individuals prefer clarity and certainty, and when neither are attainable they see confusion. However, the very process of leaving Africa means that ambiguity is also the driving force of life itself. The individual migrants, as they ultimately find out, succeed because they fall on their protean self, imitating the Greek sea god who can acquire different shapes. They are adaptable, flexible, and mobile. In other words, the new African diaspora has exhibited enormous capacity for change and transformation. These immigrants lack the impulses of fundamentalism and totalism that process reality in just one way and pursue it with all necessary means; rather, they fall instead to protean impulses that accept multiple truths, multiple pathways, the ambiguity of life, and the ambiguity of culture. To be sure, to live with ambiguity is also to live with vulnerability.

In merging the politics of maintaining ties with the homeland with that of incorporation, the new African diaspora demonstrates the capacity to seek and use knowledge, expand the frontiers of knowledge, transfer cultural practices from Africa to the West and vice versa, and create new networks, even on the Internet. Let me highlight a few. Associations are now so many and varied: religious, cultural, hometown, ethnic, political, and academic. These associations enable ideas to circulate and allow members to connect within host countries and between host countries and Africa. The collection and distribution of large sums of money have been made possible by associations in support of multiple causes, for example, funeral ceremonies and sending corpses back to Africa, scholarships, emergency support to those in need, and support for those marking social events.

Many immigrants are creating businesses, mainly small, but targeted to specific audiences that consume African products or demand African-oriented services. Entrepreneurship, in spirit and practice, is well entrenched among blacks, as Juliet Walker has pointed out in several studies.[5] African-based grocery stores, hair salons, restaurants, and many other businesses are becoming part of the urban landscape. Medium-sized stores are emerging, most notably in health-related services, real estate, and clearing and forwarding. Occupational diplomas are becoming better integrated with the market as immigrants establish profession-based businesses.

The majority of African business owners fall into what Karl Marx termed the *petty bourgeoisie*, that is, those who operate their own businesses with their own labor and without the resources (or need) to hire additional labor; when they do, they hire very few (usually one or two), typically family members or people they know. The petty bourgeoisie enjoy the advantage of not working for others, but their inability to hire the labor of others and to control that labor may serve as an obstacle to business expansion. They are also vulnerable to a wide range of misfortunes such as illness, loss of income, and inadequate time to devote to both business and family matters. Low start-up capital and a small consumer base remain key constraints to expansion.[6] Minority-owned businesses are also undercut by national chains that can sell cheaper goods.

African businesses rely on networking to survive and succeed. Initial capital can be raised through friends and families. Savings are accumulated, not always through the formal banking systems but through age-old African institutions of cooperative networking in which individuals collect and repay credit among one another on the basis of trust. In conversations with these entrepreneurs, their motivations are clear. They seek independence, self-reliance, and the money to create lasting assets in Africa so that they can retire with comfort. Lacking access to reliable retirement plans and federal social security programs in the United States, many among them, notably traders, remit money to Africa to build houses and create businesses that they can fall back on either in old age or when they return to Africa. The engaging book *Money Has No Smell* provides data on African entrepreneurs based in New York, revealing their business practices, their struggles to make ends meet, and their connections with Africa.[7]

Many transnationalist migrants understand that society has cleavages that promote competition and rivalries. They know the advantages and problems of ethnicity. Those who were driven to leave Africa by circumstances associated with warfare and political instability fully understand the forces of ethnic nationalism. To understand ethnicities is also to understand how identities work. Ethnicities and identities need mythologies to sustain them. The advantage of knowing how system works and how cleavages set the limits to what individuals can accomplish contributes in part to success in negotiations in Western societies. Those who fail not only emphasize the crippling power of racism, but they also overemphasize the power of parents to prevent the failures of children. A number of parents are so obsessed with success—defined in terms of wealth and power—that they use extraordinary means, including violence, to instill a notion of discipline in their children so that they will acquire educational capital.

Capitalism has successfully created a powerful mythology: the playing field is even, and there is meritocracy. In the United States, meritocracy has a bumper sticker name—the "American Dream." A successful mythology, it is very much grounded in the belief of egalitarianism and social equality: one succeeds or fails in relation to one's ability and talents. The sky becomes the limit, irrespective of the starting point, as long as one works hard. America, as the land of limitless opportunity, is a mythology. Africans who come from kinship societies relocate from one mythology to another and quickly discover that the lessons in kinship may not apply to the lessons in individualism. Like all mythologies, some believe it and others do not. Mythologies, like faiths, have their followers who fully endorse them. To believers, their personal experiences support the mythology of the American Dream.

Members of the new African diaspora are equally divided between those who subscribe to this mythology and those who do not. Personal narratives have yet to move beyond private testimonies and into the public space; thus there is a limited ability to construct theories derived from the experiences of many. Nevertheless, evidence from McNamee and Miller indicates that meritocracy may be a myth: "it takes money to make money (inheritance); it's not what you know but whom you know (connections); what matters is being in the right place at the right time (luck); the playing field isn't level (discrimination), and he or she married into money (marriage)."[8] Irrespective of the position of each individual, it should be fully understood that all societies operate on the bases of both merit and nonmerit. It is important to understand and to seek the means to overcome possible impediments to success.

African immigrants clearly understand the concept of cultural capital (the acquisition of knowledge and skills to fit into a society). Indeed, they are very successful (e.g., financially, network development, attaining posts in universities and government, and the like) because of their ability to combine Western education with cultural capital. If there is tension between the established African American communities and the newer African immigrants, it is based in part on the understanding and use of educational and cultural capital. New immigrants, disconnected from the history of slavery and the civil rights movement, tend to see the maximization of opportunities to acquire and expand their educational and cultural capital as their sole strategy for attaining mobility. The immigrants seek mobility in the context of the American middle class, they seek occupations that will provide mortgages, cars, and savings to draw from to remit money to Africa. In trying to balance financial demands in the United States and Africa, they have to distribute their income in a creative manner that may prohibit spending on vacations and expensive restaurants.

Thus far I have been homogenizing the experiences of millions of people that are divided by nationality, ethnicity, religion, age, and gender. Now I want to limit myself to the academics. I shall chose two case studies that represent intellectual production by the members of the new African Diaspora in order to reflect on their contributions, the impact they are making, their voices and agencies.

This scholarship may provide connecting threads, and overcome the spatial, cultural, and racial chasm imposed by the location of Africans in different parts of the world. The case studies present scholars who are committed not only to their disciplines but also to black folks who are speaking and writing from an Africa-centered platform. Development and progress are issues that cannot be divorced from the narratives and analysis of our two case studies. The two scholars conceive of scholarship in terms of interdisciplinarity of subjects and approaches, the diversity of peoples and cultures and the theories to study them, and the challenges faced by peoples of Africa and the African diaspora. Both of them work at the University of North Carolina at Charlotte.

The New African Diaspora and Knowledge Production: Tanure Ojaide, Poet and Literary Critic

Professor Tanure Ojaide is one of the few African poets living in the African diaspora, and the most distinguished. His contributions can be categorized as African and African diasporic. He is part of the new African diaspora; a person who lives in the United States but returns to Africa all the time: a constantly recurring trip to the source of his knowledge. His home is neither Africa nor the United States. He lives in both, he contributes to both, and he explains both: each one to itself, and each to the other. Perhaps his background prepared him for these eclectic and dynamic contributions. Born in colonial Nigeria, he became a teenager soon after the country attained independence, listening to different stories of how the British governed his country on the one hand, and the stories of the first set of Nigerians in power preparing to lead their country to a civil war (1967–70) on the other. He survived it all, later migrating to Syracuse, New York, where he obtained his doctorate in English. The search for education has provided him with a transatlantic biography, one that is voluntary, but not without knowledge of the preceding, involuntary transatlantic biographies. Indeed, irrespective of when African scholars relocate to the United States, they all tend to be familiar with the rudiments of race relations. At a minimum, they are familiar with the transatlantic slave trade, Pan-Africanism, the biographies of Marcus Garvey and W. E. B. Du Bois, the Cold War, and African American contributions to decolonization and apartheid in South Africa.[9] And, like Ojaide, these scholars admire the profound philosophical traditions associated with C. L. R. James, Frantz Fanon, Edward Blyden, and other notable scholars of the Pan-Africanist tradition.[10]

Figure 10.1. Professor Tanure Ojaide. Photograph courtesy of
Tanure Ojaide.

On returning to Nigeria, he moved to the northeast to teach at the University of Maiduguri, observing Nigerian politics and probably not immune to the politics of the two neighboring countries of Chad and Niger. In this part of the world, it is not possible to escape the power of Islam. Thereafter, he moved to the United States, and he has been teaching at the University of North Carolina at Charlotte since 1993. Throughout his prodigious career, he has published many books and hundreds of poems and essays. His works have also been recognized in competitions: he was the 1987 recipient of the African Regional Winner of the Commonwealth Poetry Prize, and in 1988 he won the BBS Arts and Africa Poetry Award.

Living in the United States has had a transformative impact on Ojaide, not only in terms of his prolific output but also in the quality and content of his work. He sees the world with multiple gazes and countless insights. He understands Africa from his diasporic location, and he understands the diaspora from his African background; he fuses the knowledge of both to insert them into a universal language and grammar. Ojaide has refused to surrender his intellectual commitment to the uplifting of Africa and people of African descent, setting his ideas in the paradigm of liberation pedagogy and emancipatory humanism. His poems reveal multiple journeys: away from home and back; the fusion of near and far places; and the blending of families with communities, communities with nations, and nations with the world. His journeys are full of surprises and the chemistry of joy and pain, energy and fatigue. Confinement can occur even in free places, alienation can become the theme of self-reflections, darkness can come even when there is light, and separation from something, whatever that is, cannot be avoided.

His poems are full of images of happy and troubled minds, the poor suffering various agonies and the dispossessed, and the ruthlessness of power. As I read one of his poems, I saw a humanlike apparition appear from a dark corner that stared me in the eyes with a gaze that commanded me to do something positive. I am not superstitious, and I quickly interpreted what I saw as an emergency call to action, a positive reflection about community engagement. This is the power of Ojaide's words: they create flashes of light and inspiration that instigate our liberation—racial liberation, ethnic liberation, universal liberation, humanitarian liberation.

Ojaide presents us with not only the challenges of modern Africa but also the beauty of its peoples and places, the richness and depth of its history, and the diversity and brilliance of its culture. An Urhobo man from southwestern Nigeria, he has portrayed the art of his people as vibrant, linking art with society and communication; his art is a "moral medium."[11] Many African societies, as with the Urhobo about whom he speaks, live in the world of the metaphysical and physical at the same time, balancing the requirements in both to live a peaceful life. If art imitates life, life, too, can imitate art—gods and humans can dress alike and eat the same food!

The theme of power—its abuses, uses, manifestations—shapes the content of many of his poems. When African countries were under military regimes (from the 1960s to the 1990s), Ojaide wrote devastating poems on the deadly role of the soldiers, the police states that they established, and their thirst for blood. They killed without apology or remorse, he lamented. Blood and the smell of foul blood was everywhere. The more they killed, the more they wanted to kill—unbothered by the smell, the violence, the atrocities. In "When Soldiers Are Diplomats,"[12] he mocks the deception of giving authoritarian generals civilian jobs. The diplomat could dress well, smile broadly, even speak with finesse, but the "savage sophisticraft"[13] does not forget the gun in his pocket—and is eager to use it. In an antimilitary poem, "State Executive,"[14] he chastises the generals in power for killing critics, devastating the opposition, and destroying scholars. In "From Liberation," a poem written in 1997, Ojaide portrays Nigeria as a failed state. With a bleeding heart, he calls for an immediate change:

> Let this season end, let the hope-bereft land revive
> after recovery all will be on guard against
> another infection of illiterate gunnery;
> let this season end, even if it has to be
> with the libation of the despoiled land
> with the head vulture's own blood.[15]

In a poem dedicated to Jack Mapanje, the Malawian professor jailed for political reasons from 1987 to 1991, he sounds combative and aggressive, saying that no punishment, not even the accusation of treason, should stop one from seeking the means to overthrow an illegitimate government. He commends the efforts of Mohandas Gandhi (1869–1948), who led the Indian struggles for independence against Britain. A nonviolent man, Gandhi was assassinated.

So also were Murtala Mohammad of Nigeria and Thomas Sankara of Burkina Faso, two promising African leaders, the former in 1976 and the latter in 1987. Emboldened by these assassinations, Ojaide overcomes his fear, turning himself into a "human" in a fighting spirit to promote justice, unity, and the recovery of his nation. In his struggles, he hopes to create new warriors who will re-create the land. Depressed and angry, he chooses to give up his own life and his own blood, to abandon talking, to become possessed by the "Daemons of resistance," and to keep fighting until there is change. In "My Next Step," he poses the question "For how long will eyes stand bullshit? . . . [and] watch rather than break up the offensive dance of those sworn to break rules?"[16] Here is a revolutionary call to action, warning us all of the danger of tolerating dictatorship, saying that if we do not rise up, we will lose everything. His poem speaks to the events in the Middle East in 2010, and, when Africa follows, it will become the war anthem.

In spite of all the agonies, he enjoins us to seek peace in nature and celebrate the wonders of land and hills, the greens, the plateau. In "City in My Heart," written in Jos in 1993, his sense of emotional balance reaches a peak, elevated by the land's beauty, the nature that gives peace, contentment, and warmth. In this poem one can actually feels the hills! Earlier in 1990 he had celebrated the joy of nature:

> What will we look up to without birds
> beating their wings above our heads,
> what will we look up to without trees
> thrusting their arms into the sky,
> what will we look up to without the crest of hills?
> Our roots drive deep into the soil;
> they sustain us in our search for fortune.[17]

The poet-preacher can also become a praise singer, eulogizing the good person and good deeds. He may also choose to become motivational, even if in a pessimistic mood. In a poem titled "No,"[18] Ojaide warns against the excessive urge and need to please everyone at all times, thus destroying oneself in the inability to decline proposals. He warns against showing, as did Okonkwo's in *Things Fall Apart*, either excessive displays of strength to one's enemies or excessive generosity to one's friends; in the latter case, showing false empathy or lavishing unnecessary praise on friends who can later turn foes. A poet has become a preacher, warning individuals to check their own feelings and emotions and not to respond to the reckless demands of others.

In understanding the diaspora, Ojaide uses a powerful phrase, "branches of the same tree," to connect Africans with African Americans. From the Harlem Renaissance to recent writings, a number of African American literary writings have tapped into African ideas, stories, and other aspects of African culture and folklore to produce an African American literary tradition. Ojaide moves beyond the ideas of cultural affinities, which he acknowledges to be important, to show how African American literary traditions avoid being absorbed into European cultures by adopting a host of strategies. Using the themes of identity, poverty, and self-assertion, he has analyzed poems that engage these three themes to compare works generated by Africans and those by African Americans. He regards the postemancipation experience of African Americans as the equivalent of the postindependence experience of Africans, experiences that created "situational similarity" that led to creative works that do resemble one another in content and form. Drawing from the works of African diasporic poets, notably Arna Bontemps, Sonia Sanchez, Carolyn Rodgers, and Audre Lorde, he shows how their work exhibits the consciousness also found in the works of African poets.

In the manifestation of this consciousness, "blackness" becomes a tool to promote emancipation, to create a difference with others, to create the content to teach in schools, and to decolonize minds. Ojaide tracks the history of cultural assertiveness since the Harlem Renaissance through the civil rights era in the 1960s and 1970s, plugging the contributions of the poets he chooses into the different historical phases and showing their militancy as they oppose slavery and manifest their Africanness. As he does so, works like Arna Bontemps's "God Give to Men" are seen as part of the Négritude tradition; the poet calls for a unique black identity. Bontemps praises African cultural traditions in his poem "The Return." As in Senghor's work, Bontemps praises African heritage and calls on African Americans to return to their African roots. Ojaide considers the poetry of Carolyn Rodgers from the 1970s, especially her collection *How I Got Ovah*, to show how she advocates support for black institutions. All the poets speak to harsh conditions, make political statements, and seek an end to poverty and powerlessness. "The history of African Americans," Ojaide concludes, "is inextricably linked to that of Africans. As African literature, for instance, reflects African history, so does African-American literature reflects Black history."[19]

Africa and the African diaspora are fused in his work in terms of his cosmopolitanism, rhetorical style, and the agony of a reality fixed in poverty. The vision and spirit of the African to analyze Africa can become converted to surrealism to explain the African diaspora. There is often pain in his voice, but the pain reflects sensitivity and passion about individuals. When he writes about Africa, he often uses a disguise, as if covering his face with a mask, but his body is located in the distant land of the developed country. He will then become enraged, defending the dispossessed, the weak, the suffering. The people have been betrayed, and Ojaide condemns those who have done so and points to their injustice. Ojaide is in search of a humane society in Africa and the African diaspora.

Ojaide is also a literary critic. He has written on other poets, as in his analysis of the work of Syl Cheney-Coker of Sierra Leone, who wears the mask of a crucified Christ to criticize his country.[20] In an essay on Wole Soyinka, Ojaide shows how Soyinka's poetry is shaped by two forces: first, love of ceremony, worldview, and Yoruba myths, superstitions, and beliefs; and second by Western literary traditions and Christianity. Ojaide does not see any conflict in the use of foreign and indigenous materials; rather he believes it gives "variety and vitality to the poetry."[21]

The New African Diaspora and Knowledge Production: Akin Ogundiran, Historical Archaeologist

Akin Ogundiran has shown how the histories of Africa and the Americas are connected and embedded in one another. His complicated archaeological field research has supplied evidence to show how societies in West Africa were transformed by the Atlantic economy, revealing that what were previously understood as "local histories" are actually integral to global economic and political forces. In an essay on the Yoruba-Edo hinterland in the seventeenth and eighteenth centuries, he supplies data and analysis on the Okun people, showing how their state formation and transformation connected with the "expanding commercial relations on the coast, the networks of trading contacts between the coast and the hinterland, and the dynamics of political transformations of the period."[22]

As Ogundiran's statement is further validated by the original products of his excavations and solid ethnography, we begin to note that

Figure 10.2. Professor Akin Ogundiran and his wife, Mrs. Lea Koonce Ogundiran. Photograph courtesy of Akin Ogundiran.

Okun, and even hundreds of other villages and towns in West Africa, were living in the "shadow of the Atlantic economic system."[23] The degree to which these places were affected varied, reflecting the extent to which their production and consumption were integrated with the Atlantic economy. The impact on their material cultures was evident in the spread of such items as cowries, tobacco, corn, beads, textiles, and metals, all of which became key products in daily use and consumption patterns. These new products, coming from abroad and traded regionally and locally, show the formation of new tastes and habits.

New tastes and habits, I would like to argue, are also about new and expanding institutions of production and distribution. The products would not just have to be bought within a regional network of trade but also circulated to generate capital, which was then invested into power. The commodities had to be processed and connected with other materials to generate newer products, as in turning cotton into cloth, mixing alcohol with plants to produce herbal medicines, and the like. In the process, production created new forms of social capital that had consequences on how communities were organized and how institutions reproduced themselves. For one thing, differential access to the goods would suggest the nature of stratification and power but could also have triggered competition for the control of markets, resources, and power. As evidence elsewhere has shown, as in the case of the Old Oyo Empire, kingship could have consolidated its hold on power and centralized the access to guns and gunpowder, both of which were needed for state expansion and consolidation. The poor would be defined not necessarily as those without access to locally grown food, but rather without access to imported objects.

From his evidence, Ogundiran surmises that the Okun altered the technology of producing iron, which was possible by imitating imported iron objects. Tobacco pipes were made, as the habit of smoking spread from the late sixteenth century onward. This and other examples show how West Africa was not just being drawn into early capitalism, but was also becoming an economic frontier connected with American plantations and European manufacturing businesses. Europeans and Americans seeking profits made commercial connections with Africa, thus pressuring Africans to respond to them and fulfilling the task allocated to Africans in a global division of labor.

Ogundiran's study ultimately forced me to reread Immanuel Wallerstein's *The Modern World System*,[24] in which the combination of class, capital, and nature reveal the working of an expansive global capitalist network. Wallerstein linked agro-ecological transformation to the transition from feudalism to capitalism, and pointed to serious contradictions in feudalism. Ogundiran sees ruptures as well in the case of West Africa, in the extent to which its connections to the Atlantic trade began to transform its societies. He is right to point to technological changes, not just in new products but in reconfigured objects as well. One of the main processes in world history after the nineteenth century, as noticed in Ogundiran's excavation works, was the spread of various new technologies in connections with crops, guns, and gunpowder. As he noticed, the products also triggered production and organizational changes. For example, he observes that tobacco growing and tobacco use were actually widespread in different parts of Africa. He noticed how the trade in tobacco, which is a powerful stimulant, grew along with the consumption of tea, coffee, and chocolate, which were sweetened by the increasing availability of sugar. Maize spread as well, putting more land under cultivation and leading to new maize-derived foods such as porridge and flour. African productive capacity probably increased as more land and labor were devoted to the cultivation of maize and cassava.

The most decisive impact might have been the introduction of guns and gunpowder, which in turn led to the proliferation of gun-related technologies and products. No doubt the nature of warfare was transformed; we saw the intensity of this change among the Yoruba during the nineteenth century with the dramatic rise in the capacity to destroy. Samuel Johnson captured the wars so brilliantly and engagingly in his contemporary accounts of the era.[25] Johnson noticed the trends in the use of gunpowder and guns and how access to them induced intergroup conflicts. To pay for guns and gunpowder, kings and chiefs had to tighten their control of markets and trade routes. As we saw in the nineteenth century, they diverted a large number of war captives to domestic production in an effort to integrate themselves more fully with the market in order to make more money to buy imported items and gunpowder. The chiefs and kings took a more active role in commerce. As for the war captives, the chiefs and kings put them to work as a slave labor force.

In the cumulative body of his work, Ogundiran has focused on underinvestigated aspects of West African history, as well as undertheorized topics and fields. In doing both, he transcends the training and orientation offered to historical archaeologists in West

Africa, and he also transcends conceptually based but empirically
deficient studies in the United States. He fills the gap and marries
two orientations: empirically rich studies and fertile theorization.
Using Yoruba data, he has successfully synthesized the history of
the long precolonial period with theories drawn from studies on
Atlantic history and the African diaspora. The transitional phases
in the precolonial era that he notes, as in his example of the Oyo,[26]
are innovative, urging us to rethink our parameters about concep-
tualizing historic timelines.

Ogundiran may disagree with me, but I observe new elements suggested by his data. I see very strongly Marxist ideas around value, in
which the value of labor is connected with the imperatives of capitalism to shape the nature of change. In connecting West Africa to
the Atlantic economy, Ogundiran is pointing to what could be characterized as the "metabolic rift"[27] between supply and demand;
African economies are on the supply side of the global division of
labor that compelled them to produce for the Atlantic economy and,
at the same time, to consume products from external sources. This
division of labor, and the productive mechanism unleashed by the
demand side, ultimately had implications for all aspects of institutions. Ogundiran has to grapple not only with the meaning of "local
history," but also with the definition of the "world" in which the local
is situated against the background of rapidly changing events. And
if, as he treats the local, he engages in issues around production
and trade—as all his writings indicate—he is forced to engage in the
understanding of how society relates to nature: that is, how humans
ultimately relate to their environments, using and destroying them at
the same time, and sometimes renewing them as well.

His data suggest that he could also do a set of fine essays on "political ecology," using the products of his excavations to tell us more
about socioecological changes in West Africa since the fifteenth
century. Let me draw from his recent essay on Oyo to explain. As
Robin Law noted, the foundations of Oyo as an imperial power were
laid during the sixteenth century. It became and remained a strong
empire until its fall in the early nineteenth century.[28] Its expansion
manifested not just the traits of an empire, but also the way many
states behaved in the context of emerging capitalism in the early
modern period and in encounters with capitalism in the context of
the Atlantic world after the fifteenth century. The nucleus of Oyo
was in the northwest of Yorubaland, but it subsequently incorporated

other groups and exercised power over a large area, becoming by the end of the sixteenth century, according to Ogundiran, the "largest political unit in West Africa south of River Niger."[29]

The strategies of this expansion were multiple, and Ogundiran has isolated one element: "colonization," which he defines as shifting a population from the core to the frontiers and then extracting resources from it in the form of market dues and tolls. He excavated at Ede-Ile (part of Upper Osun), which he regards as the first site to be colonized during the sixteenth century. The basis of Ogundiran's argument rests on drawing from "the perspective of the landscape as a socially constructed space in the negotiation of political and economic relations, usually between unequal powers."[30] As his data unfold, details emerge about how Oyo was able to manipulate Ede-Ile's landscape and its resources for imperial aggrandizement. Ceramics, horse remains, and landscapes dominate his excavations—what I will call the cluster of "political ecology." Ceramics indicate an extensive industry connected to available clay resources but also to trade in a "ceramic sphere" in which the objects had to be exchanged. Used for a variety of everyday purposes—cooking, decoration, containers, lamps, and the like—they reveal everyday stories and the culture of connections between the center and its colonies. Noting the widespread planting of baobab trees, he interprets it as an attempt by Oyo to change the landscape of its colony by taking the product of the savanna to the rainforest. With regard to horse remains, he sees this as evidence of the need to secure Ede-Ile by building a cavalry both to strike fear in people's minds and to use against them if necessary.

He definitely speaks to the concept of the "preindustrial," the period between the late fifteenth and early nineteenth centuries, to which Fernand Braudel has devoted three massive volumes.[31] Rather than see the period as essentially driven by the Europeans, Ogundiran confers agency to Africa. It received products and ideas, but it transformed both. In return Africans essentially gave labor and the ideas that we now label as "Africanisms" in the New World. This connection means that we have to rethink the entire idea of "traditional Africa," since it has been integrated with the Atlantic World for far longer than previously imagined. Framing West Africa as disconnected from the global impulses and as "exotic" becomes even more grossly misleading. The changes that others witnessed elsewhere also impacted West Africa, some negatively, such as population loss. Ogundiran discusses many of these changes and shows that some were actually rapid and intense.

The conditions that triggered the capitalist expansion drew Africa into the European world and Atlantic economy. Global sea passages linked the Atlantic world together, providing an enormous advantage to Europe, which had invested in maritime activities. "A reliable ship," writes J. H. Parry, "competently manned, adequately stored, and equipped with means of finding the way, can in time reach any country in the world which has a sea coast, and can return whence it came."[32] Europeans reached the West African coastline, and the region became connected with the Atlantic World. Ogundiran shows how the hinterland was not disconnected from the coast. The extensive global interactions created a world economy by connecting many economies in different parts of the world through long-distance trade. Overland routes were limited compared to global maritime trade. Rare commodities, bulky items, and human products could be traded over long distances, from deep inside the West African hinterland to faraway Brazil. Land use was remarkably transformed, especially in the Americas where settlers on the frontier expanded production, which required more labor and more markets to dispose of their products. The Dutch moved to South Africa, and internal colonization took place in various parts of the world as market forces and powerful states pressured people to move or to produce. Tendencies that later led to the Yoruba wars of the nineteenth century or the outbreak of the Islamic jihad in the savanna were being laid by the processes of changing land use. Monetary systems emerged and became global; West Africa relied on the cowries imported from outside the region. Bigger and more stable states emerged as part of the process of this early modern history, benefitting from the increasing economic activities. Empires like Oyo and Benin flourished, resembling others in Europe and elsewhere that showed large size and complex organization. The stronger empires tried to be stable and were able to become more efficient in building military systems that also enhanced their capacity to control markets and trade routes. If Africa lost people, other parts of the world gained; some calculations put the global increase in population to between 350 and 550 million over a three hundred year period.[33]

Ogundiran is not saying that the Yoruba, Edo, and others do not constitute social, cultural, and political units—as nationalist historiographers, including myself, have presented them—but rather that they were not autonomous from larger forces that shaped the early modern period. He himself has contributed to locating states in their regional context, as in his analysis of the imperialist expansion of the Old Oyo Empire into Upper Osun in Central Yorubaland.[34] However, when his fieldwork yielded such items as cowries, glass beads, and tobacco pipes, he exposed patterns of integration within a regional market and between a regional market and the Atlantic World. The objects reveal the emerging patterns of taste that were beyond the ability of the local economy to satisfy. The cowry-currency network was certainly not local, as Ede-Ile could not have produced the cowries; it needed linkages with a bigger market to have access to those cowries. The movements of a population, even when it was part of an imperialist design of colonization, as in his example of Oyo, does show that a number of those who moved had economic interests to pursue; they especially sought the means to participate in economic activities that were integrated to the larger Atlantic commerce. Colonization enabled Oyo, as Ogundiran argues, to provide the security and space to control trade routes and markets that linked the hinterland, via the Ijebu, with the coast.

The Two Case Studies in Context

It is clear that the new African diaspora is comprised of different categories of people divided by ethnicity, nationality, gender, and class. The numbers run into millions. There are transnational networks of migrants between which knowledge circulates. The category that I have focused on here is that of knowledge-cum-creative generator. There is an established "knowledge community" dealing with the knowledge of the self, knowledge about new homes, knowledge about migrations, knowledge about the African diaspora, and knowledge about change, new vision, and new pathways. Larger currents in the disciplines enrich this knowledge (as in Ogundiran connecting ideas drawn from the literature on the Atlantic World to his studies of the Yoruba).

The knowledge generated by the new diaspora overlaps with the older knowledge in terms of themes—slavery, race relations, colonization—but moves us to newer ideas of globalization, new networks of local and regional engagements, re-Africanizing black American intellectual traditions, and engagement with new technologies to deliver development-based ideas. The transnationalists want to tap into knowledge of the past to revise knowledge of the present. Their own memories, shaped by the experience of voluntary migration, are connected with those of forced migration of the Atlantic slave trade and colonization by the European empires. Perhaps as members of a post–civil rights era, they hold no psychological complexes about their color and race, thus departing from some elements of the African American experience characteristic of the highly racialized eras. The scholars of the new African diaspora manifest the ideology of development and power of black people but do not necessarily seek psychological means to overcome the trauma of enslavement and colonization. The environments in which diaspora scholars grew greatly shaped their voices. The conditions of their people and the underdeveloped states in Africa affect their creative imaginations and scholarly production. Whether as poets or historians, they seem united by the need to speak out in exposing mismanagement, corruption, and injustice. They use the language of brotherly love, hoping for change in the poor areas of the African diaspora and Africa.

It is important to underscore that this knowledge is often different from others; it is marked mainly by moving away from what may be characterized as "black orientalism," which frames knowledge of Africa in relation to preconceived notions of Africa and received knowledge of the Africa invented by Europeans in the context of slavery, racism, colonialism, and neocolonialism. Knowledge circulated about Africa in the United States can sometimes be predicated on stereotypes, old wives' tales, and fables about Africans in private homes, barbershops, and street corners. This cumulative body of circulated oral stories is powerful in terms of shaping images, expectations, and even the valuation of Africa. Ojaide and Ogundiran's foundational template is not based on stereotypical imaginings of Africa. In the stereotypical template, one seeks knowledge of Africa to either validate or invalidate the stories that have previously circulated, that is, to connect or disconnect a preexisting orality from an academic ontological engagement. Birth and firsthand experiences have shaped the ontological reality of Ojaide and Ogundiran; stories and stereotypes have shaped the ontological reality of many African Americans, stories that are not always positive.

Nevertheless, there is also the more powerful influence of how others have shaped the image of Africa. The slave trade and its legacies have shaped not only the African American self-image but also the understanding of Africa itself. Here lies another critical difference in which Ojaide and Ogundiran's experiences are disconnected from overly racialized origins and ontologies. In a racialized image of Africa, Africans and Africa are presented to African Americans as inferior and deficient. Ojaide and Ogundiran may be disappointed with the performance of leaders and the failure of institutions, but their comments and criticisms are not derisive of peoples and cultures and neither do they portray Africans by the negative image of the "dark continent."

In talking about Africa and the black experience, the writings of Ojaide and Ogundiran are influenced by humanitarian and universal concerns, the redemptive vision of power to bring about change, the brotherhood of humankind that can do away with evil and oppression. Their own individual experiences are important, but it is clear that their concerns are driven by the larger issues of nationality, race, identity, and development. Whether as poetry or history, they offer guidelines to understand human continuity and change. Ogundiran tells us about communities and ideas before our time. The stress on continuity is in itself a theory of symbolic immortality; we are told that both our ancestors and we are alive. As Ojaide tells us about ourselves here and now, our collective experiences and culture connect us with our history, symbolizing the very essence of our immortality that links us with the past. If others want to see themselves as strong nations in the image of gods with power, Ojaide and Ogundiran remind us that we are travelers with limitations in an ever-changing world.

We face a crossroads and new paths as transnationalists in a globalized world. The global economy is interlocked, and Africa and the diaspora are very much embedded in it. We want to be active within this global economy, not as suppliers of slaves and labor, or as producers of cash crops, domestic servants, and other exploitable categories, but rather as creators, inventors, managers, leaders, and entrepreneurs in control of the economic forces that shape our lives. The integration of Africa with its diaspora—in knowledge production and policies—must reinforce ideas of empowerment within the global economy. Powerful global forces may try to impose limits on us, just as they have done for centuries in the creation of Atlantic and colonial economies, but we have to fashion a new beginning in which we constitute the center and not the periphery.

There are several ways to strengthen the connections between Africa and its diaspora, and vice versa, and then use these connections to generate relevance, progress, development, and peace. First, we as scholars have to keep extending the frontier of knowledge, use our resources to transform scholarship in Africa, and ensure that our studies also inform mainstream scholarship. We must be fully inserted into all the mainstream knowledge systems and must struggle to be at the center. While we should continue to support area studies, we have to understand their limitations in academies that use the universalism of ideas as a key source of power. Africa is part of universal knowledge, and not so-called local knowledge with less value. This advancement of the universality of African/African diaspora knowledge (about them and by them) must be presented in such a way that the academic world, irrespective of location, will see both the value in and the necessity of the knowledge being generated.

To individuals, the acquisition of quality education remains the main source of mobility, especially to the segment of the population lacking access to inheritance and start-up capital to establish businesses on their own. This education has to be based on various components: the acquisition of knowledge in various disciplines; the acquisition of skill sets connected with occupations in the formal and informal sectors of the economy; and the cultivation of emotional intelligence to process data and information in a careful, objective, rational manner.

As scholars, our research and the ways we teach must reflect not only the concerns of our specific disciplines but also the concerns of the universities where we work, the locations where we live, our communities, and the people that constitute our communities and colleagues. We have the special role of linking the Americas with Africa, the academy with the public, knowledge with occupations. On our campuses, we have to represent the very best in the understanding of Africa, people of African descent, and the value of diversity and culture. Beyond college campuses, we need to allow entrepreneurs, politicians, and policymakers to benefit from our knowledge. As cultural brokers, we must bring knowledge of Africa to the Americas and that of the Americas to Africa. Insularity must give way to internationalization. As we promote study abroad programs for Americans to go to Africa, Africans must come to the United States as well. In addition, there must be domestic programs that teach students about different and diverse communities within and beyond their regions.

The suggestions on education combine merit and nonmerit factors of success. Quality education will ensure the understanding of the very process of development, even the ability to question the ideology of meritocracy and confront it with alternatives. Abilities and talents have to be discovered, then cultivated and put to use. As all first-generation migrants genuinely understand and practice, there is no shortcut to success, no substitute for hard work. Since the 1980s, a large number of immigrants still belong to the first generation. As they succeed, many will leave inheritances to their children as a "non-merit" factor to not only consolidate but also expand the wealth and knowledge base of their successors. We are already noticing the trend in the placement of Africans in all the major colleges and institutions across the United States. Focused and interested in degrees tied to occupations, the evidence is becoming clearer that the second generation may acquire greater influence than the first.

Second, knowledge must be converted into value-added knowledge for institutions and people to grow. The growth can be by way of humane values, the cultivation of cosmopolitan minds, the ability to understand the complexity of society, the management of resources and people, and the promotion of global peace. To be sure, many will expect far more tangible things by way of technical advancement, the elimination of poverty, and massive development. It is not selfish for some people to demand that the knowledge we generate transform Africa and black people. If they are transformed, the entire world is transformed: the number of poor will be reduced by millions, migrations will be reduced, interstate relations will improve, and market and democratic spaces will expand.

Third, we have to theorize more on the nature and uses of power with the goal of seeking the means for more migrants to be part of the institutions and structures of governance. Without power, it is difficult to control resources and create appropriate mechanisms of allocation. Power is difficult to acquire without social capital. Immigrants find it very difficult to acquire social capital, that is, an extended network of highly connected people. Social capital is an integral part of how the institutions of society work in relation to the acquisition of power and wealth. Immigrants can access the churches, but they tend to be their ethnic churches—not the country clubs and spaces to trade information and create entry points to obtain resources.

Fourth, we have to increase the rates of business ownership and then generate more sales, hire more people, and create more profits. For success to occur, we must understand the importance of financial and human capital and seek the means to create start-up capital that can make businesses more competitive. The possibility of creating higher start-up capital lies in only one strategy: the ability to pool and combine resources. Just as we have been successful in forming religious and ethnic associations, we have to move beyond both to create business associations. Through the acquisition of greater managerial skills and capital, there is now a large pool of immigrant petty bourgeoisie who can move to the next stage in the Marxist categorization: entrepreneurial capitalists who work in their own businesses and who are also able to hire the labor of others. In other words, the entrepreneur-capitalists are able to use the proletariat (those who sell their labor) to create more capital.

Finally, be it in politics or business, alliances have to be forged, the creation of what Martin Luther King Jr. once described as the "network of mutuality." This network will be in stages, within cities, between cities, and between hosts and homelands. The USA-Africa Dialogue discussion group is an initiative that has created a Pan-Africanist framework with a global reach; it has become the most successful in using the Internet to link black people in different continents in order to document, interpret, and disseminate the experiences of the new African diaspora. The alliances need to revive some of the agenda of older Pan-Africanist networks that sought the elimination of the exploitation and domination of black people. The members of the new diaspora must support those of the older diaspora to attain empowerment and full citizenship. Networking has to be conceived in terms of the creation of support mechanisms within the United States, and of development mechanisms between the United States and Africa.

Both Ojaide and Ogundiran, two key members of the new African diaspora, are already showing us the way, through knowledge acquisition and dissemination, to move forward in the context of globalization, transformation, empowerment, and visibility. Thus the infrastructures of capacity building are being created and consolidated. Ogundiran has shown how the study of Africa can interface with that of Europe and the Americas, giving us ideas on how we can even begin to rethink how we teach and organize the disciplines, and how some area study programs can be more creative. Ojaide has linked the community with the academy by means of poems that seek our activist engagement to put the ivory tower in the service of the community. He shows how creative people are important in the conceptual values that they bring to the table, and in their portrayal of marginalized subjectivities. In Ogundiran and Ojaide, combined knowledge reveals ideas on culture, race, people, and aspirations in ways that help us talk about subjects and issues that are crucial to the pedagogy of the black experience. Intellectual power is the very first condition for both economic and political power. As we generate sound scholarship, as the two case studies have shown, we are laying a solid foundation of intellectual power to transform lives and societies.

11

Nollywood and the Creative World of Aderonke Adesola Adesanya

The African Impact on Global Cultures

This chapter focuses on two key examples of the manifestation of African culture in the African diaspora: the rapid spread of Nollywood movies to other parts of the world and the work of a new generation of transnationalist diaspora artists based both in Africa and throughout the Western world. These two examples and other topics related to culture and cultural production, such as identity, religion, art, and poetry, illustrate how various aspects of African culture are spreading to other parts of the world.

Nollywood

Nollywood, now ranked as the third largest movie production industry in the world after Hollywood and Bollywood, is predominantly based in Nigeria, and it has become truly global. It has become arguably the most powerful contemporary form of spreading African worldviews, recuperating older values, propagating newer ones, and celebrating multivalent stories. Nollywood films have traveled widely and combine an adept manipulation of African languages with images and scenes that reveal African landscapes and storylines that are grounded in the rich valences of African culture. One can purchase the films in stores in European and American cities as well as across Africa. Given the large number of films and topics, I will draw examples from the Yoruba productions to avoid excessive generalizations.

In one sense, Nollywood unites the Yoruba. The producers and actors are mostly Yoruba, the contexts of the stories are Yoruba, and the primary consumers are Yoruba. Where witches and juju suddenly appear, no one is lost—at least within the context of a Nollywood storyline. And yet, in another sense, Nollywood sells Yoruba to the world, tasking its audience to experiment with new contexts and meanings while cautioning those same audiences not to impose criticisms on storylines governed by a logic that is new or strange to them or that works from a totally different set of cultural assumptions. When non-Yoruba do their alternative reading of Nollywood, they are often compelled to assess the contexts and texts as either primordial or modern, which only reinscribes the aesthetics of difference. The audiences' unwillingness or even inability to understand the storylines sometimes leads to the denigration of the culture that produced them, even if the external analyses are reductionist and misleading because they narrowly frame cultural products as "primitivism" or "nativism."

Nollywood presents the notion of a "new Yoruba" in urban and rural locations. Lagos is central to this definition; it is a place awash with money, big cars, and big houses, where big men and women spend lavishly. The new Yoruba tap into older and newer cultures and into local and global ones. A person can move from the village to Lagos and, weeks later, be on his or her way to London only to be forced back home soon afterward from the effects of powerful juju, or witchcraft, obtained from a diviner who lives in a nice house and drives a jeep. The new Yoruba do not live in one culture but are sandwiched among other, sometimes even three or more, cultures.

Nollywood manifests both the degenerative and regenerative sides of culture, and one can find ample examples to support both notions. Nollywood projects and subverts cultures and power at the same time. Cutting across eras, from the traditional to the more recent, many films have portrayed the power and violence of the nation-state, the cruelties and brutalities of political leaders, and the failure of state institutions to generate development. Many films have ridiculed excesses while praising generosity. Evocative stories have brought to light the dehumanizing habits of the rich and powerful—for example, those who traffic in human organs to gain wealth and power. Creative stories warn against inauthentic living, ridicule abuses, and punish characters who live immoral lives and make selfish choices. One corrupt individual can bring misfortune to an entire family or community. Nollywood indicts the rich and the powerful for being unkind to the poor and powerless. Death is ever present, and it is utilized to portray and punish evil and to remind everyone about the ultimate end of humanity.

Nollywood has transported Yoruba societies and cultures inside and outside of Nigeria to other parts of Africa and the West. Full of ambiguities, we see the Yoruba in their best moments and in their nakedness: as active and passive, as powerful and traumatized citizens within the larger political space of Nigeria. Authentic Yoruba, full of wise sayings and proverbs, are often contrasted against a newer generation, often presented as inauthentic because of its inability to speak flawless Yoruba and for its shameful violation of the cardinal principles associated with quintessential *omoluwabi*. In such character-ologies, we are moved to pity the inauthentic generation as it struggles for assimilation into an ill-defined Western world. It is portrayed as degenerate. Its members smoke, abuse their bodies with drugs, dress indecently by exposing their breasts or chests, and utter careless speech among other myriad inanities. Even bestiality becomes the non-Yoruba. Nollywood, however, seldom subverts cultural hierarchies, as it always privileges the wisdom of elders, the authority of kings and chiefs, and control over children and women.

Money matters! Nollywood does not always explain how the Yoruba become rich, but it frowns on using magic, especially human body parts, for money. While those who do so get rewarded, they are ultimately exposed, indicted, and punished. Punishing the get-rich-quick Yoruba privileges regeneration over degeneration.

Satire is also a powerful tool in Nollywood, and it allows drama and narrative to demolish the false pretenses of the Nigerian nation-state, the corrupting elements of Westernization, and the vulgarity of modernity. In many films, we are clearly warned to celebrate tradition and to engage with a cultural patrimony that relies on the past to prevail over the destructive path of the present. For example, in Tunde Kelani's *Arugba*, celebration of the Osun festival turns into political satire, tapping into the depth and richness of an age-old religious tradition to comment on the secularist politics of the post-1990s era. In blending fact with fiction and fantasy with reality, *Arugba* cleverly formulates a hybrid narratology of the decadence of power mediated by the restorative power of mythology. In *Arugba* and various other films dealing with the theme of power, Nollywood shows unfulfilled dreams but is careful not to take away hope. As grim as a situation may be, Nollywood often resolves it with hope, as if making a statement that the Yoruba spirit cannot be conquered and cannot be killed. As hope is about to be dashed and everything appears lost, the *Babalawo* (diviner) will consult Ifa to seek prevention. Sacrifices become regenerative devices to restore order.

Far more than written texts, Nollywood spreads Yoruba worldviews and culture inside and outside of Africa. No doubt there are those who would disagree with a great deal of which cultural elements are spread and emphasized. For instance, divination and diviners have been invested with all sorts of meanings as miracle workers, magicians, charm makers, evil doers, con men, wise men, saviors, and the like. The Qur'an and Bible have profoundly influenced the culture. In some movies, when the screenwriter runs out of ideas to close the story or resolve the conflicts, he or she can bring in an all-wise Imam or Pentecostal priest. In the Christian-derived films, the power of Jesus is superior to that of the diviners, and characters who draw on so-called Yoruba culture are portrayed as evil. Whether it is for good or bad, the films turn to the understanding of older cultures, contemporary realities, and gossip to create new stories.

Whether you like Nollywood or not, it has certainly become one of the most verdant pastures of Yorubanness. It has shown the capacity to further accentuate and consolidate the global dimensions of the Yoruba diaspora. Through the utilization of technology, it has initiated a new tradition of contemporary literacy and orality, one in which visuality and orality are married for maximum impact.

Nollywood is now being produced in the United States. The same stores that carry films made in Nigeria also carry those produced for the American audience. To take one example, *Virginia Is for Lovers*, a story of love and the complications of marriage, portrays the lives of contemporary Africans in an American setting. The DVD cover gives a summary of the film without revealing the answers:

> The issue of a man and a woman as best friends has always been on our minds. In other words can a man and a woman be close friends without being in love? Or is there any such thing as a platonic relationship. Now before you say anything please enjoy this romantic drama between Michael Collins (Desmond Elliot) and Stacey Thompson (Ginnefine Kanu) who are both raised in Virginia (United States), have been friends since childhood and had always helped each other. Now eventually how does Michael's wife Chobis (Hassanatu Kanu) and

her best friend Kim (Veeda Darko) feel about this and how it relates to their marriage, friends and family relations.[1]

Africa is implicated in the characters' marriages, creating a hybridity of ideas on multiple issues: romance, marital responsibility, imagined kinship, the impact of money, and the like. *Virginia Is for Lovers* is targeted at a younger generation of Africans living in the West. It is part of a growing body of work in which the signifier in black profane discourse is being rejected and replaced with something positive. The way of life captured in *Virginia Is for Lovers* is accomplished by language in which the range of meanings adheres to standard English usage. If signifying in black speech reveals tensions in society and in racial and class divisions, serious and mundane issues in *Virginia Is for Lovers* are presented in the language of a rising middle class. Africa and the experience of immigrants are not presented as esoteric, but as real; they are not intellectualized as a past heritage, but as a living culture. Western values are not being rejected, but are appropriated and adapted, thereby rejecting the binary opposition between the values to be encouraged in being black and those to be repudiated by imitating whiteness. Tensions are mediated by popular culture and the market rather than by race and class. The images of the 1970s are gone. There is no revolutionary talk, as in the past; there is no dirty characterization of blacks as wig-wearing whores and conk-haired hipsters.

Virginia Is for Lovers reveals how creativity can capture a moment, and it allows us to compare and contrast peoples of different generations as well as the different historical eras that shape their attitudes. The black middle class represented in the creative work of the Harlem Renaissance is not the one represented in the film. The rage of the class and racial wars of the past involved statements about Africa, the transatlantic slave trade, slavery, the trauma of emancipation, and the sufferings of the civil rights movement. If in the past many had to reject their origins because of the trauma of slavery, many of the present are affirming their origins. The suffering and pain of the past required confrontation with the heritage of slavery, which included accepting or rejecting Africa. In *Virginia Is for Lovers*, assimilation is celebrated, and the Western conception of romance is accepted. The trope of success and failure can become repetitive, as in the annual repetition of festivals and rituals, but such repetition should not be confused with the lack of theoretical sophistication or creative imagination. A film or work can be mediocre, but the repetition of its theme is not responsible for the mediocrity.

On the issue of repetition, I am reminded of a statement by James A. Snead: "In any case, let us remember that, whenever we encounter repetition in cultural forms, we are indeed not viewing 'the same thing' but its transformation, not just a formal ploy but also often the willed grafting onto culture of an essentially philosophical insight about the shape of time and history."[2] *Virginia Is for Lovers* weaves the trope of friendship and love into a repetitive cultural form, using the signifier of affection and marriage to narrate the experience of contemporary migrants.

Immigrant Communities

Just as Nollywood has inserted the Yoruba and other African immigrants into contemporary culture, so too have a large number of contemporary Africans living in different parts of the West inserted African culture into Western culture. They are creating, on a daily basis, a triangulated reality of the African by drawing from African tradition within the context of a postcolonial world but using ideas derived from modernity. Their numbers keep increasing. They have a notable presence in major cities such as London, New York, Chicago, Baltimore, Dallas, and Houston.

One can find in all of these cities stores owned and operated by Africans. An African language is the primary language of communication between customers and store owners, but any of the Western languages may also be used. The stores offer insight into the migration and spread of African culture and clues to unfolding changes.[3] Established food items such as yam, cassava, corn, palm oil, stock fish, dry fish, beans, *gari*, and *elubo* are found side-by-side with newer items like Quaker Oats, custard, bread, tea, coffee, evaporated milk, corned beef, and sardines. The stores carry Nollywood films made in Lagos and also films created in the United States that are imitative of Hollywood and Bollywood. The US films tell stories of migrations, romantic love, married life, cheating, and of drug trafficking, a get-rich-quick, underground economy that always ends in trouble.

There are beauty items, and two of the most popular come directly from Nigeria: *ose dudu* and *ori*. *Ose dudu*, labeled "black soap," has

Figure 11.1. Mr. Michael Palas Nti, store manager, Africacarib Market, Austin, Texas. Photograph courtesy of Colemar Nichols.

been made for centuries using a combination of palm kernels, palm oil, and other ingredients. *Ori* is shea butter, and its positive impact on the skin has been popularized even in the Western media. Wigs and hair extensions hang in visible parts of the store; some come from Nigeria but more than a few are made in China.

The stores also market beauty items such as bleaching materials divided into two categories: prohibited ones, which are hidden, and the "toners" that are displayed on the shelves. "Whitening" the skin, an attempt to change skin color from black to a shade of yellow, red, and sienna, is practiced among a number of Yoruba, notably women. Skin color is related to the conception of beauty and the politics of race. Among some men, light-skinned women christened as *omo pupa* women tend to attract greater attention than dark-skinned ones (*omo dudu*). Thus, the *omo dudu*, seeking to attract and compete with her competitors, bleaches her skin.

Moreover, as a color, black has been associated with negativity— "black market," "black mind," "black maria," "Black Friday," and so on. Satan is black, and the angels are white. Racialized societies reward the light-skinned with better jobs and pay and characterize the dark-skinned as inferiors. In defining and maintaining white privilege, black skin has been abused and insulted. Consider Edward E. Telles's comments about skin color in *Race in Another America*:

> Both the United States and Brazil were colonized by a European power that dominated militarily weaker indigenous populations and eventually instituted a system of slavery that relied on Africans. In the Brazilian case, European colonists and their descendants enslaved and imported seven times as many Africans as their North American counterparts. In the late nineteenth and early twentieth centuries, both countries also received millions of immigrants from Europe as they sought to industrialize. Since then, the light-skinned descendants in the United States and Brazil have come to dominate their darker-skinned compatriots through discriminatory practices that derive from a racial ideology, creating what sociologists call racially stratified societies. Both societies have experimented with affirmative-action policies to promote blacks and members of other disadvantaged groups, beginning in the 1960s in the United States and only recently in Brazil. However, the major similarities between these two large multiracial countries regarding race may end there. For one, the vast majority of persons in the United States with any African origin are categorized as black. In Brazil, large numbers of persons who are classified and identify themselves as white (*branco*) have African ancestors, not to mention the brown (*pardo, moreno*), mixed race (*mestiço, mulato*), and black (*preto, negro*) populations. Unlike in the United States, race in Brazil refers mostly to skin color or physical appearance rather than to ancestry.[4]

Africans cannot be isolated from these racialized hierarchies or from ideologies of white supremacy, even in Cuba where Fidel Castro attempted to use a socialist ideology to create a race-free society.[5] Coping strategies vary, and bleaching may be one of them, although the chemicals used for it contain large doses of mercury, which are dangerous.[6] The skin, as part of the body, is an identity. The women are consciously defining themselves to others, projecting aesthetics as a politics of representation. The woman who bleaches has a narrative—unspoken and interior—but those who speak about her, in the form of gossip, put forth exterior extraordinary theatrical statements, suggestive of a promiscuous combination of Yoruba with non-Yoruba values. Some may disingenuously argue that bleaching is done only for the cosmetic purpose of "looking good" rather than engaging in the politics of the body.

The body is a zone of politics, whether an individual is conscious of or accepts it or not. For example, I am conscious of always wearing

African attire to work, to teach and to lecture in Western institutions. My dress and my ideas align within the politics of culture and reject the cultural arrogance of others. Nevertheless, a body and the dress that adorns it can create identity and cultural warfare, as in the case of veiling by Muslims in Western societies. The African persona—the language, accent, dress, and food—projects a specific identity and can unleash both positive and negative comments and conflicts.

The attire on my body communicates politics without using words. In circumstances where it is interpreted as overwhelming and the persona is overdetermined, one becomes a symbol of a political identity with a history and a memory. The same person with the same attire in Ibadan, Nigeria, would be read differently than if he or she were in Austin, Texas—even within an immigrant milieu. In the latter, he or she stirs culture in the direction of assertive politics, disquiets the Western gaze, and makes the gaze—not the person—the subject of analysis. A gaze is a probe, an inquisition, even a manifestation of power, all combined to wonder about the subjectivity of an individual: his or her values, agenda, clowning, defects, and affirmation of difference. An elegant Yoruba *buba* worn at a formal Western function may be misinterpreted as the superficiality of a persona, so that the person wearing the *buba* may feel it necessary to defend or protect himself as he answers questions about his nationality and background. Although black is as a racial category in American society, the Yoruba *buba* renders him a foreign black, a non-American, perhaps even a recent immigrant. The *buba* leads to an open-ended tale that should be told with vigilance.

Members of the second generation, or children of Yoruba immigrants—if they wear the *buba* at all—wear it mainly in inconsequential locations, thus making a statement that it lacks the status to command attention in the corporate world or to mix with Western wear at major social functions. Children of immigrants relate to Africa and the culture of their hosts more in the context of assimilation than from a position of cultural assertiveness. The African who manifests Africanness may interpret the gaze that stares at her as one of adulation or it might make her feel ashamed or confused. When a loss of African identity is forced, it can provoke anger or shame in the individual. It is counted as a loss if she accepts assimilation into Euro-American cultural identity as a more-desired option. Perhaps to make herself more comfortable with the compromise, she may dismiss the subliminal pressure to belong, to become assimilated, to become "civilized."

In a related vein, a variety of African Christianity is spreading that taps into African culture to localize the Gospel. Within these diaspora churches, ideas about witchcraft, sorcerers, and the "evil eye" can be found. The Bible acquires the power of magic, divination, and healing. Biblical words can lead to miracles, as psalms are chanted like incantations, as in the examples of Yoruba *ayajo, ogede,* and *ofo.* The spread of African Pentecostalism to the West, as in the case of the Cherubim and Seraphim churches and, most recently, of Pastor Enoch Adejare Adeboye's the Redeemed Christian Church of God, is equally a spread of African culture, manifested in ideas of spiritual power, dreams, and trances. Possession by the Holy Spirit, belief in witchcraft and *omo araiye* (evil doers), and divination practices are grounded in biblical revelations, and the power of prayer is closely akin to that of incantations.[7]

Among the immigrants are a respectable number of college professors. These scholars capture events, trends, and history, and they use the methodologies and rules of their disciplines to analyze Africa. Irrespective of their disciplines, in distilling what they do, the representation of African cultures seeks to affirm tradition, change, and modernity. Hybridity has become the core principle of knowledge in presenting Africa to non-Africans, in mainstreaming Africa into knowledge production, and in using Africa as a case study to test various universal ideas. African scholars make general contributions to the understanding of black nationalism and draw from traditions and powerful mythologies created in a timeless past. The case study below illustrates my points.

Aderonke Adesola Adesanya: Artist, Cartoonist, and Poet

Just as Nollywood is spreading, so also is African art, especially in the private homes of African migrants who collect it, most notably street and tourist art, and who decorate their homes with photographs and images. My example dwells on the paintings and poetry of Dr. Aderonke Adesola Adesanya of Nigeria, who has taught at the University of Ibadan in Nigeria, and currently teaches at James Madison University in Harrisonburg, Virginia, in the United States. An art historian, artist, and cartoonist, she acquired fame in her early twenties as a cartoonist for two Nigerian newspapers, the *Tribune* and *Vanguard.* She was later to take a PhD in African art, focusing on the wood carvings of Lamidi Fakeye, a distinguished Yoruba carver.[8] She coedited a book on migration and coauthored a long book of poetry. She has done art exhibitions and poetry recitations in addition to teaching a variety of courses at the college level. Her publications and creative output have brought her tremendous attention in various countries, and she ranks as one of the most important Nigerian artists and art historians, enjoying both national and international visibility.

If Yoruba Orisa traditions and healing illustrate the transfer of culture and its repackaging from Africa to the Americas, and *Virginia Is for Lovers* presents the love lives of transnationalists, the art of Adesanya takes us back to Africa to relate art and poetry to culture, the indigenous to the modern. I have selected samples of her work done over a ten-year period in different locations, dwelling on various themes.

Yoruba Mythologies and Cultures: Opon Ifa

The Yoruba of Nigeria feature prominently in Adesanya's scholarship and creative writing. Not only are most of her major academic essays drawn from the Yoruba, so also is her poetry and a number of paintings. The paintings tend to illustrate many of the cultural patterns and characteristics about which she has written, and they touch on customs, ceremonies, festivals, modernity, and women.

Religion features prominently in her paintings. Figure 11.3, *Opon Ifa* (Ifa divinatory tray), draws from the centrality of divination in a traditionally Yoruba setting to make statements on a contemporary scholar. *Opon Ifa* is used for divination purposes. Ifa embodies *imo* (knowledge/understanding), *ogbon* (wisdom), and *oye* (insights) on which the life of the Yoruba world is sustained. Put in another way, the divination tray is *opon imo* (receptacle of knowledge/understanding), *opon ogbon* (repository of wisdom), and *opon oye* (storehouse and platter of insights) of which the deity Ifa is the custodian and its priesthood the *babalawo* or *iyalawo*. The indigenous Ifa receptacle, typically carved in wood, does have the face of Esu-deity at the centerpiece and edge of the tray. Esu is the Yoruba god of the crossroads, accepted by and assimilated into the religious ethos of devotees in the diaspora. However, Esu is labeled as the "trickster" by some and misleadingly as "Satan" by Christians looking for a linguistic equivalent to the biblical Satan. The grafting of the image of Esu-deity on

Ifa receptacle is in acknowledgment of its tremendous ability to facilitate or mar a pressing project. Without invoking and acknowledging Esu in the customary incantatory prologue of divination, there will be no accessibility to the rich resources of information from Orunmila, the custodian of Ifa. Hence, Adesanya inscribes the image of the deity on the rim of the receptacle in the painting. Adesanya also places the usual sixteen nuts, at times cowries, which facilitate entry into verses and their hidden meanings, at the center of the tray.

Adesanya's oil painting of *Opon Ifa* deliberately transmutates the original concept for the purpose of refracting new meaning. Here the Ifa tray is the universe that is supervised or policed by the invisible eyes of Esu, one of the important ministers of the Supreme Being. The map of Africa, which replaces the usual sixteen cowries, underlines the orthocentrality of the African continent in relation to natural and human resources and as the possible last hope of the human race. Given that it was presented to Toyin Falola in 2010 by his friends to commemorate his publishing more than one hundred books and articles, the Ifa tray art piece could have been informed by two factors: the celebrant's last name Falola, which has an *Ifa* prefix (lola) or the fact that if Falola could accomplish the extraordinary task of publishing over a hundred scholarly and artistic works, he might just as well have been an Ifa-incarnate.

Masquerade (fig. 11.4) captures a long-held idea on masquerades, an established way of venerating ancestors.[9] Masks and memorial effigies have been created to generate consciousness around the dead and to link the dead with the living. Known as the *egungun*, these annual celebrations in many Yoruba cities unite the people. They also provide an opportunity for performance, as the masquerades and the living could dance and exchange pleasantries. The emphasis in figure 11.4 is on the mask, which is usually made by a carver. In addition to this human-made item, one observes the vegetal, as in the case of the figure to the left with raffia attached to the mask. In combination, the masquerade is wearing an *ago*, which distinguishes him from the normal human being. The ensemble she created here is meant to be pleasing while also communicating the point that the person wearing the mask cannot be known. Their four large eyes can penetrate while remaining unseen. In *Ancestors* (fig. 11.5), she unites the dead with the living, taking all to the palace of the king where conflicts are settled, peace treaties negotiated, and joy manifested in discussions on progress. Both figures 11.3 and 11.4 are united in focusing attention on aspects of the Orisa tradition among the Yoruba—ideas and practices that have been extended to the African diaspora. Ifa, *Opon Ifa*, and *egungun* can be found in different parts of the Americas.

The Ritual of Reinvention and Renewal

In the fashion typical of African artists, whether in the homeland or in the diaspora, Adesanya excavates ideas and images from the rich archives of Yoruba and other African cultures, unpacking folklore and vintage forms to explore their potential in envisioning new forms and to enrich her work. This is what takes place in *Time Traveller* (fig. 11.6), a work pregnant with multiple motifs. In the earlier work *Rites, Ritual, and Renewal* (fig. 11.7), she revisits tradition, drawing on older religious beliefs that have survived until today. In both *Time Traveller* and *Rites, Ritual, and Renewal*, she focuses on sites of cultural memory and power where the indigenous thrives in the celebration of rites of passage, the recognition of leadership, the beginning of a venture, the establishment of alliances, and more.

In *Time Traveller*, Adesanya takes motifs from different African culture groups, most notably the Yoruba and Fulani, to create a complex work on mythologies that link the worlds of the living with the spiritual and the environment with the people. In this complicated work, she wades into the murky, controversial world of terrestrial travels and spatial fractures with thoughtful lines imposed above unreadable minds and fragmented bodies. The very heart of the painting is rather intensive; it highlights the pivotal minds of a hidden he and a disguised she. The he manifests a double identity—a sort of a guru with an undefined race that invokes the apparati of the Yoruba cult of secrecy (*ogboni*). The staff, which is made out of iron, is both a figuration and signification of power: how a metal, whose production is ritualized, becomes further embedded in a religious system where everything is explained in spiritual terms. Denis Williams is right when he states: "Power inherent in the unfamiliar and intractable metal is to be controlled not so much by means of analyzing the process of its operation as by propitiation and prayer addressed to the orisa, or god, who has been able to tame such power."[10] Ogun, the god of metal, represents the work of science and technology, from needles to airplanes. But in Adesanya's work, Ogun is the spirit, the god to be invoked. Artifact and mental fact become blended to reveal a philosophy.

The woman in *Time Traveller* is reflective; her ideas are refracted from an empty space and draw energy from the spiritualized man behind her. He possesses an arrogant gaze into what appears to be a predictable future. An elephant emerges in the woman, which is a metaphor of strength but one that works in reverse: the elephant can metamorphose into a woman. Also, the woman, when energy is needed, sheds her human flesh to become the strongest persona in the jungle. Her strength is not destructive like that of the lions and tigers that eat their neighbors, but is rather a gentle force that walks quietly and merely grazes. The elephant tusk symbolizes energy. At the same time, a decorated calabash floats in air. The imagery, presented in a disguised form, may have tapped into Adesanya's unconscious, represented in poems on women where she deploys a similar combination of Yoruba and English words to portray a strong woman who is ready to spring into action at rather short notice: "Formidable foe / Wrapped in riotous tornado."[11]

Both the man and the woman appear to defy gravity. She levitates into the sky before the womb in which they are both imprisoned breaks into a world underneath. The mutable boundaries above seem cautioned by the subtle, faded envelope opened on two wide sides. They are forever "unclosed," becoming an ideological metaphor of the complex interplay of those overwhelming forces that shape movements. Adesanya endorses ritualistic and essentialist beliefs, thus bringing the value of African indigenous spirituality and theology back to the forefront at a time of rising Christian fundamentalism. Set in a modernist context, the man and his ritual objects are not primitive, but forward-looking: They actually appear to be intellectualizing a body of ideas. We are left guessing about the outcome of his introspection.

Tension and Politics: Face Off and Hack Down the Enemy

The painting *Face Off* (fig. 11.8) is a commentary on British colonial rule in Nigeria, and appropriately chosen as the cover image of *Colonialism and Violence in Nigeria*.[12] The book examines the question of power and identity and specifically the tension between colonial power and the colonized subjects that occurred during the colonial period and as its aftermath. While the agenda of colonial power was to dominate the colony, divide and rule the subjects through various means, "civilize" the subjects, and appropriate the resources in the colony, its activities were met with opposition by the colonial subjects who chose to assert their rights as citizens. As a result, many riots and conflicts occurred between the Nigerians and British: one ethnic group against another, Islamic north against Christian south. Most of the uprisings were triggered by the policies of the British colonizer, and the British eventually withdrew their military power. Riots and protests were common—from the culturally rooted Yoruba riots in the west and the religious skirmishes with the Muslims and Hausa in the north, to the confrontations with the Igbo in the east and other ethnicities in the Delta states. Amazingly, besides encompassing all the major ethnic groupings and regions in Nigeria, these conflicts also covered the three most explicit British inculcations: cultural, religious, and economic.

Obviously, the colonial period from the 1880s to 1960 was marked by various confrontations that sometimes produced bloodshed. In the inset placed in the center of the painting *Face Off*, two men, one white-skinned and the other dark-skinned, meet eye-to-eye. The theater of their conflict is presented in the background, and the foreground is dotted by distorted forms that speak to the violence that characterized different periods of colonial and postcolonial rule. The artist's choice of the warm colors red and yellow is a deliberate one, as these convey the metaphors of heat, anger, restlessness, and bloodshed.

Hack Down the Enemy (fig. 11. 9) visualizes the conflict beyond the colonial era, especially the riotousness and violence that characterize postcolonial Africa. In the gray and red tones of the picture's plane, two hackneyed forms mounted on horses engage in mortal battle. The painting reflects the violence exhibited in the disturbing characteristics of civil wars in many countries, the genocide in Rwanda, and apartheid in South Africa. Adesanya continued the theme of violence in *Invaders and Predators* (fig. 11.10), a powerful critique of the military in power, political authoritarianism, and excessive abuse of power. Overfed and corrupt men are disguised in the left side of the painting while the traumatized ponder their survival strategies.

Women, Identity, and Politics

An artist exists within a political space and, as such, it is often difficult to ignore the ideas and experiences that stimulate political consciousness. While Adesanya balances creativity with politics, she totally frees herself from the encumbrances of power elites, as her art is not dependent on their patronage. Whether her art recalls traditional canons or articulates erotic images, they are evidently her creations and not responses to the dictates of the rich or superior patrons who choose and dismiss art depending on their various interests and aesthetic taste. As she told me in an interview:

> I believe an artist has autonomy once his/her means of sustenance is not solely dependent on income from sales of art works. Since I belong to this category, I simply create my art based on my creative impulses and my responses to my immediate environment. When I need to deploy my art to sanction excesses and aberrations within my immediate milieu, I do so without any remorse or apprehension. I do not make art to entertain (it may be pleasing to viewers and in the process entertain them but this is not the primary objective); rather, I make it to interrogate my society and to comment on the social reality of my time. I believe that this is my social responsibility.[13]

She likes to engage the notion of identity in both her scholarship and creative work.

For instance, gender identity and discourse of power were the cornerstones of the *Virginia* cartoon series that she crafted for over ten years and that were reprinted in the Nigerian newspaper *Vanguard.* *Virginia* is both the name of the central character in the cartoons and the title of the cartoon series. Virginia's character, experiences, and daily interactions with society were entry points for Adesanya to comment not only on topical issues discussed in the news media but also the narratives of other peoples' lives. Some of the cartoon strips' readers have posed questions as to whether *Virginia* reflects Adesanya's own experiences, and she offers: "Art is truth migrated into the world of imagination and imagination teased from reality. When an artist creates *truth* as told in images s/he creates an embodiment of life lived within and without. It is in the performance of truth that the energy of the work of art comes alive." She holds the notion that the work of an artist cannot be totally separated from her because her creativity is ultimately enriched by personal experiences, explorations, and research.

As such, the images Adesanya creates in mostly two-dimensional formats using a variety of media (such as oil, pastel, watercolor, pen and ink, and charcoal) are commentaries on identity. Subjects and objects in motion fascinate her, which inspired a series of paintings she developed about objects in motion in the late 1990s and early 2000s. She even concentrated on painting polo riders and dancers, which culminated in such works as *Polo Riders* (fig. 11.11), *Women on Galloping Horses* (fig. 11.12), *Benin Dancers* (fig. 11.13), *The Dancers* (fig. 11.14), and *Boaters* (fig. 11.15).

Her art also highlights aspects of culture, as seen in *The Dancers* and *Boaters*—and in *Women's Work?* (fig. 11.16), *Tete-a-Tete* (fig. 11.17), and *Elders Alive in the Niger Delta* (fig. 11.18).[14] Dance, movement, and synergy permeate various aspect of African culture. The scintillating cultural performances that she observed as she grew up left rich templates in her memory that she continues to draw from. As she says of her inspirations, "I recall the measured and calibrated gaits, the sumptuous ensemble that dancers wear to add spectacle to their repertory, and the electrifying atmosphere that enervates the spirit."

Some of her works tap into these and other experiences, making visible the vibrant energy of culture, the resilience of a people in the face of enormous challenges in life. *Elders Alive in the Niger Delta* focuses on the attractive, endearing, and enduring aspects of the Niger Delta region, a perspective different from the hostile and violent portrayals that one encounters in popular media. *The Dancers* shows a people who have decided to set aside their pains and travails in order to embrace the beauty of life; the dexterous, rigorous rhumba allows them a way to enrich the life of their community.

In several paintings she depicts women in various activities at work and at leisure, while her cartoons, numbering more than three thousand over a ten-year period, have made many social and political statements on gender and politics. The cartoons stratify society and culture into high and low, and also create a parody of urbanized women. Her poems are critical of patriarchy and politicians, affirming the statement that scholarship for black women is an opportunity to make political statements about society and male domination.[15] While drawing on indigenous idioms, she is aware of the larger currents in the West and seems to combine them, as in a painting of women on horseback playing polo. This painting connects with ideological expressions in the years of African decolonization, notably those of Kwame Nkrumah and Amilcar Cabral. *Unity and Struggle* by Amilcar Cabral is a work written at a time of both anger and hope— anger directed at the Portuguese brutalities and exploitation of his people, and hope directed at the possibility of a new future following decolonization. Cabral admonished Africans that part of the strategy to obtain their freedom also entailed fully understanding the positive contributions that the oppressor's culture offered: that liberation is an "act of culture."[16] Women on horseback playing polo are, no doubt, an "act of culture" in a Cabralian notion of liberation.

Subverting Conventions

Certain imaginations respond to observable realities. This response is certainly what one sees in *Benin Dancers*, which evolved from Adesanya's observance of day-to-day activities. Apart from the portraits of elites and of market scenes that characterize the works of early contemporary Nigerian artists such as Ben Enwonwu, Akin Lasekan, and later artists, dance forms are another topicality that artists have explored to a great extent. Enwonwu arguably pioneered the genre with his African dance series and dance forms series.[17] *Benin Dancers* actually came from direct observation and from photographs of a Benin cultural troupe that performed at one of the many academic and cultural events held at the Institute of African Studies at the University of Ibadan, Nigeria. However, Adesanya's interest in making the work stems from her art school training and dovetails with the fact that paintings of dancers or dancing figures are a common theme in contemporary African art; they are popular subjects of art students in art schools. In making dance forms, the female figure is a popular subject often employed by artists, perhaps because the female body lends itself to a remarkable range of dexterity and maneuverability or even because of the spectacle presented by an ensemble of dancing women. Both motivations deepened her fascination with the women she painted in *Benin Dancers*.

Women's Womb and the World (fig. 11.19) is a semiabstract acrylic painting that Adesanya created in 2007.[18] It was inspired by a visit to the home of some new colleagues during Thanksgiving. She met their son and his wife, who was heavy with child at the time. She decided to put down her memory of the mother-to-be carrying her body and its burden of joy with such strength during the last few days before delivery. Adesanya explained, "I reflected on so many issues concerning life, reproduction, family values, and particularly the centrality of women to the continuity of life and their sacred sacrifice in that life-giving process."

The womb, as Nana Amponsah describes it, is a powerful site of politics and memory. It can be politicized at the level of the family by social demands for many children, and particularly in African patriarchal settings by emphasis on the desire for male children. As Amponsah points out, "cross-culturally, the female body has been politicized through narratives of power, culture, tradition, modernity, race, disempowerment, and empowerment."[19] Adesanya seems more concerned with the joy and burden of pregnancy than the politics of the womb.

Acada Woman (fig. 11.20) is one of her paintings that challenges established stereotypes and patriarchal structures, critiques entrenched norms, and rethinks gender. "Acada" is the label for African women with university educations and those who tend to be bookish after graduation. By virtue of the visual vocabulary of her art—whether cartoons, paintings, drawing, or poetry—she has been termed both a feminist and a nonconformist radical artist. While I cannot say that she is looking in the same mirror in which her critics and enthusiasts view her, she is, first of all, true to her creative consciousness and to the realities of her world and experiences. She is persuaded by her personal convictions, which ultimately come to the fore in her creative expressions.

Limitless ideas are conceivable in *Acada Woman*. Adesanya takes on three cogent issues prevalent in her part of the world. First, she considers the subjectivity of patriarchal culture that believes productivity, and indeed fruitfulness, are mainly anchored by reproductive power—the ability to have offspring to carry on one's lineage. In traditional African society, success is often measured by the number of children sired by a man. On this count, she avers that productivity—and by extension success—should not be determined by one's reproductive power or even individual achievement; rather fruitfulness can be measured by other yardsticks, including the success of those one has been able to mentor. In proposing a rethinking of the ideology of productivity peculiar to African culture, she states that the hallmark of productivity is the success in the lives of those we mentor, whether they are biological children or not.

Second, she analyzes the reckless denigration of female intellectuals by a society that believes they are overly ambitious and attributes their unmarried or childless state as a confrontational position. Within *Acada Woman*, the subject's eyes—which peer into a text opened on her lap, to the pile of books arranged to her left in the background, to the multiple forms that cover different parts of her body—convey the central message that the value of the female goes beyond her biological, reproductive role. The capabilities of the intellectual woman transcend her ability to make babies; her intellectual power and other talents have the capacity to impact humanity more than has been acknowledged.

Finally, by depicting the acada woman in the nude, she takes a swipe at the pretensions of Nigerian society on the subject of morality and its propensity to equate nudity with immorality or insanity. A society that accommodates nudity in traditional art but winces at similar topicality in contemporary art can be described as overtly pretentious and practicing an aesthetic double standard. Rather than equate nudity with obscenity, Adesanya recalls more traditional contexts in which it connoted purity—a central idea in traditional societies that condoned the practice of maidens dancing naked, especially during puberty ceremonies. *Acada Woman* is essentially her metaphor of purity, and her conception of a blend of intellectual power with vintage femininity.

Society can sometimes be offended by the creative sensibilities of artists just as artists can be infuriated by the overarching control that the public wants to have on their creativity. Adesanya's reflections are informed by an experience that she narrated to me. Sometime in 2005, a male visitor who belonged to a conservative religious persuasion visited her apartment. He saw one of her paintings, *Rape of Innocence* (fig. 11.21), on her wall and perfunctorily asked her when (and not why) she hung it on the wall. "My senses," she remembered, "immediately became alert to the various layers of meaning that could be derived from the work and the debate that the speaker was beginning to tease." The painting shows two figures, a male and a female, intertwined with three women who appear to be moving across the picture's plane of predominant red color. Certain things were apparent to Adesanya: Even though nude images have always been explored and encountered in traditional African art in general and Nigerian art in particular, their encounter in contemporary art is always viewed with subjectivity or, at the extreme level, disdain. It was apparent that the person posing the question about the nude images could not comprehend why Adesanya chose to hang it there. He did not wish to say, why did you hang it there? lest he offend her. Instead, he posed the question in a diplomatic way, when did you hang it on the wall? so that she could be immediately drawn into a deeper

conversation about it. She simply could not fathom what the time factor had to do with the hanging of the painting. Her art hangs in her
sitting room because it is her work, and she likes it there! When she
put it there was her choice.

Adesanya surmised that what the speaker actually wanted to know
is why she chose to depict a nude male and females. She answered
her visitor's question but left no room for further conversation, as she
knew his religious sensibility would cloud his judgment and would
not allow for an objective inquiry. The controversy about the subject
of nude forms in art affects both training and practice. She recol-
lected how, as a student at the Obafemi Awolowo University, Ile-Ife,
Nigeria, a model that used to pose in a life drawing class was dis-
suaded from continuing by some people in her class who felt the job
was a lowly and immoral one, not unlike being a prostitute.

The combination of culture and ideology represented in Adesanya's
art and poems signifies the contemporary reality of and the emerging nature of change in Africa. I think that she is searching for effective tropes of disalienation in aesthetics to transform gender relations
and to make national politics more representative, responsible, and
responsive. In framing modernity, her predecessors, as in the work of
Enwonwu, dealt with the tropes of modernity and alienation.[20] If Wole
Soyinka settled for Ogun, the Yoruba god of iron, using him to frame
an African tragic/tragic Africa discourse, Adesanya seems to have settled for Oya, the river goddess, in her cartoons of well-dressed, sophisticated, urban women to frame issues of modernity.[21] The cartoons may
appear postmodernist to the neotraditionalists, and her assumptions
about the possibility of cultural autonomy for women may be misun-
derstood, given that she deploys the media to communicate her message about the West's impact on society.

However, Adesanya is not alone in wrestling with the problem of
how to use cultural autonomy as a solution to some aspects of Africa's
problems. In her case the problem is complicated by the desire to
reconcile women's place with postcolonial situations. Great thinkers such as Frantz Fanon, Amilcar Cabral, and Agostinho Neto have
addressed similar problems in the larger context of development
and in minimizing dependence on the West. In an essay, the linguist
Olaoba F. Arasanyin related the difficulty of creating a language
policy in an Africa whose legacy of colonization has left it with "an
alien political character" that leaves it vulnerable to powerful pressures acting outside of its boundaries.[22] Wole Soyinka, as in his attack

on Négritude, is dismissive in presenting African reality in narrower forms. Cultural autonomy for Africans is elusive within the context of globalization, just as cultural autonomy is challenging for women within the context of patriarchal, indigenous traditions and in the face of Christianity and Islam.

Furthermore, Adesanya's work seems to advocate an agenda of liberal humanism. I use the term "liberal humanism" both intentionally and critically to point to the inadequacies of liberalism to confront violence and inequality. Recalling past Yoruba traditions, especially the representation and invocation of Orisa, represents a statement about the continuity of the past. However, as we consider her paintings, poetry, and cartoons, we see in the corpus of her work instances of both subversion and transgression. Her truth is not anticolonial, but antipostcolonial, although I must point out that the term "postcolonial" does not have a straightforward meaning in the body of her work. Reading her images as texts, mythological patterns of figuration stress the opportunities and challenges of modernization in the lives of women, though not in terms of any complete break with the past. The openendedness that her creativity suggests invokes a Bakhtinian concept of indeterminacy of dealing with an "evolving contemporary reality" where art operates in a "zone of contact with the present in all its open-endedness, a zone that was first appropriated by the novel."[23] Her paintings are fresh, like her poetry, and the trajectory of their representations is clearly moving toward cultural and gendered significations of the postcolonial moment.

Creativity, Politics, and Empowerment

I now want to combine and collapse the various examples of the spread of African cultures to the Americas during the slave trade (see chapters 6, 7, and 8), Nollywood, and art to reflect on the contributions of Africans to global cultures. I will do so in a holistic framework set in the context of changing historical eras. The survival of African practices during the era of slavery allows us to talk about Africanization and re-Africanization, while the case of Nollywood and creativity in art leads us to talk about transnationalization and globalization.

In the African diaspora, identity emerged in the context of slavery, race, and migration. The voices speaking for members of the diaspora of slavery, represented in the emergence of African American identity in the United States and related ones in Europe, Asia, Latin America, and the Caribbean, have had to link creativity with this context. Derek Walcott makes the connections in his often-cited essay "The Muse of History":

> In the New World servitude to the muse of history has produced a literature of recrimination and despair, a literature of revenge written by the descendants of slaves or a literature of remorse written by the descendants of masters. Because this literature serves historical truth, it yellows into polemic and evaporates into pathos. The truly tough aesthetics of the New World neither explains nor forgives this history. It refuses to recognize it as a creative and culpable force. This shame and awe of history possesses poets of the Third World, who think of language as enslavement and who in a rage of identity, respect only incoherence and nostalgia.[24]

Walcott attempts a creative exorcism in *Dream on Monkey Mountain and Other Plays*, where a lead character, Makak, who lives as a "wild beast in hiding," gains his freedom, wanders through the landscape of oppression and subjugation, and ends up in Africa where he makes a symbolic execution of all those who had subjugated and oppressed his people.[25]

In seeking the means for liberation and emancipation, cultural and political ideas and actions found expression in black empowerment, black power, and black capitalism. Whether in Brazil or the United States, Africa—embodying a place, a home, a race, an ethnicity, a civilization, and more—becomes central to the formation of ideas and activism, as various people become like Makak. Africa is used to capture the imagination of people of African descent. Many writers see Africa as a source of black dignity and pride. When Africa was under colonial rule, the desire to free Africa merged into a global Pan-Africanist network to free the continent, to end apartheid, and to turn the continent into the leading place of pride for all blacks irrespective of where they lived. The Pan-Africanist agenda of creating the "United States of Africa" was rooted in the assumptions of shared cultural heritage and the common history of domination and exploitation by Europe.

A manifesto had emerged by the turn of the twentieth century: All blacks must unite to end oppression, exploitation, and discrimination; to free themselves of foreign control; and to be economically and politically strong. If blacks outside of Africa understand Africans and vice versa, progress, it was believed, would surely follow. African Americans have always been urged to remain interested in African affairs and to derive their source of pride from the continent, while Africans have been advised to reach out to African Americans to acquire skills. Projects of cultural celebration serve to encourage interactions and cement collaboration. Marcus Garvey, one of the best-known activists in the articulation of this comprehensive networking, described the unity of black people as entering "into common partnership to build up Africa in the interest of our race."[26] W. E. B. Du Bois refined many of these ideas, elevating them to higher political heights. Of course, not everyone accepted that the connections were possible: James Baldwin pointed to different historical struggles requiring different resolutions:

> The African has not yet endured the utter alienation of himself from his people and his past. His mother did not sing, "Sometimes I Feel Like a Motherless Child," and he has not all his life ached for acceptance in a culture which pronounced straight hair and white skin the only acceptable beauty. They face each other, the Negro and the African, over a gulf of three hundred years—an alienation too vast to be conquered in an evening's goodwill.[27]

Being caught in different struggles does not mean that the journeys are too far apart in their sources, paths, and destinations. Indeed, many embarked on the "trip" to Africa, even as the cynical and critical Baldwin presaged that they would not find the answers they wanted but only more questions. One reason to start from Africa is to understand the origin and context of many ideas, the milieus that produced them, and the mindset that shaped the imagination. We can understand how ideas travel and how these ideas are reformulated in other places. If ideas of survival and health were linked to a spiritual universe, it is not hard to understand why the worship of gods and goddesses would spread in other parts of the world, why Christianity would be redefined to include ideas drawn from African religions, why herbs and incantations would be used to solve health problems would not just go away, and why Nollywood cannot thrive if it eliminates beliefs in juju and witchcraft.

Not all new inventions and ideas owe their genesis to Africa; borrowing and adaptations also occur to modify the template to apply new technologies and concepts to older ideas, and to substitute new materials for older ones that are not available or adaptable. From the very moment of encounter with the West, even in plantation economies, innovations have always been part of the negotiation of interaction and survival. In creating new products and ideas, the enslaved mixed Amerindian, European, and African traditions. In colonial Africa, Africans were clever agents in translating received ideas to meet local needs. Several works have been published on the creation of an African American identity and the contributions of the enslaved to Western cultures, all of which provide data about the human agency to adapt to new environments and conditions.[28] Today such innovations continue in all aspects, from cuisine to attire, from the use of language and communication devices to using technologies to create new cultural meanings.

The possession of knowledge opens up opportunities to use capital for social and political purposes. For instance, healers and priests have always been respected. During slavery, slaves and slave masters were sometimes fearful but also in awe of conjurers who, they believed, had the poison to kill, the love potion to win affection, and the remedies to cure. Where knowledge was a threat or became connected with resistance, efforts emerged to ban practitioners, conjurers, the use of certain lyrics in music, herbs, and poisons.[29] Those with literary skills could acquire public acclaim. If associated with radical ideas, they could be perceived as a threat, as in the case of socialist-oriented activists of the twentieth century who were labeled communists as a way of imposing sanctions on them. Celebrations, notably funeral ceremonies, even turned death into victory, bluntly revealing to hegemonic power that the end would come to all and that glories await the weak and marginalized in the world that counts the most—the next![30]

Nollywood and art reveal the new currents in contemporary global forces. Millions of contemporary African migrants are agents and couriers of cultures. As constant travelers, they have enormous capital to innovate and to tap into the social power embedded in their difference. Many can be found at the crossroads of change and innovation. Millions generate hybrid knowledge in all aspects of life; their skills are varied, multilateral, and draw from many sources and ideas. Contrary to what many people think, Africans have created spaces of cultural innovation and expression all over the world, represented in scholarship, politics, inventions, music, dance, food, honor, and much more. Moving back and forth from Africa represents social power in the age of globalization where voices and beliefs can be carried. By demonstrating African cultures outside of Africa, migrants become powerful agents of communication. By recreating and producing new ideas that blend African inheritances with others, they become innovators. By taking ideas back to Africa, they become brokers, agents of globalization with the skills to announce and communicate new, and some borrowed, things. Without the large immigrant population, there would have been no *Virginia Is for Lovers*, and without the global academic marketplace, the artist Adesanya would not be in the United States creating her paintings in multiple spaces.

What is the place of African migrants in Western societies in all this? First, they serve as the connectors in taking Africa to the West by way of migration, travel, exchange of ideas, cultural transmission, attitudes, and much more.[31] Whether they build churches and mosques or markets and stores, they alter the landscape. When they wear their clothes, they alter the marketplace of attire and costumes. Few cannot but take note of the headgears, the colorful, flowing robes, and other clothing. When they speak, they enrich the language with their accents and sentences. When they talk, they show their attitudes, as in the loud and argumentative communication style of Nigerians.[32]

Second, the African migrants take the West to Africa through the same process of travel, migration, and the information highway. Following the principle of either you "make it or fake it," they lend credence to the mythology that the West is a land of opportunity. Gambians who did not finish high school eulogize the welfare system in Sweden; Nigerian cab drivers in Chicago or New York describe themselves as businessmen who make money as land pilots; and Senegalese carriers of small wares in the marginalized zone of Paris call themselves business tycoons in the making. Of course there are also many stories of success, and in many places African migrants represent one of the most successful immigrant groups. The professionals have solid, middle-class status. Hard currencies and Western goods are sent to Africa, which adds to capital assets.

Third, Africans allow us to study the activities of transnationalists and the impact of globalization. Many have created new nationalities on the Internet, as in one of the many ethnic associations such as the Igbo Progressive Union. In drawing on a network of new friends, kinship has been redefined where the fictional performs a similar role as the original African variant. The celebration of the rites of passage in elaborate forms shows how powerful fictional kinship has become. Social parties, with all the paraphernalia of live bands, excessive food and drink, and elaborate attire, show how ideas of success and public display can be transferred from Africa to the West.

Cultural presentations, while affirming difference, can also create an entry point to consider problems of stigmatization, racism, and ethnocentric attacks. To ultranationalists in the West, those who live among them must assimilate. Thus some European countries have banned veiling, imposed restrictions on certain marriage practices, criticized what they perceive as tough childrearing standards or as child labor, and the like. As ultranationalists argue, those who do not want to assimilate should leave so that the hegemonic culture is not diluted. Where Christian fundamentalists join in the discussion, they want a country where other religions, especially Islam, will have limited role and significance.

Fourth, the migrants complicate the notions of the state and nation in Africa. They can be from Ghana or Nigeria, but the powers of these states are curtailed in dealing with its own citizens. For many of them, the state means little. They would rather focus on their ethnicities, which they consider important since they represent building blocks for identity and form the standards by which they formulate associations. Their towns and cities are also important, since these are where they build houses and are buried should their bodies return home. Indeed, their parents and relations count far more than the state. Those who are firmly committed to ethnic identities have even called for secession.

Finally, the migrants widen the discourse on race. Of paramount importance in private discussions is the topic of race, which impacts the day-to-day reality of most ordinary people and the institutions and structures of society.[33] Racism can be overt and covert, open and disguised. It possesses two dimensions: the first is specific and the second general. As to the specific dimension, collaboration and conflicts between continental Africans and African Americans abound. Two separate identities united by color. However, the bridge between both is weak. As to the general, Africans are used to the politics of ethnicity and religion in Africa. As cruel and exploitative as the colonial system was, the majority of Africans outside of South Africa read about racism and apartheid in textbooks and heard stories told by a dying generation.[34] In the West, they face issues about race that they may misunderstand or misread. Thus it is not unusual for Africans to regret exile, to present exile as a condition of shame, or to express disillusionment. Where some had gone to Europe or America looking for quick success and opulent living, they may become disappointed, seeing the promises of high culture and prestige as a mirage. Migration dreams might become dampened or unfulfilled, as they experience difficulties or alienation. Disappointments may lead to trauma, painful feelings of profound cultural dislocation and mental agony, among others. The very suspicion of their presence can generate visceral reactions. Encounters with the homeland may produce suspicions in which migrants feel a sense of loss in all spaces: of being neither here nor there, an African who cannot relate to Africa or to the West. Not being African Americans, they may not be black enough. When they are black enough, the narratives of their experiences are reported by others, narrators who feel neither pain nor anguish.

Racism, like ethnicity, can attach categories to people on the basis of difference. In the case of racism, color is associated with deficiencies in intelligence, trust, efficiency, and ability. Whether in racism or ethnicity, the invention of difference, whether real (as in different color or different location) or imagined (as in the crude determination of intelligence), and the values attached to that difference, are designed to achieve various purposes. One purpose is to obtain and keep privileges of wealth and power. Thus a group in power can resort to cultural and biological differences to separate itself from others and then argue that those who are different are inferior. Second, the division enables the use of violence to create and sustain divisions and privileges. In racialized societies, attitudes and exercises of ethnocentrism and xenophobia are robbed of guilt, and the deadly apparatus of violence can be visited on the underprivileged race.

Albert Memmi, a sophisticated analyst, uses the concept of "ethnophobia" to characterize what I just referred to as "attitudes," saying that biological differences are astutely deployed to ground social and physical assault and hostility.[35] Racism then becomes an alibi for domination that rests on three interrelated legs: "There is (1) the act of definition of the other, as the power of one group over the other; (2) the fact of defining as a dependence of the dominant on the other for social identity, and the inherent hostility engendered by that dependence; and (3) the content of the definition, which becomes the legitimation of the dominance relation."[36] For Africans who leave Africa because of the problems of ethnicity, they have to confront another reality of cleavage: racism. They may exaggerate the cleavage, attributing their own inadequacies and limitations to it, or they may grapple with structures and institutions that impose boundaries. Many are successful, so successful that they also generate envy.

The movements of people and global interactions will continue to create discontent in politics and cultures. Uneven global development will mean that rich and poor people will create different cultures, that those who feel excluded from resources will grumble and formulate resistance cultures. The production and manufacture of goods will impact the environment, most especially forest depletion, which in turn might lead to rural-urban migrations. Population increase and urbanization will produce new urban cultures. Marginalized people will produce expressions of disappointment in words and actions. Such political expressions will empower ethnic movements and religious associations, thereby allowing a limitless number of organizations and millions of people to have allegiances in opposition to the state and such suprastate organizations as the World Bank.

Creativity's Agenda

One conclusion unites all the examples that I have drawn from Nollywood and Adesanya's paintings: creativity has an agenda. Various expressions are connected with identity. Self-definition enables the rejection of imposed ones, changing the paradigm of negativity to the positive. Self-definition gives power to color and supplies the energy to fight stereotypes, humiliations, and rejection. Creativity imparts its own measure of checks and balances on the process of deculturation that encounters with others can produce, enabling us to revalorize and reappropriate elements of cultures that have been discarded. Where religion and spirituality are involved, they allow beliefs to be used as cultural therapy.

Creativity provides the opportunity to create a counterdiscourse to hegemonic representations of blackness. Be they artists, singers, or poets, creativity allows black people to fight back with disdain, anger, and rationalization. They provide evidence of the civilization of the past, as in works by Du Bois and Cheik Anta Diop, and as evidenced by the possibilities of the present.

Creativity preaches the need for dignity and an identification with blackness, criticizes racism and dehumanization, and gives nationalistic support for the emergence of powerful black nations. Creativity announces success and pride; it puts on stage the richness of black cultures and the talents and skills of writers, poets, artists, and others. As the works are enjoyed and appreciated, the masters and the audience all become worthwhile collaborators in the project of progress and race uplift.

Creativity refutes racial prejudices and affirms blackness. The large body of work in black literature and African history combines to say that the black race is not infantile and inferior, that black people are intelligent and talented, that they do have a common identity, a rich heritage, and a long history. Not denying the contributions of other races, black scholars assert that all races, nationalities, and ethnicities have their geniuses who make original contributions to world heritage and civilization. Rather than support an ideology and bureaucracy to facilitate a monolithic system, the originality expressed in black creative endeavors points to diverse cultures and shows us the way out of totalitarian and repressive modes of thinking.

Creativity makes a statement that blacks are beyond labor, that is, people defined just in terms of manual exploitation, irrespective of the economic system. While some do have character flaws (as with all groups of people in any part of the world), the race cannot be stereotyped as foolish and mediocre. Richard Wright attempts in *Black Boy* to say that even the characterization of being foolish can be rejected by small acts of violence, and that ambition and identity should not be caged. As Wright attempts to aspire to greater heights, he is pulled back by negative characterization, his humanity dehumanized, his personality depersonalized, until he can stand it no more:

> I could not make subservience an automatic part of my behavior. I had to feel and think out each tiny item I brought to the whole of my life. While standing before white men, I had to figure out how to perform each act and how to say each word. I could not help it. I could not grin. In the past I had always said too much, now I found that it was difficult to say anything at all. I could not reach as the world in which I lived expected me to; that world was too baffling, too uncertain.[37]

Ralph Ellison's *Invisible Man* adopts a similar connection of creative use of violence for individual liberation.[38] Disengagement and withdrawal or silence have been represented as yet other ways out in countless blues songs, religious tracts, and poems. Even Wright hints at the use of this strategy as he withdraws deeper and deeper, agonizing that "I grew silent and reserved as the nature of the world in which I lived became plain and undeniable; the bleakness of the future affected my will to study."[39]

In closing this chapter, I am reminded of the warning by Frantz Fanon about the need to avoid intellectual dependency. What creativity has done for many poets, artists, filmmakers, and others is meet this Fanonian injunction, although there are also, of course, too many examples of mere imitation. As new knowledge, objects, and ideas are created, it becomes much harder to ridicule representation, to say that others must always speak for oneself. The monologic frame of universalism gives way to a dialogic form of diversity that, to cite Michel Foucault, "ultimately matters, a discourse against power, the counter-discourse of prisoners and those we call delinquents."[40]

As the vibrant Nollywood industry has demonstrated, Africa is a major site of creative innovations. Whether it is Candomblé in Brazil or blues music in the United States, we see examples of creativity in all parts of the African diaspora: abundant, limitless, boundless, vibrant, and energetic. European domination of Africa did not succeed in killing the music and dance, stories, festivals, or aesthetics. They have continued in various forms and have been reinvented into others. Migrations have created new opportunities. The characters in *Virginia Is for Lovers* seem to echo a prescient idea by George Lamming in *The Pleasures of Exile*, where individuals belong to wherever they are, but without forgetting their homeland in both the subliminal, psychic, and physical connections they still maintain.[41]

Creativity, in whatever form it is expressed, is not politically neutral. It is identity seeking, defining oneself and creating the boundaries of difference and meaning. Identity asserts the self—the individual, the nation, the ethnicity, the religion, the race—all with a goal of attaining recognition, visibility, and purpose. There have been literary schools and devices (such as Négritude, for instance) to generate pride for blackness; practical devices to bring creative minds together to generate unity (e.g., Festival of Black Arts and Cultures). In the musical talent of such figures as Mariam Makeba, Michael Jackson, King Sunny Ade, Fela Anikulapo-Kuti, Hugh Masekala, Asa, Sade, and the like, Ellison's invisible man acquires visible names. In the leading actors and actresses in Nollywood, LeRoi Jones Clay has become not one thunderbolt but many thunderbolts. In the persons of Nelson Mandela, Julius Nyerere, and Barack Obama, Richard Wright's *Black Boy* has now become a man, the epitome of power, dignity, and nobility.[42]

Figure 11.2. Dr. Aderonke Adesanya. Photograph courtesy of Dr. Maureen Shanahan of James Madison University, Harrisonburg, Virginia.

Figure 11.3. *Opon Ifa,* oil on board, 2010. Used with permission from the artist.

Figure 11.4. *Masquerades*, pastel on paper, 2000. Used with permission from the artist.

Figure 11.5. *Ancestor*, watercolor, poster color, pen and ink on paper, 2002. Used with permission from the artist.

Figure 11.6. *Time Traveller*, oil, pen, and ink on paper, 2010. Used with permission from the artist.

Figure 11.7. *Rites, Ritual, and Renewal,* charcoal on paper, 1998. Used with permission from the artist.

Figure 11.8. *Face Off*, oil on canvas, 2008. Used with permission from the artist.

Figure 11.9. *Hack Down the Enemy,* acrylic on paper, 2008. Used with permission from the artist.

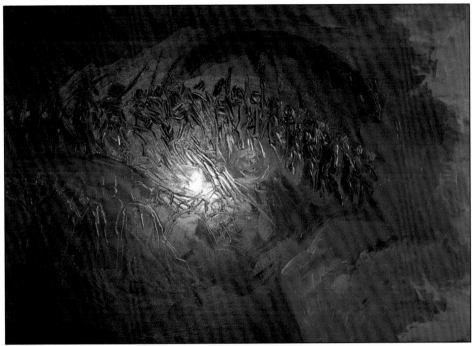

Figure 11.10. *Invaders and Predators,* oil on canvas, 2012. Used with permission from the artist.

Figure 11.11. *Polo Riders*, pastel on paper, 2002. Used with permission from the artist.

Figure 11.12. *Women on Galloping Horses*, pastel on paper, 2003. Used with permission from the artist.

Figure 11.13. *Benin Dancers*, oil and pastel on paper, 2002. Used with permission from the artist.

Figure 11.14. *The Dancers,* oil and charcoal on paper, 2006. Used with permission from the artist.

Figure 11.15. *Boaters,* pastel on paper, 2005. Used with permission from the artist.

Figure 11.16. *Women's Work?*, pastel on paper, 2005. Used with permission from the artist.

Figure 11.17. *Tete-a-Tete*, oil on canvas, 2002. Used with permission from the artist.

Figure 11.16. *Women's Work?*, pastel on paper, 2005. Used with permission from the artist.

Figure 11.17. *Tete-a-Tete*, oil on canvas, 2002. Used with permission from the artist.

Figure 11.19. *Women's Womb and the World,* acrylic on paper, 2007. Used with permission from the artist.

Figure 11.18. *Elders Alive in the Niger Delta,* pen and ink on paper, 2002.
Used with permission from the artist.

Figure 11.20. *Acada Woman,* acrylic on paper, 2007. Used with permission from the artist.

Figure 11.21. *Rape of Innocence*, oil on board, 2002. Used with permission from the artist.

12

Globalization and
Contemporary Cultures

This chapter argues that powerful forces are redefining identities within and between frontiers, producing conditions that denationalize and deterritorialize us as we travel, mix, mingle, develop a global framework, and as we reconstitute national or local identities in new spaces. New or modified identities can emerge in the context of the high influx of immigrants who struggle with the politics of incorporation, and in the context of "invisible migrants" who do not necessarily want to become citizens or make political and economic claims in host communities. Global villages are emerging with remarkable zones of discontent and crisis. The leading arenas of discontent have been economic and religious; formidable pressures turn culture into the central core of globalization itself. As my arguments advance, I will mention new opportunities and disasters, changing world politics, the nation in the context of the world, cultures and fear of cultural clashes, and new inventions and their impact.

A theme such as this requires no justification: hundreds of people have lost their lives in religious violence in different parts of Nigeria, fear of ethnic conflicts and numerous cases of ethnic cleansing have been reported, demographic shifts affect the conduct of politics and resource control, and nonstate actors, such as religious organizations, are powerful. In view of internal tumult and other recent developments, such as the failed attempt by a Nigerian in December 2009 to light an explosive to bring down a commercial plane and fears that a radicalized segment of the Islamic population may promote acts of terrorism, Nigeria has been declared a "country of interest" by the United States. Wars defined as occurring between the West and Islam in Iraq, Afghanistan, and other parts of the Middle East have as their aim the use of superior military and nuclear resources to establish hegemonic power. Global terrorism is often presented as a clash of cultures, religions, capitalism, and imperialism.

Interactions between countries mean that we must understand the determinants of foreign policy and international relations, the inter-dependency of nations and emerging new economies, the elite who manage those economies, and the culture the elite create to manage the global space. Africans live in large numbers in Western countries that benefit (and suffer) from rapid globalization. Movements of peoples and goods interlock the concerns and interests of nations, rich and poor. Countries and companies conduct negotiations on trade, prices, rights of workers, and environmental protection. Globalizing cities such as Lagos, London, and New York generate conditions that produce and re-create new identities. In these globalizing spaces, identities are deterritorialized as people mix, use a global language, and develop less of their local and national identities in their habits and lifestyles.

Millions of "invisible" migrants exist. Many have no addresses; they have become rootless, having lost relations and friends but gained new ones. Many are not interested in politics, they just want to live as contented individuals. For deterritorialized citizens, experience is valued over place of birth, and identities associated with social mobil-ity are more important than ethnicity. If some complain of alienation or the pains of exile, the deterritorialized see diverse and multicul-tural opportunities as sources of renewed energies, eclectic taste, and cosmopolitanism. To the cosmopolitans, the ability to share cultures means that national cultures, ethnic cultures, and national boundar-ies are neither sacrosanct nor distinct.

The character of a state can have deep connections to issues around culture. Once created by the European powers, African states were given various names such as Nigeria and Kenya, and they acquired their sovereignty. Each was recognized, first as a colony and later as an independent country. The colonial government negoti-ated the boundaries that contained the land of the state—without geographical boundaries, there can be no statehood. The population contained within those boundaries acquired the status of citizenship. Nationalism demanded that they defend the country's sovereignty. If conquest and violence created a state such as Nigeria, it has proved difficult to create a nation. Before they were nations, they had cultures that sustained them, although conflicts and warfare were not necessarily absent. If many people have a feeling that they are Hausa or Kataf (defined as old nations), it has never been necessarily so with Nigeria (defined as new). A new state becoming a nation is a difficult process, as it involves consensus on the cultural and political bonds among the majority of its citizens. A nation needs a political community that speaks of an identity, whether abstract or tangible. Holding a Nigerian passport, for a number of people, may be no more than the paperwork required for travel rather than evidence of a feeling of Nigerianness.

There are homogenous nation-states, but most African states are heterogeneous, which means that they can organize their conflicts and politics around precolonial nationalities. The very survival of these precolonial nationalities, as the conflicts in Liberia, Sudan, Sierra Leone, Rwanda, and other countries represent, means that modern states remain fragile.[1] Appeals to older nationalities explain the demand to create new provinces (often called "states" within specific national boundaries) within a country even when it is clear that such units are too small and lack the capacity to generate their own resources. If the precolonial nationalities appeal to the past, the modern state appeals to nationalism.

The dissolution of the postcolonial state requires a war, and a secessionist component (as in the case of Biafra or Eritrea) still requires an international recognition. Irrespective of its form, democratic or autocratic, a government manages a state. Just as the state can have a cultural character, so, too, does the government. A government could have either an Islamic character (as in Iran), a theocratic one (as in the Sokoto empire during the nineteenth century), or a secularist one. A group of politicians can create a political culture of kleptocracy that then becomes the paradigmatic framework to run the component units of government.

In a globalized world, the state is not the sole source of ideas about identity, power, and authority. To live in Nigeria does not prevent one from enjoying the products of other countries, being influenced by ideas from far and wide, or even respecting authority figures outside of Nigeria. Transborder ideas mean that we live in deterritorialized spaces. We may have fixed addresses to receive letters, but our minds are denationalized as they process ideas. New information technologies spread ideas so rapidly that the power and forces of any state cannot stop or control the consequences. Whether negative or positive, ideas about democracy, freedom, liberty, human rights, consumerism, and many more do not respect the boundaries of states as they spread rapidly and freely. Cultures and identities are no longer tied to specific spaces and localities. Also, a specific space or territory no longer has the exclusive privilege to inculcate only the values of its own group, since it cannot put its people in one big prison and prevent them from external influences.

The concepts being used to organize my data and ideas are based on the premise that culture and identity are no longer determined by one state or one locality. One territory no longer possesses the autonomy to control and shape cultures. Of course, I am sympathetic to the desire for cultural retentions and preservations of traditions,[2] but it should be made clear that emerging cultures do not owe their sources to any one geographic space. The older nations that created the traditions we cherish linked identity and culture to a specific location such that authority could come from their elders exercising and transmitting accumulated wisdom; identity could come from their gods and goddesses or from received religions such as Islam and Christianity.

Consequently, the Yoruba, for instance, can speak of a Yoruba space and a specific culture that they define as Yoruba in relation to that space. This way of thinking, perhaps established for centuries, has been challenged. Originally, the imposition of colonial rule and the creation of a modern state that submerged the Yoruba and others into Nigeria created a much bigger space. For the Yoruba to think that they can reproduce Yorubaness in its precolonial form in the Nigerian space, they have to create a nation within a nation. Authority and identity were transferred to the colonial state and later on to the postcolonial state, although the older nations protested. Identity and authority still corresponded with geography in the colonial state.

In the contemporary world, the sources of identity and authority are being contested and challenged. Nigeria as a state lacks the power to impose its definition on its people. Its control over its citizens, even within Nigeria, is limited. Extensive networks of people and ethnicities outside of Nigeria severely curtail its power.

I want to flesh out the preceding argument with five collateral ideas so that those who criticize and challenge the state can also know the limit of their own power and intellectual thinking. To start with, the Nigerian state cannot define all the various manifestations of culture. Some definitions arise outside of Nigeria itself. If youth generally like Facebook, that technology and social media are created outside of

Nigeria. Second, the state has no power to disconnect its citizens from the global networks from which they receive new ideas and manifest them. The architecture of the Nigerian state is not strong enough to prevent many people from leaving or entering the country. It also lacks the strength to combat ideas that are drawn from globalization and its new economic system, such as information from the Internet, the activities of NGOs, the creation of diasporic organizations, and the like.

Third, while the state seeks the allegiance and loyalty of its citizens, it lacks the capacity to gain their allegiance and loyalty. Indeed, citizens will not give their loyalty and allegiance because in doing so they believe the state has to give something back in exchange, such as public services and jobs, as well as an efficient infrastructure. Where non-state agencies provide those basic services and perform the equivalent of state functions, they too have a claim to that loyalty. Social movements challenge the state and get loyalty from individuals. Families do the same, so that one's father is far more important than the head of state. Religious organizations provide spiritual services, thus demanding and receiving tremendous loyalty from their members. Millions of people leave their jobs for which they are legitimately paid to attend services and revivals because they have a loyalty to religion.

Not only do alternative forms of loyalty and identity supersede the state's claims, but also the state cannot impose on citizens who have acquired the skills to question the authority of the state itself. What individuals now relate to is not the claim by the state that it has legitimate validity to exist based on law, history, and tradition, but rather that it can function effectively and that its leaders are accountable. As the state itself is challenged, especially on the grounds that it is neither accountable nor able to secure public services, new centers of identity and authority open up.

Fourth, consumption and accumulation shape many components of our identity and culture. If you have a computer and a car, they represent part of who you are. Those two objects tell us that our identity is not solely linked to a specific geography; rather, it is linked not only to Nigeria but also to consumer products from other lands. Engagements with the West and various advertisements selling Western products are aspects of culture that transfer power from national boundaries and borders to markets and places of production. If the products are mobile, so too is the identity that they represent and the culture that they make visible. The Idoma man can say that he is socialized into some aspects of Idoma culture (geography-based), but he can also purchase, if he has the money, other components of culture that he is not born with. The items that he purchases are mobile, and as he discards and acquires more, the market shapes his identity; in some cases far more than does geography. Just as an Idoma person can acquire United States citizenship, so too can he acquire alternative, additional, supplementary, and complementary identities drawn from different parts of the world. Indeed, he can acquire so many that, at some point, only his last name remains—and that is only if he so wishes to retain it!

If the resources to connect to the market are generated from occupations and companies, loyalty must be given to both, thereby consolidating how forces outside of the state shape identity and authority. The marketplace and its products are not only mobile but are also very much decentralized as individuals interact with it in different parts of the world. The ideas they communicate are clear. The centers of control in the marketplace can be traced, some even to entrepreneurs with names. "Today and the foreseeable future," concludes Richard Rosecrance, "the only international civilization worthy of the name is the governing economic culture of the world market."[3] To be sure, some may regard this statement as an exaggeration, especially religious organizations, but we need to remind them that they use the information and technologies supplied by globalization (e.g., the Internet) to do their work, propagate their message, recruit converts, and even to fight their wars.

Fifth, the limitations of globalization and the apparent failure of the state have combined to unleash alternative forms of nationalism— some virulent, some secessionist, some violent, some terroristic. The Nigerian state has encouraged the formation of ethnic militias such as the Oodua People's Congress (OPC) and the Movement for the Survival of Ogoni People (MOSOP). Small arms have spread through global sources to empower these militias. Kidnapping has become a profitable economy. Either threatened by the Nigerian state or by global forces, we see a tendency to pursue alternative survival strategies, such as strengthening or reviving older ethnic and religious identities or seeking the means to subvert them. Recourse to such ethnic lines may lead to wars, as in Rwanda, Sierra Leone, Liberia, and Chad.[4] States do collapse,[5] leaving individuals no choice but to create new, even if temporary, cultures of governance and symbols of identity. Destabilizing forces reveal many cracks in the management of global and national politics and identity.[6] Lack of economic opportunities weakens the capacity of the state to project its authority and identity. Politicians manipulate ethnic identities and virulent nationalism to remain prominent and to divert attention away from economic and political mismanagement.

There are at least a dozen issues of concern:

1. Balancing the interests of citizens and strangers in competitive economic and political spaces. Outside of small villages, primarily composed of a homogenous population, cities tend to be heterogeneous. The different people in a city such as Los Angeles speak over a hundred languages, though English is the most common language for interaction. There are more Igbo in Lagos than in many small towns and villages in eastern Nigeria.

2. Cooperation and tension between Christians and Muslims where they share common space and the members compete for resources and power. How can those divided by religion understand practices, beliefs, and behaviors different from their own?

3. Cooperation and conflicts between Islam and the West in various situations where both believe in different things and each speaks with certainty that it is right.

4. Confrontation between the religious and the secular with responses ranging from resistance to accommodation and the rationalization of practices.

5. The changing role of women in the context of tradition and patriarchy.

6. Modernity and the challenges that it poses to individuals and nations: the erosion of tradition, the constant reimagination of the future, the difficulty of balancing the ethos of community with that of individualism, and the differentiation of lives into semiautonomous spheres of family, work, occupation, leisure, and so on.

7. Consequences flowing from how the culture of global politics is structured not by democratic values but rather by militarism and militarization. In making the argument that society has to be orderly and protected, military values are promoted, leading to warfare and to the civil use of the police and army. Militarization involves the allocation of more public expenditures to the culture of violence than to other sectors because

of the belief that the use of coercive instruments can guarantee peace and security.

8. From the state to the family, from secular to religious institutions, the most pervasive determinant of contemporary culture is capitalism. Cultures at all levels have been assaulted, permeated, and assimilated by capitalism. Market values shape our ideas and affect how we think about our careers, mobility, migrations, adaptation, consumption, and value of change. Even religious authorities that preach morality and tradition do so in the context of market products, using the services of modern technology to deliver their messages with speed and efficiency.

9. As market values reveal their limitations, especially the destructiveness of these values and the damage to families and communities, alternative forms of antimarket mobilization have occurred. NGOs, antistate social movements, religious organizations, countersummit movements, and the like, have in one way or another called for alternatives to capitalism and market values. They argue about the restoration of human dignity, placing lives before profits. In calling for nonmaterialist ethics, they seek power in tradition, communities, and nonprofit-based institutions. If globalization presents millions of people as a problem, the alternative forms of organization want to see us as dignified human beings, supporting our ethical values over market values. However, ideas still have to be borrowed from technology and the marketplace to mobilize and announce alternative values and identity.

10. The constant nature of change. No matter how powerful tradition is, change is inevitable, and it will impact culture, politics, and even the sovereign state. The creation of modern Africa terminated the sovereignty of older nations and undermined the power of kings, queens, and chiefs. New economies and new elites create new culture. The Western-educated elite are replacing the queens and kings and are introducing new cultures. Today a new economic system creates new cultures and political institutions. Ideas will change, reconstituting cultures.

11. The rapidity of change brought about by technologies will affect cultural change. Every significant change will affect an aspect of culture. Changes in political and economic structures will impact the social. The Darwinian idea that change is slow

may give way to a nonevolutionary form as states and people may not be able to withstand the strong blows of new ideas that are spread rapidly by satellite television and the Internet.

12. Individuals may change faster than a nation, as they explore a variety of means (sanctioned or unsanctioned by the state) to define the self, change the self, accept/reject the self, and engage with the state itself. In Nigeria and many African countries there is a misconception that democracy brings efficiency and effectiveness to governance, ignoring the reality that the basic premise of democracy is to prevent tyranny and anarchy. As individuals realize the limitations of the state and democracy, they begin to accept the overall logic of society while adding to and complicating it. Thus individuals can adopt cultures of individualism and egocentricism (discrete, autonomous) and reject those expected by past traditions, such as holistic (where individuals link personhood to the interest of more people and the community) or sociocentric (where selfhood is defined in terms of social settings and situations) cultures.

In what follows, I will analyze some characteristics of culture in contemporary society, and the context of state and globalization within which culture operates. With Nigeria in mind, I will use the examples of religion and women—two dominant issues of concern—to illustrate many of these theoretical issues. I will close by offering a set of ideas to tap into the positive aspects of culture to create peaceful intergroup and international relations.

Cultural Portions and Cultural Politics

Culture is broad, encompassing the complexity of how the society defines itself (traditions, beliefs, behavior, and the like). UNESCO defines culture as "the whole complex of distinctive, spiritual, material, intellectual and emotional features that characterize a society or societal groups. It includes not only arts and letters, but also modes of life, the fundamental rights of the human being, value systems, traditions and beliefs." In a previous work, I have elaborated on the meanings, complications, and elaborations of culture.[8] I have also explored how African scholars have linked culture and nationalism to talk about progress and development.[9] In this chapter, I will limit myself to issues around identity, authority, and power: three elements of culture that form the basis of interpersonal and interstate relations.

Religious expression is one of the most visible cultural practices. Our people are Muslims and Christians, and a minority practice indigenous religions. Religious beliefs do shape various aspects of culture such as the organization of households, polygyny, and childraising. The expectation that religious diversity can encourage tolerance and acceptance of diverse views is not always realized, as validated by the eruption of disturbing cases of violence.

Societies cannot be studied as autonomous parochial localities. They may possess their own identities, but they inevitably have to interact with others and exchange ideas, goods, and services. Our lives are structured by both elements of commonalities (as in the religion we practice or the food we eat) and by difference (as in the specific church or mosque or our local cuisines). Irrespective of where we live, we have to encounter diversity, both horizontally, whereby others have cultures and practices different from ours, and vertically, as in the cluster of beliefs found in various places.

What frames the understanding of contemporary culture within Nigeria and other African countries is development, which in turn is underpinned by change. What our people react to includes those elements of the past that they want to retain and change. Individuals do not necessarily hold assemblies to create consensus, which may explain the divergent views and the cacophony of expressions. Reception to change can be positive or negative, peaceful or violent. A religious community may find the building of a new church desirable, but its location may be a political issue. Coming together to worship may threaten an established social order that may in turn instigate a violent reaction. The perception of development and change can be as important as the impact of development and change itself. Perceptions can be driven by established values and traditions, stereotypes, competition for resources, and political rivalries.

Change and development ultimately involve technology and industrialization in the larger context of modernity. Technology and industrialization have an immeasurable impact on culture. They do not transform lives in an equal manner. If social and economic inequities follow change, these in turn create their own impact on the culture of relations between individuals on the one hand and between regions on the other.

Citizens look to the state to generate development, to provide an environment amenable for them to function, to create the basis for change, and to provide jobs, good health care, and much more. A state may lack the capability to function well because of inadequate resources or corrupt or inefficient leadership. Where a state does not deliver the common expectations of national authority, it may undermine the overall culture of efficiency. Where the state fails, it may encourage citizens to turn deeper into the spiritual and religious realms to seek alternative answers. In places with many Muslims, we have seen a tendency to question the legitimacy and relevance of the secularist state that is unable to generate protection and economic development.

The assumptions of dividing cultures into the traditional and modern are becoming increasingly flawed on various grounds. Tradition represents modernity at a certain time. Ideas that have spread through migrations and interactions are claimed as local and presented as ageless. What the generation coming of age in the early twenty-first century refers to as tradition are practices and institutions of the post-1960 era, some traditions even refer to a more recent past. Many members of this generation have grown up in a time of flux, when new changes began to unfold before their very eyes. Similarly, what they describe as modern has within it various aspects of cultures that are fluid, that draw from the past, and that are being constantly reviewed or rethought. The society manifests the ambiguities of change and continuity, while it constantly engages in conversation about its future, worried about the challenges and gains of technologies and science. To create stability, it calls on its past, presenting aspects of institutions as "traditional" to maintain itself. It edits the past, drawing from it what it wants. What was originally foreign and modern, as in the case of religion (Islam and Christianity), can be presented as indigenous.

The modern can tap into the past to create meaning, thereby protecting the society with stable values. As more and more live in places far away from their original places of birth or acquire Western education, they can actually become rootless and seek meaning in tradition. Structural changes do occur in our lives and roles, compelling us to ask profound questions about the place of culture. Religious resurgence in different parts of the world has been attributed to the search for meaning and relevance in contemporary societies. Stress and strains trouble individuals who seek solutions in various ways: secularist or spiritualist and religious. No one must be under any illusion

Figure 12.1. Visiting professors from Canada, the United States, and the United Kingdom with young Nigerian students, Abeokuta, Nigeria, July 2012. Photograph courtesy of author.

that modern secular society has an answer to all problems, just as the traditional and religious societies also lack all of the answers. Conditions of individuals in society, old and new, are not uniform. The condition of development and modernity is also not uniform. Individuals define their interests in relation to a host of possibilities, tapping into various cultural resources to evaluate their needs and assess their success. Irrespective of where we live, as citizens or immigrants, economic actors, and political and social agents, we have worldviews that we strengthen, modify, and change as we are confronted by various situations and crises.

Small World, Big Space

A global village has emerged, united by the media, Internet, consumption, migrations, and many other elements. The objects of modernity in a home and what traders sell in the markets reveal how goods have traveled great distances—carried by fast transportation systems and obtained through transactions conducted in different currencies. Poor and rich countries interact in multiple ways and have a stake in the success of one another.

Africa has been integrated into the global world system for centuries. Much closer to the truth in evaluating the impact of this integration is that it has been a victim of global forces in terms of its incorporation into an exploitative global economic system as a supplier of labor and raw materials. As the continent moved into its modern era after European colonization, the state and the power of government have been such that the capacity to cleverly manage the impact of external forces has been limited. The slowness in the emergence of democratic institutions and governments has meant the inability to engage in dialogue to create the policies and activities to counter domination.

To effectively manage global politics and cultures, the domestic political culture has to be clearly defined and related to sustainable development. Government, laws, and policies can be shaped by tradition, beliefs about power, and behaviors of political actors. Patriarchal societies can have an authoritarian view of democracy. The individualism of Western societies has shaped its reward system, with privileges accorded to private companies. Cultural norms of corruption, sexism, and patriarchy can translate into the management of politics—even into the formulation and subversion of laws. Cultural norms can be translated so that we think that a powerful person is above the law, that laws can be interpreted to suit those in power.

Most people live within a limited space in terms of their location, worldview, aspirations, and expectations. Their village, town, or country may be the center of the world they know, understand, or even care about. Destinies are enacted within this space; children are produced and values are reproduced. One space may have a view of politics and the world that is framed by its culture and is different from others. Perhaps there is very little we can do about this limited space.

However, as we aggregate all the small spaces, we become united by living in a larger state that is diverse, heterogeneous, competitive. The knowledge that governs our behavior in our small space may not be adequate to live in that larger state. As we then aggregate the states, we can get a region, a continent, a world. We have to reconcile our location within concentric rings of geographic locations. As we become acculturated to a specific culture within our small world, the bigger space—regional and global—can function only if we accept diversity in virtually all practices. A person from a polygamous culture may come into confrontation with monogamous commitments, and both may have to relate to those who believe in same-sex practices. We cannot think of eliminating those whose beliefs and practices differ from ours.

We have to align cultural politics to the obligations and expectations to live in states, nations, and the world while maintaining personal and familial survival and advancement. We are all citizens of a state; the passport is our symbol when we go to another state. A state—with its name (Nigeria), symbols (flag), anthem, and the like—can be founded on a set of assumptions both cultural and political. Such states as Iran and Saudi Arabia have an Islamic foundation. The Sokoto empire in the nineteenth century was a theocracy. Many African countries are aggregations of former precolonial nations, and have their own established cultural practices. The modern states, created by European conquest and violence, have been struggling to generate development and stability. Elements of the practices of the past cannot be discarded, and they have implications for how contemporary societies are managed. Foreign ideas and practices cannot be prevented from making inroads, making it a necessity to accept and edit them.

The real challenge to Africa is the global context. A long history of marginalization and exploitation has been established, from the transatlantic slave trade through colonization to neocolonialism.[10] There is the power of Western domination supported by a culture of war and violence; authoritarian and patriarchal global order uses the instruments of coercion and economic inequalities to control and dominate. Those who dominate the global economy and politics are Western-based, and they use policies, some formulated in their respective countries and some by world institutions, to dominate and control. The values that are supposed to guide the world—economic equity, political democracy and participation, peace, social justice, and environmental balance—are all compromised by the domination of the rest of the world by the minority.

Africa was colonized in the last decade of the nineteenth century, which served as the basis to create new cultures and colonial modernity. In the colonial states, Africans were subjects, not citizens, and the introduction of various changes had considerable impact on previous traditions, the production of a new elite, ideas abut cultural alienation, inferiority complex, and anomie.[11] If the economy that led to that colonization necessitated territorial control, the contemporary new economy is based on technology, information, and services, all of which do not require the direct control of territories to make money and ensure the transfer of wealth from one location to another. Whereas the colonial economy required the production of groundnuts, cocoa, and other products with labor and land that are fixed in a location, the new economic system does not require the means of production to be fixed in one location; both labor and capital are very mobile. Open borders and transnational connections deliver profits to those who benefit from the new forms of information, transportation, and technology. States recognize the change as well, using the new economic system to make huge investments.

States, Borderlessness, and Power

Individuals operate within the state, defining their interactions with others in the context of laws and regulations, rights, and responsibilities. Cultures emerge as part of those interactions. States are also submerged in the larger context of the world with its visible and invisible institutions. The states, in alliance with transnational companies and a host of intergovernment organizations (IGOs), create the conditions for a global market to work, and have the power (e.g., military, regulations) to enforce global collaboration and use coercive power to punish. Powerful nations seek the means to attract resources to themselves. Cultures travel with goods and with institutions of collaboration and control. Although people tend to move more often from weaker countries to powerful ones, cultures from the powerful countries are the ones that travel more frequently to the weaker ones, which explains why there is more of Western culture in Africa than vice versa.

There is an argument that the forces of globalization are weakening the power of the state. The power of the state is becoming more diffused. Susan Stranger has made the compelling argument that the private sector and the market are taking over many of the functions of the state and that nonstate actors are actually acquiring more power.[12] The problem we face today is that the assumptions that states can control the global economy and politics as they wish are no longer possible. The idea that wealthy nations can trade with one another and that one democracy can deal with another democracy to avoid wars and minimize conflicts is undermined by the ability of globalization to create nonstate actors, economies not sanctioned or approved by the states, leaders without addresses, and a host of transsovereign crises and problems. States relate actions to sovereignty and territories and to nonstate actors who deal in drug smuggling, underground arms trade, cyber threats, prostitution, and other crimes that are not obligated to state laws. Nonstate actors have an alternative culture of order and peace. As the state loses its capacity to control and dominate in all matters and problems, local and global cultures will be shaped by the state and by nonstate actors, especially in terms of consumption habits, values of wealth accumulation, respect for constituted authorities, and the like. A drug baron may be more important than a state governor, thus affecting the culture of violence and consumption, which may clash. Even powerful warlords and heads of states have widened the basis of their networks and power by joining drug mafias. A catholic bishop may have more followers than the mayor of a city, thus affecting how values are traded. A madam controlling the international traffic of prostitutes may enjoy more clout than a civic community leader, thus affecting the content and reception of messages.

The state remains powerful. It controls the resources and the institutions of governance. Its regulations, laws, politics, and leadership have profound effects on various aspects of cultures and how cultural clashes and conflicts are mediated. It is the state, for instance, that can introduce Sharia law, although civil society can demand it. Where violence occurs because of religion or ethnicity, it is the state that uses its army and police to stop or perpetuate it.

Globalized Connectivities

The preceding indicates how other forces submerge the state in the bigger space of the marketplace, of invisible forces, of virtual space, of imagined spaces, and of denationalized geographies in relation to identity, authority, and power. A new set of connections are derived from alternative spaces and global networks. The ties between Lagos and London are much stronger than people think. Both are global cities with many functions and institutions that are regional, national, and international. The managers of the leading sectors of the economy think in terms of transborder networks; the communication infrastructures they deploy have global outreach. So also are the ties between villages and the cities part of a regional network that connects to many other countries. The cell phone is a point of contact between all parts of the world. The cell phone, the Internet, and the spread of technology have created a more connected world where economic and social ties are very dense. The European Union, for example, created "borderless" countries; citizens travel from one country to another without a visa and can work in those countries. The euro is a currency that almost 500 million people use for transactions.

The intensity of migrations within and across borders (driven by a host of factors such as war, political instability, famine, persecution, social disintegration, poverty, and the like) have created millions of people whose nationality cannot be understood within the framework of just one nation-state. Consciousness can be triple or more, suggesting a notion of both mental and physical deterritorialization. Within a state, people also move; they change jobs and locations, sell their houses and change their addresses permanently. The distance between the place of birth and the place of death can be thousands of miles.

We are confronted with a set of opportunities and challenges. The marketplace is ever extending, circulating goods from Dubai to Kaduna, from Lagos to New York. As legitimate commodities spread, so too do illegal ones such as forged currencies and drugs. The use of cocaine, marijuana, and other drugs is global, connecting the desires of youth in Chicago with those of Dar es Salaam. Sexual practices are glamorized and globalized. The pace keeps accelerating. There is competition amongst companies to seek new markets. A new economic elite is benefitting from an increasingly globalized economy. A generation of transnationalist imperialists has emerged, and they use the markets available to them all over the world to make money. The new elite considers state barriers hindrances to market expansion.

This new elite is also developing the culture that reinforces deterritorialization. It tends to study similar economic principles in elite schools, consume similar food items in similar restaurants, watch similar movies, and engage in similar vacation culture. Common culture creates common politics in a virtual space that keeps expanding.[13] Those aspiring to a higher class try to imitate the culture of the new elite.[14]

Globalization brings gains and pains. Disasters such as the spread of AIDS and environmental degradation have incalculable consequences on societies and cultures. Changing world politics impact local and global cultures. The cultural might of Islam is treated with fear in the West, where it influences military budgets and the conduct of foreign policy. The rise of China is leading to discussion about possible new forms of Asian imperialism in Africa. Controversy exists on the choice between war and peace, as this choice divided the United States and Europe during the George W. Bush administration. While the hawks in the Bush administration believed in extending American power by means of war if possible, many European leaders and their citizens wanted to leave the memory of two world wars behind. Secularist Europe also has many strong antiwar movements that seek nonmilitaristic options to attain global peace and interactions.

The confrontation between Islam and the West has dominated global politics since the fall of the Soviet Union. Samuel Huntington's "clash of civilizations"[15] has been overused as a theory in some policy-making circles to characterize the encounter. A large number of people regard the US attack on Iraq as an attack on a Muslim country with large oil reserves. The never-ending conflict between Israel and the Palestinians is analyzed by some scholars as an attempt to control the Middle East, Arabs, and Muslims. According to some citizens in the West, angry Muslims are scheming to destroy them and their civilization.

Islam will surely dominate attention in the West and will continue to be of importance in African politics and cultures. With respect to Africa, a number of people will continue to argue that ideas should be drawn from Islam to replace or reform the secularist state. A few may argue that using Islam to reform capitalism may lead to transformation. The clerics will continue to insist that the best way to counter wasteful Western consumerism is to turn to the values of modesty in Islam. Regarding Islam and the West, the linkage between the religion and terrorism will continue to generate resentments among Muslims who already think that they are being persecuted. It is apparent that some Muslim leaders, such as those in Al Qaeda, continue to believe that they have scores to settle: the humiliation caused by imperialism, the crises in the Middle East, the power of the West, and so on. These leaders align Islam with various radical and fringe elements of society.

Figure 12.2. Scholars with the Nigerian Minister of Culture, Chief Duke (*third from right*), at the Toyin Falola Annual International Conference on Africa and the African Diaspora, Lagos, July 2012. The annual conference is organized around a major theme that brings scholars from different parts of the world to an African city. Photograph courtesy of author.

Religious Traditions and Forces

No aspect of culture manifests more force and power than religion. None can match religion in its capacity to bring nations together or to disunite them. Within and between nations, religion reveals key connections to identity, nationalism, and globalization. A source of identity, religion can be used to define a group, an ethnicity, or a nation-state. A source of transnationalism, religion can contribute to the creation of a world without borders. World religions have extended the reach of globalization.

Ambiguities and contradictions define the place of religion in national and global cultures. The holy books and prophets preach peace, harmony, reconciliation, nonviolence, concern for the poor, and humanitarianism. All well and good! The interpreters of the holy books promote the vision and dreams of the founders of their religions. The evidence is abundant that they want peace and oppose taking human lives. Indeed, religious teachings do encourage and promote nonviolence.[16] However, in defending faith and expanding the frontier of a religion, competition and conflicts, even wars, have followed. Religious leaders have supported war; sometimes even praising strong political leaders who use the military for imperialism and the conquest of other lands. Those who preach peace can also preach hatred, instigate believers to violence, and call on political leaders to engage in wars. Self-interest motivates religious leaders to support war and violence.

The defense of a value or a set of values may lead to the suppression of the values of others. Societies are plural in composition and forms. The answer is actually to present the case and argument within a pluralist framework, allowing individuals to make a choice. The ability to make a choice is intimately connected to a notion of freedom: the freedom to choose a religion, a religious leader, a place of worship, or a place to live. Choice and freedom validate the power of rationality. The rigidity and authoritarianism associated with certain cultures and religions, such as Islam, can be checked by promoting pluralism and freedom to choose. The personal is political, just as the political can be personal.

In the West, it is not uncommon to speak about Islamic fundamentalism, which is an excessive characterization of Islam as violent and prone to terrorism. Analysts in the West are quick to deny the existence of Christian fundamentalism, which endorses the use of state violence and war against countries and peoples perceived as enemies. Within Western countries, Christian fundamentalism expresses itself in antigay and antilesbian, antiabortion, and politically conservative movements.

Whether Islamic or Christian, fundamentalists share certain elements in common. They preach the revival and expansion of religion, that is, of their specific faith. They want their core values to be integrated into politics. The extremists want theocracies. Moderates want more pressure on the secularist state to support their religious views. Fundamentalist views are nationalistic, grounded in strong views that their beliefs and statements are sanctioned by higher forces, that their vision is the only right one. The activities of fundamentalists are not confined within their borders. The views of religious leaders spread in different countries. Ideas and actions are sponsored and disseminated in different locations. Some of these ideas and actions are violent in nature, as with those that seek to overthrow regimes, ideologies, and state systems. Radical and violent expressions are divisive and invite counterattacks. In the case of terrorism, people are killed in the name of God.

Islam is a religion with a powerful transnational force. Its views and practices shape cultures and events. Islam has been presented as antidevelopment, but those who do so forget to mention that three-quarters of the world is labeled "developing" or "underdeveloped." For the critics of Islam, Muslim and Arab are seen as one and the same thing, such that all the negativity constructed about Arabs and Arab culture are extended to all Muslims. Arabs represent a minority of Muslims; most Muslims reside outside of the Middle East, and only about one in ten Muslims is an Arab. Politics in the Middle East is far more complicated than its framing as an Arab-Islamic issue would allow; one needs to consider imperialism, Western domination, and the politics of oil.

World religions are involved with politics: the politics of culture, the politics of governance, the politics of the state, and the politics of international relations. There is no monolithic religious political theory that guides the relationship between each religion and politics. As hostile as the presentation of one by another can be, it is not as if anyone formulated a theory of violence to kill or eliminate all of their opponents. Beliefs and politics merge to create political actions that lead to violence, distrust, prolonged hostility, and rivalries. Competition for power and wealth become sources of conflicts that may acquire religious dimensions.

Christianity has had a long history of association with politics and war. The devout are often enjoined to fight for their rights. Christians are fond of seeking passages in the Qur'an to claim that Islam supports violence, forgetting that the histories of wars commanded by God dominate the Old Testament. "When the Lord your God has given them over to you," declares Deuteronomy 7:2, "and you defeat them, then you must utterly destroy them, you shall make no covenant with them, and show no mercy to them." The cross, the symbol of peace, has also been turned into the symbol of war at various times, and war is presented as necessary to crush evil. The history of the Crusades in the twelfth century presented wars as fighting for Christ. From the sixteenth to the eighteenth centuries, war was regarded as vengeance against the ungodly and unrighteous, a view that was expressed by terrorists after the attack on the United States on September 11, 2001.

With respect to Islam, beliefs arising from its foundational principles, particularly that the religious and secular should not be separated, have been used to criticize it as antimodernization. In this case, criticism generates confusion between the premodern and the postmodern state, between the expectations of premodern society and those of contemporary society. True, Islam advocates religious expansion, but it was in the context of cohabitation and conversion. Jihads were used in some instances to expand the state, reform the religion, and create a theocracy. When a multiethnic state was created, the expectation was that a belief in Allah and commitment to the Qur'an were enough to define citizenship such that Islam (that is, religion) became the criterion rather than race, ethnicity, language, or kinship. In accepting the membership of the community, the expectations were that the principles of the faith would be promoted, that the constitution of the state was permanent, that the basis of law would be based on the Qur'an, and God (not man) was the overall head.

It is about time that both world religions stop the blame game and accept the fact that they all have some connections to the culture of violence and unhealthy political competition. "Men never do evil so completely and cheerfully," declared Blaise Pascal, the noted Catholic and celebrated mathematician, "as when they do it from religious conviction."[17] To the Islamic and Christian realist, peace and the creation of a just world require violence. The commandment not to kill, so argue the realists, is not violated when one kills to defend what is right. The question is: What is right? And is killing the right way to correct what is wrong?

Both major religions have been criticized for supporting cultures of patriarchy and domination and for preaching to the poor and the marginalized to accept political authority and economic structures. For supporting the status quo, Karl Marx and his successors have characterized religion as the "opiate of the masses," dismissing and demeaning its social principles as supportive of slavery, feudalism, and oppression.[18] It should be noted, however, that the fundamentals of religion promote the liberation of the poor and disenfranchised. The key prophets were against the unjust practices of the rich and supplied messages in support of wealth redistribution. Nigeria and other developing countries need to add to their commitment to religion a commitment to "liberation theology," a social Gospel that calls for a fight against poverty and oppression.[19] Perhaps it is about time to revive the notion of "social sin" once employed by the Reverend Martin Luther King Jr. to criticize political leaders and those in authority who close their eyes to the plight of the oppressed and marginalized. Poverty shapes the configurations of culture. Religion cannot say that it does not see the pain and cries of the people, cries that rise to the heavens, complaining of gross injustice, inhuman poverty, starvation wages, joblessness, hopelessness, malnutrition, health problems, and lack of transportation and housing.

Rather than expend energies to criticize and condemn, attack and kill, such energies should be diverted to mental liberation, the acquisition of resources to empower the poor, the recapitalization of marginalized and rural areas, and the creation of an elaborate support system for the poor. Individuals and nations can reinvent themselves if they draw from the spirit of compassion and community to elevate minds and people to abandon a path of destruction, to reject the elements of primitive atavism, and to purge culture of its anachronism and uselessness.

Women and the Palavers of Culture

Be it at the local or global levels, women have been affected by changing cultures, whether traditional or modern. Women have always been discriminated against and that discrimination is often justified by cultural practices and established traditions. Men tend to make choices for them: where they will live, how they will establish themselves, how much to invest in their education and careers. Millions of women lack the resources to pursue their work and interests. Any time that society undergoes structural changes, the woman question often arises around their social roles. In the twentieth century, when Western education was introduced to many parts of Africa, the question was whether women should go to school and, if they did, what occupations they would be allowed to pursue.

In the contemporary period, the questions that are posed relating to women include marriage, occupations, and how to balance work and family. Single women complain of the difficulty of finding men who can make and keep commitments, and those women who refuse to marry seek alternative ways to attain fulfillment. Changing occupations and marital patterns have created their own arguments as to the role of women. Millions of poor women continue to work in low-paying jobs, often performing hard domestic chores. At the same time, there are the so-called superwomen who combine everything: great occupations with great household management. Women have to manage the difficult politics of dual membership in the family of orientation (original home, in-laws, siblings, husband's siblings, and the like) and the family of procreation (husband and children). So difficult are the complications of managing the family of orientation that women, including two recently in South Africa, have been wrongly accused of witchcraft and even stoned to death.[20] Violence takes place in the family of procreation where an autocratic husband appropriates the rights to settle domestic strife with violence. A culture of phallocentrism, in various forms, allows men to have sex on demand whether the woman enjoys it or not, and too often such demands cross the line to rape. Such a culture also leads to careless politics in taking additional wives and gloating over stories of infidelity. Many women have been adept at using silence as politics, including sexual silence: a code of silence that disguises both the joy and pain of intimacy.

Women struggle with too many difficult questions: Should they marry or not? If single, should they become a second or third wife in societies that practice polygyny? If they have their children outside of wedlock, how can they work and take care of their families at the same time? Irrespective of the questions they pose, women face the challenges of living in society regardless of how they define their roles, aspirations, identity, and femininity while negotiating gender relations with men. If men tend to promote the culture of independence and separation, women seek connection and interdependence. The global system, argues Betty Reardon, links war and militarism with sexism, endowing the state and men with enormous power to use violence to oppress women.[21]

Systematic research is lacking on the various responses by women to modernizing cultures and structural changes in African contemporary societies, but honorary facts tend to suggest two categories—one traditional and the other radical-feminist. The traditional category is aligned with patriarchy, representing a unity of ungendered voices in support of age-old social hierarchies with men at the top. The practices that agrarian societies invented are transferred to the present. The radical-feminist category is one in which the power of change, modernity, and globalization reveals itself. A variety of radical orientations have emerged. The first is actually both traditional and radical, a seeming contradiction in terms, calling on women to retain central power in the household, not because they are subordinate to men but because they can be far more efficient in the management of resources. Those who make this argument do so in part because one income in the family is sufficient, and the expectation is that women can retrain and enter the workforce after they have reared their children. Some argue that they do not want their identities to be defined by their careers but rather by marriage and family. This orientation encourages normative choices to attain stability in life, in the belief that the autonomy and integrity of womanhood are not compromised. Career and occupation become secondary sources of fulfillment, while the home—where the woman receives honor as mother, wife, and counselor—is elevated. Thus, rather than femininity as subordinate to patriarchy in the traditional agrarian model, what I characterize as traditional-radical sees femininity as a household priority whereby the family becomes a social unit of power able to validate the right of women to create a meaning for their existence not defined by the needs of men.

The second category is the liberal-feminist, arguably the most common response, which calls for equal opportunities for men and women in all formal and public spheres. Where patriarchal institutions are strong, as in most parts of Africa, the liberal-feminist approach has had to contend with established, male-oriented privileges and entrenched institutions. Leading advocates have also had their characters and names disparaged. The third category is the radical-revolutionary model, which seeks to reject mainstream thinking and find new ways to live: from redefining forms of marriage and male-female relations to creating sources of independence and autonomy in financial matters and democratic expressions of sexuality. Some want to be single mothers, some want to devote their lives to their professions, and others want to forego marriage and childbearing.

Irrespective of the model and the appropriateness of each to a cultural zone, everyone (especially men) must intervene in the efforts to eradicate the oppression and exploitation of women, the personal prejudices that lead to hostility, and the institutionalization of male privileges. Specific cultural milieus must look for ways to combat the problem, and, if necessary, redefine the very premises of culture itself and expand the scope of rights and freedom. We must disarm our antiwomen attitudes by being conscious of them in ourselves and in others. We must educate the young to fight hierarchies based on gender difference, which in turn are justified on cultural grounds. Where exploitation and oppression are grounded in institutions, it may very well be that collective action will generate a revolution that will liberate such institutions from the cancer that will consume them.

Contemporary Culture: The Local and the Global

There are many complicated dimensions of culture in the contemporary era within the larger context of the local and global. Beliefs and actions can have positive and negative impacts that can divide and unite persons within and between nations. The positive impacts are many: sources of hope to billions of people, sources of construction of harmony and identity, sources to tap ideas for creativity, energy, and development. The negative forces are there as well: division among people and nations, the stereotyping of others, the manipulation of politics, and the like. Opinions and personal matters cannot be suppressed, but they can respect collective goals and the freedom of others. Lives without worldviews to shape them can be empty. Communities of memory and tradition are needed to enable individuals to relate to one another, and for one nation to deal with another.

It is certain that contemporary reality at the national and global levels is such that the forces of religion are not going to wane. Worldviews rooted in spiritual, divine, and fundamental premises are hard to reshape. Cultural cognition, of which religion forms a critical part, will continue to shape how human beings interpret daily events, the facts of life, the actions of others, and the activities of the government. Thus it remains important to understand the cultural cognition that individuals bring to the table. Whether Muslims or Christians, believers will always affirm the righteousness of their beliefs, and religious leaders will forever mobilize their followers to press on certain issues.

At all local levels, values will always be contested. Some members of the society will continue to advance the project of tradition over that of the modern, which can be characterized as the politics of orthodoxy. Those who control power need to maintain their aristocratic hold on it, and orthodoxy enables them to do so. There will be those who will advance the agenda of modernity over the traditional, as this enables them to question orthodoxy and insert themselves into democratic spaces. Tensions and challenges will continue to come in four fronts: the forms of social organization that can work in the modern world; the types of political, cultural, and religious authority; the extent of power that such authority can wield; and the teachings that are legitimate and ethical to disseminate.

The authority and weight of tradition deserve respect. Thus the issue is not that anyone is challenging established religions, established worldviews, and established cultures. However, established tradition must engage with modernity, secularity, globalization, and the future. Cultural institutions require tradition for legitimacy, but they also need adaptation to change to remain current and useful. Leaders are empowered to interpret traditions, to reconstruct the past in light of ongoing exigencies, and to invent strategies to cope with circumstances as they arise and meet the obligations of modern society.

Religious leaders must also return to those fundamentals of their religion that are opposed to violence and wars. The West now possesses sufficient chemical and nuclear resources to annihilate millions of people. Even such primitive tools as the cutlass, clubs, and knives have been used to kill thousands of people, as the case of Rwanda demonstrates. And we have seen even more barbaric forms of murder, as in Nigeria, where people's throats are slit and they are set on fire. Religious leaders must encourage antiwar and antiviolence activism and be aggressive and assertive in promoting a culture of activist pacifism. World religions promise that their worldviews will universalize us, making us citizens, not of tribes or nations but rather of faith. They promise to detribalize us, but they have succeeded in retribalizing us. In replacing our allegiance to the nation with allegiance to religion, they have created havoc. Religious competition has left deterritorialized migrants unprotected, and it has overwhelmed those who practice a minority religion. Gandhi once turned to the *Bhagavad Gita,* the Hindu treatise contained in the famous epic *The Mahabharata,* which details the encounter between the god Krishna and the warrior Arjuna, to advocate for a world without violence. I do not know what aspect of this treatise influenced him, but he could have been guided by at least one notable paragraph:

> One man believes he is the slayer, another believes he is the slain. Both are ignorant; there is neither slayer nor slain. You were never born; you will never die. You have never changed; you can never change.

Unborn, eternal, immutable, immemorial, you do not die when the body dies. Realizing that which is indestructible, eternal, unborn, and unchanging, how can you slay or cause another to slay?[22]

Nations and individuals have enormous power and talents to transform themselves. In spite of severe constraints, individuals can reject the manipulation to hate people who belong to other religions, ethnicities, and races. Men can reshape their lives and orientations to respect women, accept equality, democratize household spaces, and treat women not as sex objects but as human beings with individual destinies. Men have to recognize that women face serious difficulties in balancing work and family. In empowering women with Western education, we must do so with the awareness that the cultural ideology that defines women solely as childbearers must change and that careers and families can be combined.

Nations are obligated to interact, but they have to do so with respect. Interactions among nations will continue to be shaped by cultural, economic, and political considerations. The values of domination and control that govern the world will be harder to change until the developing world becomes developed enough to create a balance in power. Global structural change is still a long way off. It is doubtful whether the power of capitalism can ever be crushed. What is possible is to use the power of the market and technology to minimize the devastating impact of market values. There is no escape from using the facilities of the modern economic system—the technologies, the information, the market place. To use this power to greater effect, civil societies in various locations have to pull resources and mobilize to create a consensus on various aspects of identity and authority.

In teaching a new generation at all levels of the education system, it is no longer viable to limit the content and framework to a single nation; curriculum must also teach how nations interact and about the inevitable forces of globalization. One can no longer claim to be educated without understanding the building blocks of a nation, the exigencies and contingencies of development, the interdependence of nations, and the gains and losses of membership in the international community. The education and socialization of citizens must recognize that societies are diverse. Plural nations have plural views. How to manage the plurality of these views has been difficult. In Africa, ethnic stereotyping is pervasive; harmful jokes ridicule an entire group and debase their identity. In global politics the same is

Figure 12.3. A carved tree, part of a tourist attraction, especially to students who undertake summer classes in Accra, Ghana. Photograph courtesy of Ben Weiss.

true. The socialization process has to recognize the dangers posed by stereotyping. Diversity can be recognized without being maligned.

In trying to protect ourselves, the education system can create a problem. In the West, the education system focuses on the poverty of Africa and the burden and danger it represents to the West. To Americanize its own citizens, the education system extols the virtues of being an American and the glory of the United States. A patriotic position tends to create an inward-looking, parochial society where the majority of citizens know little about other places and care very little about other cultures. Other Western countries do the same. Their media portray the attitudes of politicians and reinforce the stereotypes in the way they report and analyze news. Anti-Western leaders in other places may find themselves presented as evil, warlords, or criminals. Islamic countries present the West in hostile manner, describing aspects of their cultures as decadent. The education system should seek to build bridges across cultures.

The changes that we seek at both the local and global levels can only come if we, as individuals, create a mental revolution and acquire the emotional stability to change our values, behaviors, and worldviews to accept and respect others, ensure economic and political equity, accept boundaries, promote freedom, and accept, no matter how difficult, that our personal behavior does count in the transformation of local and global culture and politics. As we transform our values and cultures as individuals, so too will our communities, nations, and the world follow our noble examples. As we create open societies, open politics, open economies, and open technologies, both local and global cultures will also become more open.

Postscript

United States Foreign Policy on Africa in the Twenty-First Century

President Barack Obama said in a speech in Accra on July 11, 2009, "The twenty-first century will be shaped by what happens not just in Rome or Moscow or Washington, but by what happens in Accra as well."[1] This is an important moment in the relations between the United States and Africa for a variety of reasons. The first is symbolic: President Obama has a direct link to African origins because his father is from Kenya. Thus he is claimed as an African son and as an African American, a dual identity and citizenship that he has to negotiate. He is clever to draw on both when political exigencies permit. He is a member of the new diaspora able to solidify his credentials by tapping into the identity of the old diaspora represented by his wife, Michelle Obama.

The second reason arises from the symbolic: What will an African/black person in power do for Africa? The expectation is that he will do much, and his administration will alter US-African relations toward a more positive direction and infuse it with more energy. This assumption is based on both the politics of kinship and of identity. The third reason correlates with the symbolic: If a black person is in power in the United States, in what ways would it affect race and race relations?[2] Some scholars originally framed his ascension to power as revolutionary, describing it in terms of a transition to a postracial era in the United States that would extend to other parts of the world. However, this has certainly not been the case. Racism is on the rise in Europe, for example, and there are many cases of racially motivated attacks. In the United States, members of the new diaspora claim that they have not seen any difference in opportunities, the liberalization of immigration rules, or easier access to visas to enter the United States.

The import of the changes in relations between Africa and the United States is related not only to Obama and his presidency, but also to a fourth reason—geopolitics. Between the Second World War and the dismantling of the Soviet Union, US-Africa relations were structured by the strategic calculations of the Cold War: East-West rivalries over the marketing of economic ideologies of capitalism and socialism, interventions in African politics, support for authoritarian leaders such as Mobutu Sese Seko of Zaire, and the elimination of radical leaders such as Kwame Nkrumah, Patrice Lumumba, and Thomas Sankara. Today, terrorism has replaced the politics of the Cold War in the aftermath of the September 11 attacks in the United States. Africa has been drawn into these geopolitical considerations. Finally, the fifth reason is that forces of social movements have been released globally; democratic spaces have expanded because of countersummit movements, antiglobalization movements, and, in general, politics from below.

Major Issues

In view of the aforementioned, the relevance of the relationship between Africa and the United States is clear enough. What then are the issues that connect both nations? Some issues are generated within Africa, and the United States has to respond to them. They include the contemporary uprisings in Tunisia, Egypt, Libya, and Syria. Often labeled the "Arab Spring Revolution," these uprisings have demonstrated the power of mass movements to change political leadership and, it is hoped, impact political culture. The United States has to take sides—either to support the political authoritarianism of sit-tight rulers or to support the masses looking for change and improvement in their standard of living. Needless to say, these revolutions will ultimately spread to other parts of Africa; it is just a matter of time.

Then there are the competitions for power that are sometimes hard to resolve and that call for peaceful resolution, as in the case of Ivory Coast and Mali. Cases of seemingly intractable conflicts in the Sudan and Uganda, and sectarian conflicts in Nigeria and other places, attract international concerns and call for mediation or intervention. As in the case of Rwanda, Liberia, and Sierra Leone, fragile states may engage in divisions, competition, and wars that are conducted with brutality.

Economic affairs within Africa constitute another body of issues: How can policies assure economic growth and sustainable development in Africa? What countries remain burdened by external debts whose loans have to be forgiven? Although the amount of aid to Africa has always been exaggerated in American popular media, how can the call for trade and investments be met? To African countries, the needs are not for charity but for opening up US markets to African goods and for investors from the United States to come to Africa.

A set of issues relates to American interests in Africa. Of preeminent importance is that of its own national security tied to terrorism and the fear of terrorism. Based on data about actual threats and analyses of Al-Qaeda and perceived dangers, the focus has been on Islam, Islamic areas, and countries with dominant Islamic populations. North Africa, the Horn of Africa, the Sahara Desert, and large countries such as Nigeria become regions of serious security concerns for the United States. Where there is evidence of political Islam, the United States sees cases such as Nigeria as a key area of interest. Thus Africa is now part of the war on terrorism both directly and indirectly.

While different from the issue of terrorism, piracy in the Horn of Africa is often presented as terroristic. Arguments and opinions are divided on this, as pirates tend to regard themselves as seeking a share of economic opportunities, compensation for the use of their water routes, and to prevent foreign companies from poaching their resources. Those opposed to pirates see them as nuisances and even terrorists who interfere with international commerce. Indeed, there are economic interests at stake. Top on the list is oil and the need to prevent any interruption in the flow of oil. Africa has rich deposits of oil, some established and some newly discovered. The United States needs the oil.

Based on the issues identified herein, the goal of US-Africa policies can be summarized as follows:

1. Find ways to establish military and strategic partnering with Africa. This entails direct involvement where possible, intelligence gathering, training African security forces, policing terrorist-infested areas, and monitoring constantly areas of perceived danger and threat.

2. Formulate strategies to ensure the constant flow of oil to the American market in order to stabilize prices and meet energy demands in the United States, thereby using Africa to minimize the threat posed by volatile politics in the Middle East.

3. Monitor threats posed by what the United States defines as oppositional and dangerous political Islam.

4. Promote bilateral and multilateral relations along strategic partnering with different nations on a number of compelling issues.

5. Pay attention to good governance with emphases on democracy and the needs of the struggling masses, human rights abuses, and poverty elimination.

6. Contribute to solutions for such diseases as malaria, HIV/AIDS, and others that kill millions of people and that reduce capacity building and productivity.

While the goals are clear, it is important to point out that policies and actions are often discussed against the background of stereotypes. There are a number of Americans who do not recognize that Africa is an ancient continent that has had great institutions and is always developing and modernizing. Indeed, some Americans believe they could go there as developers, take or buy land, put people to work like donkeys, and reap rewards. In this ideology, Africa becomes a utopia where they can get away from the chaos and confusion in their own overmodernized society, enjoy the environment of others, and be served by the uncultured natives. Many also see it as a broken continent of violence, instability, and corruption.

Prelude to the Twenty-First Century: Slavery, Colonization, and the Cold War

Relations between the United States and Africa have a longer history than is often assumed. The deep historical roots between the United States and Africa are grounded in the transatlantic slave trade. Space permits me to provide only some highlights of the slave trade and slavery in the United States. One of the major books on the history of US-Africa relations, coedited by Alusine Jalloh and Toyin Falola, discusses the signposts and the importance of the major eras, focusing on trade, migrations, the spread of Christianity, and the personalities involved. *The United States and West Africa: Interactions and Relations* also examines the forces that shaped relations between the two countries over time.[3] The ties that bind had their roots in the transatlantic slave trade, which involved the funneling of millions of enslaved Africans to the Americas, a percentage of the enslaved going to the United States.

The consequences endure through today and represent one of the major determinants of foreign policy. African Americans represent a significant number of the American public, a voting bloc, and a force in shaping the orientation of America's foreign policy. Today African Americans make up about 13 percent of the US population. Although population trends and demographics during the period of the transatlantic trade suggested that blacks would become the majority, the end of the trade and deliberate "de-blacking," that is, a conscious whitening of society, halted this trend. African presence transformed various aspects of American culture, from its cuisine to jazz music. However, more important, the struggles for civil rights in the United States and anticolonial movements in Africa were fused in a global Pan-Africanist movement.

US relations with Africa from 1885 through the 1960s were shaped by two fundamental factors: the European powers in Africa and the politics of the Cold War. Concrete and sustained policies were slow to evolve. While it was necessary that the two countries relate to each other, no coherent policies emerged. With Africa under European powers, the United States accepted Africa as an extension of Europe and looked at Africa through European eyes, feeling that its security interests were not threatened. When necessary, US companies demanded access to African markets. With the exception of links to Liberia dating back to the nineteenth century, the United States did not disturb Europe's colonization agenda, and it did not serve as a mandatory power when the League of Nations dispossessed Germany of its African colonies. Crises such as those of apartheid South Africa and the invasion of Ethiopia by Italy in the 1930s were regarded as European affairs.

Cold War politics established strategic needs that created new kinds of pressure on American policymakers, who viewed the African continent in the context of rivalry with the Soviet Union and based policies and actions on preventing the expansion of Soviet influence and socialist ideology. As long as Western Europe was in control in Africa, the United States was assured that its interests were protected. While African American leaders criticized European colonial rule, the adminstrations of President Harry S. Truman and President Dwight D. Eisenhower were restrained. The United States needed Western Europe in its rivalry with the Soviet Union, principally the protection of the NATO alliance. The support for African nationalist movements had to be carefully balanced with the maintenance of good relations with Europe. Whether it was the Mau Mau resistance in Kenya, the Algerian War of Independence, or antiapartheid struggles in South Africa, the United States did not lend its support to revolutions and radical liberation struggles. Where commercial interests were strong, as in the case of South Africa, the United States supported slow changes that would not destabilize politics and economy. In 1981 Reagan enunciated a policy of "constructive engagement" that supported the racist South African government until Congress repudiated the policy in 1986 when it passed the Comprehensive Anti-Apartheid Sanctions Act.

As part of the strategy of containing the Soviet Union, the United States was opposed to African countries that believed in the Nonaligned Movement, an alliance of countries that did not want to support either the West or the East, so as to exclude themselves from the politics of the Cold War. The United States ignored the wishes of Africans and did not consult African leaders on many issues. In line with its interest, the United States supported dictators in such countries as Cameroon, Egypt, and Ethiopia, but these leaders subverted the popular will, stole money, and violated human rights.

To advance their own agendas, a number of subsequent US presidents spoke of the concept of "selective engagement," which meant relating to specific African countries on the basis of specific economic and strategic interests. For instance, the United States established military bases in such countries as Kenya and Egypt to be able to respond to crises in those parts of Africa and the Middle East. When interests shifted or unanticipated problems loomed large, the United States also pursued a policy of disengagement, as in the case of Somalia after the failure of Operation Restore Hope. So-called crisis areas called for responses connected with American security and economic interests.[4] When the Cold War ended, policy reviews did not conclude with ideas to reinvigorate or strengthen relationships. Rather, Africa began to lose more to other continents, particularly Asia, which had greater opportunities for economic investments. One argument was that forms of support for others, notably Africa, must be balanced against the reality of budget deficits.

The post–Cold War era produced American presidents with different visions, and their impact on Africa has varied.[5] The language of diplomacy in Washington, as well as the statements on foreign policy into the twenty-first century, was on peace and political stability, democracy and development. All four policies are connected in terms of ensuring projected transformations in Africa that will ensure peace and enable a stable environment for private entrepreneurship to flourish, among other things. The US commitment to these four policies was not always strong. All together, they represent US interests without the need to use military power and coercive instruments to make them work. While there were cases of aid tied to good governance, this did not necessarily lead to the removal of bad leaders or even the end of notorious authoritarian rule.

In recent years the United States has learned valuable lessons from the wars in Iraq and Afghanistan: wars are costly and may ruin the domestic economy, public opinion shifts within a short time from support to opposition, and disengagement from wars and conflicts is extremely complicated. These lessons will affect new policies on Africa based on cost-benefit analyses and the overall outcome. Leaner resources will call for the establishment of priorities in which the Asia-Pacific region, considered to be more economically viable, is most likely to command greater attention than Africa.

The Obama Administration and Africa

The Obama administration has inherited the legacies of its predecessors, most notably those of Presidents Bill Clinton and George W. Bush. Two examples include the African Growth and Opportunity Act (AGOA) regarding trade and the Africa Command (AFRICOM) initiative. AFRICOM, a major initiative, deals with security and intelligence issues to prevent terrorism and activities defined as threatening; it aims to locate and destroy Al-Qaeda networks, keep an eye on armed rebels and pirates in Somalia, and destabilize forces in Djibouti, Ethiopia, and Kenya.

President Obama has been presented with an extraordinary platform to create a new set of development-oriented policies, but it is unclear how he intends to reform previous policies. In some cases, he is modifying them, as in dealing with the linkage between donations on health issues and abortion. In others, he is implementing them,

Figure P.1. The changing face of African cities, Accra, Ghana. Photograph courtesy of Ben Weiss.

as in the case of policies directed at terrorism and oil. New initiatives are yet to enjoy the status of what can be called an Obama doctrine.

On July 11, 2009, in his speech to the Ghanaian Parliament in Accra, President Obama laid out his views on Africa in his first visit to what he calls "sub-Saharan Africa," accepting Washington's definition of Africa that separates the black part from "Caucasian North Africa," which is lumped with the Middle East. In the speech, he notes the need for committed leadership, praising such former Ghanaian leaders as Jerry Rawlings and John Kofi Kufuor. He also notes that Africa is central to the world, basing his arguments on the clichés of globalization:

> This is the simple truth of a time when the boundaries between people are overwhelmed by our connections. Your prosperity can expand America's prosperity. Your health and security can contribute to the world's health and security. And the strength of your democracy can help advance human rights for people everywhere.

So I do not see the countries and peoples of Africa as a world apart; I see Africa as a fundamental part of our interconnected world as partners with America on behalf of the future we want for all of our children.

He follows up with his ideas on partnerships grounded in "mutual responsibility and mutual respect." These are key words, and I think that Africans have to untangle the complexities and legacies of colonialism in addition to developing their own brands of identity and nationalism.

Obama recognizes the "tragedies and triumphs of the larger African story." European rule, he admitted unequivocally, was a painful experience for his father, a cook for the British in Kenya. Obama's father was called "boy" and experienced the repression associated with the anticolonial movement. Africans rose to the challenge, going to school, fighting for independence, and asserting themselves in their own world. However, the gains of independence have been damaged by slow economies, by disease, by conflict and corruption, and Obama tries to apportion the blame:

In many places, the hope of my father's generation gave way to cynicism, even despair. Now, it's easy to point fingers and to pin the blame of these problems on others. Yes, a colonial map that made little sense helped to breed conflict. The West has often approached Africa as a patron or a source of resources rather than a partner. But the West is not responsible for the destruction of the Zimbabwean economy over the last decade, or wars in which children are enlisted as combatants. In my father's life, it was partly tribalism and patronage and nepotism in an independent Kenya that for a long stretch derailed his career, and we know that this kind of corruption is still a daily fact of life for far too many.

Obama then addressed the success stories, using the example of Ghana in building its democracy and economy, and improving governance and nation building through the efforts of ordinary men and women, especially, he notes, the "young people brimming with talent and energy and hope who can claim the future that so many people in previous generations never realized." Change would be dependent on good governance, he argued. He then presented the US agenda based on "democracy, opportunity, health, and the peaceful resolution of conflict." He defined those areas and made some vision statements.

The reality is different from the vision. Managing budget cuts during one of the most serious recessions in the United States since the 1930s has affected Africa. Spending on foreign affairs was cut by almost $8 billion in 2011, which led to cuts in support of food, medicine, and various activities of the Millennium Challenge Corporation and US Agency for International Development. Without sufficient resources, policy becomes driven less by the larger vision and more by an emphasis on key issues that have less impact on struggling Africans and less impact on what Obama identified as priorities in his major speech in Ghana. Three policy determinants overtake the larger vision: preventing terrorism, guaranteeing the supply of oil, and coping with the rising power of China.

Nongovernment Actors and Individuals

Not only nations but also people manage relationships. In addition, constituencies factor into the conduct of foreign policies. Two issues remain constant: the African American identity and the large number of contemporary immigrants. With respect to the first issue, the relationship between African Americans and Africa must be treated as one that reveals key aspects of transnational politics and history, the politics of race in the context of international relations, and the linkages between racial identity and engagement with Africa. Ideas about Africa have changed over the years. Africa has been seen as a source of redemption and liberation, a source of consciousness, and a source of creating an identity, all of which encourage African Americans to look to Africa as homeland.

The imposition of European rule in Africa and nationalist movements in Africa instigated responses in African American political communities as key leaders supported Africans in their liberation struggles. Political leaders such as W. E. B. Du Bois, Martin Luther King Jr., and others used the prisms of race and civil rights to understand and present Africa to the American public. For example, African American leaders have made statements about and taken actions regarding the Italian invasion of Ethiopia in the 1930s, the apartheid regimes in South Africa, the Algerian War of Independence, the Mau Mau rebellion in Kenya, and the overthrow and assassination of

Patrice Lumumba in the Congo. In turn, African nationalist fighters not only forged alliances with African American political leaders but both also shared ideas and strategies; the politics of civil rights in the United States and that of anticolonialism in Africa were in more than one way similar.[6]

With respect to the second issue, thousands of contemporary African immigrants in the United States are located in such cities as Chicago, Houston, New York, Dallas, Baltimore, and Washington, DC, to mention but a few. These migrants have added to our understanding of transnationalism and globalization, increasing the relevance of US-Africa relations.[7] The preceding chapters have explored the relevance of contemporary African migrants in the United States to both Africa and the host country.

Introspections and Projections

Not a few Africans, both on the continent and in the diaspora, have expressed disappointment that the Obama Administration has not done enough for Africa. His radical critics have even gone as far as saying that he is black only in name. His admirers have defended him, saying that the economic recession in the United States has left him with little to spend in support of African causes. The optimists have assured us that if President Obama has a second term, he will use political capital to turn his attention to Africa. Predictions are fraught with danger. His support for the ousting of Ghadafi in Libya has also been interpreted in various ways: some see it as an extension of Western imperialism motivated by a desire for oil, while others see it as empowering democracy. Irrespective of the opinions on Obama, it is clear that he is as yet unable to create what can be called a "punctuation moment," that is, a moment when a set of policies and actions create transformative changes that mark a clear departure from the past.

Putting aside Obama's attitude and focus, some argue that the United States should mind its own business, concentrate on its own internal affairs, and use its resources for its own citizens. With the recession in mind, made all the more visible by foreclosures, high rates of unemployment, and the anger expressed by the Occupy Wall Street Movement, some Americans say that the United States has neither the global authority nor the funds to interfere effectively in the affairs of other nations. Its energy should be focused solely on internal affairs, with the exception of extreme cases of human suffering. Even in those cases, the United States should cooperate with the United Nations to ameliorate the situation. Finally, others argue that US public policy toward Africa should be nonintrusive, that Africans should be left to grow and fail on their own. Of course, the Christian humanitarian principle must be borne in mind: give aid and assist in occasional disaster relief, but outside of such episodic moments the United States should leave Africa alone.

Thus, against the background of conflicting interpretations of Obama's administration and impact on Africa, as well as the skepticism expressed in some quarters, a number of suggestions stand out. Policies operate within intellectual and political frameworks. It remains unclear what model will eventually emerge during the second Obama administration. Will it be cooperative or collaborative? Or hegemonic? Will it be reconstructive, that is, create new thinking that would use a new political order of powerful alliances to transform Africa? Or restorative, that is, maintain aspects that have been successful over the years? Perhaps it will be a prefabrication model, which is to say that it would take what has worked in other continents and apply it to Africa. On the other hand, it might be heroic, a model that many expect Obama to follow that would include the injection of development assistance, support for the poor, and the empowerment of women and social movements that want to transform the leadership of their countries and fiercely fight corruption.

While waiting for the final model to emerge, the essential elements must include the following:

1. Make a distinction between diplomacy and philanthropy. Both are now combined in a way that the humanitarian agenda exists in the service of diplomacy, thereby undermining the good intentions, as in the case of Somalia.

2. Recognize that fragile states have the capacity to decline or collapse, and they may harbor radical cells that are very difficult to control.

3. Recognize that rapid involvement in conflict situations may lead to wars, genocide, and gross human rights abuses, and formulate, if possible, peaceful resolutions of conflicts.

4. Promote democratization and good governance in Africa as a core element of African policy. Indeed, this will be the key to winning friends among the majority of citizens.

5. Support for alleviating poverty. It may be necessary to shift money from the military-oriented approach to the development-oriented one. For instance, spend more money on research on diseases and on sanitation projects to make drinking water available in more places, which would allow children who spend hours looking for water more time to go to school.

6. Support community development in ways that improve farming systems and sales of farm products, using ideas based on local knowledge that has worked for centuries, multicrop agriculture, and socialization methods that focus on indigenous concerns and values.

7. Support disease eradication as a permanent effort, rather than temporarily responding to occasional disasters with media attention and then withdrawing. Efforts toward disease management and prevention will benefit the entire world. For example, the money spent trying to find a cure for AIDS could help not only Africans but also people worldwide.

8. Respect cultural values, as long as those values do not violate human rights.

9. Fight corruption, especially in oil rich countries. For example, enact regulations that prevent American banks from receiving money obtained from illegal activities such as bribing politicians, and freeze suspicious accounts until the sources of money are all accounted for.

Concluding Remarks

Let me close by restating key points. First, many of political and development issues in Africa cannot be fully divorced from past history, and many of the current problems are most notably the direct result of colonial interference, which means that Western countries should take some responsibility for those issues. This is not to suggest that throwing money at a number of issues, such as the prevention of disease or trying to solve the grand issues in Africa, should be done in the framework of arrogance. Such an approach would be reminiscent of a recolonization agenda or part of an even more clever design to transfer wealth from Africa to the West under the guise of globalization. The United States (and the West in general) cannot, and must not, ignore the issues that are particular to Africa.

Africa's history with Western nations cannot by any means be treated as irrelevant; neither should the consequences of this history be treated as if they are insignificant. Considering this history, it is difficult not to believe that the West should provide Africa with some form of aid—not merely via missionaries who spread Christianity, or skilled workers exported for temporary assignments, but also financial and economic aid. The United States and other European nations have, without a doubt, in some cases built up their own economies at the expense of several African nations. Any forthcoming support must avoid the civilizing themes of "Westernization" and "modernization," but rather adopt a sense of "repaying our debts to the African people," if only to ensure that the aid does not end up just as damaging as the consequences it sought to alleviate. Forms of assistance must be evaluated in terms of ensuring sustainable development.

Second, it is not true that Africa is irrelevant to US concerns and interest, both major and minor. All of the arguments advanced by those who want the United States to have a minimal interest in Africa remain: the United States should use its resources for its own people; African politics are too unstable and the United States should not be drawn into conflicts and wars that will affect it negatively; African economies are poor and have little to offer; and rich countries such as Nigeria and Angola are too corrupt to promote meaningful, sustainable development in a short time frame. Despite these arguments, it is highly unlikely that the United States will not be involved with Africa. However, these arguments will influence opinions and produce a national foreign policy whereby the United States will refuse to get involved in large-scale wars or conflicts, will calculate the danger to the lives of American citizens when it gets involved in humanitarian concerns, and will compare overall risks to the expected outcomes. Keeping terrorism in mind, US policymakers will continue to pay serious attention to political Islam and places where anti-American sentiments can incubate. Keeping oil and other minerals in mind, the United States will certainly pay attention to the growing influence of China.

Preventing terrorism is a major concern. Access to African resources such as oil, diamonds, and gold is a major consideration as well. Thus, presenting policies as if the United States gives aids to Africa without direct benefit from the continent is to mislead the public. One way to overcome the stereotype of altruistic humanitarian aid is to begin to tell the truth: the American public will benefit from Africa far more than it understands.

Third, it is critical to move initiatives and public discussion away from humanitarianism to investment that will benefit the United States and African countries. The key should be efforts toward sustainable development. The United States should contribute to Africa's development process, but not in a context in which it is criticized for either not doing enough, being a neocolonialist, or not calculating the financial benefits it obtains from Africa. Helping the continent to develop will definitely involve paying fair prices for goods, supporting women in informal economies, promoting food production, and creating an enabling environment for economic diversification. Where some countries are doing well, large amounts of capital can be injected to accelerate investment projects that will yield returns to all parties.

Fourth, individuals not associated with the government must be active in propagating compelling arguments to strengthen American relations with Africa. It should be one of the responsibilities of African scholars and opinion leaders to publicize the arguments and the reasons in multiple and diverse forms. In so doing, the talking points can include the following:

1. Economic opportunities: oil, diamonds, gold, and other minerals are part of the global trade from which the United States benefits. Thus Africa is not that destitute a place where US companies make no profits. While pointing to the dangers of exploitation, we must support trade equity and contribute to community development where such resources are extracted, and promote the interest of local companies. Fair trade should be to the benefit of both economies.

2. Terrorism remains a threat. While terrorism is of paramount concern to the United States, the majority of Africans are peaceloving and are strongly opposed to terrorism either in Africa or in the United States.

3. Weak states and crises pose a serious problem to global security. Without an effective authority, terrorist cells can grow and multiply, destabilizing the country and region. As of April 2012, Mali poses such a problem. With the fall of Ghadafi in Libya, hundreds of the mercenaries recruited by him, notably the Tuaregs, fled Mali and created antigovernment opposition forces that led to a coup and their control of almost half the country. The African Union and the United States need to respond to emerging threats to regional security. Even where

a state is stable, economic decline, corruption, and ineffective leadership generate conditions that threaten peace and encourage migrations. The overthrow of regimes in Tunisia, Libya, and Egypt is only the beginning of such occurrences.

4. Geopolitics and global competition are important. The increasing involvement of China calls for partnership and collaboration on various issues. As India and Brazil become major economic and political players, so too will they seek relevance in Africa.

5. Sustainable development is critical. If the argument can be made that poverty drives migrations, then a reverse argument can also be made that poverty reduction and elimination will reduce migration as well as criminal activities. Thus the development of Africa has positive global ramifications.

6. Medical research, notably finding a cure to diseases of global impact such as malaria and HIV/AIDS, is important.

7. Soft diplomacy, or the pursuit of various means to make friends and promote peaceful dialogue, will create more friends.

These talking points have to be presented beyond classrooms, conferences, and seminar rooms to cable television, news media, and the Internet. Changing public opinion will change the stereotypes and provide a generation of pro-Africa citizens in the United States. Simultaneously, we have to establish various associations to promote US-Africa friendship at cultural and business levels and then use larger umbrella organizations to influence policymakers and politicians. A useful model emerged in the days of the antiapartheid struggles, when the American Committee on Africa and TransAfrica both lobbied Congress. Today no single, strong voice that commands respect has emerged. Thus it is a matter of priority that we create a strong voice to define Africa's interests, shape American foreign policy in favor of Africa, and ensure that Africa is a priority in foreign relations. Our objective must be clearly defined, presented, and connected effectively with long-standing American ideals and values of democracy and free enterprise. We all seek and desire good governance, democracy, accountability, human rights, and sustainable development—all of which should be part of American policy on Africa. Our role, as scholars and opinion molders, is not to defend bad leaders but rather to expose them; it is not to justify bad policies because we would otherwise create a negative option toward Africans.

We must contribute to the expansion of democratic spaces, the activism of civil societies, and the effectiveness of the rule of law. Our energies must be deployed to ensure that the press is free and that the judiciary is not corrupt but fearless in Africa. With good governance and accountability, it is much easier for us to make our case.

The United States must pose the right set of questions for its foreign policy approach, such as how to use its resources, invest in efforts that retain global dominance, ensure the security for its citizens at home and abroad, project its power and values abroad, and support companies that seek profits. African countries, too, should pose the right set of questions. African leaders must be proactive, not necessarily reacting to superpower politics in shaping the terms of engagement; they must speak up when necessary, come together to express a common view and agenda, and prevent external intervention in their affairs. Irrespective of the policies adopted by current and future American leaders, Africans need to figure out the development of our continent independent of foreign aid and support. Foreign involvement and intervention, as we see with the Atlantic slave trade and colonization, have done enormous damage from which we are still trying to recover. While Africa cannot be isolated from the rest of the world, it must understand and process US policies (and those of all other countries) in the context of its own self-interest, namely, avoid domination and exploitation and ensure sustainable economic development and political stability. Africa's destiny must be controlled by Africans, and not by others.

Notes

Introduction

1. Zeleza, "African Diasporas," 1–19.
2. Larson, "African Diasporas and the Atlantic," 129–47. A body of new scholarship is emerging on Africans in Asia. Among others, see Jayasuriya and Angenot, *Uncovering the History of Africans in Asia.*
3. Even in the American case, the examples of black people in Canada are yet to be fully integrated into the literature. See, for instance, Mensah, *Black Canadians.*
4. Mercer, Page, and Evans, *Development and the African Diaspora.*
5. See, for instance, Jackson, *An Invincible Summer.*
6. Blyden, *African Life and Customs.*
7. Nkrumah, *Neo-Colonialism* and *Revolutionary Path.*
8. Dike, *Trade and Politics in the Niger Delta.*
9. On the various dimensions of Atlantic history, see Falola and Roberts, *Atlantic World.*
10. Among others, see Andrews, *Trade, Plunder, and Settlement;* Lane, *Pillaging the Empire,* and Rediker, *Villains of All Nations.*
11. Many books have explored the origins of the Atlantic World, such as those on the use of the sea, the role of sugar, and the role of Christopher Columbus. See, for example, Boxer, *Portuguese Seaborne Empire;* Mintz, *Sweetness and Power;* and Verlinden, *Beginnings of Modern Colonization.*
12. Smallwood, *Saltwater Slavery;* Hawthorne, *From Africa to Brazil;* and Diptee, *From Africa to Jamaica.*
13. To follow contemporary events in Africa on a daily basis, see https://groups.google.com/forum/?fromgroups#!forum/USAAfricaDialogue.

Chapter 1

1. Northrup, *Atlantic Slave Trade,* xiii.
2. Asante, *As I Run toward Africa,* 269–81.
3. Ibid., 310.
4. On a recent study of these forts and their impact, see Abaka, *House of Slaves.*
5. See, for instance, Thomas, *Slave Trade.*

6. A number of new studies are in print on Islam and slavery. Among these, see Mirzai, Montana, and Lovejoy, *Slavery, Islam and Diaspora*; and Lovejoy, *Slavery on the Frontiers of Islam.*

7. Rodney, "African Slavery and Other Forms of Social Oppression."

8. Discussions on a variety of practices can be found in Spalding and Beswick, *African Systems of Slavery.*

9. Curtin, *Atlantic Slave Trade.*

10. Manning, "Contours of Slavery," 835–57.

11. Robertson and Klein, *Women and Slavery in Africa.*

12. See, for instance, Vincent Bakpetu Thompson, *Making of the African Diaspora in the Americas.*

13. For various arguments relating to why Africans were enslaved, see, for instance, Williams, *Capitalism and Slavery*; Jordan, *White Over Black*; Davis, *Slavery and Human Progress*; and Eltis, *Rise of African Slavery in the Americas.*

14. See, for instance, Solow, *Slavery and the Rise of the Atlantic System.*

15. See, for instance, Curto and Lovejoy, *Enslaving Connections.*

16. Inikori, *Africans and the Industrial Revolution in England.*

17. See, for instance, Thornton, *Africa and Africans.*

18. Gilroy, *Black Atlantic.*

19. Rodney, *How Europe Underdeveloped Africa.*

20. Thornton, *Africa and Africans.*

21. See, for instance, Sawyer, *Slavery in the Twentieth Century*; Klein, *Breaking the Chains*; and Quirk, *Unfinished Business.*

22. Lovejoy and Hogendorn, *Slow Death for Slavery.*

23. See, for instance, Grace, *Domestic Slavery in West Africa*, 159–219.

24. See, for instance, Miers and Roberts, *End of Slavery in Africa*; and Cooper, *Decolonization and African Society.*

25. Falola and Lovejoy, *Pawnship in Africa.*

26. Sundiata, *From Slavery to Neoslavery*, 7–8.

27. Ibid., 8.

28. Lovejoy, *Ideology of Slavery in Africa.*

29. Since this chapter was completed, there have been political and social changes in both countries, most especially the division of Sudan into two countries, North and South. Perceptions about racial identities remain in both countries. In the case of Sudan, some of the incidents narrated here, in combination with wars, triggered the politics that led to secession and the decision to split the country.

30. Davies, "Mauritania Anti-Slavery Campaigner Wins Award."

31. See, for instance, Kamara, "Narratives of the Past."

32. This essay was completed before Sudan was split into two countries, North and South, because of unresolvable conflicts that included identity politics and resource allocation.

33. Beswick, *Sudan's Blood Memory*, 29–42.

34. Ibid., 198.

35. Baroness Cox, "Slavery in Sudan," testimony before US Congress House Committee on International Relations, March 13, 1996.

36. Africa Watch, *Denying "The Honor of Living."*

37. Human Rights Watch, *Behind the Red Line.*

38. Equiano, *Interesting Narrative of the Life of Olaudah Equiano.*

39. Senate Committee on Foreign Relations, *Slavery throughout the World,* 18.

40. For all their various efforts, see the website of Anti-Slavery International, www.antislavery.org.

41. Miers, *Slavery in the Twentieth Century,* 445–56.

42. Bales and Robbins, "No One Shall Be Held in Slavery or Servitude," 18–45.

43. "Nigeria's 'Respectable' Slave Trade," narrated by Allan Little, *BBC Radio 4*, April 17, 2004, 11:30 BST, transcript at http://news.bbc.co.uk/2/hi/programmes/from_our_own_correspondent/3632203.stm.

44. Munford, *Race and Reparations,* 393–439.

45. Quoted in Philips, *Reparations,* 233.

46. Ibid., 234, 237.

47. Johnson, "Colonialism's Back," 43–44.

48. On the practice of assisting slaves, prostitutes, and child labor to regain freedom, see Appiah and Bunzl, *Buying Freedom.*

49. Studies on resistance and their impact are extensive. Among others, see Howard, *Black Seminoles in the Bahamas.*

Chapter 2

1. For various accounts of the Amistad rebellion in published works, among others, see Cable, *Black Odyssey;* Jones, *Mutiny on the Amistad;* and Owens, *Slave Mutiny.*

2. Du Bois, *Souls of Black Folk,* 11.

3. Woodson, *Mis-education of the Negro,* xii–xiii.

4. Quoted in Killingray, *A Plague of Europeans,* 66.

5. Falconbridge, *An Account of the Slave Trade,* 30.

6. Kipling, "White Man's Burden," 215–17.

7. For two accessible volumes on the subject, see Falola, *Africa,* vols. 3 and 4.

8. Among others, see Achebe, *Things Fall Apart.*

9. Rodney, *How Europe Underdeveloped Africa.*

10. Falola, *Nationalism and African Intellectuals.*

11. Asante, *Afrocentric Idea.*

12. Bernal, *Black Athena*, vol. 1, *Fabrication of Ancient Greece*, and vol. 2, *Archaeological and Documentary Evidence*; Lefkowitz, *Not Out of Africa*; and Bernal, *Black Athena Writes Back*.

13. For the various representations by different authors, poets, and politicians, see Irele, *The Négritude Moment*.

14. The literature on this successful cultural tradition has become extensive. Among others, see Wintz, *Black Culture and the Harlem Renaissance*; De Jongh, *Vicious Modernism*; Lewis, *When Harlem Was in Vogue*; and Favor, *Authentic Blackness*.

15. United Nations, Charter of Courmayeur, adopted at the International Workshop of the Protection of Artistic and Cultural Patrimony, Courmayeur, Aosta Valley, Italy, June 25–27, 1992, http://www.museum-security.org/courmayeur.html (last modified December 20, 1995).

16. Falola, *Power of African Cultures*.

17. On these various back-to-Africa projects see, among others, Johnson Jr., *Retuning Home*; and Campbell, *African American Journeys to Africa*.

18. Notable examples include *Amistad*, directed by Steven Spielberg, screenplay by David Franzoni (DreamWorks SKG, 1997).

Chapter 3

1. For his poems, see Cullen and Early, *My Soul's High Song*.

2. Campbell, *Middle Passages*.

3. Du Bois, *Dusk of Dawn*.

4. Du Bois, *Souls of Black Folk*, 17.

5. Walters, *Pan-Africanism in the African Diaspora*, 385.

6. Karenga, *African American Holiday of Kwanzaa*.

7. On Pan-Africanism, see Ajala, *Pan-Africanism*; Baracka, *African Congress*; and Olisanwuche, *Pan-Africanism*.

8. Among others, see Equiano, *Interesting Narrative of Olaudah Equiano*; Turner, *Confessions of Nat Turner*; and Aptheker, *One Continual Cry*.

9. Delany, *Condition, Elevation, Emigration*.

10. See, for instance, Foster, *A Brighter Coming Day*; Cooper, *A Voice from the South*; Mildred Thompson, *Ida B. Wells-Barnett*.

11. Williams, *History of the Negro Race in America*.

12. Woodson, *African Background Outlined*.

13. Woodson, *Mis-education of the Negro*.

14. Du Bois, *World and Africa*.

15. Lewis and Bryan, *Garvey*.

16. An analysis of political strategies can be found in McCartney, *Black Power Ideologies*; Banks, *Black Intellectuals*; and Robinson, *Black Movements in America*.

17. See, for instance, Fredrickson, *Black Liberation*; and Abraham, *Politics of Black Nationalism*.

18. See, for instance, Sarbah, *Fanti National Constitution*; and Hayford, *Gold Coast Native Institutions*.

19. Horton, *West African Countries and Peoples*.

20. Blyden, *Christianity, Islam, and the Negro Race*.

21. Johnson, *History of the Yorubas*; Reindorf, *History of the Gold Coast and Asante*; and Kagwa, *Kings of Buganda*.

22. Césaire, "Notes on a Return to the Native Land."

23. Senghor, *Collected Poetry*.

24. On the nature of black leadership over time, see, for instance, Thompson, *Africans of the Diaspora*; and Cruse, *Crisis of the Negro Intellectual*.

25. The connections are clear to see in the essays in Aptheker, *Documentary History of the Negro People in the United States*.

26. Jewsiewicki and Newbury, *African Historiographies*; and Oliver, *In the Realms of Gold*.

27. Falola, *Dark Webs*.

28. Falola and Jennings, *Africanizing Knowledge*; and Falola and Jennings, *Sources and Methods in African History*.

29. Falola, *African Historiography*.

30. Alkalamat, *Introduction to Afro-American Studies*; and Adams, "Intellectual Questions and Imperatives," 210–25.

31. Among others, see Frazier, *Negro in the United States*.

32. Falola, *Nationalism and African Intellectuals*.

33. BaNikongo, *Leading Issues in African-American Studies*; and Norment, *African American Studies Reader*.

34. Bracey, Meier, and Rudwick, *Black Sociologists*; and Cross, *Shades of Black*.

35. See, for instance, Turner, *Next Decade*; Thorpe, *Central Theme of Black History*; and Thompson, *Sociology of the Black Experience*.

36. Adams, "African-American Studies and the State of the Art," 31–49.

37. The list is rather extensive. For its range, see the issues and bibliographies in Franklin and Moss, *From Slavery to Freedom*; Holt, *Black Over White*; and Joseph, *Waiting 'Til the Midnight Hour*.

38. Diop, *African Origin of Civilization*.

39. A popular work on this historiography is by the famous Guyanese historian, Rodney, *How Europe Underdeveloped Africa*.

40. Diop, *Cultural Unity of Black Africa*.

41. Mbiti, *African Religions and Philosophy*; and Abraham, *Mind of Africa*.

42. West, *Race Matters*.

43. Asante, *Kemet, Afrocentricity, and Knowledge*.

44. Richburg, *Out of America*.

45. See, for instance, Trotman, *Multiculturalism*.

Chapter 4

1. See, for instance, Mengara, *Images of Africa*.
2. See, for instance, Falola and Usman, *Movements, Borders, and Identities in Africa*.
3. Herbert, *Iron, Gender, and Power*, 12.
4. Aina, "Internal Non-Metropolitan Migration," 41–53; and Kopytoff, *African Frontier*.
5. Hance, *Population, Migration, and Urbanization in Africa*; Udo, *Migrant Tenant Farmers of Nigeria*; and Clarke and Kosinski, *Redistribution of Population in Africa*.
6. See, for instance, Connah, *Forgotten Africa*; and Manning, *Migration in World History*.
7. Lwanga-Lunyiigo and Vansina, "Bantu-Speaking Peoples and Their Expansion"; and Posnansky, "Bantu Genesis," 86–92.
8. I have coedited a set of books on migrations in recent years. Falola, Afolabi, and Adesanya, *Migrations and Creative Expressions in Africa*; Falola and Afolabi, *African Minorities in the New World*; Falola and Afolabi, *Trans-Atlantic Migration*; and Falola and Afolabi, *Human Cost of African Migrations*.
9. Elkiss, *Quest for an African Eldorado*.
10. Harding, *Other American Revolution*, 209.
11. Manchuelle, *Willing Migrants*.
12. On their contributions, see July, *Origins of Modern African Thought*; Falola, *Nationalism and African Intellectuals*; and Korang, *Writing Ghana, Imagining Africa*.
13. Falola, *Power of African Cultures*.
14. Nyerere, "Reflections on Africa," 5.
15. Valuable publications on this important organization include Akindele, *Organization of African Unity*.
16. Magubane, *Ties That Bind*.
17. See, for instance, Rev. Jesse Jackson speech, "A Moral Appeal to Resist Fascism," delivered on April 20, 1985, at the Mobilization for Jobs, Peace, and Justice, in Washington, DC.
18. See, for instance, Hill, "International Solidarity," 61–70.
19. Falola, *Nationalism and African Intellectuals*.
20. See, for instance, Elugbe and Omamor, *Nigeria Pidgin*.
21. See, for instance, Nolutshungo, *Margins of Insecurity*.
22. See, for instance, various suggestions in Howell and Allan, *Nile*.
23. Nyerere, "Reflections on Africa," 12.

Chapter 5

1. Samuel Johnson, *History of the Yorubas*, 192.

2. Impressive records can be found in Eltis, Behrendt, Richardson, and Klein, *The Trans-Atlantic Slave Trade: A Database on CD-ROM.*

3. Eades, *Strangers and Traders.*

4. Soares, *People of Faith,* 235–36.

5. Ibid., 235.

6. For an analysis of these immigrations and emigrations, see Byrd, *Captives and Voyagers.*

7. Falola and Childs, *Yoruba in the Atlantic World.*

8. Eltis, "Diaspora of Yoruba Speakers," 33.

9. Akintoye, *History of the Yoruba,* 367–68.

10. Omidire, "Agudas and Jagudas," 193–209.

11. The literature on Santeria is extensive. Among others, see Murphy, *Santeria.*

12. Verge, *Ewe.* See also Carney and Rosomoff, *In the Shadow of Slavery;* and Voeks, *Sacred Leaves of Candomblé.*

13. Sweet, *Domingos Álvares.*

14. Commonplace Book, 1736–1958, of Robert Jordan of Nansemond County, Virginia, Mss 5: 5J7664, Virginia Historical Society, Richmond, Virginia.

15. Among others, see Ohadike, *Sacred Drums of Liberation;* and Sweet, *Re-creating Africa.*

16. Heywood and Thornton, *Central Africans.*

17. Schwartz, *Born in Bondage.*

18. Carney and Rosomoff, *In the Shadow of Slavery.*

19. Moss, *Southern Folk Medicine.*

20. See, among others, Roeks, *Sacred Leaves of Candomblé;* and Weaver, *Medical Revolutionaries.*

21. Verger, *Ewe.*

22. The incantations, known as *ofo,* have been the subject of an earlier book by the same author, *Awon Ewe Osanyin.*

23. Verge, *Ewe,* 13.

24. Ibid., 16.

25. Ibid., 17.

26. Ibid., 19.

27. Roeks, *Sacred Leaves.*

28. Hall, *Social Control in Slave Plantation Societies.*

29. Carne, *Black Rice.*

30. See, for instance, Sweet, *Re-creating Africa.*

31. See, among others, Gomez, *Exchanging Our Country Marks;* Thornton, *Africa and Africans in the Atlantic World;* Sidbury, *Becoming African in America;* and Manning, *African Diaspora.*

32. Hamilton, *Voices from an Empire,* viii.

33. Landers, *Atlantic Creoles in the Age of Revolutions.*

34. Berlin, *Many Thousands Gone*, 64. Quoted in Landers, *Atlantic Creoles*, 3.

35. Landers, *Atlantic Creoles*, 5.

36. Ibid., 13.

37. Childs, *1812 Aponte Rebellion*, 35.

38. Ibid., 104.

39. Ibid., 173.

40. Ibid., 178.

41. Reis, "Slave Resistance in Brazil," 111–44.

42. Reis, *Slave Rebellion in Brazil*.

43. Childs, *1812 Aponte Rebellion*, 184–85.

44. See, for instance, Diouf, *Servants of Allah*.

45. Asa J. Davis, "Some Notes," 464–510.

46. The literature is extensive. Among others, see Joseph, *Waiting 'Til the Midnight Hour*.

47. Johnson, *Diaspora Conversions*.

48. Ibid., 188.

49. Du Bois, *Souls of Black Folk*, 364.

50. Ibid.

51. In particular, see Afolabi, Barbosa, and Ribeiro *Afro-Brazilian Mind*; Afolabi, Barbosa, and Ribeiro, *Contemporary Afro-Brazilian Literature*; and Afolabi, *Afro-Brazilians*.

52. See, for instance, Nascimento and Nascimento, *Africans in Brazil*.

53. In the Candomblé of Bahia, Brazil, St. George (São Jorge) is the syncretized "double" of the Orisa Osoosi, a divinity popular among the Ketu-Yoruba subgroup, and considered the "onile" (owner of the land) in the Afro-Brazilian Candomblé in Bahia.

54. Omidire, "Yoruba Atlantic Diaspora," 321–22.

55. Felix Ayoh' Omidire, e-mail to the author, April 21, 2012.

56. Jegede, *Incantations and Herbal Cures in Ifa Divination*.

57. Afolabi, *Golden Cage*.

58. This is a phrase by T. S. Eliot, "Tradition and the Individual Talent," 14.

59. On these goddesses, see, among others, Badejo, *Osun Seegesi*; Gleason, *Oya*; and Weaver and Egbelade, *Maternal Divinity, Yemonja Tranquil Sea Turbulent Tides*.

60. Matory, *Black Atlantic Religion*, 1.

61. Ibid.

62. Vaughan and Aldama, *Carlos Aldama's Life in Batá*, 4.

63. Ibid., 6, 7.

64. For more information, see Oyotuni's website, http://www.oyotunji.org/home.html.

65. Clarke, *Mapping Yoruba Networks*.

66. Klein, *Yoruba Bata Goes Global.*
67. Vaughan and Aldama, *Carlos Aldama's Life in Batá*, 5.
68. See, for instance, Neirmark, *War of the Orisas.*
69. Du Bois, *Souls of Black Folk*, 185.
70. Falola and Afolabi, *Human Cost of African Migrations; African Minorities in the New World*; and *Trans-Atlantic Migration*. Falola, Afolabi, and Adesanya, *Migrations and Creative Expressions in Africa*; and Yewah and Togunde, *Across the Atlantic.*
71. Wallerstein, "Evolving Role of the African Scholar," 155–61.
72. Laitin, *Hegemony and Culture.*
73. Omidire, "Yoruba Atlantic Diaspora," 321.
74. A valuable work is Walters, *Pan-Africanism in the African Diaspora.*
75. Of relevance here is the older conversation on Négritude that was transatlantic in natures. See Moore, Sanders, and Moore, *African Presence in the Americas.*
76. Johnson Jr., *Returning Home.*
77. Tokunbo is a common name given to a Yoruba child born on the other side of the Atlantic.
78. Translation: People can bear different names when they relocate to a place where they are not known.
79. Translation: One can be any name outside of one's place of birth.

Chapter 6

1. An outline history of Nigeria can be found in Falola and Heaton, *History of Nigeria.*
2. On the literature for the nineteenth century, see, among others, Ajayi and Smith, *Yoruba Warfare in the Nineteenth Century*; Ajayi, "Aftermath of the Fall of the Old Oyo Empire"; and Awe, "Rise of Ibadan."
3. Kopytoff, *Preface to Modern Nigeria.*
4. Smith, *Lagos Consulate.*
5. On the activities of these agents, see Peel, *Religious Encounter.*
6. Ajayi, "How Yoruba Was Reduced to Writing," 49–58.
7. Falola, *Yoruba Gurus.*
8. Lander, *Records of Captain Clapperton's Last Expedition to Africa.*
9. Vaughan, *Nigerian Chiefs.*
10. As in the case of such notables as Oba Okunade Sijuwade, Olubuse II, the Ooni of Ile-Ife.
11. These idioms have been subsequently collated into prints, as in the example of C. O. Thorpe, *Awon Eewo Ile Yoruba.*
12. For an elaboration, see Falola, "Missionaries and Domestic Slavery in Yorubaland," 181–92.

13. *Church Missionary Intelligencer and Record* (July 1880): 399.

14. *Church Missionary Intelligencer* (December 1849).

15. *Church Missionary Intelligencer* 1, no. 9 (January 1850): 198.

16. Ibid.

17. *Church Missionary Intelligencer and Record* (February 1878): 91.

18. CMS CA2/085 (b), Townsend to Venn, December 31, 1856.

19. CMS G/A21/4, Minute on Domestic Slavery in the Yoruba Mission, 1879, enclosure 126.

20. Johnson, *History of the Yorubas*, 626; and C.O. 147/133, Evidence of J. A. Otunba Payne, enclosed in Denton to Chamberlain (confidential), June 4, 1898.

21. C.O. 147/133, Evidence of Rev. James Johnson, enclosed in Denton to Chamberlain (confidential), June 4, 1898.

22. Ayandele, *Missionary Impact on Modern Nigeria*, 68.

23. See, for instance, the statements of two pioneer missionaries to the Ijebu in Ellis and Johnson, *Two Missionary Visits to Ijebu Country*.

24. Newton to Tapper, April 12, 1892, in *Foreign Mission Journal* 33 (July 1892), quoted in Ayandele, *Missionary Impact*, 67.

25. Johnson, *History of the Yorubas*, 643–50.

26. Ibid., 638.

27. Akinyele, *Iwe Itan Ibadan*, 213.

28. Johnson, *History of the Yorubas*, 626.

29. Pinnock, *Romance of Missions in Nigeria*.

30. Akinyele, *Iwe Itan Ibadan*, 127.

31. Oroge, "Institution of Slavery in Yorubaland"; and Mann, *Slavery and the Birth of an African City*.

32. Gibson, "Slavery in Western Africa," 41.

33. Alafin Adeyemi to Governor Carter, October 1, 1895, quoted in Pinnock, *Romance of Missions in Nigeria*, n.d.

34. O'Hear, *Power Relations in Nigeria*, 188–89.

35. Falola and Oguntomisin, *Yoruba Warlords of the Nineteenth Century*.

36. On this practice, see Bascom, *Yoruba of Southwestern Nigeria*, chapter 5.

37. Eades, *Yoruba Today*, 65–91.

38. See, for instance, O'Hear, *Power Relations in Nigeria*.

Chapter 7

1. The literature on worldview is extensive. See, for instance, Hallen, *The Good, the Bad, and the Beautiful*.

2. For a book that captures Ogun's widespread nature, see Barnes, *Africa's Ogun*.

3. For examples, see Drewal, *Yoruba Ritual*; and Ogunba, "Yoruba Occasional Festival Songs."

4. On this specialized genre, see, for instance, Akinyemi, *Yoruba Royal Poetry*.

5. Among others, see King, *Yoruba Sacred Music From Ekiti*.

6. Matory, *Black Atlantic Religion*.

7. The literature on Yoruba religions in the Americas is quite extensive. For an accessible book, see Falola and Child, *Yoruba Diaspora in the Atlantic World*.

8. See, for instance, *Orin Ibeji*, transcribed and translated by Val Olayemi.

9. Bascom, *Sixteen Cowries*.

10. On the Oyotunji, see Clarke, *Mapping Yoruba Networks*.

11. See, for instance, Abimbola, *Sixteen Great Poems of Ifa*; and Emmanuel, *Odun Ifa*.

12. On this genre, see, among others, Babalola, *Content and Form of Ijala*.

13. See, for instance, the views of Olomo, *Core of Fire*; and a contemporary presentation of the Orisa in Adewale-Somadhi, *Fundamentals of the Yoruba Religion*.

14. On these musical genres, see Waterman, *Juju*.

15. Ogunyemi, *Obaluaye*.

16. On performance within a Yoruba setting, see Barber, *I Could Speak until Tomorrow*; and Barber, *Generation of Plays*.

17. Quoted in Elebuibon, *Adventures of Obatala*, pt. 2, *Orikis by the Awise of Osogbo*, 200–201.

Chapter 8

1. See, for instance, Brotz, *African American Social and Political Thought*.

2. *Brown v. Board of Education*, 347 US 499 (1954).

3. On black movements and the various strands of opinions, see, for instance, Robinson, *Black Movements in America*; Cruse, *Crisis of the Negro Intellectual*; and Banks, *Black Intellectuals*.

4. Anderson, "Legal and Executive Journey," 361.

5. See, for instance, Ogbu, "Minority Education," 45–57.

6. See, for instance, Locke, *New Negro*.

7. Huggins, *Report to the Ford Foundation*.

8. See, for instance, Asante, *Afrocantric Idea*; and Conyers, *Africana Studies*.

9. Stewart, "Reaching for Higher Ground," 1–69, quoted in Norment, *African American Studies Reader*, xxvi.

10. See, for instance, Tushner, *Making Civil Rights Law*.

11. Hacker, "Goodbye to Affirmative Action," 21, quoted in Anderson, "Legal and Executive Journey," 367.

12. *Newsweek*, January 27, 2003, 27.

13. See, for instance, Skolnick and Currie, *Crisis in American Institutions*.

14. Herrnstein and Murray, *The Bell Curve*. See also Rushton, *Race, Evolution, and Behavior*.

15. See, for instance, West, *Race Matters*.

16. On the literature on class and privilege, see, for instance, Lenski, *Power and Privilege*.

17. See, for instance, D'Souza, *Illiberal Education*.

18. Anderson, "Permissive Social and Educational Inequality," 444.

19. See, for instance, Fredrickson, *Black Liberation*; Abraham, *Politics of Black Nationalism*; and Falola, *Nationalism and African Intellectuals*.

20. See, for instance, Magubane, *Ties That Bind*.

21. See, for instance, Hutchinson, *Disappearance of Black Leadership*.

Chapter 9

1. On their ideas, see Falola, *Nationalism and African Intellectuals*.

2. Dufoix, *Diasporas*, 3.

3. Lovejoy, *Transformations in Slavery*.

4. Thornton, *Africa and Africans*.

5. Helg, *Our Rightful Share*.

6. See, for instance, common thematic strands in Robinson, *Black Movements in America*; and Falola, *Nationalism and African Intellectuals*.

7. USA Africa Dialogue Series, http://groups.google.com/group/USAAfricaDialogue.

8. This term is borrowed from Korkin, *Tribes*.

Chapter 10

1. See the use of this terminology in Okpewho and Nzegwu, *New African Diaspora*.

2. Brotherton and Kretsedemas, *Keeping Out the Other*.

3. A solid study on this subject is by Telles, *Race in another America*. Where an ideology of socialism has been tried, evidence suggests that race issues are still difficult to eliminate. See Sawyer, *Racial Politics in Post-Revolutionary Cuba*.

4. Robinson, *Forgeries of Memory and Meaning*.

5. Walker, *History of Black Business in America*.

6. The limitations to minority business are analyzed in Fairlie and Robb, *Race and Entrepreneurial Success*.

7. Stoller, *Money Has No Smell*.

8. McNamee and Miller, *Meritocracy Myth*, 1.

9. On the most salient topics familiar to Africans, see, among others, Meriwether, *Proudly We Can Be Africans*; and Collier-Thomas and Franklin, *Sisters in the Struggle.*

10. A good introduction to this line of thinking is by Henry, *Caliban's Reason.*

11. Ojaide, "How the Urhobo People See the World through Art," 73–79.

12. In Wainwright, *Border Lines*, 105–6.

13. This word should have been "sophistocrat" or "sophisticrat," since it is odd to call a person a craft. However, poetry itself is odd, and Ojaide is using poetic license.

14. Ojaide, "State Executive," 113–14.

15. Ojaide, "From Libation," 9.

16. Ibid., 106–7.

17. Ojaide, "From Our Own Reasons," 112.

18. Ibid., 110–11.

19. Ojaide, "Branches of the Same Tree," 101.

20. Ojaide, "Half-Brother of the Black Jew," 1–14.

21. Ojaide, "Two Worlds."

22. Ogundiran, "Living in the Shadow of the Atlantic World," 97.

23. Ibid.

24. Wallerstein, *Modern World System.*

25. Samuel Johnson, *History of the Yorubas.*

26. Ogundiran, "Chronology, Material Culture, and Pathways."

27. On the elaboration of this concept, see Foster, "Marx's Theory of Metabolic Rift," 366–405.

28. Law, *Oyo Empire.*

29. Ogundiran, "Formation of an Oyo Imperial Colony during the Atlantic Age," 224.

30. Ibid.

31. Braudel, *Civilization and Capitalism.*

32. Parry, *Discovery of the Sea*, 16.

33. See, for instance, McEvedy and Jones, *Atlas of World Population History.*

34. Ogundiran, "Formation of an Oyo Imperial Colony."

Chapter 11

1. *Virginia Is for Lovers*, directed by James Oddoye (Bronx, NY: Black Star Entertainment, 2009).

2. Snead, "Repetition as a Figure of Black Culture," 59–60.

3. There is ample data to study these stores as well as street trading. For a useful study that looks at another African group, see Stoller, *Money Has No Smell*.

4. Telles, *Race in Another America*, 1.

5. On race and politics in Cuba, see Sawyer, *Racial Politics in Post-Revolutionary Cuba*.

6. Mercury poisoning can damage the kidneys, and can cause all kinds of mental and neurological symptoms.

7. See for instance, Falola, "Introduction," in *Christianity and Social Change in Africa*, 1–25; and Harris, *Yoruba in Diaspora*.

8. Adesanya, *Carving Wood, Making History*.

9. The piece is used as the cover image in Falola and Oyebade, *Yoruba Fiction, Orature, and Culture*. Also see Adepegba, "Intriguing Aspects of Yoruba Egungun Masquerades."

10. Quoted in Jeyifo, "Wole Soyinka and the Tropes of Disalienation."

11. Poetic recitation in Yoruba, Dr. Aderonke Adesanya, March 30, 2009, Austin, Texas.

12. Falola, *Colonialism and Violence in Nigeria*.

13. Interview with Dr. Aderonke Adesanya, Washington, DC, November 2010. Subsequent quotations and recollections of Adesanya are from this interview.

14. This painting has been used to illustrate the book cover by Falola and Agwuele, *Africans and the Politics of Popular Culture*.

15. Falola and Adesanya, *Etches on Fresh Waters*.

16. Cabral, *Unity and Struggle*.

17. See some examples in Ogbechie, *Ben Enwonwu*.

18. One of the two paintings that she produced during her visiting fellowship at the Institute for Advanced Study, Indiana University, Bloomington, Indiana, in fall 2007. She donated *Acada Woman* to the institute in appreciation of the time she spent there and the productive engagement she had with faculty and students.

19. Amposah, "Colonizing the Womb," abstract.

20. Ogbechie, *Ben Enwonwu*.

21. Soyinka, *Myth, Literature, and the African World*.

22. Arasanyin, "Africa and Language-Policy Inertia," 281–308.

23. Bakhtin, *Dialogic Imagination*, 7.

24. Walcott, "Muse of History," 13.

25. Walcott, *Dream on Monkey Mountain and Other Plays*.

26. Garvey, "Africa for the Africans," 75.

27. Baldwin, "Colloquim in Paris," 105.

28. Among others, see Mintz and Price, *Birth of African-American Culture*; Herskovits, *New World Negro*; and Holloway, *Africanisms in American Culture*.

29. See, for instance, such episodes in Mullin, *Africa in America*; and Reis, *Slave Rebellion in Brazil*.

30. Brown, *Reapers Garden*.

31. Jalloh and Falola, *United States and West Africa*.

32. Falola, Afolabi, and Adesanya, *Migrations and Creative Expressions in Africa*.

33. Research is just emerging on contemporary African immigrants in the West. See, for instance, Falola and Afolabi, *African Minorities in the New World*; *Trans-Atlantic Migration*; and *Human Cost of African Migrations*.

34. Falola, *Colonialism and Violence in Nigeria*.

35. Memmi, *Racism*.

36. Martinot, "Introduction: The Double Consciousness," xxvi.

37. Wright, *Black Boy*, 215.

38. Ellison, *Invisible Man*.

39. Wright, *Black Boy*, 181.

40. Foucault, *Language-Counter-Memory Practice*, 209.

41. Lamming, *Pleasures of Exile*.

42. The reference here is to LeRoi Jones (Imamu Amiri Baracka), *Dutchman*.

Chapter 12

1. Falola and Njoku, *War and Peace in Africa*.

2. Falola, *Power of African Cultures*.

3. Rosecrance, "Rise of the Virtual State," 59–60.

4. Falola and Oyebade, *Hot Spot*.

5. Zartman, *Collapsed States*.

6. See, for instance, Crocker, Hampson, and Aall, *Managing Global Chaos*.

7. UNESCO, *Final Report of the World Conference on Cultural Policies*, 41.

8. Falola, *Power of African Cultures*.

9. Falola, *Nationalism and African Intellectuals*. See also Falola and Hassan, *Power and Nationalism in Modern Africa*.

10. Falola and Child, *Changing Worlds of Atlantic Africa*; and Falola and Roberts, *Atlantic World*.

11. The literature on culture and colonialism is extensive. See, for instance, Memmi, *Colonizer and the Colonized*; and Fanon, *Black Skin, White Masks*.

12. Strange, *Retreat of the State*; and Spruyt, *Sovereign State*.

13. Rosecrance, *Rise of the Virtual State*.

14. New studies are emerging on their character, culture, and politics. Among them, see Leibovich, *New Imperialists*; and Rosecrance, "Rise of the Virtual State," 59–60.

15. Huntington, *Clash of Civilizations*.

16. See, among others, Wallis, *Waging Peace*; Runyon, *Theology, Politics, and Peace*; Meen and Gustafson, *Religious Challenge to the State*; Zisk, *Politics of Transformation*; and April Carter, *Peace Movements*.

17. Pascal, *Pascal's Pensées*, 894.

18. Marx, *On Religion*.

19. See, for example, Cone, *Black Theology of Liberation*; and Rowland, *Cambridge Companion to Liberation Theology*.

20. See, for instance, the *Los Angeles Times*, February 1, 2012.

21. Reardon, *Sexism and War System*.

22. The translation is from Easwaran, *Bhagavad Gita*, 90–91.

Postscript

1. "President Addresses the Ghanaian Parliament in Accra," July 11, 2009, Accra, Ghana, http://www.uspolicy.be/headline/obama's-speech-ghana. All subsequent quotations from President Obama are from this speech.

2. See a set of discussions in Zeleza, *Barack Obama and African Diasporas*.

3. Jalloh and Falola, *United States and West Africa*. See also Duignan and Gann, *United States and Africa*.

4. Bender, Coleman, and Sklar, *African Crisis Areas*.

5. Adebajo, *Curse of Berlin*.

6. Among others, see Anderson, *Eyes Off the Prize*.

7. Afolabi and Falola, *African Minorities in the New World*.

Bibliography

Abaka, Edmund. *House of Slaves and "Door of No Return": Gold Coast/Ghana Slave Forts, Castles & Dungeons, and the Atlantic Slave Trade*. Trenton, NJ: Africa World Press, 2012.

Abdullah, Zain. "African 'Soul Brothers' in the 'Hood': Immigration, Islam, and the Black Encounter." *Anthropological Quarterly* 82, no. 1 (2009): 37–62.

Abimbola Wande. *Sixteen Great Poems of Ifa*. Paris: UNESCO, 1975.

Abraham, Kinfe. *Politics of Black Nationalism: From Harlem to Soweto*. Trenton, NJ: Africa World Press, 1991.

Abraham, William E. *The Mind of Africa*. Chicago: University of Chicago Press, 1962.

Achebe, Chinua. *Home and Exile*. Oxford: Oxford University Press, 2000.

———. *Things Fall Apart*. London: Heinemann, 1958.

Adams, Russell L. "African-American Studies and the State of the Art." In *Africana Studies: A Survey of Africa and the African Diaspora*, edited by Mario Azevedo, 31–49. Durham: Carolina Academic Press, 1998.

———. "Intellectual Questions and Imperatives in the Development of Afro-American Studies." *Journal of Negro Education* 53, no. 3 (1984): 210–25.

Adepegba, Cornelius Oyeleke. "Intriguing Aspects of Yoruba Egungun Masquerades." *Nigerian Field* 55 (1990): 3–12.

Adewale-Somadhi, A. M. *Fundamentals of the Yoruba Religion*. San Bernadino, CA: Ile Orunmila Communications, 1993.

Adi, Hakim. "The African Diaspora, 'Development,' and Modern African Political Theory." *Review of African Political Economy* 29, no. 92, Africa, the African Diaspora, and Development (June 2002): 237–51.

Adogame, Afeosemime, U. Roswith, I. H. Gerloff, and Klaus Hock. *Christianity in Africa and the African Diaspora: The Appropriation of a Scattered Heritage*. London: Continuum, 2008.

Afolabi, Niyi. *Afro-Brazilians: Cultural Production in a Racial Democracy*. Rochester, NY: University of Rochester Press, 2009.

———. *The Golden Cage: Regeneration in Lusophone African Literature and Culture*. Trenton, NJ: Africa World Press, 2001.

Afolabi, Niyi, Márcio Barbosa, and Esmeralda Ribeiro, eds. *The Afro-Brazilian Mind: Contemporary Afro-Brazilian Literary and Cultural Criticism*. Trenton, NJ: Africa World Press, 2007.

———. *Contemporary Afro-Brazilian Literature*. Trenton, NJ: Africa World Press, 2007.

"African Diaspora." *African Arts* 10, no. 1 (1976): 83.

Africa Watch. *Denying "The Honor of Living": Sudan, A Human Rights Disaster.* New York: Human Rights Watch, 1990.

Agorsah, Kofi. "The Archaeology of the African Diaspora." *The African Archaeological Review* 13, no. 4 (1996): 221–24.

Aina, Tade Akin. "Internal Non-Metropolitan Migration and the Development Process in Africa." In *The Migration Experience in Africa*, edited by Jonathan Baker and Tade Aina, 41–53. Uppsala: Nordiska Afrikainstitutet, 1995.

Ajala, Adekunle. *Pan-Africanism: Evolution, Progress, and Prospects.* London: Andre Deutsch, 1973.

Ajayi, J. F. Ade. "The Aftermath of the Fall of the Old Oyo Empire." In *History of West Africa.* edited by J. F. Ade Ajayi and Michael Crowder, 11:136–45. London: Longman, 1974.

———. "How Yoruba Was Reduced to Writing." *Odu: Journal of Yoruba Studies* 8 (1961): 49–58.

Ajayi, J. F. Ade, and R. S. Smith. *Yoruba Warfare in the Nineteenth Century.* Cambridge: Cambridge University Press, 1965.

Akintoye, S. Adebanji. *A History of the Yoruba.* Dakar: Amalion Publishers, 2010.

———. *Revolution and Power Politics in Yorubaland, 1840–1893.* London: Longman, 1971.

Akinyele, I. B. *Iwe Itan Ibadan, Iwo, Ikirun ati Osogbo.* Ibadan: self-published, 1911.

Akinyemi, Akintunde. *Yoruba Royal Poetry: A Socio-historical Exposition and Annotated Translation.* Bayreuth: Eckhard Breitinger, Bayreuth University, 2004.

Akyeampong, Emmanuel. "Diaspora and Drug Trafficking in West Africa: A Case Study of Ghana." *African Affairs* 104, no. 416 (2005): 429–47.

Alabi, Adetayo. "On Seeing Africa for the First Time: Orality, Memory, and the Diaspora in Isidore Okpewho's 'Call Me by My Rightful Name.'" *Research in African Literatures* 40, no. 1, Oral Literature and Identity Formation in Africa and the Diaspora (2009): 145–55.

Alkalamat, Abdul. *Introduction to Afro-American Studies: A People's College Primer.* Chicago: Peoples College Press, 1986.

Anderson, Beverly J. "Permissive Social and Educational Inequality Forty Years after *Brown.*" *Journal of Negro Education* 63, no. 3 (1994): 443–50.

Anderson, Carol. *Eyes Off the Prize: The United Nations and the African American Struggle for Human Rights, 1944–1955.* New York: Cambridge University Press, 2003.

Andrews, Kenneth R. *Trade, Plunder, and Settlement: Maritime Enterprise and the Genesis of the British Empire, 1480–1630.* Cambridge: Cambridge University Press, 1984.

Appiah, Kwame Anthony, and Martin Bunzl, eds. *Buying Freedom: The Ethics and Economics of Slave Redemption.* Princeton: Princeton University Press, 2007.

Apter, Andrew H., and Lauren Hutchinson Derby. *Activating the Past: History and Memory in the Black Atlantic World.* Newcastle: Cambridge Scholars, 2010.

Aptheker, Herbert. *A Documentary History of the Negro People in the United States.* New York: The Citadel Press, 1951.

———. *One Continual Cry: David Walker's Appeal, Its Setting and Its Meaning.* New York: Published for A.I.M.S. by Humanities Press, 1965.

Arasanyin, Olaoba F. "Africa and Language-Policy Inertia: The Historical Genesis." In Falola and Hassan, *Power and Nationalism in Modern Africa,* 281–308.

Arthur, John A. *African Diaspora Identities: Negotiating Culture in Transnational Migration.* Lanham, MD: Lexington Books, 2010.

———. *The African Diaspora in the United States and Europe: The Ghanaian Experience.* Aldershot, England: Ashgate, 2008.

Asante, Molefi K. "African Renaissance Conferences of the 21st Century: Dakar and Salvador in Perspective." *Journal of Black Studies* 37, no. 2 (2006): 169–76.

———. *The Afrocentric Idea.* Philadelphia: Temple University Press, 1987.

———. *As I Run toward Africa.* Boulder, CO: Paradigm, 2011.

———. *Kemet, Afrocentricity, and Knowledge.* Trenton, NJ: Africa World Press, 1990.

Awe, B. A. "The Rise of Ibadan as a Yoruba Power in the Nineteenth Century." PhD diss., Oxford University, 1964.

Axel, Brian Keith. "The Context of Diaspora." *Cultural Anthropology* 19, no. 1 (2004): 26–60.

Ayandele, E. A. *The Missionary Impact on Modern Nigeria, 1842–1914: A Political and Social Analysis.* London: Longman, 1966.

Babalola, S. A. *The Content and Form of Ijala.* Oxford: Oxford University Press, 1966.

Badejo, Diedre. *Osun Seegesi: The Elegant Deity of Wealth, Power, and Femininity.* Trenton, NJ: Africa World Press, 1996.

Bailyn, Bernard. *Atlantic History: Concept and Contours.* Cambridge: Harvard University Press, 2005.

Bakhtin, Mikhail. *The Dialogic Imagination: Four Essays.* Edited and translated by Michael Holquist and Caryl Emerson. Austin: University of Texas Press, 1986.

Bales, Kevin, and Peter T. Robbins. "No One Shall Be Held in Slavery or Servitude: A Critical Analysis of International Slavery Agreements and Concepts of Slavery." *Human Rights Review* 2, no. 2 (2001): 18–45.

Ball, Erica, Melina Pappademos, and Michelle Ann Stephens. *Reconceptualizations of the African Diaspora.* Durham, NC: Duke University Press, 2009.

BaNikongo, Nikongo, ed. *Leading Issues in African-American Studies.* Durham, NC: Carolina Academic Press, 1997.

Banks, William M. *Black Intellectuals: Race and Responsibility in American Life.* New York: W. W. Norton, 1996.

Baracka, Amiri, ed. *African Congress: A Documentary of the First Modern Pan-African Congress.* New York: William Morrow, 1972.

Barber, Karin. *The Generation of Plays: Yoruba Popular Life in Theatre.* Bloomington: Indiana University Press, 2000.

———. *I Could Speak until Tomorrow: Oriki, Women, and the Past in a Yoruba Town.* Washington, DC: Smithsonian Institution Press, 1991.

Barnes, Sandra, ed. *Africa's Ogun: Old World and New.* 2nd ed. Bloomington: Indiana University Press, 1997.

Bascom, William. *Sixteen Cowries: Yoruba Divination from Africa to the New World.* Bloomington: Indiana University Press, 1980.

———. *The Yoruba of Southwestern Nigeria.* New York: Holt, Rinehart, and Winston, 1969; reprint, Prospect Heights, IL: Waveland Press, 1984.

Bauböck, Rainer, and Thomas Faist. *Diaspora and Transnationalism: Concepts, Theories, and Methods.* Amsterdam: Amsterdam University Press, 2010.

Bender, Gerald J., James Smoot Coleman, and Richard L. Sklar. *African Crisis Areas and U.S. Foreign Policy.* Berkeley: University of California Press, 1985.

Berlin, Ira. *Many Thousands Gone: The First Two Centuries of Slavery in North America.* Cambridge: Harvard University Press, 2000.

Bernal, Martin. *The Archaeological and Documentary Evidence.* Vol. 2. Rutgers: Rutgers University Press, 1991.

———. *Black Athena: The Afroasiatic Roots of Classical Civilization.* Vol. 1, *The Fabrication of Ancient Greece, 1785–1985.* New Brunswick, NJ: Rutgers University Press, 1987.

———. *Black Athena.* Vol. 2, *The Archeological and Documentary Evidence.* New Brunswick, NJ: Rutgers University Press, 1991.

———. *Black Athena Writes Back: Martin Bernal Responds to His Critics.* Durham: Duke University Press, 2001.

Beswick, Stephanie. *Sudan's Blood Memory: The Legacy of War, Ethnicity, and Slavery in Southern Sudan.* Rochester, NY: University of Rochester Press, 2004.

Birdsall, Nancy, Milan Vaishnave, and Robert L. Ayres, eds. *Short of the Goal: U.S. Policy and Poorly Performing States.* Washington, DC: Center for Global Development, 2001.

Blackshire-Belay, C. Aisha. "The African Diaspora in Europe: African Germans Speak Out." *Journal of Black Studies* 31, no. 3 (2001): 264–87.

Blake, Cecil. "An African Nationalist Ideology Framed in Diaspora and the Development Quagmire: Any Hope for a Renaissance?" *Journal of Black Studies* 35, no. 5 (2005): 573–96.

Blakey, Michael L. "Bioarchaeology of the African Diaspora in the Americas: Its Origins and Scope." *Annual Review of Anthropology* 30 (2001): 387–422.

Blyden, Edward Wilmot. *African Life and Customs*. London: C. M. Phillips, 1908.

———. *Christianity, Islam, and the Negro Race*. London: W. B. Whittingham, 1887.

Bob-Milliar, George M. "Chieftaincy, Diaspora, and Development: The Institution of Nkosuohene in Ghana." *African Affairs* 108, no. 433 (2009): 541–58.

Bodry-Sanders, Penelope. *African Obsession: The Life and Legacy of Carl Akeley*. Jacksonville, FL: Batax Museum Publishing, 1998.

Bond, Patrick. *Looting Africa: The Economics of Exploitation*. New York: Palgrave Macmillan, 2006.

Bonnett, Aubrey W., and Calvin B. Holder. *Continuing Perspectives on the Black Diaspora*. Rev. ed. Lanham: University Press of America, 2009.

Borstelmann, Thomas. *Apartheid's Reluctant Uncle: The United States and Southern Africa in the Early Cold War*. New York: Oxford University Press, 1993.

———. *The Cold War and the Color Line: American Race Relations in the Global Arena*. Cambridge: Harvard University Press, 2003.

Boxer, Charles R., ed. *The Portuguese Seaborne Empire, 1415–1825*. New York: Alfred A. Knopf, 1975.

Boyd, Antonio Olliz. *The Latin American Identity and the African Diaspora: Ethnogenesis in Context*. Amherst: Cambria Press, 2010.

Bracey, John, August Meier, and Elliot Rudwick, eds. *The Black Sociologists: The First Half Century*. Belmont, CA: Wadsworth. 1971.

Brands, H. W. *The Specter of Neutralism: The United States and the Emergence of the Third World, 1947–1960*. New York: Columbia University Press, 1989.

Braudel, Fernand. *Civilization & Capitalism, 15th–18th Century*. 3 vols. New York: Harper and Row, 1981–84.

Bressey, Caroline, and Hakim Adi. *Belonging in Europe: The African Diaspora and Work*. New York: Routledge, 2010.

Brits, Japie. "Despatching Apartheid: American Diplomats in South Africa, 1948–1953." *South Africa Historical Journal* 46, no. 1 (2002): 175–202.

———. "Tiptoeing along the Apartheid Tightrope: The United States, South Africa, and the United Nations in 1952." *The International History Review* 27, no. 4 (2005): 754–79.

Brotherton, David C., and Philip Kretsedemas, eds. *Keeping Out the Other: A Critical Introduction to Immigration Enforcement Today.* New York: Columbia University Press, 2008.

Brotz, Howard, ed. *African American Social and Political Thought, 1850–1920.* New York: Transaction, 1992.

Brown, Audrey Lawson. "Afro-Baptist Women's Church and Family Roles: Transmitting Afrocentric Cultural Values." *Anthropological Quarterly* 67, no. 4 (1994): 173–86.

Brown, Kenneth L. "Ethnographic Analogy, Archaeology, and the African Diaspora: Perspectives from a Tenant Community." *Historical Archaeology* 38, no. 1, Transcending Boundaries, Transforming the Discipline: African Diaspora Archaeologies in the New Millenium (2004): 79–89.

Brown, Vincent. *The Reapers Garden: Death and Power in the World of Atlantic Slavery.* Cambridge: Harvard University Press, 2008.

Bruner, Edward M. "Tourism in Ghana: The Representation of Slavery and the Return of the Black Diaspora." *American Anthropologist* New Series 98, no. 2 (1996): 290–304.

Byfield, Judith A., LaRay Denzer, and Anthea Morrison. *Gendering the African Diaspora: Women, Culture, and Historical Change in the Caribbean and Nigerian Hinterland.* Bloomington: Indiana University Press, 2010.

Burin, Eric. *Slavery and the Peculiar Solution: A History of the American Colonization Society.* Gainesville: University Press of Florida, 2005.

Byrd, Alexander X. *Captives and Voyagers: Black Migrants across the Eighteenth-Century British Atlantic World.* Baton Rouge: Louisiana State University Press, 2009.

Cable, Mary. *Black Odyssey: The Case of the Slave Ship Amistad.* New York: Penguin, 1977.

Cabral, Amilcar. *Unity and Struggle.* Edited by Michael Wolfers. London: Heinemann, 1980.

Campbell, James T. *Middle Passages: African American Journeys to Africa, 1787–2005.* New York: Penguin Press, 2006.

Carney, Judith A. *Black Rice: The African Origins of Rice Cultivation in the Americas.* Cambridge: Harvard University Press, 2001.

———. "The Role of African Rice and Slaves in the History of Rice Cultivation in the Americas." *Human Ecology* 26, no. 4 (1998): 525–45.

Carney, Judith A., and Richard Nicholas Rosomoff. *In the Shadow of Slavery: Africa's Botanical Legacy in the Atlantic World.* Berkeley: University of California Press, 2009.

Carotenuto, Matthew, and Katherine Luongo. "Dala or Diaspora? Obama and the Luo Community of Kenya." *African Affairs* 108, no. 431 (2009): 197–219.

Carrington, Ben. *Race, Sport, and Politics: The Sporting Black Diaspora.* London: SAGE, 2010.

Carter, April. *Peace Movements: International Protest and World Politics since 1945*. New York: Longman, 1992.

Carter, Donald Martin. *Navigating the African Diaspora: The Anthropology of Invisibility*. Minneapolis: University of Minnesota Press, 2010.

Chester, Edward W. *Clash of Titans: Africa and U.S. Foreign Policy*. Philadelphia: Orbis Books, 1974.

Childs, Matt D. *The 1812 Aponte Rebellion in Cuba and the Struggle against Atlantic Slavery*. Chapel Hill: University of North Carolina Press, 2006.

Chivallon, Christine. "Can One Diaspora Hide Another? Differing Interpretations of Black Culture in the Americas." *Social and Economic Studies* 54, no. 2 (2005): 71–105.

Clarke, J. I., and L. A. Kosinski, eds. *Redistribution of Population in Africa*. London: Heinemann, 1982.

Clarke, Kamari Maxine. *Mapping Yoruba Networks: Power and Agency in the Making of Transnational Communities*. Durham, NC: Duke University Press, 2004.

Clarke, Kamari Maxine, and Deborah A. Thomas. *Globalization and Race: Transformations in the Cultural Production of Blackness*. Durham, NC: Duke University Press, 2006.

Clough, Michael. *Free at Last?: U.S. Policy toward Africa and the End of the Cold War*. New York: Council on Foreign Relations Press, 1992.

Collier-Thomas, Bettye, and V. P. Franklin, eds. *Sisters in the Struggle: African American Women in the Civil Rights–Black Power Movement*. New York: New York University Press, 2001.

Cone, James H. *A Black Theology of Liberation: Twentieth Anniversary 'with Critical Responses*. Maryknoll, NY: Orbis Books, 1990.

Connah, Graham. *Forgotten Africa: An Introduction to Its Archaeology*. London: Routledge, 2004.

Conniff, Michael L., Thomas J. Davis, and Patrick James Carroll. *Africans in the Americas: A History of the Black Diaspora*. New York: St. Martin's Press, 1994.

Conyers, James L., ed. *Africana Studies: A Disciplinary Quest for Both Theory and Method*. North Carolina: McFarland, 1997.

Conyers, James L. *Racial Structure and Radical Politics in the African Diaspora*. New Brunswick, NJ: Transaction Publishers, 2009.

Cooney, Frank. *Studies in Race Relations: South Africa and USA*. Glasgow: Pulse, 1986.

Cooper, Anna Julia. *A Voice from the South, by a Black Woman of the South*. Xenia, OH: Aldine Printing House, 1892.

Cooper, Frederick. *Decolonization and African Society: The Labor Question in French and British Africa*. New York: Cambridge University Press, 1996.

Copson, Raymond W. *The United States in Africa: Bush Policy and Beyond*. New York: Palgrave Macmillan, 2007.

Corbould, Clare. *Becoming African Americans: Black Public Life in Harlem, 1919–1939.* Cambridge: Harvard University Press, 2009.

Counts, James Early. "'Culture [Wars]' and the African Diaspora: Challenge and Opportunity for U.S. Museums." *Issue: A Journal of Opinion* 24, no. 2 (1996): 31–33.

Crabb, Cecil V., Jr. *The Doctrines of American Foreign Policy: Their Meaning, Role, and Future.* Baton Rouge: Louisiana State University Press, 1982.

Crocker, Chester, Fen Osler Hampson, and Pamela Aall, eds. *Managing Global Chaos.* Washington, DC: US Institute of Peace, 1996.

Cross, William E. Jr. *Shades of Black: Diversity in African-American Identity.* Philadelphia: Temple University Press, 1991.

Cruse, Harold. *The Crisis of the Negro Intellectual: A Historical Analysis of the Failure of Black Leadership.* New York: Quill, 1967.

Cullen, Countee, and Gerald Lyn Early. *My Soul's High Song: The Collected Writings of Countee Cullen, Voice of the Harlem Renaissance.* New York: Doubleday, 1991.

Cunliffe, Philip. *Critical Perspectives on the Responsibility to Protect: Interrogating Theory and Practice.* Hoboken, NJ: Taylor & Francis, 2011.

Curry, Dawne Y., Eric D. Duke, and Marshanda A. Smith. *Extending the Diaspora: New Histories of Black People.* Urbana: University of Illinois Press, 2009.

Curtin, Philip D. *The Atlantic Slave Trade.* Madison: University of Wisconsin Press, 1969.

Curto, Jose C., and Paul E. Lovejoy, eds. *Enslaving Connections: Changing Cultures of Africa and Brazil during the Era of Slavery.* New York: Humanity Books, 2004.

Davies, Carole Boyce. *Encyclopedia of the African Diaspora: Origins, Experiences, and Culture.* 3 vols. Santa Barbara, CA: ABC-CLIO, 2008.

Davies, Carole Boyce, Meredith Gadsby, Charles Peterson, and Henrietta Williams, eds. *Decolonizing the Academy: African Diaspora Studies.* Trenton, NJ: Africa World Press, 2003.

Davies, Desmond. "Mauritania Anti-Slavery Campaigner Wins Award," *PANA* (London) November 18, 1998.

Davis, Asa J. "Some Notes on the Life and Times of an Afro-Brazilian Abolitionist of Yoruba Descent." In *The Proceedings of the Conference on Yoruba Civilisation Held at the University of Ife, Nigeria, 26th–31st July, 1976.* Edited by I. A. Akinjogbin and G. O. Ekemode, 464–510. Ife: University of Ife, 1976.

Davis, Darién J. *Beyond Slavery: The Multilayered Legacy of Africans in Latin America and the Caribbean.* Lanham, MD: Rowman & Littlefield, 2007.

Davis, David Brion. *Slavery and Human Progress.* Oxford: Oxford University Press, 1984.

Dayal, Samir. "Diaspora and Double Consciousness." *Journal of the Midwest Modern Language Association* 29, no. 1 (1996): 46–62.

Delany, Martin. *The Condition, Elevation, Emigration, and Destiny of the Colored People of the United States.* Originally printed in Philadelphia, by the author, in 1852. Reprint with an introduction by Toyin Falola. New York: Humanity Books, 2004.

Demissie, Fassil. *African Diaspora and the Metropolis: Reading the African, African American, and Caribbean Experience.* London: Routledge, 2010.

Dickson, David. *United States Foreign Policy toward Sub-Saharan Africa.* Lanham: University Press of America, 1985.

Dike, K. O. *Trade and Politics in the Niger Delta, 1830–1885: An Introduction to the Economic and Political History of Nigeria.* Oxford: Clarendon Press, 1956.

Diop, Cheikh Anta. *The African Origin of Civilization: Myth or Reality.* Westport, CT: Lawrence Hill, 1974.

Diouf, Sylivane A. *The Cultural Unity of Black Africa.* Chicago: Third World Press, 1978.

———. *Servants of Allah: African Muslims Enslaved in the Americas.* New York: New York University Press, 1998.

Diptee, Audra. *From Africa to Jamaica: The Making of an Atlantic Slave Society, 1775–1807.* Gainesville: University Press of Florida, 2010.

Drachler, Jacob, ed. *Black Homeland/Black Diaspora: Cross-Currents of the African Relationship.* Port Washington, NY: Kennikat Press, 1975.

Drewal, Henry John. *Sacred Waters: Arts for Mami Wata and Other Divinities in Africa and the Diaspora.* Bloomington: Indiana University Press, 2008.

Drewal, Margaret Thompson. *Yoruba Ritual: Performers, Play, Agency.* Bloomington: Indiana University Press, 1992.

D'Souza, Dinesh. *Illiberal Education: The Politics of Race and Sex on Campus.* New York: The Free Press, 1991.

Du Bois, W. E. B. *Dusk of Dawn: An Essay toward an Autobiography of a Race Concept.* New York: Harcourt Brace, 1940.

———. *The Souls of Black Folk.* New York: Fawcett, 1961.

———. *The World and Africa.* New York: International Publishers, 1975.

Dudziak, Mary. *Cold War Civil Rights: Race and the Image of American Democracy.* Princeton: Princeton University Press, 2011.

Dufoix, Stéphane. *Diasporas.* Translated by William Rodarmor. Berkeley: University of California Press, 2003.

Eades, J. S. *Strangers and Traders: Yoruba Migrants, Markets, and the State in Northern Ghana.* Trenton, NJ: Africa World Press, 1994.

———. *The Yoruba Today.* Cambridge: Cambridge University Press, 1980.

Easwaran, Eknath. *The Bhagavad Gita.* Petaluma, CA: Nilgiri Press, 1985.

Edwin, Shirin. "African Muslim Communities in Diaspora: The Quest for a Muslim Space in Ken Bugul's 'Le baobab fou.'" *Research in African Literatures* 35, no. 4 (2004): 75–90.

Elebuibon, Ifayemi. *The Adventures of Obatala.* Pt. 2, *Orikis by the Awise of Osogbo.* Lynwood, CA: Ara Ifa Publishing, 1998.

Eliot, T. S. "Tradition and the Individual Talent." In *Selected Essays.* London: Faber and Faber, 1951.

Elkiss, T. H. *The Quest for an African Eldorado: Sofala, Southern Zambezia, and the Portuguese, 1500–1865.* Waltham, MA: Crossroads Press, 1981.

Ellis, H. J., and James Johnson. *Two Missionary Visits to Ijebu Country [Report on a missionary tour through a portion of Ijebu-Remo made between 3rd and 29th August, 1892 by The Rev J. Johnson and The Establishment of the Wesleyan Mission in Ijebu-Remo from the Diary (Dec. 1892–1893) of The Rev. H. J. Ellis].* Ibadan, Nigeria: Daystar Press, 1974.

Ellison, Ralph. *Invisible Man.* New York: Random House, 1952.

Eltis, David. *The Rise of African Slavery in the Americas.* New York: Cambridge University Press, 2000.

Eltis, David, Stephen Behrendt, David Richardson, and Herbert Klein. *The Trans-Atlantic Slave Trade: A Database on CD-ROM.* Cambridge: Cambridge University Press, 1999.

Elugbe, Ben, and Augusta Omamor. *Nigeria Pidgin: Background and Prospects.* Ibadan: Heinemann Educational Books, 1991.

Emmanuel, Abosede. *Odun Ifa: Ifa Festival.* Lagos: West African Book Publishing, 2000.

Epperson, Terrence W. "Critical Race Theory and the Archaeology of the African Diaspora." *Historical Archaeology* 38, no. 1, Transcending Boundaries, Transforming the Discipline: African Diaspora Archaeologies in the New Millenium (2004): 101–8.

Equiano, Olaudah. *The Interesting Narrative of the Life of Olaudah Equiano, or Gustavus Vassa, the African.* London, 1789.

Esedebe, P. Olisanwuche. *Pan-Africanism: The Idea and Movement, 1776–1963.* Washington, DC: Howard University Press, 1982.

Evans, Ivan Thomas. *Cultures of Violence: Lynching and Racial Killing in South Africa and the American South.* Manchester: Manchester University Press, 2009.

Fairlie, Robert W., and Alicia M. Robb. *Race and Entrepreneurial Success: Black-Asian and White-Owned Businesses in the United States.* Cambridge: The MIT Press, 2008.

Falconbridge, Alexander. *An Account of the Slave Trade on the Coast of Africa.* London: Society for the Abolition of the Slave Trade, 1788.

Falola, Toyin, ed. *Africa.* Vols. 3 and 4. Durham: Carolina Academic Press, 2002–4.

———, ed. *African Historiography: Essays in Honor of J. F. Ade Ajayi.* London: Longman, 1993.

———. *Christianity and Social Change in Africa: Essays in Honor of J. D. Y. Peel.* Durham: Carolina Academic Press, 2005.

————. *Colonialism and Violence in Nigeria.* Bloomington: Indiana University Press, 2009.

————, ed. *Dark Webs: Perspectives on Colonialism in Africa.* Durham: Carolina Academic Press, 2003.

————. "Missionaries and Domestic Slavery in Yorubaland in the Nineteenth Century." *Journal of Religious History* 14, no. 2 (1986): 181–92.

————. *Nationalism and African Intellectuals.* Rochester, NY: University of Rochester Press, 2001.

————. *The Power of African Cultures.* Rochester, NY: University of Rochester Press, 2003.

————. *Yoruba Gurus: Indigenous Production of Knowledge in Africa.* Trenton, NJ: Africa World Press, 2000.

Falola, Toyin, and A. Agwuele, eds. *Africans and the Politics of Popular Culture.* Rochester, NY: University of Rochester Press, 2009.

Falola, Toyin, and Adebayo Oyebade. *Hot Spot: Sub-Saharan Africa.* Westport, CT: Greenwood Press, 2010.

————, eds. *Yoruba Fiction, Orature, and Culture: Oyekan Owomoyela and African Literature and the Yoruba Experience.* Trenton, NJ: Africa World Press, 2011.

Falola, Toyin, and Aderonke Adesola Adesanya. *Etches on Fresh Waters.* Durham: Carolina Academic Press, 2008.

Falola, Toyin, and Aribidesi Usman, eds. *Movements, Borders, and Identities in Africa.* Rochester, NY: University of Rochester Press, 2009.

Falola, Toyin, and Christian Jennings, eds. *Africanizing Knowledge: African Studies across the Disciplines.* London: Transaction, 2002.

————, eds. *Sources and Methods in African History: Spoken, Written, Unearthed.* Rochester, NY: University of Rochester Press, 2002.

Falola, Toyin, and Kevin D. Roberts, eds. *The Atlantic World, 1450–2000.* Bloomington: Indiana University Press, 2008.

Falola, Toyin, and Matt Child, eds. *The Changing Worlds of Atlantic Africa: Essays in Honor of Robin Law.* Durham: Carolina Academic Press, 2009.

————, eds. *The Yoruba Diaspora in the Atlantic World.* Bloomington: Indiana University Press, 2004.

Falola, Toyin, and Matthew Heaton, *A History of Nigeria.* Cambridge: Cambridge University Press, 2008.

Falola, Toyin, and Niyi Afolabi, eds. *The Human Cost of African Migrations.* London: Routledge, 2007.

————, eds. *African Minorities in the New World.* London: Routledge, 2008.

————, eds. *Trans-Atlantic Migration: The Paradoxes of Exile.* London: Routledge, 2008.

Falola, Toyin, Niyi Afolabi, and Aderonke Adesanya, eds. *Migrations and Creative Expressions in Africa and the African Diaspora.* Durham: Carolina Academic Press, 2008.

Falola, Toyin, and Paul E. Lovejoy, eds. *Pawnship in Africa: Debt Bondage in Historical Perspective.* Boulder, CO: Westview, 1994.

Falola, Toyin, and Raphael Chijioke Njoku, eds. *War and Peace in Africa.* Durham: Carolina Academic Press, 2010.

Falola, Toyin, and Sallah Hassan, eds. *Power and Nationalism in Modern Africa: Essays in Honor of Don Ohadike.* Durham: Carolina Academic Press, 2008.

Fandrich, Ina J. "Yorùbá Influences on Haitian Vodou and New Orleans Voodoo." *Journal of Black Studies* 37, no. 5 (2007): 775–91.

Fanon, Frantz. *Black Skin, White Masks.* New York: Grove Press, 1967; originally published in 1952.

Favor, J. Martin. *Authentic Blackness: The Folk in the New Negro Renaissance.* Durham: Duke University Press, 1999.

Fikes, Kesha, and Alaina Lemon. "African Presence in Former Soviet Spaces." *Annual Review of Anthropology* 31 (2002): 497–524.

Forbes, Jack D. *Africans and Native Americans: The Language of Race and the Evolution of Red-Black Peoples.* 2nd ed. Urbana: University of Illinois Press, 1993.

Foster, Francis Smith, ed. *A Brighter Coming Day: A Frances Ellen Watkins Harper Reader.* New York: The Feminist Press of the City of University of New York, 1990.

Foster, John Bellamy. "Marx's Theory of Metabolic Rift: Classical Foundations for Environmental Sociology." *American Journal of Sociology* 105 (1999): 366–405.

Foucault, Michel. *Language-Counter-Memory Practice.* Edited and translated by Donald F. Bouchard. Oxford: Basil Blackwell, 1977.

Francis, David. *U.S. Strategy in Africa: AFRICOM, Terrorism, and Security Challenges.* Hoboken: Taylor & Francis, 2010.

Franklin, John Hope, and Alfred A. Moss Jr. *From Slavery to Freedom: A History of the African Americans.* 7th ed. New York: McGraw-Hill. 1994.

Franklin, V. P. "Introduction: Explorations within the African Diaspora." *Journal of African American History* 95, no. 2 (2010): 151–56.

Frazier, E. Franklin. *The Negro in the United States.* Rev. ed. New York: Macmillan, 1957.

Frazier, John W., Joe T. Darden, and Norah F. Henry. *The African Diaspora in the U.S. and Canada at the Dawn of the 21st Century.* Albany: State University of New York Press, 2010.

Fredrickson, George M. *Black Liberation: A Comparative History of Black Ideologies in the United States and South Africa.* New York: Oxford University Press, 1995.

Gaines, Kevin K. *American Africans in Ghana: Black Expatriates and the Civil Rights Era.* Chapel Hill: University of North Carolina Press, 2006.

Games, Alison. "Atlantic History: Definitions, Challenges, and Opportunities." *American Historical Review* 111, no. 3 (2006): 741–57.

Gates, Henry Louis, Jr. *Tradition and the Black Atlantic: Critical Theory in the African Diaspora.* New York: Basic Civitas, 2010.

Gerloff, Roswith. "The Significance of the African Christian Diaspora in Europe: A Report on Four Meetings in 1997/8." *Journal of Religion in Africa* 29, Fasc. 1 (1999): 115–20.

Gibson, A. E. M. "Slavery in Western Africa." *Journal of the African Society* 9 (October 1903).

Gilman, Nils. *Mandarins of the Future: Modernization Theory in Cold War America.* Baltimore: Johns Hopkins University Press, 2003.

Gilroy, Paul. *The Black Atlantic: Modernity and Double Consciousness.* Cambridge: Harvard University Press, 1993.

Gleason, Judith. *Oya: In Praise of an African Goddess.* New York: HarperCollins, 1987.

Gleijeses, Piero. *Conflicting Missions: Havana, Washington, and Africa, 1959–1976.* Chapel Hill: University of North Carolina Press, 2003.

Goldschmidt, Walter, ed. *The United States and Africa.* Westport, CT: Praeger, 1963.

Gomez, Michael A. *Exchanging Our Country Marks: The Transformation of African Identities in the Colonial and Antebellum South.* Chapel Hill: University of North Carolina Press, 1998.

———. "Of Du Bois and Diaspora: The Challenge of African American Studies." *Journal of Black Studies* 35, no. 2 (2004): 175–94.

———. *Reversing Sail: A History of the African Diaspora.* New York: Cambridge University Press, 2005.

Gordon, David F., David C. Miller Jr., and Howard Wolpe. *The United States and Africa: A Post–Cold War Perspective.* New York: W. W. Norton, 1998.

Gordon, Edmund T., and Mark Anderson. "The African Diaspora: Toward an Ethnography of Diasporic Identification." *Journal of American Folklore* 112, no. 445 (1999): 282–96.

Grace, John. *Domestic Slavery in West Africa.* London: Frederick Muller, 1975.

Gramby-Sobukwe, Sharon. "Africa and U.S. Foreign Policy: Contributions of the Diaspora to Democratic African Leadership." *Journal of Black Studies* 35, no. 6. (2005): 779–801.

Griffith, R. Marie, and Barbara Dianne Savage. *Women and Religion in the African Diaspora: Knowledge, Power, and Performance.* Baltimore: Johns Hopkins University Press, 2006.

Grubbs, Larry. *Secular Missionaries: Americans and African Development in the 1960s.* Amherst: University of Massachusetts Press, 2009.

———. "'Workshop of a Continent': American Representation of Whiteness and Modernity in 1960s South Africa." *Diplomatic History* 32, no. 3 (2008): 405–39.

Gunning, Sandra, Tera W. Hunter, and Michele Mitchell. *Dialogues of Dispersal: Gender, Sexuality, and African Diasporas*. Malden, MA: Blackwell, 2004.

Guridy, Frank. *Forging Diaspora: Afro-Cubans and African Americans in a World of Empire and Jim Crow*. Chapel Hill: University of North Carolina Press, 2010.

Haass, Richard N., ed. *Transatlantic Tensions: The United States, Europe, and Problem Countries*. Washington, DC: Brookings Institution Press, 1999.

Hahn, Peter L., and Mary Ann Heiss, eds. *Empire and Revolution: The United States, and the Third World since 1945*. Columbus: Ohio State University Press, 2000.

Hall, Gwendolyn Midlo. *Social Control in Slave Plantation Societies: A Comparison of St. Domingue and Cuba*. Baltimore: Johns Hopkins University Press, 1971.

Hallen, Barry. *The Good, the Bad, and the Beautiful: Discourse about Values in Yoruba Culture*. Bloomington: Indiana University Press, 2000.

Hamilton, Russell. *Voices from an Empire*. Minneapolis: University of Minnesota Press, 1974.

Hamilton, Ruth Simms. *Routes of Passage: Rethinking the African Diaspora*. East Lansing: Michigan State University Press, 2007.

Hance, William A. *Population, Migration, and Urbanization in Africa*. New York: Columbia University Press, 1970.

Harding, Vincent. *The Other American Revolution*. Berkeley: University of California Press, 1980.

Harris, Hermione. *Yoruba in Diaspora: An African Church in London*. New York: Palgrave, 2006.

Harris, Joseph E. "African Diaspora Studies: Some International Dimensions." *Issue: A Journal of Opinion* 24, no. 2 (1996): 6–8.

———. *Global Dimensions of the African Diaspora*. Washington, DC: Howard University Press, 1993.

Harrison, Paul Carter, Victor Leo Walker, and Gus Edwards. *Black Theatre: Ritual Performance in the African Diaspora*. Philadelphia: Temple University Press, 2002.

Haviser, Jay B., and Kevin C. MacDonald. *African Re-Genesis: Confronting Social Issues in the Diaspora*. Abingdon: UCL, 2006.

Hawthorne, Walter. *From Africa to Brazil: Culture, Identity, and an Atlantic Slave Trade, 1600–1830*. Cambridge: Cambridge University Press, 2010.

Hayford, J. Caseley. *Gold Coast Native Institutions with Thoughts upon a Healthy Policy for the Gold Coast and Ashanti*. London: Frank Cass, 1970.

Haynes, Jeffrey. *Religion, Politics, and International Relations: Selected Essays*. New York: Routledge, 2011.

Helg, Aline. *Our Rightful Share: The Afro-Cuban Struggle for Equality, 1886–1912*. Chapel Hill: University of North Carolina Press, 1995.

Henry, Paget. *Caliban's Reason: Introducing Afro-Caribbean Philosophy.* New York: Routledge, 2000.

Herbert, Eugenia W. *Iron, Gender, and Power: Rituals of Transformation in African Societies.* Bloomington: Indiana University Press, 1993.

Herbst, Jeffrey. "Analyzing Apartheid: How Accurate Were U.S. Intelligence Estimates of South Africa, 1948–1994." *African Affairs* 102, no. 406 (2003): 81–107.

———. *U.S. Economic Policy toward Africa.* New York: Council on Foreign Relations Press, 1992.

Herrnstein, Richard J., and Charles A. Murray. *The Bell Curve: Intelligence and Class Structure in American Life.* New York: Free Press, 1994.

Herskovits, Melville J. *The New World Negro: Selected Papers in Afro-American Studies.* Bloomington: Indiana University Press, 1966.

Heywood, Linda M., and John K. Thornton. *Central Africans, Atlantic Creoles, and the Foundation of the Americas, 1585–1660.* Cambridge: Cambridge University Press, 2007.

Hill, Sylvia. "International Solidarity: Cabral's Legacy to the Afro-American Community." *Latin American Perspectives* 11, no. 2 (1984): 61–70.

Hine, Darlene Clark, Trica Danielle Keaton, and Stephen Small. *Black Europe and the African Diaspora.* Urbana: University of Illinois Press, 2009.

Holloway, Joseph E., ed. *Africanisms in American Culture.* 2nd ed. Bloomington: Indiana University Press, 2005.

Holt, Thomas. *Black over White: Negro Political Leadership in South Carolina during Reconstruction.* Bloomington: Indiana University Press, 1990.

Hopkins, Anthony. *An Economic History of West Africa.* London: Longman, 1973.

Horne, Gerald. *From the Barrel of a Gun: The United States and the War against Zimbabwe, 1965–1980.* Chapel Hill: University of North Carolina Press, 2001.

———. *Mau Mau in Harlem?: The U.S. and the Liberation of Kenya.* New York: Palgrave MacMillan, 2009.

———. "Race from Power: U.S. Foreign Policy and the General Crisis of 'White Supremacy.'" *Diplomatic History* 23, no. 3 (1999): 437–61.

Horton, J. A. *West African Countries and Peoples and a Vindication of the African Race.* London: W. J. Johnson, 1868.

Howard, Rosalyn. *Black Seminoles in the Bahamas.* Gainesville: University Press of Florida, 2002.

Howell, P. P., and J. A. Allan, eds. *The Nile: Sharing a Scarce Resource.* Cambridge: Cambridge University Press, 1994.

Hubbard, James. *The United States and the End of British Colonial Rule in Africa, 1941–1968.* Jefferson, NC: McFarland, 2010.

Huggins, Nathan I. *A Report to the Ford Foundation on African American Studies.* New York: The Ford Foundation, 1985.

Human Rights Watch, *Behind the Red Line: Political Repression in Sudan.* New York: Human Rights Watch, 1996.

Hunt, Michael H. "Conclusions: The Decolonization Puzzle in U.S. Policy: Promise versus Performance." In *The United States and Decolonization: Power and Freedom,* edited by David Ryan and Victor Pungong, 19–45. New York: St. Martin's Press, 2000.

Huntington, Samuel. *The Clash of Civilizations and the Remaking of World Order.* New York: Simon and Schuster, 1996.

Hunwick, John O., and Eve Troutt Powell. *The African Diaspora in the Mediterranean Lands of Islam.* Princeton: Markus Wiener, 2002.

Hutchinson, Earl Ofari. *The Disappearance of Black Leadership.* Los Angeles: Middle Passage Press, 2000.

Inikori, Joseph E. *Africans and the Industrial Revolution in England: A Study In International Trade and Economic Development.* Cambridge: Cambridge University Press, 2001.

Irele, F. Abiola. *The African Imagination: Literature in Africa and the Black Diaspora.* New York: Oxford University Press, 2001.

———. *The Négritude Moment: Explorations in Francophone African and Caribbean Literature and Thought.* Trenton, NJ: Africa World Press, 2011.

Irobi, Esiaba. "What They Came With: Carnival and the Persistence of African Performance Aesthetics in the Diaspora." *Journal of Black Studies* 37, no. 6 (2007): 896–913.

Irwin, Ryan. "A Wind of Change: White Redoubt and the Postcolonial Moment, 1960–1963." *Diplomatic History* 33, no. 5 (2009): 897–926.

Jackson, Donna. *Jimmy Carter and the Horn of Africa: Cold War Policy in Ethiopia and Somalia.* Jefferson, NC: McFarland, 2007.

Jackson, Henry F. *From the Congo to Soweto: U.S. Foreign Policy toward Africa since 1960.* New York: Morrow, 1982.

Jackson, Jennifer V., and Mary E. Cothran, "Black versus Black: The Relationships among African, African American, and African Caribbean Persons." *Journal of Black Studies* 33, no. 5 (2003): 576–604.

Jackson, Tommie Lee. *An Invincible Summer: Female Diasporan Authors.* Trenton, NJ: Africa World Press, 2011.

Jalloh, Alusine, and Stephen E. Maizlish, eds. *The African Diaspora.* College Station: Texas A&M University Press, 1996.

Jalloh, Alusine, and Toyin Falola, eds. *The United States and West Africa: Interactions and Relations.* Rochester, NY: University of Rochester Press, 2008.

Jayasuriya, Shihan de S., and Jean-Pierre Angenot, eds. *Uncovering the History of Africans in Asia.* Leiden: Brill, 2008.

Jayasuriya, Shihan de S., and Richard Pankhurst. *The African Diaspora in the Indian Ocean.* Trenton, NJ: Africa World Press, 2003.

Jegede, Obafemi. *Incantations and Herbal Cures in Ifa Divination: Emerging Issues in Indigenous Knowledge.* Ibadan: African Association for the Study of Nigeria, 2010.

Jewsiewicki, B., and D. Newbury, eds. *African Historiographies: What History for which Africa?* Beverly Hills, CA: Sage Publications, 1986.

Johnson-Odim, Cheryl. "Mirror Images and Shared Standpoints: Black Women in Africa and in the African Diaspora." *Issue: A Journal of Opinion* 24, no. 2 (1996): 18–22.

Johnson, Paul. "Colonialism's Back—And Not a Moment Too Soon." *New York Times Magazine,* April 18, 1993, 43–44.

Johnson, Paul Christopher. *Diaspora Conversions: Black Carib Religion and the Recovery of Africa.* Berkeley: University of California Press, 2007.

Johnson, Robert Jr. *Retuning Home: A Century of African-American Repatriation.* Trenton, NJ: Africa World Press, 2005.

Johnson, Samuel. *The History of the Yorubas.* Lagos: Christian Missionary Society, 1921.

Johnstone, Andrew. *The U.S. Public and American Foreign Policy.* Hoboken: Taylor & Francis, 2010.

Jones, Howard. *The Mutiny on the Amistad: The Saga of a Slave Revolt and Its Impact on American Abolition, Law, and Diplomacy.* Oxford: Oxford University Press, 1987.

Jones, LeRoi (Imamu Amiri Baracka). *Dutchman.* London: Faber and Faber, 1964.

Jongh, James De. *Vicious Modernism: Black Harlem and the Literary Imagination.* New York: Cambridge University Press, 1990.

Jordan, Winthrop D. *White over Black: American Attitudes toward the Negro, 1550–1812.* Chapel Hill: University of North Carolina Press, 1968.

Joseph, Peniel E. *Waiting 'Til the Midnight Hour: A Narrative History of Black Power in America.* New York: Henry Holt, 2006.

July, Robert W. *The Origins of Modern African Thought.* New York: Praeger, 1967.

Kadende-Kaiser, Rose M. "Interpreting Language and Cultural Discourse: Internet Communication among Burundians in the Diaspora." *Africa Today* 47, no. 2 (2000): 121–48.

Kagwa, Apolo. *The Kings of Buganda.* 1901; reprint, Nairobi: East African Publishing House, 1971.

Kalb, Madeliene. *The Congo Cables: The Cold War in Africa—From Eisenhower to Kennedy.* New York: Macmillan, 1982.

Kamara, C. S. "Narratives of the Past, Politics of the Present: Identity, Subordination, and the Haratines of Mauritania." PhD diss., University of Chicago, 1997.

Kansteiner, Walter H., and J. Stephen Morrison. *Rising U.S. Stakes in Africa: Seven Proposals to Strengthen U.S.-Africa Policy.* Washington, DC: Center for Strategic and International Studies, 2004.

Karenga, Maulana. *The African American Holiday of Kwanzaa: A Celebration of Family, Community, and Culture.* Los Angeles: University of Sankore Press, 1989.

Kashmeri, Sarwar. *The North Atlantic Treaty Organization and the European Union's Common Security and Defense Policy: Intersecting Trajectories.* Carlisle, PA: Strategic Studies Institute, U.S. Army War College, 2011.

Keenan, Jeremy. *The Dark Sahara: America's War on Terror in Africa.* London: Pluto Press, 2009.

Killingray, David. *A Plague of Europeans: Westerners in Africa since the Fifteenth Century.* Baltimore, MD: Penguin Books Ltd, 1973.

Kilson, Martin, and Robert I. Rotberg. *The African Diaspora: Interpretive Essays.* Cambridge: Harvard University Press, 1976.

King, Anthony. *Yoruba Sacred Music from Ekiti.* Ibadan: Ibadan University Press, 1961.

King, Kenneth. *Pan-Africanism and Education: A Study of Race Philanthropy and Education in the Southern States of America and East Africa.* New York: Oxford University Press, 1971.

Kipling, Rudyard. "The White Man's Burden." In Rudyard Kipling, *Collected Verse,* 215–17. New York: Doubleday, 1907.

Kirk-Greene, Anthony. "Decolonization: The Ultimate Diaspora." *Journal of Contemporary History* 36, no. 1 (2001): 133–51.

Klein, Debra L. *Yoruba Bata Goes Global: Artists, Culture Brokers, and Fans.* Chicago: University of Chicago Press, 2007.

Klein, Martin A., ed. *Breaking the Chains: Slavery, Bondage, and Emancipation in Modern Africa and Asia.* Madison: University of Wisconsin Press, 1993.

Konadu, Kwasi. *The Akan Diaspora in the Americas.* New York: Oxford University Press, 2010.

Kopytoff, Igor, ed. *The African Frontier: The Reproduction of Traditional African Societies.* Bloomington: Indiana University Press, 1987.

Kopytoff, Jean Herskovits. *A Preface to Modern Nigeria: The "Sierra Leonians" in Yoruba, 1830–1890.* Madison: University of Wisconsin Press, 1965.

Korang, Kwaku Larbi. *Writing Ghana, Imagining Africa: Nation and African Modernity.* Rochester, NY: University of Rochester Press, 2003.

Korkin, Joel. *Tribes: How Race, Religion, and Identity Determine Success in the New Global Economy.* New York: Random House, 1994.

Krenn, Michael L., ed. *The African-American Voice in U.S. Foreign Policy since World War II.* New York: Garland, 1998.

———. *The Color of Empire: Race and American Foreign Relations.* Dulles, VA: Potomac Books, 2007.

Laitin, David D. *Hegemony and Culture: Politics and Change among the Yoruba.* Chicago: University of Chicago Press, 1986.

Lake, Anthony, and Christine Todd Whitman. *More Than Humanitarianism: A Strategic U.S. Approach to Africa.* New York: Council on Foreign Relations Press, 2007.

Lake, Obiagele. "Toward a Pan-African Identity: Diaspora African Repatriates in Ghana." *Anthropological Quarterly* 68, no. 1 (1995): 21–36.

Lander, Richard. *Records of Captain Clapperton's Last Expedition to Africa.* London: H. Colbrun and R. Bentley, 1830.

Landers, Jane G. *Atlantic Creoles in the Age of Revolutions.* Cambridge: Harvard University Press, 2010.

Lane, Kris E. *Pillaging the Empire: Piracy in the Americas, 1500–1750.* Armonk: M. E. Sharpe, 1998.

Langley, J. Ayo. *Ideologies of Liberation in Black Africa, 1856–1970: Documents on Modern African Political Thought from Colonial Times to the Present.* London: Rex Collins, 1979.

Larson, Pier M. "African Diasporas and the Atlantic." In *The Atlantic in Global History, 1500–2000,* edited by Jorge Cañizares-Esguerra and Erik R. Seeman, 129–47. Upper Saddle River, NJ: Prentice Hall, 2006.

———. "Reconsidering Trauma, Identity, and the African Diaspora: Enslavement and Historical Memory in Nineteenth-Century Highland Madagascar." *William and Mary Quarterly,* Third Series 56, no. 2, African and American Atlantic Worlds (1999): 335–62.

Law, R. *The Oyo Empire c. 1600–c. 1836: A West African Imperialism in the Era of the Atlantic Slave Trade.* Oxford: Oxford University Press, 1977.

Lefkowitz, Mary. *Not Out of Africa: How Afrocentrism Became an Excuse to Teach Myth as History.* New York: Basic Books, 1996.

Leibovich, Mark. *The New Imperialists.* New York: Prentice Hall, 2002.

Lemelle, Sidney J., and Robin D. G. Kelley. *Imagining Home: Class, Culture, and Nationalism in the African Diaspora.* New York: Verso, 1994.

Lenski, G. *Power and Privilege: A Theory of Social Stratification.* New York: McGraw-Hill, 1966.

Leone, Mark P., Cheryl Janifer LaRoche, and Jennifer J. Babiarz. "The Archaeology of Black Americans in Recent Times." *Annual Review of Anthropology* 34 (2005): 575–98.

Lewis, David Levering. *When Harlem Was in Vogue.* New York: Random House, 1981.

Lewis, Rupert. "The Contemporary Significance of the African Diaspora in the Americas." *Caribbean Quarterly* 38, nos. 2/3 (1992): 73–80.

Lewis, Rupert, and Patrick Bryan, eds. *Garvey: His Work and Impact.* Trenton, NJ: Africa World Press, 1991.

Locke, Alain, ed. *The New Negro: Voices of the Harlem Renaissance.* New York: Simon and Schuster, 1997.

Lopes, Nei. "African Religions in Brazil, Negotiation, and Resistance: A Look from Within." *Journal of Black Studies* 34, no. 6 (2004): 838–60.

Lovejoy, Paul E., ed. *Africans in Bondage: Studies in Slavery and the Slave Trade.* Madison: University of Wisconsin Press, 1986.

———. *Identity in the Shadow of Slavery.* New York: Continuum, 2009.

———. *The Ideology of Slavery in Africa.* Beverly Hills, CA: Sage, 1981.

———. ed. *Slavery on the Frontiers of Islam.* Princeton: Marcus Wiener, 2004.

———. *Transformations in Slavery: A History of Slavery in Africa.* Cambridge: Cambridge University Press, 1983.

Lovejoy, Paul E., and David Vincent Trotman. *Trans-Atlantic Dimensions of Ethnicity in the African Diaspora.* New York: Continuum, 2003.

Lovejoy, Paul E., and Jan S. Hogendorn. *Slow Death for Slavery: The Course of Abolition in Northern Nigeria.* Cambridge: Cambridge University Press, 1993.

Lukose, Ritty A. "The Difference That Diaspora Makes: Thinking through the Anthropology of Immigrant Education in the United States." *Anthropology and Education Quarterly* 38, no. 4 (2007): 405–18.

Lundsgaarde, Erik. *Africa toward 2030: Challenges for Development Policy.* Basingstoke: Palgrave Macmillan, 2011.

Lwanga-Lunyiigo, S., and J. Vansina. "The Bantu-Speaking Peoples and Their Expansion." In UNESCO, *General History of Africa*, volume 3:140–62. London: Heinemann Educational Books, 1988.

Lymna, Princeton, and Patricia Dorff, eds. *Beyond Humanitariainism: What You Need to Know about Africa and Why It Matters.* New York: Council for Foreign Relations Press, 2007.

Lynn, Martin. "Technology, Trade, and 'A Race of Native Capitalists': The Krio Diaspora of West Africa and the Steamship, 1852–1895." *Journal of African History* 33, no. 3 (1992): 421–40.

Magubane, Bernard Makhosezwe. *The Ties That Bind: African American Consciousness of Africa.* Trenton, NJ: Africa World Press, 1987.

Mahoney, Richard. *JFK: Ordeal in Africa.* New York: Oxford University Press, 1983.

Manchuelle, Francois. *Willing Migrants: Soninke Labor Diasporas, 1848–1960.* Athens: Ohio University Press, and London: James Currey Publishers, 1997.

Mann, Kristin. *Slavery and the Birth of an African City, Lagos, 1760–1900.* Bloomington: Indiana University Press, 2007.

Mann, Kristin, and Edna G. Bay. *Rethinking the African Diaspora: The Making of a Black Atlantic World in the Bight of Benin and Brazil.* Portland, OR: F. Cass, 2001.

Manning, Patrick. *The African Diaspora: A History through Culture.* New York: Columbia University Press, 2009.

————. "Contours of Slavery and Social Change in Africa." *American Historical Review* 88, no. 4 (1983): 853–57.

————. *Migration in World History.* London: Routledge, 2005.

Marable, Manning, and Vanessa Agard-Jones. *Transnational Blackness: Navigating the Global Color Line.* New York: Palgrave Macmillan, 2008.

Martinot, Steve. "Introduction." In Albert Memmi, ed, *Racism.* Minneapolis: University of Minnesota Press, 2000.

Marx, Karl. *On Religion.* New York: Shocken, 1964.

Massing, Andreas W. "Baghayogho: A Soninke Muslim Diaspora in the Mande World (Baghayogho: Une diaspora Soninké dans le monde Mandé)." *Cahiers d'Études Africaines* 44, no. 176 (2004): 887–922.

————. "The Wangara, an Old Soninke Diaspora in West Africa? (Les Wangara, une vieille diaspora Soninke d'Afrique de l'Ouest?)." *Cahiers d'Études Africaines* 40, no. 158 (2000): 281–308.

Mathers, Kathryn. *Travel, Humanitarianism, and Becoming American in Africa.* Basingstoke: Palgrave Macmillan, 2010.

Matory, J. Lorand. *Black Atlantic Religion: Tradition, Transnationalism, and Matriarchy in the Afro-Brazilian Candomblé.* Princeton: Princeton University Press, 2005.

M'Baye, Babacar. *The Trickster Comes West: Pan-African Influence in Early Black Diasporan Narratives.* Jackson: University Press of Mississippi, 2009.

Mbiti, John. *African Religions and Philosophy.* London: Heinemann, 1969.

McCartney, John T. *Black Power Ideologies: An Essay in African-American Political Thought.* Philadelphia: Temple University Press, 1992.

McEvedy, Colin, and Richard Jones. *Atlas of World Population History.* London: Penguin, 1985.

McLaren, Joseph. "African Diaspora Vernacular Traditions and the Dilemma of Identity." *Research in African Literatures* 40, no. 1, Oral Literature and Identity Formation in Africa and the Diaspora (2009): 97–111.

McNamee, Stephen J., and Robert K. Miller Jr. *The Meritocracy Myth.* Lanham, MD: Rowman & Littlefield, 2009.

Meen, Matthew C., and Lowell S. Gustafson, eds. *The Religious Challenge to the State.* Philadelphia: Temple University Press, 1992.

Memmi, Albert. *The Colonizer and the Colonized.* Boston: Beacon Press, 1967.

————, ed. *Racism.* Minneapolis: University of Minnesota Press, 2000.

Mengara, Daniel M., ed. *Images of Africa: Stereotypes and Realities.* Trenton, NJ: Africa World Press, 2001.

Mensah, Joseph. *Black Canadians: History, Experiences, Social Conditions.* Halifax: Fernwood, 2002.

Mercer, Claire, Ben Page, and Martin Evans. *Development and the African Diaspora: Place and the Politics of Home.* London: Zed, 2008.

Meriwether, James H. *Proudly We Can Be Africans: Black Americans and Africa, 1935–1961.* Chapel Hill: University of North Carolina Press, 2002.

Metz, Steve. "American Attitudes toward Decolonization in Africa." *Political Science Quarterly* 99, no. 3 (1984): 515–34.

Miers, Suzanne, and Richard Roberts, eds. *The End of Slavery in Africa.* Madison: University of Wisconsin Press, 1988.

———. *Slavery in the Twentieth Century: The Evolution of a Global Economy.* New York: AltaMira Press, 2003.

Miles, Tiya, and Sharon Patricia Holland. *Crossing Waters, Crossing Worlds: The African Diaspora in Indian Country.* Durham, NC: Duke University Press, 2006.

Miller, Ivor. "Cuban Abakuá Chants: Examining New Linguistic and Historical Evidence for the African Diaspora." *African Studies Review* 48, no. 1 (2005): 23–58.

Minter, William, Gail Hovey, and Charles Cobb Jr., eds. *No Easy Victories: African Liberation and American Activists over a Half Century, 1950–2000.* Trenton, NJ: Africa World Press, 2008.

Mintz, Sidney W. *Sweetness and Power: The Place of Sugar in Modern History.* New York: Viking, 1985.

Mintz, Sidney W., and Richard Price. *Birth of African-American Culture: An Anthropological Perspective.* Boston: Beacon, 1992.

Mizrai, Behnaz A., Ismael Musah Montana, and Paul E. Lovejoy, eds. *Slavery, Islam, and Diaspora.* Trenton, NJ: Africa World Press, 2009.

Monroe, J. Cameron, and Akinwumi Ogundiran, eds. *Power and Landscape in Atlantic West Africa: Archaeological Perspectives.* Cambridge: Cambridge University Press, 2012.

Monson, Ingrid T. *The African Diaspora: A Musical Perspective.* New York: Garland, 2000.

Moore, Carlos, Tanya R. Sanders, and Shawna Moore, eds., *African Presence in the Americas.* Trenton, NJ: Africa World Press, 1995.

Moss, Kay K. *Southern Folk Medicine, 1750–1820.* Columbia: University of South Carolina Press, 1999.

Motley, Carol M., and Kellina M. Craig-Henderson. "Epithet or Endearment? Examining Reactions among Those of the African Diaspora to an Ethnic Epithet." *Journal of Black Studies* 37, no. 6 (2007): 944–63.

Muller, Carol A. "The New African Diaspora, the Built Environment, and the Past in Jazz." *Ethnomusicology Forum* 15, no. 1 (2006): 63–86.

Mullin, Michael. *Africa in America: Slave Acculturation and Resistance in the American South.* Urbana: University of Illinois Press, 1992.

Mullings, Leith. *New Social Movements in the African Diaspora: Challenging Global Apartheid.* New York: Palgrave Macmillan, 2009.

Munford, Clarence J. *Race and Reparations: A Black Perspective for the 21st Century.* Trenton, NJ: Africa World Press, 1996.

Murphy, Joseph M. *Santeria: African Spirits in America.* Boston: Beacon Press, 1993.

————. *Working the Spirit: Ceremonies of the African Diaspora.* Boston: Beacon Press, 1994.

Nascimento, Abdias do, and Elisa Larkin Nascimento. *Africans in Brazil: A Pan-African Perspective.* Trenton, NJ: Africa World Press, 1992.

Nash, Gray B. *Red, White, and Black: The Peoples of Early North America.* 4th ed. Upper Saddle River, NJ: Prentice Hall, 2000.

Neirmark, Philip John. *The War of the Orisas: Empowering Your Life through the Ancient African Religion of Ifa.* New York: HarperCollins, 1993.

Newsom, David D. *The Imperial Mantle: The United States, Decolonization, and the Third World.* Bloomington: Indiana University Press, 2001.

Niblett, Robin, ed. *America and a Changed World: A Question of Leadership.* London: Chatham House, 2010.

Nkrumah, Kwame. *Neo-Colonialism: The Last Stage of Imperialism.* New York: International Publisher, 1966.

————. *Revolutionary Path.* New York: International Publishers, 1973.

Noer, Thomas. *Cold War and Black Liberation: The United States and White Rule in Africa, 1948–1968.* Columbia: University of Missouri Press, 1985.

Nolutshungo, Sam C., ed. *Margins of Insecurity: Minorities and International Security.* Rochester, NY: University of Rochester Press, 1996.

Norment, Nathaniel Jr., ed. *The African American Studies Reader.* Durham: Carolina Academic Press, 2001.

Northrup, David, ed. *The Atlantic Slave Trade.* Boston: Houghton Mifflin, 2002.

Nyerere, Mwalimu Julius K. "Reflections on Africa and its Future." Lecture, no. 41, Nigerian Institute of International Affairs, Lagos, 1987.

Nwaubani, Ebere. *The United States and Decolonization in West Africa, 1950–1960.* Rochester, NY: University of Rochester Press, 2001.

Oboe, Annalisa, and Anna Scacchi. *Recharting the Black Atlantic: Modern Cultures, Local Communities, Global Connections.* New York: Routledge, 2008.

Ogbechie, Sylvester. *Ben Enwonwu: The Making of an African Modernist.* Rochester, NY: University of Rochester Press, 2008.

Ogbu, J. U. "Minority Education in Comparative Perspective." *Journal of Negro Education* 59, no. 1 (1990): 45–57.

Ogundiran, Akinwumi. "Chronology, Material Culture, and Pathways to the Cultural History of Yoruba-Edo Region, Nigeria, 500 B.C.–A.D. 1800." In *Sources and Methods in African History,* edited by Toyin Falola and Christian Jennings, 33–79. Rochester, NY: University of Rochester Press, 2003.

————. "The Formation of an Oyo Imperial Colony during the Atlantic Age." In *Power and Landscape in Atlantic West Africa: Archaeological Perspectives,* Cameron Monroe and Akinwumi Ogundiran, eds. 222–52. Cambridge: Cambridge University Press, 2012.

———. "Living in the Shadow of the Atlantic World." In *Archaeology of Atlantic Africa and the African Diaspora*, edited by Akinwumi Ogundiran and Toyin Falola, 77–99. Bloomington: Indiana University Press, 2007.

Ogundiran, Akinwumi, and Toyin Falola, eds. *Archaeology of Atlantic Africa and the African Diaspora*. Bloomington: Indiana University Press, 2007.

Ogunyemi, Olatunji. "The Appeal of African Broadcast Web Sites to African Diasporas: A Case Study of the United Kingdom." *Journal of Black Studies* 36, no. 3 (2006): 334–52.

———. "The News Agenda of the Black African Press in the United Kingdom." *Journal of Black Studies* 37, no. 5 (2007): 630–54.

Ogunyemi, Wale. *Obaluaye: A Yoruba Music-Drama*. Ibadan: University Press, 1972.

Ohadike, Don C. *Sacred Drums of Liberation: Religions and Music of Resistance in Africa and the African Diaspora*. Trenton, NJ: Africa World Press, 2007.

Ohaegbulam, Festus Ugboaja. *U.S. Policy in Postcolonial Africa: Four Case Studies in Conflict Resolution*. New York: Peter Lang, 2004.

O'Hear, Ann. *Power Relations in Nigeria: Ilorin Slaves and Their Successors*. Rochester, NY: University of Rochester Press, 1997.

Ojaide, Tanure. "Branches of the Same Tree: African and African-American Poetry." In *Of Dreams Deferred, Dead or Alive: African Perspectives on African-American Writers*, edited by Femi Ojo-Ade, 101. Westport, CT: Greenwood Press, 1996.

———. "From Libation." *Illuminations: An International Magazine of Contemporary Writing* 14 (Summer 1998): 9.

———. "From Our Own Reasons." *OBSIDIAN II: Black Literature in Review* 5, no. 3 (1990): 112.

———. "The Half-Brother of the Black Jew: The Poetry of Syl Cheney-Coker." *CLA Journal* 35, no. 1 (1991): 1–14.

———. "How the Urhobo People See the World through Art." In *Where Gods and Mortals Meet: Continuity and Renewal in Urhobo Art*, edited by Perkins Foss, 73–79. New York: Museum of African Art, and Ghent: Snoeck Publishers, 2004.

———. "State Executive," *OBSIDIAN II: Black Literature in Review* 5, no. 3 (1990): 113–14.

———. "Two Worlds: Influence in the Poetry of Wole Soyinka." *Black American Literature Forum* 22, no. 4 (1988): 767–76.

Ojwang, Dan. "'Eat Pig and Become a Beast': Food, Drink, and Diaspora in East African Indian Writing." *Research in African Literatures* 42, no. 3, Asian African Literatures, Gaurav Desai, Special Guest Editor (2011): 68–87.

Okoye, Chukwuma. "The Deep Stirring of the Unhomely: African Diaspora on Biyi Bandele's 'The Street.'" *Research in African Literatures* 39, no. 2, Nigeria's Third-Generation Novel: Preliminary Theoretical Engagements (2008): 79–92.

Okpewho, Isidore, Carole Boyce Davies, and Ali Al Mazrui. *The African Diaspora: African Origins and New World Identities.* Bloomington: Indiana University Press, 1999.

Okpewho, Isidore, and Nkiru Nzegwu, eds. *The New African Diaspora.* Bloomington: Indiana University Press, 2009.

Olaniyan, Tejumola, and James H. Sweet. *The African Diaspora and the Disciplines.* Bloomington: Indiana University Press, 2010.

Olayemi, Val. *Orin Ibeji.* Occasional publication, no. 25. Ibadan: Institute of African Studies, University of Ibadan, 1971.

Olisanwuche, P. Esedebe. *Pan-Africanism: The Idea and the Movement, 1776–1963.* Washington, DC: Howard University Press, 1982.

Oliver, R. *In the Realms of Gold: Pioneering in African History.* Madison: University of Wisconsin Press, 1997.

Olomo, Aina. *The Core of Fire: A Path to Yoruba Spiritual Activism.* New York: Athelia Henrietta Press, 2002.

Omidire, Félix Ayoh'. "Agudas and Jagudas: Afro-Brazilian Returnees, Cultural Renaissance, and Anticolonial Protagonism in West Africa." In *Back to Africa.* Vol. 1, *Afro Brazilian Returnees and Their Communities,* edited by Kwesi Kwaa Prah, 193–209. Cape Town: CASAS, 2009.

———. "The Yoruba Atlantic Diaspora—Brazil, Cuba, Trinidad and Tobago." In *Teaching and Propagating African and Diaspora History and Culture,* edited by Tunde Babawale, Akin Alao, Felix Ayoh' Omidire, and Tony Onwumah, 305–26. Lagos: Centre for Black and African Arts and Civilization, 2009.

Onslow, Sue. *Cold War in Southern Africa: White Power, Black Liberation.* Hoboken, NJ: Routledge, 2009.

Oroge, E. Adeniyi. "The Institution of Slavery in Yorubaland with Particular Reference to the Nineteenth Century." PhD diss., University of Birmingham, 1971.

Orser, C. E., Jr. "The Archaeology of the African Diaspora." *Annual Review of Anthropology* 27 (1998): 63–82.

Owens, William. *Slave Mutiny: The Revolt on the Schooner Amistad.* New York: John Day, 1953.

Palmer, Colin A. "Defining and Studying the Modern African Diaspora." *Journal of Negro History* 85, nos. 1–2 (2000): 27–32.

Paris, Peter J. *Religion and Poverty: Pan-African Perspectives.* Durham, NC: Duke University Press, 2009.

Parry, J. H. *The Discovery of the Sea.* Berkeley: University of California Press, 1981.

Patterson, Rubin. "Transnationalism: Diaspora-Homeland Development." *Social Forces* 84, no. 4 (2006): 1891–1907.

Patterson, Tiffany Ruby, and Robin D. G. Kelley. "Unfinished Migrations: Reflections on the African Diaspora and the Making of the Modern World." *African Studies Review* 43, no. 1 (2000): 11–45.

Peel, J. D. Y. *Religious Encounter and the Making of the Yoruba.* Bloomington: Indiana University Press, 2000.

Pesci, David. *Amistad: The Resurrection of a Remarkable Story.* New York: Marlowe, 1997.

Petropoulos, Jacqueline. "Performing African Canadian Identity: Diasporic Reinvention in 'Afrika Solo.'" *Feminist Review* 84, no. 1 (2006): 104–23.

Pham, John-Peter. *India in Africa: Implications of an Emerging Power for AFRICOM and U.S. Strategy.* Carlise, PA: Strategic Studies Institute, U.S. Army War College, 2011.

Philips, Muyiwa, ed. *Reparations: A Collection of Speeches by M. K. O. Abiola.* Lome, Togo: Linguist Service, 1992.

Pinn, Anthony B. *Black Religion and Aesthetics: Religious Thought and Life in Africa and the African Diaspora.* New York: Palgrave Macmillan, 2009.

Pinnock, S. G. *The Romance of Missions in Nigeria.* Richmond, VA: Educational Department, Foreign Mission Board, Southern Baptist Convention, 1917.

Plummer, Brenda Gayle. *Window on Freedom: Race, Civil Rights, and Foreign Affairs, 1945–1988.* Chapel Hill: University of North Carolina Press, 2003.

Posnansky, Merrick. *Africa and Archeology: Empowering an Expatriate Life.* New York: Palgrave Macmillan, 2009.

———. "Bantu Genesis." *Uganda Journal* 25, no. 1 (1964): 86–92.

Price, Sally, and Richard Price. *Maroon Arts: Cultural Vitality in the African Diaspora.* Boston: Beacon Press, 1999.

Quirk, Joel. *Unfinished Business: A Comparative Survey of Historical and Contemporary Slavery.* Paris: UNESCO, 2009.

Rahier, Jean, Percy C. Hintzen, and Felipe Smith. *Global Circuits of Blackness: Interrogating the African Diaspora.* Urbana: University of Illinois Press, 2010.

Ralph, Michael. "Diaspora." *Social Text* 100 (Fall 2009): 94–101.

Rasmussen, Susan. "A Temporary Diaspora: Contested Cultural Representations in Tuareg International Musical Performance." *Anthropological Quarterly* 78, no. 4 (2005): 793–826.

Reagon, Bernice Johnson. "African Diaspora Women: The Making of Cultural Workers." *Feminist Studies* 12, no. 1 (1986): 77–90.

Reardon, Betty. *Sexism and War System.* Syracuse, NY: Syracuse University Press, 1985.

Rediker, Marcus. *Villains of All Nations: Atlantic Pirates in the Golden Age.* Boston: Beacon Press, 2004.

Reindorf, Carl. *A History of the Gold Coast and Ashanti* (1895). Accra: Ghana Universities Press, 2007.

Reis, João José. *Slave Rebellion in Brazil: The Muslim Uprising of 1835 in Bahia.* Baltimore: Johns Hopkins University Press, 1993.

———. "Slave Resistance in Brazil: Bahia, 1807–1835." *Luso-Brazilian Review* 25, no. 1 (1988): 111–44.

Richburg, Keith B. *Out of America: A Black Man Confronts Africa.* New York: Basic Books, 1997.

Robertson, Claire C., and Martin A. Klein, eds. *Women and Slavery in Africa.* Madison: University of Wisconsin Press, 1983.

Robinson, Cedric J. *Black Movements in America.* New York: Routledge, 1997.

———. *Forgeries of Memory and Meaning: Blacks and the Regimes of Race in American Theatre and Film before World War II.* Chapel Hill: University of North Carolina Press, 2007.

Rodney, Walter. "African Slavery and Other Forms of Social Oppression on the Upper Guinea Coast in the Context of the Atlantic Slave Trade." *Journal of African History* 7, no. 5 (1966): 431–43.

———. *How Europe Underdeveloped Africa.* Washington, DC: Howard University Press, 1972.

Roeks, Richard A. *Sacred Leaves of Candomblé: African Magic, Medicine, and Religion in Brazil.* Austin: University of Texas Press, 1997.

Rosecrance, Richard. "The Rise of the Virtual State." *Foreign Affairs* 75, no. 4 (1996): 59–60.

———. *The Rise of the Virtual State: Wealth and Power in the Coming Century.* New York: Basic Books, 2000.

Rothchild, Donald, and Edmond J. Keller, eds. *Africa-U.S. Relations: Strategic Encounters.* Boulder, CO: Lynne Rienner, 2006.

Rowland, Christopher, ed. *The Cambridge Companion to Liberation Theology.* New York: Cambridge University Press, 1999.

Ruby, Jennie. "The Black Diaspora." *Off Our Backs* 18, no. 8 (1988): 10.

Rugh, William. *The Practice of Public Diplomacy: Confronting Challenges Abroad.* Basingstoke: Palgrave Macmillan, 2011.

Runyon, Theodore, ed. *Theology, Politics, and Peace.* Maryknoll, NY: Orbis Books, 1989.

Rushton, J. Philippe. *Race, Evolution, and Behavior.* New Jersey: Transaction, 1999.

Sarbah, Mensah. *Fanti National Constitution: A Short Treatise on the Constitution and Government of the Fanti, Ashanti, and Other Akan Tribes of West Africa, Together with an Account of the Discovery of the Gold Coast by Portuguese Navigators, a Short Narration of Early English Voyages, and Study of the Rise of British Gold Coast Jurisdiction by John Mensha Sarbah.* London: William Clowes, 1906.

Sawyer, Mark O. *Racial Politics in Post-Revolutionary Cuba*. Cambridge: Cambridge University Press, 2006.

Sawyer, Roger. *Slavery in the Twentieth Century*. London: Routledge & Kegan Paul, 1986.

Schniedman, Witney. *Engaging Africa: Washington and the Fall of Portugal's Colonial Empire*. Lanham: University Press of America, 2004.

Schwartz, Marie Jenkins. *Born in Bondage: Growing Up Enslaved in the Antebellum South*. Cambridge: Harvard University Press, 2000.

Scott, James M. *After the End: Making U.S. Foreign Policy in the Post–Cold War World*. Durham, NC: Duke University Press, 1998.

Segal, Aaron. *An Atlas of International Migration*. London: Hans Zell, 1993.

Senate Committee on Foreign Relations, *Slavery throughout the World*. Hearing before the Committee on Foreign Relations, US Senate, 106th Congress, September 28, 2000, http://purl.access.gpo.gov/GPO/LPS11447.

Senghor, Léopold Sédar. *The Collected Poetry*. Translated and with an introduction by Melvin Dixon. Charlottesville: University Press of Virginia, 1991.

Sherwood, Marika. *Origins of Pan-Africanism: Henry Sylvester Williams, Africa, and the African Diaspora*. New York: Routledge, 2011.

Sidbury, James. *Becoming African in America: Race and Nation in the Early Black Atlantic*. Oxford: Oxford University Press, 2007.

Simeon-Jones, Kersuze. *Literary and Sociopolitical Writings of the Black Diaspora in the Nineteenth and Twentieth Centuries*. Lanham, MD: Lexington Books, 2010.

Singleton, Theresa A. *The Archaeology of the African Diaspora in the Americas*. Glassboro, NJ: Society for Historical Archaeology, 1995.

Skinner, Elliot P. *Beyond Constructive Engagement: United States Foreign Policy Toward Africa*. St. Paul, MN: Paragon House, 1986.

Skinner, Rob. *The Foundations of Anti-Apartheid: Liberal Humanitarians and Transnational Activists in Britain and the United States, 1919–1964*. Basingstoke: Palgrave Macmillan, 2010.

Skolnick, J., and E. Currie. *Crisis in American Institutions*. Boston: Little Brown, 1988.

Smallwood, Stephanie E. *Saltwater Slavery: A Middle Passage from Africa to American Diaspora*. Cambridge: Harvard University Press, 2007.

Smith, Malinda. *Securing Africa: Post-9/11 Discourses on Terrorism*. Farnham, UK: Ashgate, 2010.

Smith, Robert S. *Freedom's Distant Shores: American Protestants and Post-Colonial Alliances with Africa*. Waco, TX: Baylor University Press, 2006.

———. *The Lagos Consulate, 1851–1861*. Berkeley: University of California Press, 1979.

Smith, Sandra N. "Educational Development for the African Diaspora in Suriname." *Journal of Negro Education* 51, no. 2 (1982): 147–56.

Snead, James A. "Repetition as a Figure of Black Culture." In *Black Literature and Literary Theory*, edited by Henry Louis Gates Jr., 59–60. London: Methuen Press, 1990.

Soares, Mariza De Carvalho. *People of Faith: Slavery and African Catholics in Eighteenth-Century Rio de Janeiro*. Translated by Jerry D. Metz. Durham, NC: Duke University Press, 2011.

Solow, Barbara L., ed. *Slavery and the Rise of the Atlantic System*. New York: Cambridge University Press, 1991.

Soyinka, Wole. *Myth, Literature, and the African World*. Cambridge: Cambridge University Press, 1976.

Soyinka, Wole and Biodun Jeyifo. "Wole Soyinka and the Tropes of Disalienation." In *Wole Soyinka: Art, Dialogue, and Outrage: Essays on Literature and Culture*. Ibadan: New Horn Press, 1988.

Spalding, Jay, and Stephanie Beswick, eds. *African Systems of Slavery*. Trenton, NJ: Africa World Press, 2010.

Spruyt, Hendrik. *The Sovereign State and Its Competitors*. Princeton: Princeton University Press, 1994.

Staniland, Martin. *American Intellectuals and African Nationalists, 1955–1970*. New Haven, CT: Yale University Press, 1991.

Stewart, James B. "Reaching for Higher Ground: Toward an Understanding of Black/Africana Studies." *Afrocentric Scholar* 1, no. 1 (1992): 1–69.

Stoller, Paul. *Money Has No Smell: The Africanization of New York City*. Chicago: University of Chicago Press, 2002.

Strange, Susan. *The Retreat of the State: The Diffusion of Power in the World Economy*. Cambridge: Cambridge University Press, 1996.

Sundiata, Ibrahim K. *From Slaving to Neoslavery: The Bight of Biafra and Fernando Po in the Era of Abolition, 1827–1930*. Madison: University of Wisconsin Press, 1996.

Sweet, James H. *Domingos Álvares, African Healing, and the Intellectual History of the Atlantic World*. Chapel Hill: University of North Carolina Press, 2011.

———. *Re-creating Africa: Culture, Kinship, and Religion in the African-Portuguese World*. Chapel Hill: University of North Carolina Press, 2004.

Tall, Emmanuelle Kadya. "Comment se construit et s'invente une tradition religieuse: L'exemple des nations du Candomblé de Bahia (How a Religious Tradition Is Constructed and Invented: Candomblé Nation in Bahia)." *Cahiers d'Études Africaines* 42, no. 167 (2002): 441–61.

Telles, Edward E. *Race in Another America: The Significance of Skin Color in Brazil*. Princeton: Princeton University Press, 2004.

Terborg-Penn, Rosalyn, Sharon Harley, Andrea Benton Rushing, and Association of Black Women Historians. *Women in Africa and the African Diaspora.* Washington, DC: Howard University Press, 1987.

Thomas, Hugh. *The Slave Trade: The Story of the Atlantic Slave Trade, 1440–1870.* New York: Simon & Schuster, 1997.

Thompson, Daniel C. *Sociology of the Black Experience.* Westport, CT: Greenwood Press, 1974.

Thompson, J. Lee. *Theodore Roosevelt Abroad: Nature, Empire, and the Journey of an American President.* New York: Palgrave Macmillan, 2010.

Thompson, Krista A. "Preoccupied with Haiti: The Dream of Diaspora in African American Art, 1915–1942." *American Art* 21, no. 3 (2007): 74–97.

Thompson, Mildred, ed. *Ida B. Wells-Barnett: An Exploratory Study of an American Black Woman, 1893–1930.* Brooklyn, NY: Carlson, 1990.

Thompson, Vincent B. *Africans of the Diaspora: The Evolution of African Consciousness and Leadership in the Americas, from Slavery to the 1920s.* Trenton, NJ: Africa World Press, 2000.

———. *The Making of the African Diaspora in the Americas, 1441–1900.* London: Longman, 1987.

Thornton, John. *Africa and Africans in the Making of the Atlantic World, 1400–1600.* Cambridge: Cambridge University Press, 1999.

Thorpe, C. O. *Awon Eewo Ile Yoruba.* Ibadan, Nigeria: Onibon-Oje Press, 1967.

Thorpe, Earl E. *The Central Theme of Black History.* Westport, CT: Greenwood Press, 1960.

Tillery, Alvin B. *Between Homeland and Motherland: Africa, U.S. Foreign Policy, and Black Leadership in America.* Ithaca: Cornell University Press, 2011.

Tishken, Joel E., Toyin Falola, and Akíntúndé Akínyemí. *Sàngó in Africa and the African Diaspora.* Bloomington: Indiana University Press, 2009.

Trost, Theodore Louis. *The African Diaspora and the Study of Religion.* New York: Palgrave Macmillan, 2007.

Trotman, C. James, ed. *Multiculturalism: Roots and Realities.* Bloomington: Indiana University Press, 2002.

Tshimanga, Charles, Ch Didier Gondola, and Peter J. Bloom. *Frenchness and the African Diaspora: Identity and Uprising in Contemporary France.* Bloomington: Indiana University Press, 2009.

Turner, James, ed. *The Next Decade: Theoretical and Research Issues in African Studies.* Ithaca: Cornell University Press, 1984.

Turner, Nat. *Confessions of Nat Turner.* Virginia: Southampton Institute, 1831.

Tushner, M. *Making Civil Rights Law: Thurgood Marshall and the Supreme Court, 1936–1961.* New York: Oxford University Press, 1994.

Udo, R. K. *Migrant Tenant Farmers of Nigeria.* Lagos: African University Press, 1975.

Udvardy, Monica L., Linda L. Giles, and John B. Mitsanze. "The Transatlantic Trade in African Ancestors: Mijikenda Memorial Statues (Vigango) and the Ethics of Collecting and Curating Non-Western Cultural Property." *American Anthropologist,* New Series, 105, no. 3 (2003): 566–80.

UNESCO. *Final Report of the World Conference on Cultural Policies.* Organized by UNESCO in Mexico City, July 26–August 6, 1982.

Vaughan, Olufemi. *Nigerian Chiefs: Traditional Power in Modern Politics, 1890s–1990s.* Rochester, NY: University of Rochester Press, 2000.

Vaughan, Umi, and Carlos Aldama. *Carlos Aldama's Life in Batá: Cuba, Diaspora, and the Drum.* Bloomington: Indiana University Press, 2012.

Verger, Pierre Fatumbi. *Awon Ewe Osanyin: Yoruba Medicinal Leaves.* Ile-Ife: Institute of African Studies, University of Ife, 1967.

———. *Ewe: The Use of Plants in Yoruba Society.* São Paulo: Companhia das Letras, 1995.

Verlinden, Charles. *Beginnings of Modern Colonization: Eleven Essays with an Introduction.* Translated by Yvonne Freccero. Ithaca, NY: Cornell University Press, 1970.

Vestal, Theodore. *The Lion of Judah in the New World: Emperor Haile Selassie of Ethiopia and the Shaping of Americans' Attitudes toward Africa.* Santa Barbara, CA: Praeger, 2011.

Voeks, Robert A. "African Medicine and Magic in the Americas." *Geographical Review* 83, no. 1 (1993): 66–78.

———. *Sacred Leaves of Candomblé: African Magic, Medicine, And Religion in Brazil.* Austin: University of Texas Press, 1997.

Von Eschen, Penny. *Race against Empire: Black Americans and Anticolonialism, 1937–1957.* Ithaca: Cornell University Press, 1997.

Wainwright, J. A., ed. *Border Lines: Contemporary Poems in English.* Toronto: Corp Clark, 1995.

Walcott, Derek. *Dream on Monkey Mountain and Other Plays.* London: Jonathan Cape, 1972.

———. "Muse of History: An Essay." In *Is Massa Day Dead? Black Moods in the Caribbean,* edited by Orde Coombs, 1–27. New York: Anchor and Doubleday, 1974.

Walker, Juliet E. K. *The History of Black Business in America: Capitalism, Race, Entrepreneurship.* Chapel Hill: University of North Carolina Press, 2009.

Wallerstein, Immanuel. "The Evolving Role of the African Scholar in African Studies," *African Studies Review* 26, nos. 3–4 (1983): 155–61.

———. *The Modern World System.* New York: Academic Press, 1974.

Wallis, J., ed. *Waging Peace.* New York: Harper & Row, 1982.

Walters, Ronald W. *Pan-Africanism in the African Diaspora: An Analysis of Modern Afrocentric Political Movements.* Detroit, MI: Wayne State University Press, 1993.

Watermna, Christopher Alan. *Juju: A Social History and Ethnography of an African Popular Music.* Chicago: University of Chicago Press, 1990.

Waters, Robert. *Historical Dictionary of United States-Africa Relations.* Lanham, MD: Rowman & Littlefield, 2009.

Weaver, Karol K. *Medical Revolutionaries: The Enslaved Healers of Eighteenth-Century Saint Domingue.* Urbana-Champaign: University of Illinois, 2006.

Weaver, Lloyd, and Olurunmi Egbelade. *Maternal Divinity, Yemonja Tranquil Sea Turbulent Tides: Eleven Yoruba Tales.* New York: Athelia Henrietta Press, 1998.

Weik, Terrance. "Archaeology of the African Diaspora in Latin America." *Historical Archaeology* 38, no. 1, Transcending Boundaries, Transforming the Discipline: African Diaspora Archaeologies in the New Millennium (2004): 32–49.

———. "The Archaeology of Maroon Societies in the Americas: Resistance, Cultural Continuity, and Transformation in the African Diaspora." *Historical Archaeology* 31, no. 2 (1997): 81–92.

West, Cornel. *Race Matters.* New York: Vintage, 1994.

Westad, Odd Arne. *The Global Cold War: Third World Interventions and the Making of Our Times.* New York: Cambridge University Press, 2007.

White, George Jr., *Holding the Line: Race, Racism, and American Foreign Policy Toward Africa, 1953–1961.* Lanham, MD: Rowman & Littlefield, 2005.

White, Steven F. "Translating the African Diaspora." *Callaloo* 30, no. 2 (2007): 439–40.

Wiarda, Howard J. *American Foreign Policy in Regions of Conflict: A Global Perspective.* New York: Palgrave Macmillan, 2011.

Williams, Eric. *Capitalism and Slavery.* Chapel Hill: University of North Carolina Press, 1972.

Williams, George Washington. *History of the Negro Race in America,* 2 vols. New York: G. P. Putnam's Sons, 1883.

Williams, Walter L. *Black Americans and the Evangelization of Africa, 1877–1900.* Madison: University of Wisconsin Press, 1982.

Williams, Zachery, ed. *Africana Cultures and Policy Studies: Scholarship and the Transformation of Public Policy.* New York: Palgrave Macmillan, 2009.

Winders, James A. *Paris Africain: Rhythms of the African Diaspora.* New York: Palgrave Macmillan, 2006.

Wintz, Cary D. *Black Culture and the Harlem Renaissance.* Houston, TX: Rice University Press, 1988.

Wirtz, Kristina. "How Diasporic Religious Communities Remember: Learning to Speak the 'Tongue of the Oricha' in Cuban Santería." *American Ethnologist* 34, no. 1 (2007): 108–26.

Woodson, Carter G. *The African Background Outlined.* New York: Negro University Press, 1958.

————. *The Mis-education of the Negro*. Washington, DC: Associated Publishers, 1933; reprint Trenton, NJ: Africa World Press, 1990.

Woodward, Peter. *U.S. Foreign Policy and the Horn of Africa*. Farnham, UK: Ashgate, 2007.

Wright, George. *Destruction of a Nation: United States Policy toward Angola since 1945*. Chicago: Pluto Press, 2007.

Wright, Michelle M. *Becoming Black: Creating Identity in the African Diaspora*. Durham: Duke University Press, 2004.

Wright, Richard. *Black Boy*. New York: Harper & Row, 1966.

Yewah, Emmanuel, and 'Dimeji Togunde. *Across the Atlantic: African Immigrants in the United States Diaspora*. Champaign, IL: Common Ground, 2010.

Young, Jason R. *Rituals of Resistance: African Atlantic Religion in Kongo and the Lowcountry South in the Era of Slavery*. Baton Rouge: Louisiana State University Press, 2007.

Zack-Williams, Alfred B. "African Diaspora Conditioning: The Case of Liverpool." *Journal of Black Studies* 27, no. 4 (1997): 528–42.

————. "Development and Diaspora: Separate Concerns?" *Review of African Political Economy* 22, no. 65 (1995): 349–58.

Zack-Williams, Alfred B., and Giles Mohan. "Editorial: Africa, the African Diaspora, and Development." *Review of African Political Economy* 29, no. 92, Africa, the African Diaspora, and Development (2002): 205–10.

Zartman, J. William. *Collapsed States*. Boulder, CO: Lynne Rienner, 1995.

Zeinert, Karen. *The Amistad Slave Revolt and American Abolition*. North Haven, CT: Linnet, 1997.

Zeleza, Paul Tiyambe. "African Diasporas: Toward a Global History." *African Studies Review* 53, no. 1 (2010): 1–19.

————. "Rewriting the African Diaspora: Beyond the Black Atlantic." *African Affairs* 104, no. 414 (2005): 35–68.

Zisk, Betty H. *The Politics of Transformation: Local Activism in the Peace and Environmental Movements*. Westport, CT: Praeger, 1992.

Index

From the fifteenth century to the present, Africa has lost millions of its people to other parts of the world, either from the slave trade or voluntary migration. This displacement of African peoples is the most important event in modern African history, dislocating the social foundations of the continent and fashioning ties—political, economic, cultural—between Africa and other continents, mainly North America. Though the legacies of the diaspora are well known—slavery, colonialism, racism, poverty, and underdevelopment—the ways in which these forces also worked to spur the diaspora are not fully understood, by those who were part of this migration or by scholars, historians, and policymakers.

In this definitive study of the diaspora in North America, Toyin Falola offers a causal history of the western dispersion of Africans and its effects on the modern world. Reengaging old and familiar debates and framing new ones that enrich the discourse surrounding Africa, Falola isolates the thread, running nearly six centuries, that connects the history of slavery, the transatlantic slave trade, and current migrations. A boon to scholars and policymakers and accessible to the general reader, the book explores diverse narratives of migration and shows that the cultures that migrated from Africa to the Americas have the capacity to unite and create a new pan-Africanist movement within the globalized world.

Toyin Falola is the Jacob and Frances Sanger Mossiker Chair in the Humanities and University Distinguished Teaching Professor at the University of Texas at Austin.

"This *tour de force* shows mastery of the literature and the themes that connect Africa to its diaspora. A gift that will be well appreciated by both academics and nonacademics."

—Edmund Abaka, associate professor
of history, University of Miami

"In *The African Diaspora*, Falola provides a comprehensive report on continental and intercontinental African migrations and displacements, past and present. Students of African history and economics, Africana migration, critical race theory, and development studies will find it hard to ignore this enriching contribution to global Africana scholarship. Even more significant are the invaluable policy insights that policy researchers and makers can garner from Falola's gem."

—Tunde Bewaji, professor of philosophy,
University of the West Indies

"In this fascinating book, Toyin Falola, the most prolific and celebrated African historian of his generation, offers us an erudite and engaging study of African Atlantic diasporas from slavery to Obama. It brilliantly weaves together accounts of the old and new diasporas' political, social, cultural, intellectual, and artistic histories and of their enduring resilience and complex connections to their African homeland. This book immeasurably expands the analytical contours of the field of African diaspora studies. An impressive achievement."

—Paul Tiyambe Zeleza, Presidential Professor of
African American Studies and History and
dean of the Bellarmine College of Liberal Arts,
Loyola Marymount University